Unearthing Churchill's Secret Army

Unearthing Churchill's Secret Army

The Official List of SOE Casualties and Their Stories

Martin Mace and John Grehan

Pen & Sword
MILITARY

First published in Great Britain in 2012
and republished in this format in 2021 by
Pen & Sword Military
An imprint of
Pen & Sword Books Ltd
Yorkshire – Philadelphia

ISBN 978 1 39901 320 8

Typeset in 11pt Ehrhardt by Mac Style

Printed and bound in the UK by
CPI Group (UK) Ltd, Croydon, CR0 4YY.

Pen & Sword Books Limited incorporates the imprints of Atlas, Archaeology, Aviation,
Discovery, Family History, Fiction, History, Maritime, Military, Military Classics,
Politics, Select, Transport, True Crime, Air World, Frontline Publishing, Leo Cooper,
Remember When, Seaforth Publishing, The Praetorian Press, Wharncliffe Local History,
Wharncliffe Transport, Wharncliffe True Crime and White Owl.

For a complete list of Pen & Sword titles please contact

PEN & SWORD BOOKS LIMITED
47 Church Street, Barnsley, South Yorkshire, S70 2AS, England
E-mail: enquiries@pen-and-sword.co.uk
Website: www.pen-and-sword.co.uk

Or
PEN AND SWORD BOOKS
1950 Lawrence Rd, Havertown, PA 19083, USA
E-mail: Uspen-and-sword@casematepublishers.com
Website: www.penandswordbooks.com

Contents

Acknowledgements

The authors would like to extend their grateful thanks to the following individuals and organisations for their kind assistance during the course of researching and writing this book: Nicholas Andrews (Records and Enquiries Manager) and Peter Francis (Head of External Communications) at the Commonwealth War Graves Commission, not least for their help in compiling the casualty lists, but also for permission to quote information on the memorials and cemeteries from the Commission's website; the staff of The National Archives at Kew; Norman Brown of the Royal Pioneer Corps Association; Harry Verlander; Les Tanner of ww2connection; Peter Osborne of Independent Books; and Leanne Mace, Sara Mitchell and Denis Mace for all their work on preparing the manuscript.

Jacket image: 'Loire Rendezvous'. By the renowned aviation artist Philip E. West, this painting depicts Westland Lysanders of 161 (Special Duties) Squadron turning onto their final course to a clandestine landing field somewhere in occupied France during a full moon period in 1943. Based at RAF Tempsford, Bedfordshire, and often operating from Tangmere to shorten the flight, the pilots flew a dead reckoning course to their first turning point, usually on the River Loire, The moonlit town of Blois is easily distinguishable by its château, churches and bridge with the Forest of Chambord beyond. The agents in the rear cockpit prepare themselves by torchlight for the forthcoming landing. (*Courtesy of SWA Fine Art: www.swafineart.com*)

List of the Casualties Commemorated by the Commonwealth War Graves Commission as Serving with SOE

ADLER, Gabriel
AGAZARIAN, Jack Charles Stanmore
ALEXANDRE, Roland Eugène Jean
ALLARD, Elisée Albert Louis
AMPHLETT, Philip John
AMPS, James Frederick
ANTELME, Joseph Antoine France
AUSTIN, John Patrick Standridge
BARRETT, Denis John
BEAUREGARD, Alcide
BEC, Francisque Eugene
BENOIST, Robert Marcel Charles
BERLINER, Egon Friederich Paul
BERTHEAU, Louis Eugene Desire
BIÉLER, Gustave Daniel Alfred
BLOCH, André
BLOCH, Denise Madeleine
BLOOM, Marcus Reginald
BORREL, Andrée Raymonde
BOUGUENNEC, Jean
BUTTON, Harold Victor
BYCK, Muriel Tamara
BYERLY, Robert Bennett
CARELESS, Alfred
CAUCHI, Eric Joseph Denis
CLECH, Marcel Remy
CLEMENT, George
COPPIN, Edward Cyril
DAMERMENT, Madeleine Zöe
DAREME, Pierre Edouard
DEFENCE, Marcel Enzebe
DEFENDINI, Alphonse
DEMAND, George William Hedworth
DENISET, François Adolphe

DETAL, Julien Theodore Joseph
DOWLEN, Roland Robert
DUBOUDIN, Emile George Jean
DUCLOS, Philip Francis
FINLAYSON, David Haughton
FOX, Marcel Georges Florent
FRAGER, Henri Jaques Paul
GAILLOT, Henri Hubert
GARDNER, Denis
GARRY, Emile August Henri
GEELEN, Pierre Albert Hubert
GOUGH, Victor Albert
GRAHAM, Harry Huntingdon
GROVER-WILLIAMS, William Charles
    Frederick
GYORI, Issack
HAMILTON, John Trevor
HANAU, Julius
HAYES, Victor Charles
HILL, William Arthur
HOFFMAN, Ernst
HUBBLE, Desmond Elis
INAYAT-KHAN, Noor
JOHANSEN, Hans Robert Filip
JONES, Sidney Charles
JUMEAU, Clement Marc
KASAP, Jechel Usher
KEUN, Gerald Philip George
LANGARD, Raymond
LANSDELL, Armand Richard
LARCHER, Maurice Louis Marie Aristide
LAYZELL, Gordon Edward
LECCIA, Marcel Mathieu René
LEDOUX, Jacques Paul Henri

LEE, Lionel
LEFORT, Cicely Margot
LEIGH, Vera Eugenie
LEVENE, Eugène Francis
LORD, Christopher James
MACALISTER, John Kenneth
MAITLAND-MAKGILL-CRICHTON,
   David
MAKOWSKI, Stanisław
MALRAUX, Claude Raymond
MARTIN-LEAKE, Stephen Philip
MAYER, James Andrew John
McBAIN, George Basil
MELLOWS, Thomas Anthony
MENESSON, James Francis George
MICHEL, François Gérard
DE MONTALEMBERT, Arthur Franz,
MULSANT, Pierre Louis
MUVRIN, Nick
NEWMAN, Isidore
NICHOLLS, Arthur Frederick Crane
NORMAN, Gilbert Maurice
OGDEN-SMITH, Colin Malcolm
OPOCZYNSKI, Abraham
PALMER, Sir Anthony Frederick Mark
PARDI, Paul Baptiste
PERTSCHUK, Maurice
PICHL, Otto
PICKERSGILL, Frank Herbert Dedrick
PLEWMAN, Eliane Sophie
PRASSINOS, Mario Lambros Achilles
RABINOVITCH, Adolphe
RAFFERTY, Brian Dominic
RECHENMANN, Charles Théophile
REIK, Chaviva
REISZ (REISS), Stephan Rafael
RENAUD, Jean

RENAUD-DANDICOLLE, Jean Marie
ROBERTS, Sidney George
ROCKINGHAM, David William
ROLFE, Lilian Verna
ROWDEN, Diana Hope
RUDDELAT, Yvonne Claire
SABOURIN, Roméo Roger
DE SAINT-GENIÈS, Baron Marie Joseph
   Gonzagues
SARRETTE, Paul François Marie Charles
   William
SAVON, Gilbert Joseph
SCHWATSCHKO, Alexandre
SEHMER, John
SELBY, Neil Beauchamp
SERINI, Enzo
SEVENET, Henri Paul
SIBREE, David Whytehead
SIMON, Jean Alexandre Robert
SIMON, Octave Anne Guillaume
SINCLAIR, Jack Andrew Eugene Marcel
SKEPPER, Charles Milne
STEELE, Arthur
SUTTILL, Francis Alfred
SZABO, Violette Reine Elizabeth
SZENES, Hannah
TESSIER, Paul Raymond Elie
TROTOBAS, Michael Alfred Raymond
UNTERNAHRER, Yolande Elsa Maria
VASS, Alexander Francis
VIVIAN, Guy Joseph
WALLACE, David John
WHITTY, Valentine Edward
WILKINSON, Edward Mountford
WILKINSON, George Alfred
WORMS, Jean Alexandre
YOUNG, John Cuthbert

Foreword

By Harry Verlander, Jedburgh Team *Harold* and Special Force 136 Burma

Before the Second World War there were virtually no 'Special Forces' as we have now come to know them. Great belligerent armies flogged it out in the field but, towards the end of the First World War, a degree of mobility had come to warfare in the shape of the aircraft and the motor vehicle. Communications had also come on in leaps and bounds and those out of direct contact with their HQ could now feed information back and receive new orders by radio telegraphy and, later, radio telephony.

Conditions became ripe for small groups to begin operating far and wide behind enemy lines and gave birth, in the Second World War, to units such as the Long Range Desert Group, Special Air Service, Commandos and the Special Operations Executive.

Each had a different development and was shaped for certain jobs, dictated by the circumstances of the ever changing war. The SOE was formed on the direct orders of Churchill who wanted a clandestine army '... to set Europe ablaze'. Its mission was to encourage and facilitate espionage, sabotage and reconnaissance behind enemy lines, liaising with the resistance and other subversive forces already in existence.

Like the other Special Forces, the SOE were sworn to secrecy and because of this neither I nor my colleagues could speak of what we had done for seventy years; unlike our French and American counterparts who were released from their secrecy after thirty years. Similarly, because we operated in such small units, and never really came into contact with other teams, we knew very little about our colleagues and it wasn't until a few years ago, when I was invited to attended some reunions and celebrations, that I first met other members of the SOE who, subsequently, became friends – our own Band of Brothers.

I am sure the reader can appreciate that because of the two factors I have mentioned above, it would have been very easy for those who gave their lives on these clandestine operations to be completely forgotten; indeed immediately post war most of the Special Forces were axed on the pretext that there were '... too many private armies'.

It is therefore a pleasure for me to introduce to you this work by John Grehan and Martin Mace, which records the fate of those SOE agents who died on active service. Without such a reference the names of so many brave people might have slipped slowly into obscurity. Now, at least, those who study our history will have a reference point for which I, for one, am grateful. Thank you, John and Martin.

Harry Verlander
August 2011

Introduction

Death Be Proud

The weak autumn sun cast thin shadows across the manicured lawns that encompassed the circular structure. On either side of the formal entrance stood two low stones, each of which bore the same inscription – 'Memorial to the Missing'.

We were at the Brookwood Military Cemetery in Surrey, the centrepiece of which is the Memorial to 3,500 men and women who died for the Allied cause during the Second World War and have no known grave. These people come from every branch of the United Kingdom and Commonwealth land forces; from the Royal Artillery, the county infantry regiments, the Royal Tank Regiment, the Intelligence Corps and, of course, the General List.

There is also one panel, just one, which shows E. Serini as being a member of the Special Operations Executive (SOE). What is remarkable about this is that amongst the names carved on the memorial is one of the most famous members of the SOE, Violet Szabo, yet she is commemorated under her parent unit of the First Aid Nursing Yeomanry (FANY).

Further inspection revealed other known members of the SOE, all of which are named on the memorial under other units. That some people should be recognised as SOE and others not was an anomaly that demanded further investigation.

Our mission began then, on that day. We wanted to know how many agents had lost their lives whilst operating with the SOE. We found that, of all the books published on the Special Operations Executive, this was a subject that had been conspicuously neglected. But by its very nature the SOE was a secretive organisation, so if their memorials or graves did not show them as being SOE how could we know how many of these incredibly brave people had been killed in that dark world in which they worked? Who were they? How did they die? Where did they die? It was a mystery that we were determined to solve.

We had to start our research somewhere, so we turned to the only official register of the British and Commonwealth dead – the records of the Commonwealth War Graves Commission. From these we were able to identify those men and women who had died, according to the official records, whilst in service with the Special Operations Executive. This list numbered 140.

However, our investigation revealed that there were far more individuals who died in service with the SOE than the official list of 140. Beyond even these there were countless numbers of locally-recruited sub-agents that suffered imprisonment, torture and even death because of their involvement in and support of SOE agents and their activities. How many will never be known.

We also found that two of the agents recorded as killed in action actually survived the war and that the date of death, and even the names, of some others has been inaccurately recorded – such was the secrecy under which they operated and so hard did the Germans and the Japanese try to conceal the atrocities they had committed.

Equally the British Government of the time never acknowledged their clandestine activities. The agents themselves were well aware that neither their relatives, nor the general public, might ever learn of either the work they had undertaken or of how they met their end.

Now, at last, their stories can be told.

Chapter 1

So Secret a Service

The Special Operations Executive was born out of the ashes of defeat. The summer of 1940 saw Britain forced onto the defensive and fighting for its very survival. But the irrepressible Churchill was determined to carry the war to the enemy, however unlikely this may have appeared in that bleak period of Britain's history. He knew, nevertheless, that for a long time most of the fighting would be conducted by 'guerrillas, special agents, revolutionaries, and saboteurs'. It was, as William Stevenson (code name *Intrepid*) put it, 'time we learned to fight with the gloves off, the knee in the groin, the stab in the dark.'[1]

Even before the collapse of France the Chiefs of Staff had submitted to the Cabinet a paper suggesting that Germany could be defeated by a combination of economic warfare and subversion and that a special organisation was needed to co-ordinate the latter activities.

Following a ministerial meeting on 1 July 1940, the Minister of Economic Warfare, Hugh Dalton, consolidated the views of his colleagues in a note to the Foreign Minister, Lord Halifax: 'What is needed is a new organisation to co-ordinate, inspire, control and assist the nationals of the oppressed countries who must themselves be the direct participants. We need absolute secrecy, a certain fanatical enthusiasm, willingness to work with people of different nationalities, complete political reliability.'[2]

Eight days later, another meeting was held to talk through these proposals with Churchill, following which a formal document was prepared. This was accepted by Churchill on 22 July and, with the now famous exhortation to 'Set Europe Ablaze', the Special Operations Executive was created to 'co-ordinate all action by way of subversion and sabotage' under the control of Hugh Dalton's ministry.

The objective of this new force was to make contact with people in the occupied nations who might be willing to participate in subversive activity. 'The plan', wrote Major General Sir Colin Gubbins KCMG, DSO, MC, who became its Director in August 1943, 'was to encourage and enable the peoples of the occupied countries to harass the German war effort at every possible point by sabotage, subversion, go-slow practices, *coup de main* raids, etc., and at the same time to build up secret forces therein, organised, armed and trained to take their part only when the final assault began ... in its simplest terms, this plan involved the ultimate delivery to occupied territory of large numbers of personnel and quantities of arms and explosives.'[3]

For this the agents would need to be trained in armed and unarmed combat, and in sabotage techniques. They were taught how to withstand interrogation, how to deliver secure messages, how to avoid detection. They were issued with forged identity papers made out in their false new names, and they were issued with plenty of money.

Their training was conducted at numerous locations across the United Kingdom. They underwent commando training at Arisaig in Scotland, where they were taught armed and unarmed combat skills by the likes of William E. Fairbairn and Eric A. Sykes, former Inspectors in the Shanghai Municipal Police. They then attended courses in security and 'tradecraft' at what were called the 'finishing schools' around the Beaulieu estate in Hampshire. Finally, they received specialist training in skills such as demolition techniques or Morse code telegraphy at various country houses in England and parachute training (if necessary) at the Special Training School STS 51 and 51a situated near Altrincham, Cheshire with the assistance of No.1 Parachute Training School at RAF Ringway (now Manchester Airport). A commando training centre similar to Arisaig was later set up at Oshawa, for Canadian members of the SOE.

SOE headquarters in London was split into sections, each one dealing with a different country. These were departments for Abyssinia, Albania, Czechoslovakia, Belgium, Denmark, Germany, Greece, Hungary, Italy, Netherlands, Norway, Poland, Romania, South-east Asia and Yugoslavia. There was a slightly different arrangement for France where there was a competing organisation. This was the Gaullist RF Section (Résistance Français) which, whilst nominally part of the SOE, operated independently and was staffed almost exclusively with French nationals. For this reason it does not form part of this study.

There were several subsidiary SOE headquarters and stations set up to manage operations that were too distant for London to control. SOE's operations in the Middle East and Balkans were controlled from a headquarters in Cairo which, in April 1944, became known as Special Operations (Mediterranean). A subsidiary headquarters was later set up in Italy under Cairo's command to control operations in the Balkans. There was also a station near Algiers, established in late 1942 and codenamed *Massingham*, which operated in southern France.

An SOE station, which was first called the India Mission and was subsequently known as GS I(k) was set up in India late in 1940. It eventually moved to Ceylon and became known as Force 136. A mission was also set up in Singapore but it was not able to form any resistance movements in Malaya before the Japanese overran the country. Force 136 took over its surviving staff and operations.

Operations in the field, particularly those in France, were generally organised into separate networks, or circuits (*réseaux* in France). These circuits were normally set up by three agents – the organiser, who was the senior person in the team, plus his courier and his wireless operator.

The organiser was responsible for arming and supplying the local Resistance cells within his group. This was done by sending encoded messages by his wireless operator for boats or aircraft to deliver the munitions at pre-arranged times and places. The organiser would then select targets in his area for the cells to attack – though often, especially in the later years of the war, targets would be chosen by London. These were usually railway lines, power stations, dams and even factories. Women were often recruited as wireless operators and especially as couriers in France (where the mail was subject to censorship) because it was difficult for young men to travel around without being stopped and questioned.

In countries such as Albania and Yugoslavia, where the terrain was more challenging and the political situation between the various resistance groups was complex, the missions, such as they were, were organised along a variety of different lines with no common structure. Similarly, in the Far East, where conditions were even more difficult, the teams were all-male and were put together in an *ad-hoc* fashion to suit the situation on the ground.

At its outset there was no name for this ultra-secret organisation. Indeed its very existence was never publically acknowledged until after the war. As its longest-serving executive director, Colin Gubbins, explained: 'I do not believe that theatre commanders, as they came to be called, or even Resident Ministers, were ever informed officially by the War Cabinet of the creation of SOE in July 1940; and secondly they were not given any inkling of the charter upon which it was founded. From the beginning quite excessive secrecy was enjoined on SOE itself from above ... In this connection I cannot at the same time find anybody who was ever informed officially or in writing what the charter of the SOE was. I think that SOE was looked upon as a sort of branch of the secret service, and of course a secret service with no written charter.'[4]

SOE was part of the Ministry of Economic Warfare, known as Military Operations 1 (Special Projects). It was divided into three branches: SO1, SO2 and SO3. The operational arm was SO2 and it was this branch, under the control of its executive director, which became the principle body of the SOE.

During its brief period of existence the SOE had three directors all of whom adopted the initials 'CD' to conceal their identities and to maintain continuity. This practice was extended throughout the SOE with each staff post represented by a symbol that had no obvious connection with the position held.

The historian Nigel West used the SOE's Polish country section as an example to demonstrate this: the section itself was MPP, the Head of Department was MP, his two senior staff officers were MPJ and MPF. Other posts were, Operations, MPC, Training, MPG, Movements and Supplies was MPN and Intelligence was MPX.1. This meant that an individual could well be known by more than one symbol during his service with SOE and it was these symbols that were used in all communications and internal communications.[5]

Such was the degree of secrecy surrounding the organisation it actually operated under the cover title of the 'Inter-Service Research Bureau'. This was so that no-one would question the comings and goings of so many people in different service uniforms. The people who worked there referred to it amongst themselves as 'The Org', or 'The Firm', or 'The Racket'.

The SOE was, as its principle historian, Professor M.R.D. Foot, bemoaned, an unusually complex organisation '... and its complexities have not been made any easier to unravel by the dense fog of secrecy in which it lived. In that fog few fragments of it have still to be hidden, and wisps of fog still keep getting in the way of the seeker of past truth.'[6]

With their headquarters at 64 Baker Street in London the SOE happily adopted the nickname of 'The Baker Street Irregulars', after the gang of street urchins that Sherlock Holmes employed 'to go everywhere, see everything and overhear everyone'. Ironically, the one place that they could not go was their own headquarters. This was in case any of them saw details that could be extracted by torture. It was the SOE's cardinal rule that the people in the field should know only enough to enable them to carry out their duties.

In its formative months recruitment was a major problem – one can hardly advertise for a service that is supposed to be secret. The type of people recruited into the SOE ranged from 'safe-crackers, forgers and professional bank robbers', to 'men and women of such distinction in public life that their involvement is unmentionable to this day'. Presumably the professional criminals were equally unwilling to reveal their names to a wider audience.

Secrecy within the SOE was taken to such extremes that Maurice Buckmaster, the head of the French Section, could not tell even his wife the true nature of his employment. Mrs Buckmaster only discovered where her husband was working when, on a trip to London, she accidently stumbled upon her husband's workplace when the family dog sniffed out his master's scent.

*   *   *

Though there were some early attempts by the SOE at developing an organisation in Occupied Europe (Georges Bégué being the first agent parachuted into France in May 1941), its operations only really began in earnest in 1942.

In the main theatre, France, this started with the arrival of Francis Suttill. He was the man, it was expected in Baker Street, who would recruit large numbers of loyal French men and women across France and build the framework around which the great Resistance movement would be created. His circuit was PROSPER and his objective was to prepare the French for D-Day when they would rise up and help the Allied armies drive the Germans out of their country.

In those optimistic days it was thought that the Allied invasion would take place in 1943. It was never imagined that the agents would have to survive in German-occupied France until 1944. The Germans had an extensive and efficient counter-espionage organisation and the chances of agents remaining undetected for almost two years were slim. Indeed, not one of the circuits set up in 1942 was still in existence in 1944.[7]

At its peak, the SOE employed some 13,000 agents and staff (10,000 men and 3,000 women), and it has been estimated that it supplied and supported around a million sub-operatives across all theatres and regions around the world. Yet information about the arrest and death of the lost agents are in many cases extremely difficult to ascertain. Missing agents were not even included in the published War Office casualty lists, appearing only on a separate 'Secret' casualty list.[8]

The reasons for this are easy to understand. Firstly, there was no complete central record of agents that were employed or engaged by the SOE and the fact that agents were recruited both inside and outside the UK meant that such a register could never have been compiled. Many of the locally-recruited agents never actually set foot in Britain and consequently do not appear on official SOE or CWGC records.

Secondly, as Buckmaster himself conceded, 'We did not keep elaborate records, for the more there was on paper, the greater the chance of something going astray. It was therefore our policy to destroy all records after an appropriate time had elapsed.'[9]

To add to what M.R.D. Foot called 'the density of the clouds of unknowing', before leaving the UK to begin their active service, the agents had to dispense with everything that might reveal their true identities. This meant a change of name, known as the 'Documentary' name, the adoption of an alias or 'Fieldname', as well as an 'Operational' name. It would also be coupled with a cover story to support the new identity. Even during training in Britain a false name was used. In all fairness, the use of codenames was not merely to confuse the enemy, it also enabled people to hold conversations in difficult circumstances without fear of their true meaning being understood.[10]

The agents' families were given little or no indication of the type of work the men and women were engaged upon, being told simply that it was 'of a hazardous nature'. Usually they were not even aware of where or when their husbands, wives or children were sent into the field.

Though agents trained together in groups, they were discouraged from meeting other agents in the UK, and whilst at Baker Street or in one of the section houses, agents were often 'spirited' from one room to the next to avoid unnecessary contact. Of course agents did meet and inevitably they would talk to each other. But there was one subject about which discussion was absolutely forbidden – they must never tell anyone where they were going.[11]

It was also standard SOE protocol to keep each cell as independent as possible in the field. This ensured that if one circuit was compromised it would not necessarily lead to the fall of any other circuits. The wisdom of this policy became apparent when the most important circuit in northern France, Francis Suttill's PROSPER circuit, expanded very rapidly and encompassed many sub-circuits. The result was that when PROSPER was broken by the Gestapo a great many agents were compromised.

Even when it was known for certain that an agent had been captured by the Germans the incident was kept as quiet as possible. 'There should be no publicity of any kind,' was the usual SOE instruction following the arrest of any agent, 'and if any intimation is sent to the next of kin they should be forbidden to publish it and warned they ought not to convey the information to anyone.'[12]

It was also deliberate Nazi policy to conceal the fate of such prisoners. In an order issued by Hitler on 7 December 1941, and signed by *Generalfeldmarschall* Wilhelm Keitel, captured political activists or Resistance fighters in German-controlled territory were to disappear into the 'Night and Fog' (*Nacht und Nebel*). The idea behind this terrible order was to deter opposition to German rule as the victims would be swept away never to be heard of again.

The *Nacht und Nebel* decree has manifested itself in the inaccurate recording of some details of the missing SOE agents. The date of Yvonne Rudellat's death is given by the Commonwealth War Graves Commission as 30 April 1945, yet it seems probable that she died around a week earlier. The date of one of the most famous female SOE agents, Noor Inayat-Khan, is recorded by the CWCC as being 6 July 1944. This is because it was believed at one time that she had been one of four female agents killed at Natzweiler-Struthof concentration camp. It has since been discovered that she was shot on 13 September 1944 at Dachau.

News of the capture of an agent could also be extremely misleading, as the agent known as Benoit (Benjamin Cowburn) explained: 'As soon as an agent was taken the most extraordinary rumours would immediately begin to circulate. The person who brought the news of the arrest would often give you all the details of how it occurred, whose fault it was, where the captive had been taken, where he was being detained, the size of his cell and what he got for breakfast. A few days later someone else would give you an entirely different version on each point.'[13]

Whilst the SOE generally operated independently of the other armed forces it relied heavily upon the Royal Navy and particularly the RAF for logistical support. The SOE had its own Special Duties squadrons allocated to it, which were used for the infiltration and exfiltration of agents. The RAF was also employed dropping arms and equipment to agents and their teams in the field and when the aircraft were deployed on these flights the same heavy veil of secrecy shrouded the entire operation as in every aspect of the SOE's work. Firstly the aircraft would be sent from their usual RAF base to another airfield from where they would mount the mission. Then, in their squadron's Operations Record Book, where normally information about the sortie would be detailed, was simply written 'SOE operations'.

The SOE actually suffered a number of casualties even before any of its agents had been sent into the field. On the night of 5/6 May 1941, just as F Section was ready to infiltrate its first half-a-dozen agents into France, three of them were killed and two others wounded in the section house during an air raid on London. The sixth agent, a wireless operator called Georges Bégué, was out of the flat at the time of the bombing. He went on to become F Section's first agent to be parachuted into France.

Another agent was lost by F Section – quite literally. A man, who was a professional gambler, was sent into France with a large sum of money. He was supposed to use these funds to obtain information on ration cards, permits and other official controls. This individual made his way down to the French Riviera and neither he, nor the money, was ever seen by the SOE again. As Buckmaster wrote in 1958, 'I suppose he is knocking around somewhere in the world's gambling centres, but he must be doing better for he has never set foot again in this country in search of further funds.'[14]

* * *

Severe interrogation or quite possibly torture was the inevitable consequence of capture by the enemy. The agents were not uniformed combatants and the protection usually afforded prisoners of war did not apply to spies, which the agents were generally considered to be. Though the agents were trained in dealing with harsh treatment the controllers knew that many of their people would succumb and reveal all they knew to the Gestapo. All they asked their agents to do was to try and hold out for forty-eight hours to give the other members of their cell a chance to get away.

Just what the captured agents were likely to suffer was recorded by one of those that survived internment and torture by the Gestapo. Odette Sansom GC, MBE, was tortured by the Gestapo at their French headquarters in Paris. The first treatment she endured was a red-hot poker pressed against her spine. When that failed to break her resolve, the Germans pulled out her toenails with a pair of pliers – all ten of them.[15]

Another agent that survived not only torture but even the notorious concentration camp at Buchenwald was Wing Commander Forest Yeo-Thomas GC, MC & Bar, *Croix de Guerre, Légion d'honneur*. He has left us a description of another favourite torture technique employed by the Gestapo. This was the *baignoire* in which the victim was submerged in a bath of cold water to the point where he was drowning. He would then be pulled out and revived. The questioning would then continue and if the interrogator did not get the information, the process would be repeated.

'I was helpless,' wrote Yeo-Thomas. 'I panicked and tried to kick out, but the vice-like grip was such that I could hardly move. My eyes were open, I could see shapes distorted by the water, wavering above me, my lungs were bursting, my mouth opened and I swallowed water. Now I was drowning. I put every ounce of my energy into a vain effort to kick myself out of the bath, but I was completely helpless and, swallowing water, I felt that I must burst.

I was dying, this was the end, I was losing consciousness, but as I was doing so, I felt the strength going out of me and my limbs going limp.' At this point he was pulled back out of the bath to face his interrogator once again.[16]

To help them if the torture became intolerable, or if they believed that they would be unable to endure any torture when captured, the agents were given cyanide pills – known as the 'L' (for lethal) pill. These pills were very small and could be concealed in a ring or in a lipstick. The pills were not to be swallowed but instead were to be sucked in the mouth until they dissolved. Death would occur in thirty seconds and, the agents were assured, was painless. Some of the cyanide pills produced for the SOE had an insoluble coating and could be safely carried in the mouth. The cyanide would only be released when the agent bit through the outer coating.

A very high proportion of those agents that were captured were killed by the Germans because they did not want any of these people to disclose the treatment they had received whist in captivity. The manner in which many of them died, however, requires further explanation.

The majority of them were hanged, on specific instructions from Hitler, with nooses made of piano wire. This was meant to make their deaths as slow and degrading as possible. Why this was so was explained by Himmler: 'The mere slaughter of the *Fuhrer*'s enemies was of no importance to him. They should die, certainly, but not before torture, indignity and interrogation had drained from them that last shred and scintilla of evidence which should lead to the arrest of others.'[17]

*   *   *

In 1946 the SOE was closed down for good, winding up its operations, as Nigel West put it, 'with inordinate haste, destroying documents wholesale'. Before being dismissed its staff members were sworn to secrecy. When Elizabeth Nicholas attempted to uncover information on the fate of the French Section agents in 1958 she found that, 'Every obstacle is now placed in the way of those who wish to write of the unlucky ones – those who lost their lives when serving with SOE; those whose story if published, would be painted in more sombre colours.'[18]

It was in some measure to protect the memory of those unlucky ones that the general public was not given permission to view any of the SOE's records and it was only because questions had been raised in the House of Commons about the loss of so many agents that an official history was written. Published in 1966 it was the first detailed account of the main theatre of SOE operations, France.

Even then this book was only a partial examination of the SOE operation and one of the most important of the staff members at Baker Street, Vera Atkins, was scathing in her condemnation of M.R D. Foot's book *SOE in France*. 'Some consider it the Bible,' she said to historian Sarah Helm in 1998. 'It's about as accurate as the Bible.'

Foot made no pretence about the difficulties under which he worked. As he explained, when the organisation was being wound up the files were 'roughly weeded' by staff officers who had helped complete them. The number of documents that remained was subsequently reduced a further two times. With respect to the French Section, Foot wrote, 'many of the files on particular circuits and operations, almost all messages exchanged with the field, all the training files, and some important papers on the early development of SOE have thus disappeared.'[19] In a recently-revised edition, with more files being opened to the public, Foot had been able to rectify some of the shortcomings of his original version.

A genuinely official account of the whole of the SOE administration was produced shortly after the war. Commissioned by Major General Gubbins, it was written by William Mackenzie who was given unrestricted access to the SOE's surviving archives and was permitted to interview personnel. An in-house production that was classified as secret, it was not made available to the general public until 2000. Whilst it is an important study, it was written with specific objectives in mind. These were 'how the SOE had come into being, what it had been for, and how it had worked'.

In its 800 pages there is little space devoted to individual agents. Mackenzie also makes it quite clear that he experienced great difficulty piecing together the details for his history from the SOE files.

'This material is in great confusion,' he wrote in the Preface. 'Partly through inexperience, partly for reasons of security, SOE began life without a central registry or departmental filing system.' When Buckmaster was challenged about the incomplete state of F Section's files he replied that those who finished their daily work at any time between three and five in the morning felt 'little desire to tabulate the events of the day in order to earn the gratitude of some hypothetical historian of the future'.[20]

The historians of the present, no longer hypothetical, are further hampered in their research by the sad fact that there was a fire at Baker Street early in 1946 in which a great many documents were destroyed. Marcus Binney quotes an unpublished paper which claims that Norman Mott, the head of the SOE Liquidation Section in Baker Street, had once stated: 'The entire contents of my office where I was holding a considerable number of operational files ... In addition, all the handing-over briefs from the SOE Country Sections were destroyed as well as a good deal of material relating to investigations into blown *réseaux*.'[21]

What remains is, according to one source, no more than fifteen percent of the original total. Part of the reason for this is that many records were destroyed during the war for fear that they would fall into the hands of the enemy. This happened in Singapore immediately before the Japanese seized the island in 1941 and in the summer of 1942 in Egypt. It is said that there were 'clouds of smoke' hanging over Cairo as secret papers were hurriedly burnt by British military and governmental officials when it was thought that Rommel's *Afrika Korps* was about to capture the city.[22] Indeed, some accounts state that 1 July 1942 was afterwards known as 'Ash Wednesday' for this reason.

The estimate of the small percentage of the SOE's records that have survived to the present day is supported by the National Archive guide *SOE Operations in Western Europe*. Its authors state: 'As with most of the SOE records, these are only a fraction of what originally existed. There is evidence of fire and water damage in many of the papers. As there was no central registry and no indication of the file series it is difficult to estimate overall losses, which have been put as high as eighty five percent.'[23]

It was not until 2003 that the first of the around 8,000 surviving SOE Personal Files were released through the National Archive. This, at last, enabled us to progress. Slowly over the succeeding years, more and more of the persnnel files have been opened. Yet some of the SOE files, almost seventy years on, are still closed to the general public. This occurs where the papers in the file may contain information on people still alive, even though the individual to which the file relates may be dead.

Further complications occur in the files of the National Archive in that some names are spelt differently from those given by the CWGC and some are logged under names that the individuals adopted during their SOE service. Such, indeed, was the secrecy pervading the whole of the SOE operation and organisation that some people with names or backgrounds similar to other operatives became confused with those other agents.

Take, for example, the case of Jean Renaud-Dandicolle. He operated under the names J. Danby, Dandy, Jean Renaud, Jean Larrue and J. Demirmont. If this is not enough to confuse the unwary researcher, there is another agent who died whilst serving with the SOE called Jean Renaud. To make matters worse both of them, remarkably, had been awarded the Military Cross. On top of this there were at least four agents whose fieldname was Jean and another whose fieldname was Renaud!

The information found within these files is also far from complete. Some contain a wealth of detail about the individuals, their background, their training and their operational instructions. Others, sadly, have just a few papers with tantalisingly few real facts. Such words as 'believed', 'suspected' and 'possibly' occur all too frequently.

For many families the fate of their loved-ones was never positively confirmed. Take the above-mentioned Jean Renaud. In August 1945 his father tried to establish the facts surrounding his son's disappearance. He sent a letter to the French authorities that included the following words: 'We have received no definite answer and we do not know whether to infer that our son is alive or dead. Now that the European war is over, and in the case of the secret services of "Jean" having demanded a silence which we have never ceased to observe in his own interests, we suppose that there is no reason why you should not inform us definitely. It is understood that if a certain secrecy must be observed, we would do it willingly. It would be enough for us to know whether Jean is still alive.'[24] Sadly, as we now know, Jean was killed.

On 21 August 1944, Gubbins sent a circular to all country section heads demanding that the fate of all those who had worked 'so devotedly and gallantly' for the SOE should be investigated. Only in the French Section was there someone with the drive and energy to undertake this task thoroughly, and this was Flight Officer (later Squadron Officer) Vera Atkins.

For many months after the end of the war in Europe Atkins doggedly pursued and interrogated both surviving SOE agents, former Gestapo personnel and concentration camp officials throughout Germany. As regards the missing agents of other sections, the fate of many remains obscure.[25]

* * *

France was the most important SOE arena, and the most dangerous for its agents. Almost a quarter of F Section's agents in France failed to return and Maurice Buckmaster estimated that the losses incurred within F Section were 'equivalent to those sustained by a regiment of the line in constant action'.

They inevitably form the largest group investigated in this book. As the head of F Section, Buckmaster knew only too well the dangers his agents faced. 'In no other department of war did so much courage pass unnoticed,' he wrote after the war. 'In no other department of war were men and women called upon to die alone, to withstand agony of mind and body in utter solitude, to face death, often ignominious and pain-racked, uncertain whether they might not have saved themselves by the revelation of petty secrets. In no other department of war were civilians asked to risk everything.'[26]

This is the story of those 140 men and women who did risk, and lose, everything.

Notes

1. Stevenson, *A Man Called Intrepid*, pp.72 and 105.
2. Dalton, *The Fateful Years*, p.368; Butler, *Grand Strategy*, pp.53-4.
3. Cookridge, *Inside SOE*, p.13.
4. Auty & Clogg, *British Policy*, p.3. There was a 'charter' put onto paper on 19 July 1940 as the 'War Cabinet Home Defence (Security) Executive, Special Operations Executive'. This was published in the year 1992 by Nigel West in *Secret War* and in 2000. Mackenzie, *Secret History of SOE*, pp.753-5.
5. West, Appendix 1, pp.329-334.
6. Foot, *SOE: The Special Operations Executive*, p.8.
7. Jones, *Quiet Courage*, pp.50-7.
8. TNA HS9/30/1.
9. Buckmaster, *They Fought Alone*, p.63.
10. Foot, *SOE in the Low Countries*, p.29.
11. The time when the agents awaiting transport out to their theatre of operations were most likely to come into contact was at the SOE holding flat in Orchard Court. The man in charge of the flat, a man called Park, would, 'move people from briefing room to briefing room (and into the bathroom) with the agility of characters in a French farce.' Buckmaster, pp.52-3.
12. TNA HS9/908/1.
13. Cowburn, *No Cloak, No Dagger*, p.118.
14. This person was called Nigel Low, Buckmaster, pp. 45-6; Howard, *Undercover*, p.191.
15. J. Tickell, *Odette*, p.222-5.
16. M. Seaman, *Bravest of the Brave*, p.140.
17. J.W. Wheeler-Bennett, *Nemesis of Power*, p.662, quoted in Foot, *SOE in France*, p.373.
18. West, p.318; Nicholas, *Death Be Not Proud*, p.19.
19. Binney, *The Women Who Lived for Danger*, pp.338-40.
20. Howard, p.187.
21. Binney, *op cit*.
22. Sutherland, *He Who Dares*, p.71.
23. Dear, p.211.
24. TNA HS9/391/7.
25. Foot, *SOE in the Low Countries*, p.426.
26. Buckmaster, p.203-4.

Chapter 2

Carve their Names with Pride

The Lost Agents of the SOE as recorded on the Commonwealth War Graves Commission Register

ADLER, Gabriel

Date of death:	1 June 1944
Place of death:	Rome, Italy
Rank:	Lieutenant
Parent unit:	General List
Service number:	246996
Decorations:	None recorded
Date joined SOE:	21 September 1942
Code names:	Gabriele/Bianchi/John Armstrong
Nationality:	Hungarian
Age at time of death:	Twenty-four
Date of birth:	15 September 1919
Place of birth:	Satu-mare, Hungary (Ceded to Romania in 1920)

Location of memorial: Cassino, Italy

On 10 January 1943, Gabriel Adler was infiltrated by submarine into the Cagliari area of Sardinia to undertake Operation *Avocat*, his part of which was to implement a wireless plan called *Moselle*. As soon as he was landed he was seized by Italian troops and was imprisoned at Cagliari. His wireless set was with him when he was arrested and attempts were made by the Italian military intelligence agency SISMI (*Servizio per le Informazioni e la Sicurezza*) to play this back to London.

In May or June 1943 he was transferred to the Regina Coeli prison in Rome, which was taken over by the German *Sicherheitsdienst* (SD) following the Italian surrender. He was interrogated by the SD but gave away no important information and even managed to convince the Germans that he was British. As he had never started his mission in Sardinia he was not considered to be a threat to the Germans and, after his interrogation, he was left alone, though remained incarcerated in Regina Coeli. After approximately a year in Rome it was reported that a 'John Armstrong' was in prison at Lake Bracciano, which is some 35 miles outside the Italian capital.

After the liberation of Rome by Allied forces in June 1944, considerable efforts were made to find out what had become of Adler. It was discovered that he had been one of eighty prisoners selected by the Gestapo from the cells at Regina Coeli on 3 June 1944 to be moved to northern Italy ahead of the Allied advance.

This group was assembled in the courtyard of the prison and their hands tied behind their backs. They were put onto trucks, having been told that they were to be taken to the SD headquarters at the Via Tasso in Rome (now home to the Historical Museum of the Liberation) and then onto Florence. At 00.30 hours on the 4th, a second batch of prisoners was assembled in the same fashion as the earlier group; hands tied and put onto the trucks.

A few of the captives believed that they were not being transferred, rather that they were being taken away to be killed. Consequently, shortly after leaving the confines of the prison they made a bid for freedom. Shots were fired but some of them managed to escape.

A further report indicated that the first batch of prisoners removed from the prison had also tried to escape when the convoy of trucks was the subject of an Allied air attack. Little attempt was made to stop the escapees by the guards who were just ordinary Italians simply glad to get away from Rome. There was no word specifically about Adler.

Later, however, a large number of bodies were taken to the Santo Spirito Hospital in Rome. One report stated that none of the bodies was Adler's. At the time Adler was known to be wearing battle dress over which was a pair of ski-ing trousers and a wind jacket, and none of the bodies wore such clothing. A contradictory report, this time from a New Zealand priest who was at the hospital, said that he saw a placard attached to one of the bodies which read 'Unknown English soldier'.

When the Allies reached Rome, the Regina Coeli was empty. Witnesses stated that even as the last of the German vehicles was leaving, the remaining prisoners were being released.

With such a mass of conflicting evidence, the officers investigating the fate of Adler concluded that: 'Most probably he is dead, but this conclusion has only been reached by a process of conjecture, and by eliminating other alternatives.'

AGAZARIAN, Jack Charles Stanmore

Date of death:	29 March 1945
Place of death:	Flossenbürg, Germany
Rank:	Flight Lieutenant
Parent unit:	Royal Air Force
Service number:	71106
Decorations:	Mentioned in Despatches, *Croix de Guerre*, *Legion d'Honneur*
Date joined SOE:	30 May 1942
Code names:	Marcel/Usher/Jacques Chevalier
Nationality:	British
Age at time of death:	Twenty-nine
Date of birth:	28 August 1915
Place of birth:	Stanmore, Middlesex, UK

Location of memorial: Brookwood, UK

A director of a Physio-Therapeutic organisation until 1940, Jack Agazarian, the second of six children born to an Armenian father and a French mother, was extremely well-liked by his trainers, being repeatedly described by them as 'intelligent, witty, brilliant and clever'. The only flaw in his character that they identified was that when in the company of women, his 'incorrigible chivving [*sic*] of them makes him a target of their vanity and arouses the amused interest of others'.

His first SOE mission began when he was parachuted into France to join the PHYSICIAN circuit on 29 December 1942. He worked as a wireless operator in Paris for six months. The Gestapo knew that he was transmitting and were constantly, and often closely, on his trail. Despite these dangers he remained in regular contact with London. On several occasions he narrowly escaped arrest, eventually becoming so badly compromised that he was forced to leave France in June 1943.

Although the Gestapo had a photograph of him and were still actively searching for him, he agreed to return to France just a month later to join another circuit as their wireless operator. He left for this second mission on 22 July 1943, joining the PROSPER circuit.

A few weeks after his arrival, his circuit chief, Nicholas Bodington, received a message asking him to attend an important rendezvous. The address of the meeting place (the flat of a Madame Ferdi-Filipowski in the Rue de Rome) was radioed to him via fellow agent Norman Gilbert from London. It was thought that the address might have been blown so Agazarian, in order to protect Bodington, volunteered to go in his place.

The meeting place was indeed under German surveillance and upon his arrival Agazarian was arrested. After his capture he was taken to Avenue Maréchal Foch and then the *Maison de Correction* at Frèsnes, Val-de-Marne near the city of Paris, which became the largest criminal prison in Europe. He remained at Frèsnes for several months before being transported to Flossenbürg Concentration Camp in Bavaria, Germany.

After the American 90th Infantry Division (part of the US Third Army) liberated Flossenbürg on 23 April 1945, they were able to secure the details of all the prisoners – with the exception of the British captives, the records of whom had been destroyed by the *Schutzstaffel* (SS). According to the testimony of one of the survivors from the camp, who was a Czech national, there were fifteen British prisoners and only one of these – a Thomas Swan of Glasgow – was still alive when the camp was liberated.

A Danish officer in the cell next to Agazarian later reported that on the morning of his execution he tapped a message in Morse code on the adjoining wall: 'I believe this is our turn. Cheerio, and give my love to my wife.' Happily, this message was indeed passed onto Mrs Agazarian, who also worked for F Section.

Agazarian was recommended by his Section Head for a medal, with these words: 'This officer showed outstanding bravery in returning to France though known to the Gestapo, and his self-sacrifice in volunteering to take his commanding officer's place at a dangerous rendezvous is worthy of the highest praise. It is strongly recommended that he receive the Military Cross.'

Unfortunately, the MC cannot be awarded posthumously and this request was denied. This led to the head of the SOE Major General Gubbins himself intervening on Agazarian's behalf, proposing the award of the MBE. The only award he would be granted was that of a Mention in Despatches.

ALEXANDRE, Roland Eugène Jean

Date of death:	September 1944	
Place of death:	Gross-Rosen (now Rogoźnica) Poland	

Rank:	Lieutenant
Parent unit:	General List
Service number:	306148
Decorations:	None recorded
Date joined SOE:	23 December 1943
Code names:	Astre/Roland Esnault
Nationality:	French
Age at time of death:	Twenty-three
Date of birth:	30 June 1921
Place of birth:	Jouy-à-Josas, France

Location of memorial: Brookwood, UK

Roland Alexandre was born in France, but educated at Shoreham Grammar School and Brighton Technical College before joining General Aircraft Ltd at Feltham in Middlesex as an aircraft fitter. His SOE assessors regarded him as being a little too young to operate on his own, but considered he would make a reliable assistant to an experienced organiser. His only failing was an entirely forgivable, but excessive, interest in the opposite sex.

His role was to re-establish contact with the circuits in the Nantes and Angers areas, both of which had all but ceased to operate due to the effectiveness of the Gestapo in that part of France. The organiser in Angers became known to the Germans and he went to live in Nantes, handing over to a new man sent out from Baker Street. Then, in May 1943, the Nantes organiser was arrested and the net started to close around the Angers' circuit. The organiser was evacuated back to the United Kingdom by Lysander.

Back in London both these organisers said that, despite the setbacks, the area they had left offered 'considerable opportunities'. The Nantes group, for example, had put together a plan to take possession of the city's port, which stands on the banks of the Loire, on D–Day, whilst the Angers group had arranged to cut the railway line and the telephone communications. All that these groups needed were the arms and equipment and the go-ahead from London.

Once he had settled himself into his new surroundings Alexandre was expected to get the circuits going again, continue with the supply drops and put into place the various plans. He was given 200,000 francs and told that he could spend 150,000 francs a month without reference to his Section Head. He was also given one very specific instruction – to avoid the wife of one of the circuit's organisers, known as Madame Wilkinson, because she was 'most talkative and dangerous on security grounds'.

Alexandre was advised to concentrate his efforts against railway targets and, interestingly, this was because Baker Street had persuaded the RAF to abandon attacks on French locomotives and trains by fighters and fighter-bombers. Major General Gubbins had convinced the RAF that not only was the SOE more effective than the fighters in these kind of actions but also that this would prevent the loss of valuable pilots and planes.

He was dropped by parachute on 8 February 1944, with his radio operator, the American Robert Byerly, and two other agents, Francis Deniset and Jacques Ledoux, near Poitiers. They were supposed to have been met on landing by Emile Garry's PHONE agents but this circuit had been penetrated and all four were immediately arrested.

Alexandre was initially imprisoned at Frèsnes. At first it was reported that he had then been moved to a fortress-style camp called Ravitch (Ravitsch) on the Polish / Silesia border and was last seen alive there on 11 September 1944, though it was said that he was being very badly treated.

This information was later found to be suspect, and his name now appears on the memorial at Gross-Rosen as one of the agents killed there in September 1944. Typical of the confusion surrounding the fate of missing agents is that the CWGC give his date of death as 19 May 1944.

ALLARD, Elisée Albert Louis

Date of death:	14 September 1944
Place of death:	Buchenwald, Germany
Rank:	Lieutenant
Parent unit:	General List
Service number:	313354
Decorations:	None recorded
Date joined SOE:	December 1943
Code names:	Henrique/Charles Montaigne
Nationality:	French
Age at time of death:	Thirty-eight
Date of birth:	14 July 1906
Place of birth:	Vieux Conde, France.

Location of memorial: Brookwood, UK

Elisée Allard joined the French Army in 1937 and fought with distinction in the Battle of France, being wounded and decorated before being taken prisoner by the Germans. He was transported to Germany where he was put to work in a factory in Kaiserslautern.

After one failed attempt, Allard managed to escape and made his way through France to the unoccupied zone. Here he began his Resistance activities at Limoges where he worked as the secretary to Marcel Leccia in the *Maison des Prisonniers de Guerre*, which was an organisation that assisted with the repatriation of prisoners of war returning from Germany.

When the Germans moved into the unoccupied zone in November 1942, Leccia and Allard decided to try and reach Britain. They set off across the Pyrénées on foot in December 1942. Soon after entering Spain they were captured and imprisoned. They spent almost a year in and out of various prisons throughout Spain until they escaped and made their way to Portugal, eventually reaching England by ship from Lisbon.

Allard began his SOE training and assessment in December 1943. He was highly regarded by his assessors who saw him as 'certainly giving the impression of a man who is 100 percent reliable'. He had a 'very pleasant manner, and a cool, cautious temperament'. Though he was quietly humorous and very well liked by the rest of his training group, it was very apparent to the assessors that he was not a leader. He was a quiet man who liked to remain in the background and let others take the lead. He would therefore, ran the final report on Allard, 'make a splendid second in command'.

He was utterly devoted to Leccia and he asked if he could continue to work with Leccia on his next mission. This was granted and the two men left for the field on 5 April 1944, along with the Belgian, Geelen, to start the LABOURER circuit around Touraine and Paris. The group would be composed of Leccia's friends and relations all of whom knew each other well. They parachuted into the Creuse (a department in central France named after the Creuse river) and were taken to a safe-house. They brought with them a large sum of money for the F-Section agent Pearl Witherington and the STATIONER circuit.

The men were in Paris soon after landing in France to meet with contacts in the capital when they were arrested. It transpired that one of Leccia's friends was working for the Germans.

Allard was reported to have been seen in Cherche-Midi prison (this was a jail in Paris for military prisoners) on 9 May 1944, being then transferred to Frèsnes on 30 June. He was eventually moved to Buchenwald where he was one of sixteen agents hanged without trial on the night of 11/12 September 1944.

AMPHLETT, Philip John

Date of death:	29 March 1945	
Place of death:	Flossenbürg, Germany	

Rank:	Lieutenant
Parent unit:	General List, No.2 Commando
Service number:	270979
Decorations:	Mentioned in Despatches
Date joined SOE:	10 August 1942
Code Names:	Taxidermist/Phillipe Jean Chiraux
Nationality:	British
Age at time of death:	Twenty-three
Date of birth:	15 April 1921
Place of birth:	London

Location of memorial: Brookwood, UK

The son of an army major, Philip Amphlett had not settled into any particular career after leaving school and his last employment before joining the British Army was that of a commercial traveller. In this capacity he had travelled many times to France but, despite this, his French vocabulary was deemed weak.

His reports during his SOE training were not very favourable. 'Amphlett, is unsuitable for this kind of work,' ran one report. 'His general attitude was slovenly, and he appeared to lack determination or the offensive spirit necessary for this type of work.' Yet, as a former Commando, he was strong and agile and the report from the Physical Training instructor was highly complimentary.

Consequently, it was decided that Amphlett would be better suited in direct action rather than general covert work and he was parachuted into France on 16 August 1943, as part of the SCULLION II *coup-de-main* team to attack the distillation plant at *Usines et Raffineries des Telots* synthetic oil plant near Autun. The first attempt at sabotaging this plant earlier in the year, Code named SCULLION 1, having failed.

The operation was not a great success but this was not due to any failings on the part of the field team. The operatives had been provided with demolition charges that were inadequate for the job, and little real damage was done. Amphlett performed his part of the operation well, which led to him being recommended for a Mention in Despatches 'for his bravery and initiative during a hazardous operation in enemy-occupied territory'. The wording of his citation explained how: 'Amphlett showed very great daring and *sang-froid* in the execution of his particular tasks. The leader in the party paid tribute to the speed and accuracy with which Amphlett placed his charges on the target.'

After the operation he was to make his way back to Britain and was last seen at Dijon on 23 August 1943. Only two men from the raiding party reached England and nothing more was known in London of Amphlett's whereabouts. He was listed simply as 'missing' and his pay abruptly terminated. More than a year later, with his bank account about to fall into the red, Baker Street decided to inform the War Office that Amphlett was 'missing in action' so that he could receive his normal pay. As nothing could be revealed about the nature of his work, his status could not be published in the open Casualty Lists.

It was later learnt that he had been captured trying to leave France. He was taken initially to Frèsnes and then to Flossenbürg where he was executed. In October 1945 Vera Atkins wrote to Major Amphlett telling him of some information that she had recently received about the 'exemplary courage' of the British agents that had been held at Flossenbürg and their 'uncompromising attitude towards their jailors'.

AMPS, James Frederick

Date of death:	29 March 1945
Place of death:	Flossenbürg, Germany
Rank:	Lieutenant
Parent unit:	Royal Artillery
Service number:	241288
Decorations:	None recorded
Date joined SOE:	16 December 1942
Code Names:	Tomas/Chemist/Jean Marechal
Nationality:	French
Age at time of death:	Thirty-eight
Date of birth:	21 April 1906
Place of birth:	Rueil-Malmaison, France
Location of memorial:	Brookwood, UK

James Amps was born in Rueil-Malmaison in the western suburbs of Paris, and at the age of thirteen became an apprentice to a racehorse trainer in Chantilly. Through this work, Amps eventually became a professional jockey.

With the situation in Europe deteriorating, Amps made his way to Britain in April 1940 and enlisted with the Royal Artillery – his brother, Brigadier J.W. Amps, was already serving with 268 Coastal Battery, Royal Artillery in the Orkney Islands. Amps served with an anti-aircraft battery in the Shetlands until he was considered for the SOE at the beginning of 1942.

Though described by his SOE assessor as being 'illiterate' Amps was also considered to be 'physically tough' and have 'plenty of guts'. He damaged his knee during parachute training in June 1942 and the injury was such that at first looked as if it would require an operation. Nevertheless, he recovered satisfactorily and was able to be parachuted into northern France on the night of 1/2 October of that year.

He was to be a key operative in the important PROSPER network and would act as second in charge to Major Francis Suttill. 'In principle,' he was informed, 'you will work one part of the population whilst PROSPER works another. You have been shown and know all the details of PROSPER's mission, its objects and their order of importance, policy in regard to attacking targets and necessity for maintaining at all times your communications with London.' It was most unusual for an assistant to be so fully informed but the reason why Amps was treated differently was that if anything should happen to Suttill, Amps would be expected to take over command of the vital PROSPER circuit.

We are fortunate that his operational instructions still survive. They provide us with a rare glimpse into the way the agents had to work in Occupied France in these very early days of the SOE when there was no effective Resistance movement and no-one to welcome them when they landed in the dark.

He and Suttill were to be dropped 'blind' in the countryside outside Paris: 'You will then go to Paris by train, and PROSPER [i.e. Suttill], your circuit chief, will decide which of you is to go to one of the two addresses which he has, in order to obtain absolutely recent information on conditions, use of food cards and the best place where you can live, at any rate during your early part of your time in the field.'

They were given the two addresses in Paris and told how to identify themselves. At the first address they were to say that they were friends of Charles Young and 'how sorry they were to hear that his dog was dead'. At the other address they would make themselves known by saying 'de la part de Charlot'.

If contact was lost with PROSPER there was a pre-arranged rendezvous at a café on the Rue Caumartin every day at midday and remain there for only ten minutes. A local girl, referred to only as Monigue (who would also act as his courier), would pass there at that time each day. Amps was also given a 'post-box' to send reports back to London as well as a safe-house where he could hide if being chased by the Gestapo.

His family was still living in France and when Amps first went missing it was reported that he had not been arrested and that he was merely 'inactive' and living peacefully with his wife, Odette, in Paris. Indeed, a report from Paris dated 18 May 1943, stated: 'Amps is no good. Recommend he be left in peace and used for one or two minor jobs only.' Apparently he handled written messages with difficulty and was no good with codes.

He was duly left unemployed and it was presumed that he was still with his wife when he was arrested. He was taken to Frèsnes jail in September 1944 before being transferred to Flossenbürg. He was executed here on 29 March 1945.

ANTELME, Joseph Antoine France

Date of death:	19 May 1944
Place of death:	Gross-Rosen (now Rogoźnica) Poland
Rank:	Major
Parent unit:	General List
Service number:	239255
Decorations:	OBE, *Croix de Guerre Avec Palme, Legion d'Honneur*
Date joined SOE:	1941
Code names:	Dumontet/Athos/Ratier Antoine/ Joseph Marie Fernand
Nationality:	British
Age at time of death:	Forty-four
Date of birth:	12 March 1900
Place of birth:	Curepipe, Mauritius

Location of memorial: Brookwood, UK

Joseph Antelme was recruited by the SOE in November 1941 whilst in the South African artillery in Durban, South Africa. After his successful contribution to Operation *Ironclad*, the British take-over of Madagascar in 1942, Joseph Antelme volunteered to continue working with the SOE in France. One of fourteen Franco-Mauritians who served in SOE during the Second World War, Antelme went into France in November 1942 with the job of contacting French officials to arrange finance and protect supply lines for the Allied troops after the D-Day landings.

He went back to the UK in March 1943 returning to France in May that year to join Francis Suttill's PROSPER circuit. He also carried with him messages from Winston Churchill to former French Prime Ministers Édouard Herriot and Paul Reynaud, inviting them to come to Britain.

Disaster struck the PROSPER network before Antelme could make contact with the French politicians when Suttill was arrested in June 1943. Although he was fortunate enough to escape the first round-up of agents following Suttill's arrest, he was now on the run. He was equally fortunate to be able to return to England as planned by Lysander on 20 July 1943.

When he arrived back in London in mid-July, the normally confident and resilient Antelme was a shaken man. He had only escaped capture because he was out of Paris at the time of the arrests of the PROSPER agents. The tale he had to tell, of mass arrests and reports of shootings, was indeed a shocking one. The arrests appeared systematic and based on sound information. It appeared to those running F Section that someone's resolve had broken and they were revealing everything they knew.

They were not aware, of course, about the duplicity of Henri Déricourt who was being run as a double agent by *SS-Sturmbannführer* Karl Bömelburg, head of the Gestapo in France. Déricourt, who was the SOE's chief air movement's officer in northern France, became one of the organisation's most controversial characters and despite his admission after the war that he assisted the Germans, he was never punished. Through Bömelburg's department, the Germans were informed of the arrival and departure of agents organised by Déricourt. Usually agents would be allowed to depart unmolested, so as not to arouse any suspicions in London, and agents that had landed were not arrested until the aircraft had departed.

In February 1944, rested and resolved, Antelme was parachuted back into France with two other agents. With him was Madeleine Damerment, who was to act as his courier, and Lionel Lee, his radio man. Antelme's role on this, his third mission in France, was predominantly to investigate the PARSON circuit based at Rennes, which London suspected was in enemy hands. Antelme was also to arrange a double Lysander operation near Le Mans and then set up a new circuit (SURVEYOR) at any place he decided upon near, but to the south of, Paris.

The three agents were to be met by a reception committee arranged via the radio of Noor Inayat-Khan which, for some time, had been a subject of concern at Baker Street. There was a strong chance that Inayat-Khan's PHONO circuit was controlled by the Germans and that the three agents would fall straight into the arms of the Gestapo. In case this might happen, Antelme was advised to 'cut completely with the PHONO circuit on landing'.

After a number of delays due to bad weather, the skies cleared and the trio set off from RAF Tempsford on 29 February. Upon his return, the pilot of the Handley Page Halifax reported that all had gone to plan. The plan that succeeded, however, was that of the Gestapo into whose arms he landed.

Antelme was still in a 'towering' rage at being taken by the Germans when he arrived at 84 Avenue Foch in Paris. He was so well known to the Gestapo that they merely brushed aside his attempts at disguising his identity. Yet he was able to convince them that he was sent back into France to work under Emile Garry and that Garry was to have briefed him on his new mission.

Antelme was moved to Gross-Rosen concentration camp where he was executed in May 1944.

AUSTIN, John Patrick Standridge

Date of death:	4 April 1945
Place of death:	Zwolle, Netherlands
Rank:	Sergeant
Parent unit:	Royal Berkshire Regiment
Service number:	5348971
Decorations:	Mentioned in Despatches
Date joined SOE:	1944
Code names:	Bunny
Nationality:	British
Age at time of death:	Twenty-two
Date of birth:	September 1922
Place of birth:	United Kingdom

Location of memorial: Hattem, Netherlands

John Austin was sent into Holland as the radio operator of the DUDLEY Jedburgh team with Dutchman Major Brinkgreve and American Major Olmsted. Their objectives included the organisation and equipping of the Resistance movement in Overijessal in the central eastern part of the country and to prepare plans for the defence of bridges essential for the Allied forces in their advance into Germany in conjunction with Operation *Market Garden*.

They were dropped by a Short Stirling bomber into eastern Holland on 11 September 1944, in uniform. Though this had been standard policy for many of the Jedburghs in France it was impractical in a small country like the Netherlands and they had to obtain civilian clothing before they could move around more freely.

They arrived with containers full of arms, which were quickly hidden away. The local (self-appointed) Resistance leader had a very imperfect group under his command and Brinkman soon found that nothing was known of the German troops in the area or of any enemy supplies or depots in the area. The next day Austin received his radio sets.

Brinkgreve soon had things organised and on 17 September they were informed of the start of *Market Garden*, the bold Allied plan to seize the bridges over the Rhine. They were told to keep all the roads clear of civilians and to guard the bridges in their area. This they achieved but *Market Garden* failed and the Allies were unable to penetrate as far as Overijessal.

With the fighting continuing around Arnhem there was increased enemy activity and whilst travelling along one road they encountered an SS roadblock. They dare not stop to be inspected so the driver crashed through the road block whilst the agents, including some local Dutch fighters, opened fire. Five Germans were wounded or killed in the brief but fierce engagement. The agents subsequently learned that another car of the same make approached the road block later in the day and was attacked by grenades and machine-guns. When the Germans went to investigate the wrecked car they found to their dismay an SS officer, an SD officer and their driver all dead.

The Jedburgh team and their Dutch colleagues seemed to have had a remarkably successful time in Holland. They organised sabotage operations and were involved in a number of battles with the Germans. Their activities also included robbing the bank at Almelo, where they made off with more than 50,000 guilders. This money had been taken from the Dutch by the Germans and was being held at Almelo prior to its removal to Germany.

During the week of 24 September to 1 October they were able to bring together all the Resistance groups in the region, which amounted to 3,500 men who were ready for immediate action. Another 12-15,000 could be mobilised should the Allies force the passage of the Rhine.

Towards the end of November the Jedburgh team and 116 others, including evaders from the 1st British Airborne Division, which had become trapped behind enemy lines, attempted to cross over the Rhine. Only seven succeeded. The remainder were killed or captured. The latter included Sergeant Austin.

He was imprisoned at Zwolle. On 4 April Austin and five Dutch prisoners were taken from their cells and shot. Though at first there was some suggestion that Austin may have been shot in an escape bid, it seems this was in fact a reprisal measure for an attack that had been carried out earlier against an important German official.

BARRETT, Denis John

Date of death:	5 October 1944
Place of death:	Buchenwald, Germany
Rank:	Flight Lieutenant
Parent unit:	Royal Air Force Volunteer Reserve
Service number:	71108
Decorations:	Mentioned in Despatches, *Croix de Guerre*
Date joined SOE:	23 November 1943
Code names:	Honoré/Innkeeper/Charles Meunier
Nationality:	British
Age at time of death:	Twenty-seven
Date of birth:	23 November 1916
Place of birth:	Paris, France
Location of memorial:	Runnymede, UK

Born in Paris to British parents, Denis Barrett was a tailor in the French capital before joining the RAF in 1929. His ability to speak French eventually saw his transfer to the SOE.

During his subsequent assessment, one SOE trainer considered him to be 'intelligent, practical, resourceful, observant, has plenty of initiative and is well able to look after himself'. It was decided that he would be suitable to lead a small group.

He was first parachuted into the Aube department in the north-east of France in April 1943 as the wireless operator to a circuit in the Troyes area. He worked there until November 1943 when he became so seriously compromised that he had to leave France, returning with nine others to the UK.

He returned to England by Lysander and, after further training, was parachuted back into France in early March 1944. Once again he was to work as a wireless operator, this time for a new circuit (MINISTER) in the Seine–et–Marne.

His circuit organiser described Barrett thus: 'A grand officer. The ideal W/T operator. Technically perfect. Security first class. Willing to undergo any hardship for the safety of his mission. Unselfish, courageous, outstandingly efficient. A very honest and reliable man, with imagination and guts. One of the best men we ever put into the field.'

Barrett had two wireless sets, one he kept in Troyes, the other in the country outside the town. The Gestapo knew that there were agents transmitting from Troyes and they had direction finding vans circulating the town. In addition to this they had German operators situated around the town trying to pick up any transmissions. After another agent was arrested in Troyes whist transporting his wireless set, Barrett decided to cease transmissions from the town and use only his country set.

For a month he cycled from Troyes to his set in Dierry, successfully avoiding the German patrols on all the main roads – there were even times when he cycled past stationary direction finding vans that were listening out for his signals! Regardless of his efforts at concealment Barrett was eventually arrested whilst actually making a transmission.

Typical of the confusion surrounding the activities of the SOE is that the organisation's historian M.R.D. Foot wrote that Barrett was captured whilst part of a group that was on its way to extricate an SAS party that had got into difficulties in the forest of Fontainebleau.

He was taken to Avenue Foch where his name was found marked on the wall after the war. He was later moved to Frèsnes and then to Buchenwald. According to Foot, Barrett was amongst the first fifteen of thirty-one agents to be hanged at Buchenwald in the first week of September 1944. However, this does not correspond with the details in his personal file, which give the same date of 5 October that is recorded by the CWGC.

The latter date is supported by Nigel Perrin in his book *Spirit of Resistance* who states that Barrett was one of the second group of eleven removed from Block 17 on 4 October 1944 and killed throughout the course of that night. He was shot.

BEAUREGARD, Alcide

Date of death:	20 August 1944
Place of death:	Montluc, France
Rank:	Lieutenant
Parent unit:	General List, 2nd Canadian Division Signals
Service number:	D/56546
Decorations:	Mentioned in Despatches
Date joined SOE:	19 August 1943
Code names:	Cyrano/Burglar/André Beauregarde
Nationality:	Canadian
Age at time of death:	Twenty-seven
Date of birth:	25 March 1917
Place of birth:	Roxton Falls, Canada

Location of memorial: Bayeux, France

Canadian Army Signalman Beauregard was sent into France on 8 February 1944, as radio operator for the LACKEY circuit in the Saone-et-Loire department near Lyon. He was described by his training assessor as 'a man of very limited intelligence' yet it was also conceded that he was able to 'make the most' of those limited abilities. His willingness to learn made him 'just worth using'.

As a member of the 2nd Canadian Division Signals, with both electrical and radio training and relations still living in Brittany, he was ideal for a place in the field but only, his assessor stressed, 'as a very short-term W/T operator, but under no other circumstances'. Beauregard's assessor clearly underestimated his capabilities as he went on to perform successfully in the field in conditions of grave danger for five months.

Beauregard had damaged his ankle during parachute training at Ringway so he was landed at Azay-sur-Cher, east of Tours, by Lysander with Jules Lesage (*Cosmo*). The pair's mission was to reinforce the DITCHER circuit. Lesage, however, had made a number of enemies during his first tour of duty in Lyons and none of his former colleagues were willing to work with him again.

Regardless, Beauregard worked on, until he was caught by direction-finding equipment in July 1944. He was taken to Fort Montluc in Lyon – a former military prison used by the Gestapo between 1942 and 1944 for an interrogation centre and internment camp for those waiting for transfer to concentration camps. A report of Beauregard's arrest, which is still in his personal file in the National Archives, was sent to London on 2 August when it was stated that in prison he 'seemed to have lost his reason'. He was, it was thought, shot in the fort on 20 August 1944 – just four days before the prison was liberated by Allied and FFI (*Forces Françaises de l'Intérieur*) forces. This is also the explanation of his death that is given by M.R.D. Foot.

However, more research by the organisation *Libre Résistance*, has suggested an entirely different story. Early on the morning of Sunday, 20 August 1944, the Germans and the *Milice* selected 120 of the inmates from Montluc and crammed them into two buses – buses that still bore the legend 'Gendarmerie Nationale'. They were driven out to the abandoned Fort Côte Lorette at Saint-Genis-Laval, a few miles south-west of Lyon.

Once the prisoners were inside the building of the fort the Germans opened fire. For three-quarters of an hour the executions continued. The mayor of Saint-Genis-Laval, along with the local Gendarmerie, attempted to halt the killings and eventually the Germans stopped shooting. But they had placed explosives around the building and these were detonated. Three men managed to jump out through a window, two of whom were killed. Just one man survived the massacre to tell the tale.

The dead, which included Beauregard, were buried locally on the 23rd in the presence of the entire population of Saint-Genis-Laval – and in front of the Germans. In 1946, the municipality of Saint-Genis-Laval decided to erect a monument in honor of victims of the massacre. It was inaugurated on 28 September and each year since, a commemorative ceremony has taken place on the nearest Sunday to 20 August.

BEC, Francisque Eugene

Date of death:	16 June 1944
Place of death:	Forêt de Charnie, France
Rank:	Second Lieutenant
Parent unit:	General List
Service number:	322014
Decorations:	Mentioned in Despatches, *Legion d'Honneur*, *Croix de Guerre*
Date joined SOE:	20 February 1944
Code names:	Hugues/Borer/Raymond Perrin/Francisque Eugène Labrousse
Nationality:	Dual British and French
Age at time of death:	Thirty-eight

Date of birth: 18 October 1905
Place of birth: Palmers Green, UK

Location of grave: Le Mans, France

Though born in England, Francisque Bec received his secondary education in Boulogne and served with the French Air Force between 1925 and 1927. At the outbreak of war in 1939, Bec joined the French Army and was subsequently attached to the British Royal Army Service Corps in France in a liaison capacity.

He was demobilised from the French Army following the fall of France and, after working in a variety of jobs in Grenoble, he crossed into Spain and made his way to Gibraltar. He eventually reached the United Kingdom in September 1942.

Bec began his SOE training in early March 1944. His assessors considered Bec to be 'very slow, painstaking and conscientious, but has a tendency to make mistakes'. Despite this poor assessment, Bec was parachuted into France on 28 May 1944, as an arms instructor to the HEADMASTER 2 circuit in the Sarthe department.

This was a difficult area for the Resistance movement as the population was mainly agricultural and had not suffered from the German occupation. Indeed, in many respects it had profited by it. Not only did this make recruitment difficult but it also limited the places where arms and equipment could be dropped. Nevertheless, along with his circuit chief, Major Chris Hudson, Bec developed two fairly large Resistance groups in the Forêt de Charnie and the Forêt de Bercé. From these bases the groups carried out sabotage in and around Le Mans.

Surprisingly, unlike many other areas in France, news of the Allied landings in Normandy had an adverse effect on the morale of the people around Le Mans. The prospect of having to actually fight the German occupiers led to some in the Resistance here getting 'cold feet'.

Bec was killed on 16 June 1944, when his group was attacked in the Forêt de Charnie by a large German force. The previous night a small party from the HEADMASTER 2 circuit was walking through the woods when they ran into group of Germans. They were captured and duly handed over to the Gestapo.

One of the prisoners, a man called Philippe, gave away the location of the Resistance base in the forest and the following day a body of around 100 German troops attacked Bec's encampment. Taken by surprise, Bec's men were compelled to disperse but only after inflicting heavy casualties amongst the attackers – including the German commanding officer and fourteen of his men. Unfortunately Bec and two of his group were caught in an ambush and all three were cut down by machine-gun fire.

At first Hudson had thought that Bec was 'lacking in those [qualities] essential to our work, personality and energy … he appeared 'dépaysé' [out of his element]'. Following the events of 16 June 1944, though, he reported that: 'He died bravely, and at the end showed evidence of a power of command he had previously lacked.' For his actions that day, Francisque Bec was recommended for a Mention in Despatches.

The bodies of the SOE and Resistance men killed in the fighting were later recovered by their comrades and taken to Le Mans cemetery where they were buried. The ceremony was photographed and copies sent back to London where they were forwarded to Bec's father in Ruislip. The photographs showed three coffins, two draped with the Tricolour, the other with the Union Flag. The graves were covered in flowers, to prove, as Buckmaster wrote, 'how greatly the French appreciated the gallantry of those British officers who had volunteered to work with them'.

BENOIST, Robert Marcel Charles

Date of death:	14 September 1944
Place of death:	Buchenwald, Germany
Rank:	Captain
Parent unit:	General List
Service number:	301112
Decorations:	Mentioned in Despatches, *Médaille de la Résistance Française*
Date joined SOE:	August 1943
Code names:	Lionel/Clergyman/Daniel Perdridge/Roger Marcel/Robert Bremontier
Nationality:	French
Age at time of death:	Forty-nine
Date of birth:	20 March 1895
Place of birth:	Rambouillet, France

Location of memorial: Brookwood, UK

Robert Benoist was recruited into the SOE by former racing driver William Grover-Williams, a friend from his pre-war motor racing days. Benoist himself became a world champion whilst driving for the French Delage team in 1925. He established a small Resistance circuit – CHESTNUT – from his private estate near Rambouillet some 25 miles to the south-west of Paris.

His wireless operator, Dowlen, lived by himself at Pontoise and it was there that he was caught at his set by a German direction-finding team. Thirty-six hours later Benoist's brother, Maurice, who was a peripheral member of the CHESTNUT circuit, was arrested at his flat in Paris.

Under torture, Maurice was forced to reveal where other members of the circuit were being housed and this led to the arrest of Grover-Williams. It seems that Maurice Benoist was recruited as a double agent and that he subsequently helped the Germans – actions which included the betrayal of his brother Robert.

It was just three days after Maurice had been taken into custody, on 2 August 1943, when Robert Benoist was arrested; it occurred in the same street in which Grover-Williams had been captured. Four Germans bundled him into a large car; two of them sat either side of him in the back but they did not handcuff him. They also failed to shut one of the back doors properly, and this was noticed by Benoist. When the car rushed round a corner, Benoist flung himself against the German on that side and together they rolled out into the road. Benoit ran off and disappeared.

Despite his remarkable escape, Benoist soon found that all his friends' houses were under surveillance. However, he was able to hide in his secretary's apartment until Henri Déricourt was able to get him to Britain by Lysander on the night of 19/20 August. Maurice Benoist's complicity in his brother's arrest was confirmed when he was released by the Gestapo a few days later.

Benoist returned to France on 20/21 November 1943, this time to re-start the CLERGYMAN circuit around Nantes. With Denise Bloch as his wireless operator, he first made his way to his estate where there were still arms dumps and men willing to use them again.

Once he had got his circuit fuctioning once more, he and Bloch moved up to Nantes. He returned to the UK for a 'consultation', before being airlifted back into France with instructions to prepare for D-Day. He was given high-voltage electrical pylons and railways in the Nantes region as targets for and after D-Day and was told to prepare for conducting 'anti-scorch activities'.

Benoist and Bloch were both arrested on 18 June 1944. Benoist was the first to be captured when he went to Paris to visit his dying mother. The following day the Germans raided the Benoist château and seized Denis Bloch.

Along with thirty-seven other agents, Benoist was executed at Buchenwald in September 1944 – Benoist was in the first group of sixteen called out of Block 17 on 9 September. It was subsequently reported that the victims were sadistically beaten before being hanged.

'He was indisputably courageous,' wrote Buckmaster in recommending Robert Benoist for a posthumous award, 'quick-witted and tough.' In his honour, the village of Auffargis in north-central France has named a street after him.

BERLINER, Egon Friederich Paul

Date of death:	4 April 1945
Place of death:	Buchenwald, Germany
Rank:	Lieutenant
Parent unit:	General List
Service number:	322825
Decorations:	None recorded
Date joined SOE:	May 1943
Code names:	Flying Officer F.M. Chigwell/Frederick Michael O'Hara/Frederico Hoffer/Fredrich Knoll
Nationality:	Austrian
Age at time of death:	Twenty-two
Date of birth:	9 May 1923
Place of birth:	Vienna, Austria
Location of memorial:	Cassino, Italy

Egon Berliner was the son of an Austrian Jewish family which, in the middle to late 1930s, began to experience problems with the Nazi authorities. In August 1938 he had a fight with a Hitler Youth and was chased for some three hours by SS men before he managed to give them the slip. From that time on, Berliner vowed to escape to Britain.

In May 1939 he arrived home to be told by the porter of his block that there were two men waiting for him. So Berliner put his escape plan into action. He had obtained a Jewish passport with which he was able to travel out of the country. The Austrians were quite happy to let Jews out of their country but there were restrictions on Aryans. He arrived in the United Kingdom in September that year – just as the war began.

As a foreign national he was interned in May 1940 and sent to Canada. He returned from there to Britain in April 1941, joining the Pioneer Corps a month later. He was transferred to the SOE in May 1943.

Though his assessors considered Berliner to be 'self-confident, tough and determined', they were puzzled by his 'absence of any particular ideals or loyalties', which was odd considering his background. Operationally, his task was to make contact with a communist group in Innsbruck in Austria and to see if it could be developed into a Resistance organisation. Though it was not thought that there was much chance of this operation succeeding as none of the population were likely to oppose the Nazi authorities, Baker Street considered it was worth risking one agent – but only one.

Selected as that 'one', on 28/29 July 1944, Berliner was dropped into the southern Tyrol with another agent, though the latter would only escort him as far as Innsbruck. But his mission was not successful and in September he was forced to return to the Allied lines in northern Italy.

Undeterred, he returned to Austria to investigate the Social Democratic movement in Graz, Austria's second-largest city. Again his mission (code named Operation *Evansville*) was unsuccessful and he fled to the Koralpe, a mountain range in southern Austria. In April 1945 he was arrested by the SS at Maribor whilst attempting to cross the River Drave into Yugoslavia. According to one report he was actually betrayed by a local opposition group with whom he had made contact.

Berliner was interred in the Gestapo's Paulusthorgasse prison in Gratz. On arrival he was beaten and questioned for two hours. This was the only interrogation he had to endure but he was then placed in the condemned cell with a number of others.

At 20.30 hours on Tuesday 4 April 1945, SS-*Oberstumführer* Herz of the Graz Gestapo entered the cell and read out a list of names. The men were put on a lorry to be taken to the SS barracks in Wetzelsdorf. Though the Austrians said that the lorry received a direct hit from an Allied bomb and all the prisoners were killed, they were in fact executed and buried locally. Berliner was one of them.

BERTHEAU, Louis Eugene Desire

Date of death:	Between 7 May 1945 and 15 May 1945
Place of death:	Sandbostel, Germany
Rank:	Lieutenant
Parent unit:	General List
Service number:	329598
Decorations:	Mentioned in Despatches, *Médaille de la Résistance Française*, *Legion d'Honneur*
Date joined SOE:	17 March 1944
Code names:	Pélican/Petit Fils
Nationality:	French
Age at time of death:	Twenty-five
Date of birth:	18 November 1919
Place of birth:	Olivet, Loiret, France

Location of memorial: Brookwood, UK

Louis Bertheau was recruited in France for the SOE by Henri Peulevé to act as a wireless operator for his AUTHOR circuit. Bertheau was a twenty-four-year-old former French Air Force radio operator and thus ideally suited for the job.

When the French Army was demobilised by the Germans he moved with his wife to Meymac near Ussel in the Haute-Corrèze region of Central France. Here he offered his services to the local Resistance, eventually being passed onto Peulevé. After only one month's training Bertheau was considered satisfactory and he was soon transmitting to London from Meymac.

From the very first he was under constant threat of capture from the German detection-finding vans that patrolled the streets below his base, as well as spotter aircraft that circled the sky above. Such was the sophistication and intensity of the German surveillance techniques that Baker Street recommended that operators remain on line for no more than five minutes at a time. Despite the danger Bertheau worked up to nineteen hours a day without a break.

On Tuesday 21 March 1944, Peulevé needed to send an urgent message to London. He duly made his way to Bertheau's hide-out on the Route du Tulle in the city of Brive. At around 15.30 hours, two black Citroëns pulled up outside Bertheau's building. One uniformed officer and three others in civilian clothes climbed out of the cars and ran to the house. They burst through the unlocked front door and rushed upstairs to find a group of four men standing around a wireless set.

A neighbour called Adrien Dufour had watched the comings and goings at the house and had believed that the place was being used by a group of Jewish black marketers. He had tipped off the *Milice* who passed the information onto the Gestapo.

Bertheau was in the act of transmitting when the *Milice* officer and the Gestapo entered the room. He had the presence of mind to send a rapid signal 'nous somme pris!' ('We are taken') as the astonished *Milice* took in the unexpected sight that greeted them.

They were marched away in pairs and put into the two cars. The men had not been searched and Peulevé was able to stuff some of the papers he was carrying behind the seat of the car.

The men were taken to the *Waffen-SS* barracks in Tulle and the next morning transferred to the Gestapo headquarters at Limoges before being taken by train the following day to Paris. Later Bertheau was deported to Germany, being incarcerated in the concentration camp at Sandbostel near Bremen. He died there in the hospital from typhus on 7 May 1945, just days after its liberation.

Adrien Dufour, the man who had denounced Bertheau and his colleagues, was later arrested and sentenced by a Limoges court to twenty years' hard labour. Despite been sent to Buchenwald concentration camp, Major Henri Leonard Thomas Peulevé DSO, MC, *Croix de Guerre*, *Legion d'Honneur*, *Médaille de la Résistance Français* survived the war.

BIÉLER, Gustave Daniel Alfred

Date of death:	5 September 1944
Place of death:	Flossenbürg, Germany
Rank:	Major
Parent unit:	Le Régiment de Maisonneuve, Canadian Army
Service number:	Not recorded
Decorations:	DSO, MBE , *Croix de Guerre*
Date joined SOE:	Not recorded
Code names:	Guy/Musician/Guy Morin
Nationality:	Canadian
Age at time of death:	Forty
Date of birth:	26 March 1904
Place of birth:	Beurlay, France

Location of memorial: Grosebeek, The Netherlands

Though born to British parents in France, Gustav Biéler emigrated to Canada at the age of twenty, where he settled in Montréal. He first worked as a school teacher and then as an official translator for Sun Life Assurance, eventually becoming a Canadian citizen.

On the outbreak of the Second World War, although married with two children, Biéler joined the Canadian Army and was eventually posted to Britain. His wife Marguerite Geymonat remained in Canada and worked as a broadcaster to the troops in Europe on Radio-Canada International. Because of his familiarity with France and his fluency in both French and English, Biéler was a natural candidate for service in the SOE. Known to many by his wartime nickname of 'Guy', it is noted in one account that Buckmaster once referred to Biéler in his file as 'the best student SOE had'.

He was sent into the field on 28 November 1942, with wireless operator Arthur Staggs and Michael Trotobas (see later entry) to head up the MUSICIAN circuit. But it was not until March 1943 that Biéler established his own contacts and started working in the Saint-

Quentin/Valenciennes region. The reason for this was that Biéler had hurt his back when he parachuted onto rocky ground in the dark and had spent some months in Paris recuperating.

He performed his first acts of sabotage in May 1943, organising thirteen cuts in important rail lines. For one period the main line from Saint-Quentin to Lille was sabotaged by his teams about once every two weeks. He also arranged the sabotage of the Saint-Quentin canal lock gates, effectively blocking one route by which the Germans sent submarine parts down to the Mediterranean. His operations grew, and eventually he mustered twenty-five Resistance teams scattered over different areas of northern France. They became highly effective, destroying fuel storage tanks, bridges and the electric tractors used to tow barges on the shipping waterways.

Though operating far from the PROSPER *réseaux*, he became linked with that circuit because the radio operator given to Francis Suttill proved incompetent and he was forced to send his messages through PROSPER. It was only when Yolande Beekman was sent out to join Biéler that he had his own capable operator. But, by then, he was known to a number of people in PROSPER; it would prove a fatal connection.

On 13 January 1944, Biéler and Beekman were arrested at the Café Moulin Brulé in Saint-Quentin. It is said that because he tried to resist arrest he was tortured, though most likely the Germans simply wanted to extract as much information as possible. However, it does seem that he was subject to particularly bad treatment.

It is known that he was held in 4 Place des États Unis but was transferred to Flossenbürg (cell no.23) on 9 April 1944. The torture continued, yet his unflinching demeanour gradually earned the respect of his guards. When the crippled and emaciated Canadian was taken out to be shot by firing squad the Germans gave him a guard of honour.

Today the main street of the little village of Fonsommes near Saint-Quentin is called the Rue du Commandant Guy Biéler after this 'formidable' man and in Canada the veterans residence in Montréal is named after him as is the beautiful Lake Biéler.

BLOCH, André

Date of death:	11 February 1942	
Place of death:	Fort Mont-Valérian, France	
Rank:	Lieutenant	
Parent unit:	General List, Royal Fusiliers	
Service number:	184314	
Decorations:	Mentioned in Despatches, *Médaille de la Résistance Française*	
Date joined SOE:	19 February 1941	
Code names:	George/Draughtsman/André Jean Bernard	

Nationality: French
Age at time of death: Twenty-seven
Date of birth: 19 June 1914
Place of birth: Paris, France

Location of memorial: Brookwood, UK

André Bloch (who served as Alan George Boyd), was a former lawyer who spent one year in the French Army before becoming an infantry liaison officer with the British Expeditionary Force in France in 1939.

When he joined the SOE, Bloch was trained as a wireless operator. These operatives were taught how to disguise addresses in their reports. For addresses in Paris, for example, they had to pick the 9th street after the real one in volume 2 of the 1939 Paris telephone directory. They then had to add 9 to the number of the building and put that figure before and after the name of the street. The city itself was to be omitted entirely.

It was essential for anyone who wanted to move around in France to have a valid identity card. It was found that in small towns the cards were validated at the town hall where some 'awkward' questions might be asked. But in Paris it was a simple operation.

This was explained by one agent during his de-brief back in England: 'At the Gare d'Austerlitz there is a notice with the magic words "Here identity cards can be validated". You produce your card to a man at a table, who has a stamp, and if the card is of the right age, it will be stamped.' No questions are asked.

After his training André Bloch was part of a six-man parachute drop from an Armstrong Whitworth Whitley bomber south of Châteauroux on the night of 6/7 September 1941. As a valuable wireless operator (at first he was the only SOE wireless operator in Occupied France), he was promptly taken by SOE agent Pierre de Crevoisier de Vomécourt to help with his AUTOGIRO circuit, which eventually settled around Le Mans. This was SOE's first Resistance network in Occupied France.

Exactly a month later Bloch began his transmissions. For several weeks, his work continued seemingly without problems – until 12 November 1941, that is. This is the date on which his last message was received in London.

The story of Bloch's arrest was explained by Pierre de Vomécourt: 'He happened to be Jewish and this was all too obvious in his appearance. To send us Bloch was yet another example of London's incredible ignorance of the realities of life in Occupied France. Less than a month after he arrived he was denounced as a Jew by one of his neighbours. When the Germans came to his house to arrest him they howled with delight to find his transmitter. Expecting merely to arrest a Jew, they had found themselves a radio operator.'

Bloch was initially imprisoned at Le Mans. It was reported that he was badly beaten in captivity but that he never divulged anything to his interrogators. According to a report complied after the war 'his great courage and self-sacrifice in enduring the torture saved the lives of his comrades'. In the recommendation for a Mention in Despatches to be granted to Bloch it was stated that 'the Gestapo despaired of eliciting any information from him and he was executed on 11 February 1942'.

BLOCH, Denise Madeleine

Date of death:	5 February 1945
Place of death:	Ravensbrück, Germany
Rank:	Ensign
Parent unit:	Women's Transport Service (FANY)
Service number:	F/27
Decorations:	*Legion d'Honneur, Croix de Guerre Avec Palme, Médaille de la Résistance Française (Avec Rosette)*
Date joined SOE:	21 July 1943
Code names:	*Ambroise*/Micheline Claude Rabatel
Nationality:	French
Age at time of death:	Twenty-nine
Date of birth:	21 January 1916
Place of birth:	Paris, France

Location of memorial: Brookwood, UK

Denise Bloch was killed alongside Violette Szabo in Ravensbrück in February 1945. Born in Paris to a Jewish family, she was involved in the Resistance in France becoming a radio operator for SOE agent Brian Stonehouse in Lyons.

Stonehouse was captured on 24 October 1941, and Denise went into hiding. In early 1943 she was contacted by SOE agents George Starr and Philippe de Vomécourt and resumed her work with the SOE in the South of France.

It was eventually decided that she should go to Britain to further her training and to be fully enrolled into the SOE. To do this she had to cross into Spain. On 29 April 1943, in the company of another agent, Maurice Dupont, she walked for seventeen hours over the Pyrénées, before undertaking a twenty-one day journey to London via Gibraltar and Lisbon.

Baker Street regarded Bloch as being too well known by the Gestapo for her to be any further use in France and it was some months before Buckmaster relented and permitted her to commence training. It was, therefore, not until 2 March 1944, that she was landed back in France at Soucelles near Nantes along with another agent Robert Benoist.

She joined the CLERGYMAN circuit as a courier, encoder and wireless operator. Denise was taking an extraordinary risk in returning to France. Benoist was captured on 18 June 1944, and Denise was seized the next day following a raid by the Gestapo on a château (the Villa Cécile) belonging to the Benoist family near Rambouillet. She was just unfortunate to be there at that particular time, having lunch.

She was taken to Frèsnes prison and endured interrogation at the infamous Gestapo headquarters at 84 Avenue Foch. The actual organisation that devoted its efforts against the SOE, particularly in the early years, was the *Abwehr*, the German military counter-intelligence organisation. Initially the *Abwehr* was housed in the former Sûreté headquarters in the Rue de Soussaies, transferring in 1942 to 82 Avenue Foch. What the French Resistance and most people called the Gestapo was the *Sicherheitdienst*, or SD, and this was established in Paris under SS-*Sturmbannführer* Hans Joseph Kieffer in 84 Avenue Foch.

This building was used for imprisonment and interrogation of many of the foreign agents captured in France. The second floor was occupied by the SD's wireless section headed by Dr Josef Goetz and the fourth floor was used by Kieffer himself. The fifth floor was where the agents were held and interrogated.

On 8 August 1944, Denise, in the company of Violet Szabo and Lilian Rolfe, was sent to Ravensbrück (known to the French as *l'Enfer des Femmes* – the Women's Hell). The journey took twelve days. They travelled by train to Metz where they were disembarked and kept in stables overnight. Eventually they were imprisoned at Ravensbrück where the three SOE girls were able to share a bunk together. After just three weeks the girls were shipped out to Torgau and then on to Königsberg.

At Königsberg the women were put to work on a project to help build a new airfield. This involved the clearing of trees and digging ground that was frozen hard. The women suffered terribly from exposure in the freezing temperatures. There was no heating in their huts and their food consisted of potato or beet peelings boiled in water with a little bread – one loaf had to be shared amongst fourteen prisoners. Many of the women workers collapsed and died where they worked amongst the trees.

On the evening of 19 or 20 January 1945, the three SOE girls were told to be ready to return to Ravensbrück at 05.00 hours the next morning. For the journey they were given a change of clothes. When they arrived back at the concentration camp they were put into solitary confinement for a few days before being transferred back to the main part of the camp. Just a few days later all three were shot.

BLOOM, Marcus Reginald

Date of death:	6 September 1944
Place of death:	Mauthausen, Austria
Rank:	Lieutenant
Parent unit:	General List
Service number:	236314
Decorations:	Mentioned in Despatches
Date joined SOE:	24 February 1942
Code names:	Urbain/Bishop/Michel Blount
Nationality:	British
Age at time of death:	Thirty-six
Date of birth:	24 September 1907
Place of birth:	London, UK

Location of memorial: Brookwood, UK

Born into an orthodox Jewish home in Tottenham, north London, Marcus Bloom was sent to France to run the Paris branch of the family mail order business in the 1930s. He returned to England in 1938 and had volunteered for service within forty-eight hours of the declaration of war.

Bloom was recruited into the SOE on 24 February 1942. He was trained as a wireless operator and landed in France by boat via Gibraltar. With the code name *Urbain*, Bloom worked for the PRUNUS circuit where he received the instructions for an attack on the Toulouse Powder (explosive) factory. The attack was successful and for his part in this he was Mentioned in Despatches.

A comment in one SOE file, relating to Bloom, states: 'The risk of sending to the field this officer with his imperfect French and his Anglo-Saxon Jewish appearance, was only justified by an extreme penury of WT operators. He was very courageous and fought to the finish ... it is clear he did a good job for many months.'

His luck would not last. One day in early April 1943 the house in which he was hiding, the Château d'Equerre near Fonsorbes in the Haute-Garonne, south-western France, was surrounded by the SS. Bloom and his comrades had been betrayed.

All the principle members of the team were captured. Suddenly Bloom and a Spanish member of his group, Robert, made a break for freedom. Despite the fact that they were handcuffed together, the pair ran into a surrounding wood, firing pistols at the pursuing Germans. In this manner they managed to cover an astonishing nine miles, having crossed a river seven times to throw the Germans off their trail.

Robert, however, became exhausted and suggested going to the *Gendarmerie de Murray* (near Toulouse) where the *Capitaine* was a known Gaullist. Unfortunately, when they arrived at 05.00 hours, a different officer was on duty who said he would fetch the *Capitaine*. But he disappeared and instead the Gestapo arrived.

Bloom was taken to Frèsnes prison and then onto Avenue Foch for interrogation. According to Leopold Turcan, another Resistance fighter who was also present, Bloom, after his initial interrogation where he gave only his name, rank and number, was marched down a corridor to another room and shoved violently inside. He was pushed into a chair in the middle of the room by two men in suits. One man stood in front of him and again Bloom refused to answer questions, upon which he was struck fiercely in the face by the back of the Gestapo man's hand. Again he refused to answer questions and so the second man came from behind and pointed a revolver at Bloom's temple.

Yet again he refused to answer and he was struck on the head by the butt of the gun. He fell to the floor, blood running down his face, as one of the men kicked him. The interrogators left the room and another guard helped Bloom up and he was driven back to Frèsnes.

Sometime in 1944 Bloom was sent to the camp at Ravitch (Ravitsch), before being marched to Gusen, a satellite camp of Mauthausen, near Linz in Austria. It is understood that there were other Allied agents at Gusen. They were dressed in blue prison uniform, with a white triangle marked with the letter 'I' on the back. They were all kept together in the same wing of the camp.

On 2 September 1944, this group was taken by lorry from Gusen, through the village of Mauthausen and up the hill to the notorious death camp. Here they were housed in what was usually a transport depot. The camp records indicate that forty-seven 'Allied soldiers' were received on that day, of which thirty-nine were Dutch, seven were British and one was American.

On the third afternoon of their incarceration in Mauthausen, each man was ordered to open his shirt and numbers from one to forty-seven were painted on their chests. It has been said that this was the order in which they were to be shot, though it is now believed that this was in fact done for the camp records before the bodies were cremated. Marcus Bloom was number twenty-nine.

This group of prisoners was then taken to a quarry at the edge of the camp. Though there were numerous witnesses to the executions that followed, the details vary considerably from one account to the next. What is certain is that the men were taken to the bottom of the quarry and ordered to carry large stones up the 186 steps that led to the top.

Camp guards and SS lined the steps to drive the prisoners on with sticks and clubs. SS photographers recorded the appalling scene, which they claimed showed the prisoners running up the steps trying to escape. This gave the camp authorities, in their distorted vision, the 'proof' they required. As the men stumbled and fell through exhaustion they were shot.

Marcus Bloom was amongst the first to die. One version of what happened in the quarry notes that after the first two men had been shot, it was Bloom's turn. He ran up the steps with a rock but suddenly turned and threw his rock at the guard striking him fully in the chest; he fell tumbling to the bottom of the steps. Marcus then made a defiant run for it up the stairway of death, but a machine-gun cut him down.

This shocking ritual continued until 15.00 hours – but not all the prisoners had succumbed. The survivors returned under heavy SS guard, carrying the bodies of their comrades on carts into the main camp where they spent the night.

The survivors, quoted as twenty-seven in number, were brought back to the quarry the following day and the slaughter recommenced until all forty-seven were dead. Many of the men refused to go through the ritual of the first day and simply walked up to the entrance and presented themselves to the guards to be shot.

Amongst the many tributes to this SOE agent is an unsigned testimonial provided by his colleagues in the PRUNUS circuit. It ends with the following passage: 'His great courage and composure always hugely inspired all those who knew him. We mourn the loss of this congenial and courageous officer. He fought a gun battle with the Gestapo, although heavily outnumbered, until running out of ammunition, killing several of them. He is remembered here by us all with enormous respect.'

BORREL, Andrée Raymonde

Date of death:	6 July 1944
Place of death:	Natzweiler-Struthof, France
Rank:	Lieutenant
Parent unit:	Women's Transport Service (FANY)
Service number:	F/3
Decorations:	*Croix de Guerre*
Date joined SOE:	15 May 1942
Code names:	Denise/Whittbeam/Denise Urbain
Nationality:	French
Age at time of death:	Twenty-four
Date of birth:	18 November 1919
Place of birth:	Louveciennes, Yvelines, Paris, France

Location of memorial: Brookwood, UK

Andrée Borrel escaped from France to England in 1942, having already been involved with the Resistance in smuggling shot-down Allied airmen out of France. As the first SOE woman to be parachuted into France (along with fellow agent Lise de Baissac), Borrel was to prepare the way for Francis Suttill to set up the first F Section circuit. Her role was to be Suttill's personal courier. Suttill's alias was 'Prosper', from which the circuit took its name.

Borrel was described by Suttill as 'really in every way the best of all of us'. It has been said that Suttill's French accent was so poor he would not have been able to set up his organisation without Borrel's help as a negotiator.

Together Suttill and Borrel travelled throughout central France posing as an agricultural salesman and his assistant whilst engaged on covert operations. This included recruiting more people for his group, sabotaging railway lines and arranging aerial drops of weapons and explosives. It is recorded that the various PROSPER cells received 240 containers of arms and munitions during the first five months of 1943.

However, in June of that year, it became clear that the Gestapo had discovered the identity of at least some of the PROSPER group. On 25 June a 'flash' message was received in the signals room in London from Paris. The message said that Suttill, his main radio operator Gilbert Norman (Archambaud) and Borrel had 'disappeared, believed arrested'.

Four days earlier, on the evening of 22/23 June Borrel had been staying with Gilbert Norman in his supposed 'safe house' when the Gestapo came knocking. Both were arrested.

After many months imprisoned in France, Borrel was sent to the civilian prison at Karlsruhe in the south-west of Germany near the Franco-German border. Soon, though, she was on her way with three other women to the concentration camp at Natzweiler-Struthof situated in the Vosges Mountains of Alsace.

Borrel's departure from Karlsruhe on the morning of 6 July 1944 – exactly one month after the Allied landings in Normandy – was observed by another of the prison's inmates, a

French political prisoner called Lisa Graf. She provided this description of Borrel: 'Denise, a young woman with black hair, blue eyes, pale skin, wearing a grey coat and short blue socks, with navy-blue shoes that had rubber soles.'

Natzweiler-Struthof was first established by the SS in May 1941 and, until the camp was liberated on 23 November 1944, an estimated 52,000 people had passed through its gates and approximately 25,000 of these were killed.

Natzweiler was principally a male camp and the arrival of four women was a notable event – even to the extent that the women were driven by car through the camp to their barrack quarters rather than forcing them to walk through the camp where their presence would be seen by all the inmates.

The women were accompanied by a man from the Karlsruhe Gestapo who allegedly told the camp *Kommandant* that Berlin had issued orders for the women to be killed at once. The women were marched down the *Lagerstrasse*, the path that ran down the centre of the camp – unlike the Gestapo, the SS were not concerned about who saw the women.

One of those who saw the women, Roger Linet, noticed that 'they seemed young, they were fairly well groomed, the clothes were not rubbish, their hair was brushed and each had a case in her hand'. The women, it seemed, had no idea of what awaited them, unlike those that watched them walk by.

According to the statement made by one of the camp doctors, Dr Werner Rohde (who was replacing the out-going Dr Plaza), the order had been given to kill the women that night by hanging. Straub, the camp executioner, objected, arguing that hanging British and French women would cause '*ein grosses theater*' – a big fuss. Another way had to be found.

It is so disturbing to learn, some sixty-five years later, how the Germans calmly went about finding a solution to the problem of how to kill these four girls without making a 'big fuss'.

It was decided that the most suitable method would be by lethal injection. Sarah Helm, in her book *A Life in Secrets*, quotes the statement given by a medical orderly, Emil Bruttel. This man recalled receiving a telephone call from Dr Plaza that evening: 'He told me to look in medical stores and see how many capsules of Evipan there were. I told him there were just enough for the normal requirements of the operating theatre. Then Plaza rang down again. He said: "Look and see if we have any phenol and how much there is.' I reported back that we had about 80cc."

Plaza told Bruttel to bring the Phenol, a 10cc syringe and two larger-gauge needles down to the prison block. Soon the sound of the fires being lit in the crematorium reverberated around the camp.

Meanwhile, Georges Boogaerts, a Belgian doctor who had been given charge of the prisoners' hospital, had managed to make contact with the girls. The windows of the hospital faced directly towards the prison block some 25 yards away and Boogaerts was able to call across to the women, one of whom, he recalled, was dark-haired and called herself 'Denise'. Though she would soon die, Andrée Borrel had not merely 'disappeared'. Her treatment at the hands of the Nazis was now a thing of record.

The women were given a meal of thin soup and bread – their last meal – and then they were moved into separate, single cells that were so small it was impossible for them to stand. An early curfew of 20.00 hours had been imposed and now all the prisoners were in their barracks.

Bruttel and another hospital orderly, Emil Forster, took the phenol and the syringes and met up with the officers who were to conduct the executions. Meeting up by the prison entrance, the orderlies walked down the *Langerstrasse* with Plaza and Rohde, the camp's adjutant, *Obersturmbannführer* Ganninger, and a number of the *Blockführers.*

The execution party entered the crematorium building at the end of the path and went into a small room, where the doctors explained to the others exactly how they were to conduct the killings. The women were to be brought one at a time into the room. Each would then be made to lie on a bed, at which point one of the doctors would perform an intravenous injection into her arm. In every case 10cc of phenol (carbolic acid) would be used.

One by one the young, unsuspecting girls were taken into the room. When one of them asked why they were being injected, she was told that it was for typhus. Only this one of the four (and we cannot be certain which one), her suspicions now aroused, attempted to struggle.

After being injected the drugged women were carried into the adjacent room where they were laid down and undressed. They were then dragged along the corridor to the oven where they were placed on a 'transporter' and pushed inside. The bodies were laid out alternately, i.e. the first one went in feet first, the next one went in head first, and so on.

Accounts of the cremation mention the fact that one of the women may still have been alive when she was pushed into the oven. The following explanation was given by one of the other prisoners in the camp – Walter Schultz – who had been told the story by the man in charge of the oven, Peter Straub: 'When the last woman was half way in the oven (she had been put in feet first) she came to her senses and struggled. As there were sufficient men there they were able to push her into the oven, but not before she had resisted and scratched Straub's face.' According to this account, the woman had shouted '*Vive la France*' as she went to her death.

Whenever the oven door was opened an increased draught drove the flames out of the top of the chimney. Four times that night, at fifteen-minute intervals, the flames shot up into the dark sky for all to witness.

When all the bodies had been burned the doctors left the crematorium. As they walked away from the murder scene they talked about what had happened. They said that they had originally intended to use Evipan but because there was too little in stock they had resorted to phenol. As if to justify the murders to each other they discussed their belief that the women had been killed because they were spies – and they comforted themselves by describing their method of execution as being more 'humane' than hanging.

BOUGUENNEC, Jean

Date of death:	14 September 1944
Place of death:	Buchenwald, Germany
Rank:	Lieutenant
Parent unit:	General List
Service number:	257217
Decorations:	MBE
Date joined SOE:	18 November 1942
Code names:	Max/Butler/Francis Garel
Nationality:	French
Age at time of death:	Thirty-two
Date of birth:	25 July 1912
Place of birth:	St-Eloy, France

Location of memorial: Brookwood, UK

The background of Jean Bouguennec, a journalist before the war, was the subject of some concern at Baker Street. When he arrived in Britain, someone who had had contact with him in France (a Communist supporter called Simone Hartogg) stated that, using the name Garel, he had claimed to have been working with the Resistance in the Dordogne area since 1941. Supposedly he was captured by the Vichy police who agreed to release him when the British paid a ransom of 25,000 Francs. Bouguennec, however, said that after his arrest by the Vichy police he was imprisoned at Mauzac from where he managed to escape before the ransom was paid. He then succeeded in making his way to Britain via Spain.

It was also alleged that in July 1937 he was sentenced to death by the French on charges of espionage. According to the French press at the time he was involved in an MI5 plot organised from London concerning biological warfare.

When this came to light during his SOE vetting process, he claimed that it was not him but another Jean Bouguennec. Eventually this, and his other stories, was accepted and in January 1943 he began his SOE training and assessment. He was described as being 'a typical journalist ... full of anecdote, out of the way information and smiling cynicism'.

On 23 March 1943, he was parachuted into France to start a new circuit (BUTLER) in Brittany, but broke his ankle on landing. After his recovery he built up two important groups, one based at Château du Loire and the other at Sablé-sur-Sarthe. He organised a number of successful supply drops and with the explosives he received carried out several attacks on the railways in the region. On one occasion Bouguennec personally led an attack that resulted in three locomotives being completely destroyed between Sablé and Angers.

He was arrested by the Gestapo along with two other agents (Marcel Fox and Marcel Rousset) whilst having lunch at the house of Lucile Blanchard on 7 September 1943. It is thought that they were betrayed by one of the circuit members. Initially held in Avenue Foch, on 18 April 1944, he was moved to Ravitsch in Poland, returning to Paris and internment at the Gestapo torture cells at 3 bis Place des États Unis on 19 May. On 8 August 1944, he was transported to Buchenwald – a move that effectively sealed his fate.

Despite his uncertain background, Bouguennec, who served as Francis Garel, proved to be an exceptional agent. He had made such an impact that his section chief in recommending him for the Military Cross wrote: 'A very brave man indeed. Straight, honest and hard-hitting. One of the most fearless men we have ever had. His vast prison experience made him a kind of martyr. A truly remarkable leader.'

Gubbins, however, did not put Bouguennec's name forward for an MC, deciding instead to recommend only a Mention in Despatches. 'During the twelve months he spent in captivity,' wrote Gubbins, 'he was subject to severe torture and appalling hardships, which he bore with outstanding courage, giving a magnificent example to his fellow prisoners and even earning the respect of the Gestapo.'

Then, on 27 July 1945, Gubbins amended his statement: 'Since this citation was prepared, it has been learnt that, after severe hardship and unspeakable torture, he was executed on 14 September 1944. It is recommended that Lieutenant Garel be appointed a Member of the Order of the British Empire.' It was at Buchenwald where Bouguennec/Garel was murdered.

As the award of an MBE could not be granted posthumously Gubbins arranged for this decoration to be dated on the day before Bouguennec was killed. He was duly appointed an MBE with effect from 13 September 1944.

BUTTON, Harold Victor

Date of death:	12 October 1944
Place of death:	Llesh, Albania
Rank:	Sergeant
Parent Unit:	2nd Royal Tank Regiment, Royal Armoured Corps
Service number:	7948572
Decorations:	None recorded
Date joined SOE:	1943
Code names:	None recorded
Nationality:	British
Age at time of death:	Twenty-one
Date of birth:	4 November 1922
Place of birth:	Needham Market, UK

Location of memorial: Tirana, Albania

Sergeant Harold Button was parachuted to Biza in north-western Albania at 22.00 hours on 15 October 1943. He was the wireless operator of a three-man Force 399 team; which was to undertake liaison work with the local Resistance fighters.

Despite the British Government's intention to remain neutral in Albania and to support those forces fighting the Germans regardless of their political persuasion, the Mission in northern Albania, under the command of Major Neil McLean, repeatedly advised the arming of Abas Kupi's nationalist, i.e. anti-Communist, forces as distinct from anti-Nazi.

As the Germans began their withdrawal from Albania in the summer of 1944 it became clear that the Communists were the strongest of the Resistance groups and that McLean's support for Kupi would place the SOE Mission in danger. It was decided, therefore, to withdraw McLean's team and this included Sergeant Button.

The Graves Registration investigation into his death provided the following report: 'On the night of 12/13 October 44, Sergeant Button, in company with forty other men of various nationalities, was on the seashore of the Albanian coast awaiting the arrival of MTBs to evacuate them [this was Operation *Elbert*]. Two seamen reached the shore after thirty minutes delay, dragging a waterlogged assault craft with them. They explained that owing to the heavy surf, which was breaking about 80 yards from the shore, great difficulty was experienced in getting the boats ashore and several had sunk.

'In view of the urgency for evacuation it was necessary to start embarking, which continued for the next two hours until only Sergeant Button with his W/T equipment and five others remained ... Sergeant Button and two Russians boarded the next boat and it was seen disappearing into the darkness apparently in good order.

'Five minutes later cries for help were heard by those remaining on shore so they waded out up to their necks through the surf and met the two seamen in charge of Sergeant Button's boat who explained that the boat had become waterlogged and sunk. Every effort was made to find them, and the naval officer in charge sent other boats to search but no trace was found. It was not possible to use searchlights owing to the close proximity of the enemy.'

Neither Button nor the two Russians with him in the boat could swim – the latter had not even seen the sea before in their lives. There had been 'great panic' on the boat as it took on water. The two sailors crewing it were in a poor state when they got back to the shore, having almost been pulled down themselves by their terrified passengers. Eventually one of the Russians was found clinging to the boat, but Button, who was heavily dressed and had a haversack on his back, and the other Russian had disappeared.

Other members of the SOE's Albanian mission participated in the search for Button's body. At the time he drowned he had been carrying code books which, if they fell into the hands of the Germans, might compromise others. The Germans did in fact find the body.

BYCK, Muriel Tamara

Date of death:	23 May 1944
Place of death:	Romorantin, France
Rank:	Section Officer
Parent unit:	Women's Auxiliary Air Force
Service number:	9111
Decorations:	Mentioned in Despatches
Date joined SOE:	July 1943
Code names:	Violette/Benefactress/Michèlle Bernier
Nationality:	British
Age at time of death:	Twenty-five
Date of birth:	4 June 1918
Place of birth:	Ealing, London
Location of grave:	Pornic, France

It was Easter Day, 9 April 1944, when Muriel Byck landed on French soil. Because of a torn leg muscle she could not use a parachute, so she was taken by Lysander to act as the radio operator for Philippe de Vomécourt's VENTRILOQUIST circuit.

She operated successfully until the middle of May. Such was her dedication, it is said that she maintained an hour-to-hour link with London and when there were no transmissions she worked as a courier, alerting sabotage teams. She worked her wireless in a shed behind a garage of a French resister. The garage was often visited by Germans asking for repairs to their vehicles.

The strain of being in such close proximity to the enemy finally drove Byck to move to the house of a blacksmith named Jourdain at Vernou. One morning whilst there, she appeared unusually quiet during breakfast. Byck stated that she had a headache and felt rather tired. So after the meal she said that she would go and lie down in her room for a while. But just as she was turning to leave she collapsed onto the floor.

Muriel was carried up to her bed – where de Vomécourt found her a little later. She was still breathing but unconscious. Whatever he tried, Byck was unresponsive. De Vomécourt decided that he had to contact a doctor. It took three calls before a doctor – Dr Andrieux, a Resistance supporter – could be found. When he arrived and examined Byck he declared that she was seriously ill and urgently needed hospital treatment. Muriel Byck had meningitis.

Historian Beryl Escott explained what happened next: 'Now they were in a dilemma. The Germans kept a careful watch on any persons admitted to hospital – a check meant to catch such people as Muriel or Philippe – and he knew that their papers would not stand up to such close scrutiny. Could he afford the risk? In the face of a question of life or death there seemed little choice. He telephoned for an ambulance.'

The hospital at Romorantin was run by nuns. It seems possible that the nuns were aware of the nature of the person they were helping, but they said nothing. De Vomécourt wanted to stay close to Byck in case she unconsciously gave herself away. Muriel was examined by one of the doctors who declared that her only chance of survival was a lumbar puncture. De Vomécourt was asked if he would give permission for such a procedure. He agreed.

De Vomécourt remained with Byck throughout the operation. She never regained consciousness. It seems that Byck had suffered meningitis as a child but had not mentioned this when she joined the SOE in case she was rejected because of the possibility of its reoccurrence, which sadly turned out to be the case.

De Vomécourt now had the sad task of arranging the funeral. In case the Gestapo took an interest in the event de Vomécourt refused to allow anyone else connected with her Resistance work to attend the funeral and she was buried under her cover name of Michèlle Bernier and placed in a zinc coffin in case her body could later be moved. It has been stated that the Germans arrived at the cemetery during the ceremony but they waited until its conclusion before taking any action. This allowed de Vomécourt to escape over a wall.

BYERLY, Robert Bennett

Date of death:	8 May 1945	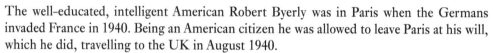
Place of death:	Gross-Rosen, Poland	
Rank:	Lieutenant	
Parent unit:	Royal Canadian Corps of Signals	
Service number:	C. 32458	
Decorations:	None recorded	
Date joined SOE:	3 July 1943	
Code names:	Gontrand/Biologist/Robert Antoine Breuil	
Nationality:	American	
Age at time of death:	Twenty-nine	
Date of birth:	20 March 1916	
Place of birth:	Drexel Hill, Pennsylvania, USA	

Location of memorial: Brookwood, UK

The well-educated, intelligent American Robert Byerly was in Paris when the Germans invaded France in 1940. Being an American citizen he was allowed to leave Paris at his will, which he did, travelling to the UK in August 1940.

In April 1941 he enlisted with the Canadian Army but he soon found his army employment uninteresting and he sought adventure. He found this with the SOE and during his training he declared that he was happy and excited having at last found something that interested him. Strangely, he did not want himself to be considered an American – he wanted to be a 'European'. He was, it was noted at the time, very pro-British.

Byerly was regarded as being somewhat effeminate in appearance by the tough SOE trainers but they were keen to stress that he did not lack courage or determination. Though a former journalist and teacher he was not considered to be forceful enough to be a circuit organiser. It seems that he had travelled widely throughout North America and Europe and had never had to work too hard to make a living coming as he did from 'prosperous background and gently nurtured'. Yet having been a signalman with the Royal Canadian Corps of Signals he was perfectly suitable for employment as a wireless operator.

Byerly was dropped into France, near Poitiers, on 8 February 1944. With him were three other men, one of whom was R.E.J. Alexandre who was to set up the SURVEYOR circuit in conjunction with Joseph Antelme's railwaymen friends. Byerly was to be the circuit's wireless operator with the secondary role of recruiting and training locals in the same role.

Soon after these agents had landed, Byerly's set was heard in Baker Street; but it was evident that something was wrong. The men were dropped into a reception organised by the PHONO circuit and it was later discovered that this circuit was controlled by the Germans. All the agents were arrested upon landing.

Byerly had been given a number of special messages to transmit if he was not under arrest. These instructions had been given verbally, so there was no written record that could be seized. Byerly's transmissions included none of these messages, so it was presumed, correctly as it transpired, that he was in German hands.

For a short while London continued to communicate with Byerly's set in the hope of gleaning some information on what had happened to the four agents. When no positive news was forthcoming, Baker Street stopped replying to the supposed transmission from Byerly. Soon afterwards the transmissions stopped and his wireless set was never used again.

All four men from the drop, Byerly, Alexandre, François Deniset and Jacques Ledoux, were seized and imprisoned in Paris. Byerly, along with another agent from the Canadian Army, François Deniset, was held at 3 bis Place des États Unis. In the summer of 1944 he was transferred to Gross-Rosen where he and the other three men that had landed in France with him in February 1944 were executed.

CARELESS, Alfred

Date of death:	20 October 1943
Place of death:	Tragjas, Albania
Rank:	Captain
Parent unit:	Royal Armoured Corps
Service number:	243988
Decorations:	None recorded
Date joined SOE:	1943
Code names:	None recorded
Nationality:	British
Age at time of death:	Thirty
Date of birth:	23 May 1913
Place of birth:	Jarrow, UK

Location of memorial: Tirana, Albania

Alfred Careless left for operations in Albania as part of the SAPLING Mission (Code named SAPLING 7) on the night of 19/20 October 1943. The dropping ground was on top of a mountain (Mount Mrite) near Tragjas after fears that the town itself might be vulnerable to German patrols.

The aircraft they were travelling in was a Handley Page Halifax of 148 (Special Duties) Squadron. No.148 Squadron was reformed at RAF Gambut in Libya on 14 March 1943. Tasked to undertake the Special Duties role, it was equipped with Handley Page Halifaxes and Consolidated B-24 Liberators. It became responsible for supplying Partisan groups throughout the Balkans and as far afield as Poland, as well as undertaking normal bombing missions when not otherwise occupied.

On the night of 19/20 October 1943, the Halifax reached the drop zone and flashed the identification letter of the day, which was answered from the ground. The aircraft then flew off to circle round to make its first pass. Its engines were throttled back.

As it came back towards the dropping ground the engines were suddenly heard to open up and a few seconds later the aircraft crashed into the side of the mountain below the dropping ground. The time was 00.45 hours. The subsequent report on the incident stated that it appeared that the 'plane lost height during its circuit in the dark and the initial verdict was that this was due to pilot error. All the personnel in the aircraft were killed.

The leader of the circuit he was to join, Major Jerry (or Gerry) Field, went down the mountainside to bury the dead. He found that the Partisans were more interested in looting than dealing with the bodies. Field, it was reported, was 'very disillusioned at the waste of British life on behalf of the Albanians who did not appreciate our sacrifice on their behalf'.

Field was so disgusted with the incident that ten days later he wrote: 'The Albanians are lazy, liars and thieves and personally I think we are wasting our time doing anything for them ... When SAPLING 7 crashed they stood about and would not help me to dig graves for the mangled bodies I found ... joking and grumbling that their material was lost and that there were no parachutes for them to buy.'

The report from Major Field on the crash drew the following conclusion: 'Badly mutilated bodies Captain Careless and Sergeant Williams only found in tail wreckage, others completely destroyed by fire. Two possible causes [of crash] to me: 1. Careless, not dressed for jump, despatcher with pilot when target seen, pushed past to warn others, causing the dive. 2. Pilot blinded by rising moon, failed to see top of mountain.'

CAUCHI, Eric Joseph Denis

Date of death:	5 February 1944	
Place of death:	Montbéliard, France	
Rank:	Lieutenant	
Parent unit:	General List	
Service number:	279563	
Decorations:	Mentioned in Despatches	
Date joined SOE:	9 May 1943	
Code names:	Pedro/Messenger/Louis Jean Caudron	
Nationality:	British	
Age at time of death:	Twenty-six	
Date of birth:	11 August 1917	
Place of birth:	Syros, Greece	
Location of grave:	Perreuse, France	

The first impression that former tobacco grower and exporter, Eric Cauchi, presented to his SOE assessors was that he was rather slow witted, but they soon realised that he was of above average intelligence. He was under training at the same time as Elaine Plewman, whom he took a particular interest in. It was noticed that he rarely went out unless Mrs Plewman was also going out. This friendship was discussed by the assessors but they decided that it did not represent a security risk.

Cauchi was parachuted into the Jura Mountains on 13 August 1943, to act as the arms instructor to the JUDGE circuit in and around Dijon. He successfully arranged a number of supply drops but in November the organiser, John Young, was arrested. Following this Cauchi was being actively searched for by the Germans, so he escaped to Switzerland.

Meanwhile, another senior agent, Julius Hanau, stepped in and incorporated the JUDGE group into his STOCKBROKER circuit. Cauchi returned to his circuit in January 1944 and worked under Hanau's orders but operated independently, taking control of the remnants of the JUDGE circuit.

Cauchi was killed on 5 February 1944, when he failed to stop at a *Feldgendarmerie* street control in Montbéliard. The Germans pursued him, eventually surrounding him and two others in the Café Grangier on the road between Sochaux and Montbéliard.

The Germans then attacked the café with firearms; Cauchi tried to escape, firing at the Gestapo. A number of Germans were wounded but Cauchi was shot in the chest by machine-gun fire. He died in the street two hours later. The other two men were killed in the café, one of whom, it was later discovered was Jean Simon.

This very brave, rather impetuous officer, wrote Buckmaster in recommending Cauchi for a Mention in Despatches, 'took unkindly to discipline and restraint, but always responded to an appeal for effort. His headstrong qualities led him into a trap, but the betting is that he would have risked the trap for the sake of revenge anyway. Most gallant and a great loss.'

CLECH, Marcel Remy

Date of death:	24 March 1944
Place of death:	Mauthausen, Austria
Rank:	Lieutenant
Parent unit:	General List
Service number:	225589
Decorations:	*Médaille de la Résistance Française*
Date joined SOE:	3 February 1942
Code names:	*Bastien*/Georges Jean Clermot
Nationality:	French
Age at time of death:	Thirty-eight
Date of birth:	11 October 1905
Place of birth:	Finistère, France

Location of memorial: Brookwood, UK

Former taxi driver and Leading Seaman in the French Navy, Breton-born Marcel Clech was one of the earliest of F Section's agents, beginning his training in July 1941. He undertook two missions in France. His first mission began on 9 April 1942, when he arrived at Agay on the Côte d'Azur via Gibraltar. The Lyons/Tours area became his operational zone. During this time he earmarked suitable landing zones in the area and began transmissions as a wireless operator.

In November 1942 he went to a small village near Beaugency for a week. When he returned to his original address in Tours he found the entire street cordoned off. Some fifty Germans in civilian clothes (presumably Gestapo) were searching every house – they were looking for a radio transmitter. Consequently, Clech 'went to ground', eventually returning to Britain by Lysander on 13 April 1943.

Once in the UK Clech was thoroughly debriefed, during which he provided a great deal of important detail about life in France at that time. Such information enabled the SOE staff to fit and equip agents in a manner in keeping with their surroundings in France. Anyone wearing clothes no longer available in France would be certain to attract the attention of the authorities. Clech was able to advise the people at Baker Street that because of a shortage of leather all new shoes were being made with wooden soles and that leather suitcases are completely unobtainable. He was also able to bring back his identification card and examples of other documents that would be essential for any agent to move around in France.

Clech was also able to describe the radio detection-finding vehicle used by the Gestapo. This was a small, low, enclosed mid-blue coloured truck with *Wehrmacht* plates. It was driven by a man in civilian clothes. Most people were completely unaware of its true purpose.

For his second mission, Clech was taken by Lysander to a point that was 9 miles east-south-east of Tours. From there he had to make his way to Paris. Intended to be the wireless operator for Sidney Jones (alias *Elie*) as part of the INVENTOR circuit, he was given both a primary address and a secondary address in case the former was compromised. There were also 151,335 Francs for his personal use, for which he was expected to keep an account of his expenditure.

If Clech found himself unable to transmit and felt himself in danger, he was given an address in Lisbon to which he could send a coded letter. Baker Street would then make arrangements for extracting him.

As it transpired Clech was unable to transmit for some time and he had to use Jack Agazarian (PROSPER circuit) to send his messages. Though contact with another circuit was dangerous, he managed to conceal his identity. He was then able operate himself, which he did from 10 September 1943, until his arrest just nine days later, sending seven messages in that time.

Clech was captured shortly after Sidney Jones and his courier Vera Leigh were both arrested in Paris. Though Clech's arrest was probably as a result of the collapse of an associated circuit (PROSPER) or as a result of the infiltration of Henri Frager's network, it is possible that it was simply due to the success of German direction-finding. It is thought that for a period of time after his arrest that he was being controlled by the Gestapo.

Little is known of Clech's fate following his arrest, other than he was subsequently sent to Mauthausen Concentration Camp where he was killed. This wasn't discovered until November 1945, after the camp was liberated by men of the US 11 Armoured Division and its records examined. These documents were found to be surprisingly complete and they showed each person's name, nationality, date of birth, date of death and in some cases the reason why the person was being held.

CLEMENT, George

Date of death:	7 September 1944
Place of death:	Mauthausen, Austria
Rank:	Lieutenant
Parent unit:	107th (5th Battalion The King's Own Royal Regiment (Lancaster)) Regiment, Royal Armoured Corps
Service number:	259937
Decorations:	Mentioned in Despatches
Date joined SOE:	16 January 1943
Code names:	Edouard/Driver/Georges Jean Clermont
Nationality:	Russian
Age at time of death:	Twenty-six
Date of birth:	20 October 1917
Place of birth:	Petrograde, Russia

Location of memorial: Brookwood, UK

George Clement, who was born in Pretrograde, Russia, a week before Stalin seized power, had been an undergraduate at Brasenose College, Oxford, before he was conscripted. He was seen as being 'very English public school and university in his bearing, conversation and social form'.

He was the wireless operator for François Vallée's PARSON network, which operated around Rennes. Clement was parachuted into France along with another PARSON member-to-be, Henri Gaillot, on 24 July 1943.

The circuit was soon putting together a number of different teams. By the middle of August, Vallée was able to report through Clement that he had organised several sabotage groups of a dozen men each in the area bounded by Saint-Brieuc, Rennes and Nantes. He also declared that he had a few guerrilla groups at his disposal ready and waiting for instructions from London. The circuit received four drops of arms.

A report from France in January 1944 states that he was arrested at 10.00 hours on a Sunday in the middle of December (most likely the 21st) at St Braz-des-Ifs. The rest of the circuit escaped and went to ground. M.R.D. Foot wrote that Clement was caught whilst transmitting on 28 November.

Following his arrest – the circumstances behind which are not known – Clement was taken to Rennes prison. It is stated by a number of agents that he then collaborated with the Germans and that he was spotted assisting the Germans on a bogus reception committee.

It seems that the first transmission he made after his arrest (on 4 January) was without the necessary security checks. After that a few more transmissions were sent that included these checks. It is possible that Clement felt that with his first omission he had alerted Baker Street. Despite these allegations he was recommended for a Mention in Despatches. Clement had worked for five months under difficult and dangerous conditions and contributed much to the success of the PARSON circuit.

He was moved to Frèsnes and later sent to Mauthausen concentration camp. He was shot here on the second day of the mass murders in September 1944 – see the previous entry for Marcus Bloom.

COPPIN, Edward Cyril

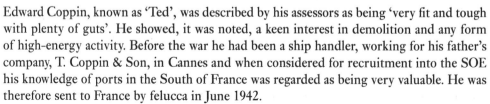

Date of death:	23 September 1943
Place of death:	Possibly Ravensbrück, Germany
Rank:	Lieutenant
Parent unit:	RASC
Service number:	231091
Decorations:	Mentioned in Despatches, *Croix de Guerre*
Date joined SOE:	12 February 1942
Code names:	Olivier/Bay/Jean Pierre Vidal
Nationality:	British
Age at time of death:	Twenty-eight
Date of birth:	20 May 1915
Place of birth:	Brightlingsea, UK

Location of memorial: Brookwood, UK

Edward Coppin, known as 'Ted', was described by his assessors as being 'very fit and tough with plenty of guts'. He showed, it was noted, a keen interest in demolition and any form of high-energy activity. Before the war he had been a ship handler, working for his father's company, T. Coppin & Son, in Cannes and when considered for recruitment into the SOE his knowledge of ports in the South of France was regarded as being very valuable. He was therefore sent to France by felucca in June 1942.

Under the general control of Henri Frager's DONKEYMAN circuit, Coppin was the organiser of a group in the port of Marseilles. He was given the additional role of being the liaison link between the Marseilles and Chaminade groups.

Over time, Coppin built up a successful sabotage group amongst railway workers in the area. One of his organisation's most notable achievements occurred in the autumn of 1942 when it diverted trains that were destined for Germany. By switching the points they were able to send the trains in the opposite direction – towards the Spanish border. They also specialised in derailments, which they achieved by smearing the rails in heavy fat.

Coppin's knowledge of shipping enabled him to arrange a delivery of equipment for his circuit by sea to the coast near Antibes. He had organised his circuit so well that the groups trained and equipped by him continued to operate successfully even after he was arrested, along with his courier, at the house where he was living on 23 April 1943.

There is enormous confusion over the fate of Coppin. This has resulted from the use of his cover-name, Olivier. This was also the name of an explosives agent, Lieutenant Michael Reeve, who was sent to help Michael Trotobas (see below). It is widely thought that this latter person was Ted Coppin and that he betrayed Trotobas.

Nothing was known about Coppin after his arrest until 22 November 1946. On this date his father wrote to the War Office to say that a woman, a Mme Experton, who had been in prison with Coppin had contacted his family with the news that their son was alive somewhere. This woman also claimed that Coppin had initially been held in the Saint-Pierre prison in Marseilles.

Here the SOE agent was placed in a filthy, vermin-infested cell. He suffered terribly humiliating treatment and was brutally tortured but, despite this, he refused to talk. The proof of this is that no-one from his group was subsequently arrested. There was also evidence that Coppin was sent to Ravensbrück (possibly, though not for certain, via Frèsnes) arriving there at 04.00 hours in the morning of 3 February 1944. When his fate was investigated, no evidence could be found to support this theory. As far as anyone is aware, the twenty-eight-year-old was executed at Ravensbrück where he died in September the previous year.

His Section Chief recommended Coppin for an MBE; all he received was a Mention in Despatches.

DAMERMENT, Madeleine Zöe

Date of death:	13 September 1944
Place of death:	Dachau, Germany
Rank:	Ensign
Parent unit:	Women's Transport Service (FANY)
Service number:	F/37
Decorations:	*Legion d'Honneur, Croix de Guerre, Médaille de la Résistance Française*
Date joined SOE:	1 July 1942
Code names:	Solonge/Jacqueline Duchateau Martine Dussautoy
Nationality:	French
Age at time of death:	Twenty-six
Date of birth:	11 November 1917
Place of birth:	Tortefontaine, France

Location of memorial: Brookwood, UK

Madeleine Damerment had been involved in the Resistance in helping rescue Allied prisoners in the areas around Lille, working with the PAT escape line and assisting Michael Trotobas. One day the Gestapo visited her home, asking for her whereabouts. Luckily she was out at the time, but she decided it would be wise for her to escape to the Unoccupied Zone.

Damerment continued to work for the Resistance in the South of France but one of the members of her group became a Gestapo informant and so she left for England, via Spain and Portugal. She is credited with assisting seventy-five Allied airmen escape back to the United Kingdom.

Baker Street had no hesitation in accepting Damerment and she was soon being trained to be a courier for a new circuit called BRICKLAYER. This organisation had been established by Noor Inayat-Khan following the collapse of the Suttill's Paris-based PROSPER circuit.

Madeleine, along with France Antelme and a wireless operator called Lionel Lee, was dropped by parachute some 20 miles east of Chartres on 29 February 1944 – straight into the arms of the waiting Gestapo.

Taken to Avenue Foch, Frèsnes and then to Karlsruhe, Damerment was put in a cell with a German women who was a political prisoner. It is said that she was not ill-treated during her stay at Karlsruhe.

On the morning of 12 September 1944, Damerment was transported with Plewman, Beekman (Unternahrer) and Inayat-Khan to Dachau. They were driven from Karlsruhe to the train station where they caught the early train to Munich, arriving late that afternoon. The girls had no indication of the fate that awaited them. They travelled in an ordinary compartment with three Gestapo officials and were able to chat freely amongst themselves. They changed to a local train to Dachau, located some 20 miles north-west of Munich, and arrived there after dark. They had to walk to the camp, which they reached about midnight.

The Karlsruhe Gestapo officer, *Kriminalsekretaer* Christian Ott, made this statement about the deaths of the four women when interviewed after his capture by the Allies at the end of the war:

'The four prisoners had come from the barrack in the camp, where they had spent the night, into the yard where the shooting was to be done. Here he [his colleague Max Wassmer] had announced the death sentence to them. Only the *Lagerkommandant* and two SS men had been present.

'All four had grown very pale and wept; the major [Madeleine Damerment] asked whether they could protest against the sentence. The *Kommandant* declared that no protest could be made against the sentence. The major then asked to see a priest. The *Kommandant* refused this on the grounds that there was no priest in the camp.

'The four prisoners now had to kneel down with their heads towards a small mound of earth and were killed by the two SS, one after another by a shot through the back of the neck. During the shooting the two Englishwomen held hands and the two Frenchwomen likewise. For three of the prisoners the first shot caused death, but for the German-speaking Englishwoman [Beekman] a second shot had to be fired as she still showed signs of life after the first shot.' The time was approximately 10.00 hours.

DAREME, Pierre Edouard

Date of death:	4 March 1945
Place of death:	Germany
Rank:	Lieutenant
Parent unit:	General List
Service number:	294285
Decorations:	King's Medal for Courage
Date joined SOE:	8 September 1943
Code names:	Edouard Tridonani/Jacques Andres
Nationality:	Italian
Age at time of death:	Thirty-two
Date of birth:	12 February 1913
Place of birth:	Montreux, Switzerland

Location of memorial: Brookwood, UK

Pierre Dareme's true name was Edouard Tridondani. He was born on 12 February 1913, at Montreux, Switzerland, to an Italian father and a Swiss mother. He was a keen skier, taking part in competitive championships.

Dareme became an engineer at a Ford garage in Montreux before being conscripted into the Italian Army in 1934. When Italy invaded Abyssinia in 1935 his unit was posted to Asmara in Eritrea. Being opposed to Fascist principles he deserted in 1937 and made his way into Sudan. He found work as a clerk in Khartoum for a year before travelling to Egypt where he became an engineer at Zaccari in Alexandria, the following year.

Because of his anti-Fascist views and because he was a deserter, Dareme was evacuated by the Italian Consul from Alexandria to Cairo in 1940 when Italy declared war on Britain. He offered his services to the SOE in Cairo but no role could be found for him.

Eventually it was decided to send him to the UK where he might be usefully employed. His journey began with a flight to Lagos, where he found a ship that took him to Britain via Freetown. He arrived in the UK in April 1943 and was formally accepted into the SOE for training the following September.

In training he proved adept at demolition but being a skier and mountaineer with a knowledge of the French Alps he wanted to work in that area. He was generally found to be a quiet and reserved character and 'too negative' to be a leader. It was decided that he would be ideal as a saboteur or as an assistant to a 'stronger' man.

Before Dareme was used in such a role he was parachuted into France near Toulouse in September 1943 to test an escape route in the south of the country. His officer's report of this episode read as follows: 'Through no fault of his own he was unable to contact the address given to him and was therefore forced to remain in France until another address could be sent to him, in order that he should contact the [escape] line. During this trying period Tridondani kept cool-headed and quiet and was able to make his escape on receipt of the new address. He returned to this country in January 1944 and owing to the completion of his successful test many Allied airmen and agents made good their escape from German hands.'

For his second mission he was infiltrated back into France on 9 April 1944, as a lieutenant to an organiser involved in 'clandestine communications'. Shortly after his arrival he was arrested in Perpignan at a control check of passengers at a bus stop. According to his personal file he was arrested 'due to disobeying orders', the reason for this being that Dareme was using an identity card that he had forged himself.

Nothing further was ever heard of him and there the matter rested with SOE. However, post-war research suggests that an Edouard Tridondani, prisoner number 30258, died at the work camp for the Watenstedt-Salzgitter steel works in Lower Saxony on 4 March 1945. The camp at Watenstedt was administered by the much larger concentration camp at Neuengamme. German records indicate that a large group of French prisoners, mostly members of the Resistance, arrived at KZ Watenstedt in late May or early June 1944 from a holding camp in Compiègne.

It is possible that Dareme was part of this transport and that if he was indeed prisoner number 30258 then it is likely he was buried at the Jammertal *Ausländerfriedhof* in Salzgitter.

The date of death listed by the Commonwealth War Graves Commission, of 9 April 1944, is therefore to be considered incorrect.

DEFENCE, Marcel Enzebe

Date of death:	8 June 1944
Place of death:	Gross-Rosen, Poland
Rank:	Captain
Parent unit:	General List
Service number:	257910
Decorations:	Mentioned in Despatches
Date joined SOE:	Not recorded
Code names:	Dédé/Weaver/Maurice Doare/ Michel Delaplace
Nationality:	French
Age at time of death:	Twenty-four
Date of birth:	1920
Place of birth:	Paris, France
Location of memorial:	Brookwood, UK

Marcel Defence (aka Dédé) was a young Frenchman born in Paris. His French father had emigrated to Scotland where Marcel had become a Glasgow dock engineer.

Recruited into the SOE, Defence was dropped into France in May 1943 to join the Paris detachment of the extensive SCIENTIST circuit. As a trained wireless operator he was to work under Marc O'Neil who, despite his name, was a former major in the French Army. Defence's task was to help save this group from the unfolding disaster that had befallen PROSPER.

All went well at first and O'Neil returned to the United Kingdom for a few weeks in August 1943, leaving the circuit in the hands of André Grandclément, who was also a former army officer. During O'Neil's absence the Gestapo was given Grandclément's address in Bordeaux, which was the main base of the SCIENTIST group, by a sub-agent who was captured during a series of 'experimental' arrests in the area.

Though Grandclément was out when the Germans raided his house, they found a list of names written in an easily-deciphered code. As soon as the Germans had broken the codes, the arrests began – scores of them.

Grandclément himself was caught in the round-up. During his interrogation he was persuaded by the Bordeaux Gestapo chief, Friedrich Dhose, that it was in his and his country's interests to help the Germans. Dhose's arguments were so persuasive that Grandclément was completely taken in and he actively collaborated to such an extent that he was released and allowed to move around freely.

He went to call on one of the local Resistance helpers and to his surprise found there, amongst others, Marcel Defence. Grandclément, believing in his new-found cause, tried to convert Defence and the others. Though he could not convince them to change allegiance he told them that he was going to reveal to the Germans where all the circuit's arms dumps were located. Grandclément was lucky to leave the house alive (though he, his wife, and his bodyguard, Marc Duluguet, were subsequently executed in July 1944 on the orders of *Actor* – the SOE agent Roger Landes).

Defence was then involved in a desperate race to remove as many of the caches as possible before the Germans could intervene. Defence then rushed up to Paris to warn the recently returned O'Neil, who rapidly wound up what remained of SCIENTIST. Defence escaped to Britain by sea.

On 7 March 1944, Defence returned to France as the wireless operator for Octave Simon. Together they were to re-start the SATIRIST circuit around Beauvais. The pair had expected to be met by a reception committee arranged by Francis Garel's BUTLER circuit, but instead they landed straight into a German reception committee – Garel and his wireless operator had been captured six months earlier, and the Germans had been operating BUTLER's captured wireless set to convince F Section into despatching further agents and stores.

After initially being held at Place des Etats-Unis in Paris, Defence was transferred to Ravitsch concentration camp. By the end of the war in Europe hundreds of thousands of people had been sent from France to the German camps and some 200,000 had been killed, nearly half of whom were resisters – including more than 100 SOE agents. One of that number, Marcel Defence, was moved from Ravitsch to Gross-Rosen where he was executed.

DEFENDINI, Alphonse

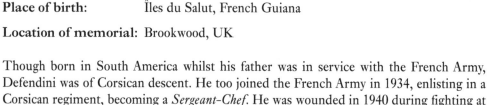

Date of death:	14 September 1944
Place of death:	Buchenwald, Germany
Rank:	Lieutenant
Parent unit:	General List
Service number:	301258
Decorations:	Mention in Despatches, *Médaille de la Résistance Française*
Entered SOE Service:	11 April 1944
Code names:	Priest/Jules/Angehand
Nationality:	French
Age at time of death:	Thirty-four
Date of birth:	4 December 1909
Place of birth:	Îles du Salut, French Guiana

Location of memorial: Brookwood, UK

Though born in South America whilst his father was in service with the French Army, Defendini was of Corsican descent. He too joined the French Army in 1934, enlisting in a Corsican regiment, becoming a *Sergeant-Chef*. He was wounded in 1940 during fighting at Chemin des Dames near Soissons in the Aisne.

Defendini returned to Corsica – which was occupied at that time by the Italians – where he became involved with the Resistance movement. He was particularly active during the liberation of the island in November 1943. After the expulsion of the Germans from Corsica, Defendini made his way to Britain at the end of that year and volunteered to continue his Resistance work in France.

He was landed on the Brittany coast on 29 February 1944, being given the task of organising a Resistance group (PRIEST) in the Meuse department centred around Verdun. He had been given a list of railway lines to be sabotaged on D-Day.

It had been intended that Defendini was to be met on arrival by personnel from Frank Pickersgill's ARCHDEACON circuit. It was later learnt that this group was under German control and it was presumed that Defendini was arrested soon after or upon arrival.

However, it is now believed that he was seized by the Gestapo when he went to what was thought to be a safe-house for a meeting with Roger Sabourin (see below). Initially Defendini was taken to 3 bis Place des États Unis and later moved to Frèsnes prison (initially placed in Cell 28) where, despite being tortured, he gave nothing away.

Remarkably, it seems Defendini was able to persuade one of the prison guards, a Russian, to smuggle out a number of letters. Surprisingly, these eventually found their way to Britain. Calling the Gestapo 'Germaine' and the Russian guard 'her maid', he wrote the following: 'You know the temperament of my mistress Germaine. If by ill luck Germaine realised that I was tricking her and the maid was my accomplice, she – Germaine – would still have the strength to shoot me. I am obliged to remain with her but I hope that her end is near' – the letter was written two days after D-Day.

Defendini went on to write that 'Germaine put me through the hoop for a long time [i.e. he was tortured] and then, as everything comes to an end sooner or later, she dropped the subject'.

At least one of these letters was addressed to fellow SOE agent Henri Frager. Defendini planned to attempt an escape and he asked Frager to try and send him 'two small revolvers with ammunition, some cyanide of mercury poison, four metal saws and a plan of the prison with the guard posts and sentry positions'. In his notes he was able to provide the outside world with valuable information about other captured agents.

His morale was said to be excellent and he even started to dig an escape tunnel. However, it is known that he was still at Frèsnes in January 1945, though he was then transferred to Buchenwald where he was hanged.

DEMAND, George William Hedworth

Date of death:	29 March 1945
Place of death:	Flossenbürg, Germany
Rank:	Lieutenant
Parent unit:	General List
Service number:	250965
Decorations:	Mentioned in Despatches
Entered SOE service:	1942
Code names:	Edmonde/Stevedore/Pierre Strube
Nationality:	British
Age at time of death:	Twenty-three
Date of birth:	24 July 1921
Place of birth:	Durham, UK
Location of memorial:	Brookwood, UK

George Demand took part in both SCULLION I and SCULLION II sabotage missions against the synthetic oil plant of Les Talots near Autun, a town in the Saône-et-Loire département in Burgundy. His role was that of radio operator for the team. The first SCULLION attack took place on 18 April 1943, but they found the plant too well guarded (Patrick Howarth suggests that this might have been because the Germans had been alerted to the possibility of an attack), and the team leader, Hugh Dormer, aborted the mission.

Dormer believed that the plant could still be attacked with success and he asked for a second chance. This time Demand was dropped into France four days ahead of the rest of the seven-man team to prepare for the mission. The other members of SCULLION II landed on 16 August 1943. They attacked the plant, successfully laying their explosives, though with limited effect.

None of the team was fluent in French and following the attack, five of the team, including George Demand, were captured by the Germans. Only Hugh Dormer and Sergeant Charlie Birch escaped back to Britain.

After some months in Frèsnes prison, Demand and the other prisoners were sent to Flossenbürg, being executed just weeks before the end of the war.

Dormer wrote in his diary that the work of the SOE, 'often breeds a race of professional mercenaries who love war'. The prospect of leading 'armed bands of hungry, desperate men eager for revenge', he continued, 'was a nightmare which had often haunted him'. As a result he decided to return to more open forms of warfare and he joined the Guards Armoured Division for the D–Day landings.

DENISET, François Adolphe

Date of death:	8 May 1945	
Place of death:	Gross-Rosen, Poland	
Rank:	Captain	
Parent unit:	Royal Canadian Artillery	
Service number:	Not recorded	
Decorations:	None Recorded	
Entered SOE service:	10 October 1943	
Code names:	Jean Jacques/Mariner/Francois Dussault	
Nationality:	Canadian	
Age at time of death:	Twenty-seven	
Date of birth:	3 October 1917	
Place of birth:	St Boniface, Manitoba, Canada	

Location of memorial: Brookwood, UK

Deniset was a French Canadian who was completely bi-lingual in English and French. He began his SOE training in October 1943.

Deniset was considered a 'very intelligent mature-minded man, serious and of good motivation' by his assessors and it was believed that he 'should do good work in the field and make many friends there'. Even though he received considerable praise, a subsequent report stated that 'whilst he has certain powers of leadership and has a pleasant and unaggressive manner ... his personality lacks the forcefulness to be fully effective ... and would be best used as an instructor or a subordinate organiser'.

Another problem was that whilst Deniset's French was excellent, he had no knowledge of France whatsoever. He was surprised, for instance, to learn that the French drank coffee out of glasses in cafés. It was therefore decided that he did not have the knowledge to be a circuit organiser but that he would make an ideal lieutenant. As a result, Francois Deniset was detailed to join the PHONO circuit in the Chârtres area as Emile Garry's second in command and arms instructor.

He was given a list of locomotive sheds, railways and roads to destroy, which he was to pass onto Garry. Deniset was parachuted into France on 8 February 1942, with three other agents near Poitiers, but the PHONO circuit was under German control and he was arrested on arrival.

It is known that the Germans that captured Deniset came from Paris and that he was interned for some time in Frèsnes. This huge prison complex was at that time the largest in Europe. Built at the end of the nineteenth century it comprised of three, four-storey cell blocks with connecting structure at right-angles. Prisoners were exercised in the courtyards between the blocks. Though generally much like any other prison, Frèsnes also had a number of underground punishment cells – *cellules de force* – which were used to punish prisoners or, in the case of some of the SOE agents, to try and break their resistance. These cells had no lighting, no beds and no water. They were dirty, cold and damp and prisoners were kept in solitary confinement, their only contact being the guard who brought them the weak soup upon which they had to survive.

Survive Frèsnes he did and on 2 June 1944, Deniset was seen by other captured SOE agents in 3 bis Place des États Unis. When it was known in London that Deniset had been captured, Buckmaster recorded the following: 'A very good and promising officer. It is a tragedy that he never had a chance to show his worth. I felt he was one of the best we should ever have had, from his character at any rate, I judged him to be a great potential leader.'

After the war F Section experienced great difficulty in uncovering the ultimate fate of Deniset. It was discovered that he eventually found himself in Ravitsch concentration camp though it is recorded that he was executed at Gross-Rosen.

DETAL, Julien Theodore Joseph

Date of death:	14 September 1944
Place of death:	Buchenwald, Germany
Rank:	Lieutenant
Parent unit:	General List
Service number:	309881
Decorations:	None recorded
Date joined SOE:	1944
Code names:	Roderique/Biologist/Julien Hamont
Nationality:	Belgian
Age at time of death:	Not recorded
Date of birth:	1915
Place of birth:	Not recorded

Location of memorial: Brookwood, UK

Belgian-born Detal was parachuted into France with Philip Duclos on the Leap Year night of 29 February 1944. They were to set up DELEGATE with their objective being to disrupt communications between Brittany and the rest of France. Twelve drops of stores were planned to provide DELEGATE with the munitions to carry out its mission.

They landed in a field arranged by the BUTLER circuit, which was ran by Marcel Rousset who had worked in a network on the fringe of the PROSPER network in the Sarthe. Rousset had been arrested on 7 September 1943, and, inevitably, Detal and Duclos landed straight into a German reception committee. Both were subsequently imprisoned in Paris.

On 8 August 1944, Detal was one of a number of agents moved via the transit camp at Compiègne to join other French resisters at Paris's Gare de l'Est. The others they were being grouped with had come from Frèsnes jail and Avenue Foch.

The prisoners were handcuffed together in pairs and put onto a train carriage, which was divided into two compartments with grilles over the windows and guarded by *Feldgendarmerie*. There were thirty-seven men altogether crowded into the two compartments designed to accommodate just eight people each. A small group of women agents, including Violet Szabo, was placed in a separate compartment.

The train left Paris and moved very slowly east – towards Germany. The journey continued through the night, with no thought given to providing the male prisoners with any food or drink. By the afternoon of the second day, as the train was approaching Châlons-sur-Marne, it was attacked by the RAF. Explosions and cannon fire rocked the train, which shuddered to a halt. In the terror and confusion of the attack, three of the men suffered seizures, the result of their weakened condition.

Witnessing the state of the men, Szabo, along with Denise Bloch and Lilian Rolfe, crawled along the floor from her compartment to give water to the men in both compartments. These remarkable women shared not just their water but also their compassion and through the noise of the battle shouted words of encouragement to the men.

The destination of the group of men was Buchenwald. Here they were stripped, all the hair on their heads and bodies shorn, and were given prison rags to wear. They were then placed in Block 17 where conditions, particularly the food, were better than that experienced in such places as Frèsnes. They were kept apart from the other prisoners and treated quite differently. The agents were not ordered to turn out for the morning roll-call with the other internees, nor were they expected to work or forced to queue in the canteen as their food was brought to them. Such treatment gave the men hope that they would eventually be released.

At 13.30 hours on 9 September 1944, the names of sixteen of the group of agents, including that of Julien Detal, were read out and the men were taken from Block 17. They were never seen again and it was later learnt that after being savagely beaten they were all hanged in the prison's crematorium.

DOWLEN, Roland Robert

Date of death:	29 March 1945	
Place of death:	Flossenbürg, Germany	

Rank:	Lieutenant	
Parent unit:	General List	
Service number:	241045	
Decorations:	Mentioned in Despatches	
Date joined SOE:	27 April 1942	
Code names:	Richard/Chandler/Francois	
	Antoine Perrier	
Nationality:	British (Naturalised 1936)	

Age at time of death:　Thirty-six
Date of birth:　12 October 1907
Place of birth:　Sicily

Location of memorial: Brookwood, UK

Little is now known about Roland Dowlen's early life, though it is recorded that he initially enlisted in the Royal Army Service Corps in 1941.

The details of his SOE assessment (which began on 27 April 1942) reveal a quiet, though resourceful, man. Of particular credit was his sense of security that he had made 'his second nature'. He was given much praise by his instructors, yet the following note was placed on his Baker Street file: 'A curiously evasive officer, whom nobody could get to know intimately. Pleasant, shy, uneffusive. A scoutmaster, but you wouldn't have guessed it. I find it curiously difficult to evaluate this officer.'

He was landed in France by Westland Lysander on the night of 17/18 March 1943, along with three other agents, two in each of two aircraft. Dowlen's mission was to join Grover-Williams' CHESTNUT circuit in the Paris area as its radio operator.

The CHESTNUT circuit was a very small team, consisting of the three former racing drivers Grover-Williams, Robert Benoist and Jean-Pierre Wimille, who used their wives and one or two female friends as their couriers. During the four months that Dowlen operated as the circuit's radio operator he successfully sent thirty-nine messages. These included some excellent information gathered through Benoist's and Wimille's private connections in Paris.

He lived away from the others of the group at Pontoise, in the north-western suburbs of Paris, in a villa rented from another member of the circuit. It was there that he was caught by an *Abwehr* direction-finding team whilst operating his set. M.R.D. Foot gives the date of his arrest as 31 July 1943, whereas a note in Dowlen's personal file states 12 August.

After his arrest, six messages were sent using Dowlen's captured machine. It seems that Dowlen may have transmitted these, but if he did so it was under duress. The messages stopped on 1 October.

He spent eighteen months in captivity in France, both at 84 Avenue Foch and 3 bis Place des États Unis, before being transferred to Germany. Dowlen was eventually killed at Flossenbürg. For his 'bravery and self-sacrifice' Dowlen was awarded a posthumous Mention in Despatches.

DUBOUDIN, Emile George Jean

Date of death:	22 March 1945
Place of death:	Buchenwald, Germany
Rank:	Captain
Parent unit:	General List; 45th Training Regiment RA
Service number:	183055
Decorations:	None recorded
Date joined SOE:	13 February 1941
Code names:	Alaine/Playwright/Jacques Dupre
Nationality:	French
Age at time of death:	Thirty-seven
Date of birth:	23 May 1907
Place of birth:	Halluin

Location of memorial: Brookwood, UK

Emile Duboudin, who graduated with a BA in Economics, worked for Crédit Lyonnais for nine years before the war, becoming fluent in both German and English. Duboudin joined the French artillery upon mobilisation at the outbreak of war. He rose to the rank of lieutenant and became a member of the French liaison team with the British Expeditionary Force. He married an English girl called Dolan and adopted the name of John George Dolan during his service with the SOE.

His first mission for the SOE began in 1941 when he was landed by the Special Services vessel HMS *Fidelity* on 19 September 1941 on the Loire coast under the name of Alaine. He went into the field, according to his own interpretation of his instructions, to make contact with the local Resistance movement. He established the SPRUCE *réseaux*, the first of its kind in Lyons. Baker Street afforded priority to this circuit and soon it was reinforced with more agents from the UK as well as more money (Peter Churchill, for example, brought with him 300,000 Francs in January 1942).

Duboudin, though 'a brave and shrewd man', lacked the ability to get on with his comrades and one by one his fellow agents sought other circuits they could join. As a result he was recalled to London 'for a rest'.

He went back to France on 23 March 1943, having been granted his wish of a higher rank (i.e. captain). It was said that he would undertake work of a 'higher nature' reflecting his advanced rank.

Duboudin's brother was in charge of the signals at the Gare du Nord and they had met in Paris shortly after landing in France. He went back to his brother's house where he collected some of his belongings. He said that he would come back again, but he did not do so. The next that his brother knew about Duboudin was that he was in Frèsnes prison, where he went to visit him on 9 December 1943. He had been in solitary confinement for six months. It is known that he was tortured but that he proved to be 'extremely un-co-operative'.

Duboudin was moved to Compiegne in January 1944 and then to Weimar in March. From here he was transferred to Buchenwald and then the Dora V2 rocket factory at Nordhausen, a sub-camp of the Dora-Mittelbau concentration camp, in June to undertake forced labour.

He had been able to write to his brother a number of times during this period, the last letter being dated 31 July 1944. He was then transferred to Buchenwald, eventually being worked to death at Elbrich labour camp, succumbing to under-nourishment and pleurisy. He was moved to the camp hospital suffering from acute bronchopneumonia. On 19 March 1945, the pleurisy took hold. He became delirious on the 21st and a 'violent' temperature set in. He never regained consciousness and it was said that he died in the arms of another inmate from the French Resistance, a certain Michel de Beauvais.

DUCLOS, Philip Francis

Date of death:	27 June 1944
Place of death:	Gross-Rosen, Poland
Rank:	Lieutenant
Parent unit:	General List
Service number:	294482
Decorations:	None recorded
Date joined SOE:	5 June 1943
Code names:	Christian/Stockman/Phillippe Morvant
Nationality:	British
Age at time of death:	Twenty-one
Date of birth:	29 January 1923
Place of birth:	Paris, France.

Location of memorial: Brookwood, UK

Born in Paris to Mauritian parents, Philip Duclos was only sixteen-years-old at the outbreak of war in September 1939. When the Germans invaded France the following May, Duclos and his mother moved out of the capital. Mme Duclos eventually returned to Paris, but young Philip was determined to try and reach Britain to join the Free French Forces. He was stopped by his mother only when she pointed out to him that he was still too young to be accepted.

Duclos agreed to stay in France to complete his education and the pair were able to cross into the Vichy zone and settle down in Nice. On 21 August 1942, Duclos made his bid to cross into Spain and down to Gibraltar – by bicycle.

Predictably, he was arrested in Spain and imprisoned at Barcelona jail. After six months he was released and he was at last able to continue on to the United Kingdom.

Though he was still very young and had no previous military experience, his determination to reach Britain and become involved in the war could not be denied and he began his SOE training on 5 June 1943. His assessors regarded him as being very kind-hearted and easy going. During his waking hours he was very security-minded but unfortunately he talked, in French, in his sleep.

Duclos was sent into the field on 29 February 1944, with Julien Detal, to form the DELEGATE circuit. He was to act as Detal's lieutenant and arms instructor. However, the Germans were waiting as they landed.

He was imprisoned at Frèsnes and Avenue Foch. Following the start of the liberation of France in June 1944, the Gestapo evacuated Paris, moving the captured SOE agents, including Duclos, to Germany. The Gestapo's final act was to transmit a message on a captured SOE set to F Section in London: 'Many thanks [for the] large deliveries arms and ammunition ... have greatly appreciated good tips concerning your intentions and plans.'

It is believed that Philip Duclos was executed at a satellite camp of Sachsenhausen located at Gross-Rosen.

FINLAYSON, David Haughton

Date of death:	1 August 1944
Place of death:	Gross-Rosen, Poland
Rank:	Lieutenant
Parent unit:	General List
Service number:	306891
Decorations:	None recorded
Date joined SOE:	25 July 1943
Code names:	Guillaume/Friar/Daniel Henri Garcie
Nationality:	British
Age at time of death:	Twenty
Date of birth:	23 September 1923
Place of birth:	Anglet, near Bayonne, France

Location of memorial: Brookwood, UK

Young David Finlayson was born to English parents in France where he was educated until the age of thirteen. His family eventually returned to the UK and David studied Engineering at Wolverhampton Technical College. Being bilingual he made an ideal potential SOE recruit.

Finlayson began his SOE training on 25 July 1943. His assessors regarded Finlayson as, 'a pleasant type of student officer, who is keen and intelligent, picks up instructions well and though rather young is in general a satisfactory student and would be suitable as a member of a "*coup-de-main*" party'.

At the age of just nineteen Finlayson was far too young to be placed in charge of a circuit. However, he proved to have a good technical mind and he enjoyed working by himself – attributes that made him ideal for the role of a wireless operator. As a result, he was sent into France on the night of 2/3 March 1944, to act as the wireless operator to Maurice Lepage's (*Colin*) LIONTAMER circuit in the Valenciennes area. He was also given the supplementary task of recruiting and training local operators.

Nothing certain was ever heard from Finlayson after his arrival in France. Though a number of messages were sent on his wireless set, none of them included the special messages that he had been given verbally. What probably happened when he landed in France is revealed in a note on his personal file: 'Finlayson and his organiser [Lepage] and lieutenant [Edmond Lesout] were received by the MUSICIAN circuit, which is now known to have been controlled by the Germans. Immediate arrest must be assumed. Telegrams continued to arrive on his plan until the end of May, all of which must have been under German control.'

At the bottom of the report his Section Head in London wrote the following: 'Very bad luck. An unfortunate affair. He was a good man.'

As late as January 1946 there was still no definite information concerning Finlayson. It has since been discovered that he was executed at Gross-Rosen.

FOX, Marcel Georges Florent

Date of death:	29 March 1945
Place of death:	Flossenbürg, Germany
Rank:	Lieutenant
Parent unit:	General List
Service number:	257605
Decorations:	Mentioned in Despatches, *Legion d'Honneur*, *Croix de Guerre avec Palme*
Date joined SOE:	25 August 1942
Code names:	Ernest/Publican/Maurice René Beauvais
Nationality:	French
Age at time of death:	Thirty-five
Date of birth:	22 March 1910
Place of birth:	Lisbon, Portugal

Location of memorial: Brookwood

Marcel Fox worked at the London branch of Crédit Lyonnais from 1930 until the declaration of war in 1939. He then immediately made his way to France to join the French Army, all at his own expense.

He was posted to the sector of the Maginot Line around the Fort du Hackenberg where the British troops were stationed from December 1939, being a liaison officer with the BEF. He saw considerable front line action and was later arrested by the Germans, though he subsequently escaped.

Fox returned to France and resumed working for his old company. He became friends with Emil270 Duboudin and when Duboudin joined the SOE, Fox became his second in command of the SPRUCE circuit. However, Fox had to resign from his position at the bank when money and some SPRUCE circuit documents went missing from his office. Determined to find out who had stolen these items, he put the matter in the hands of detectives only to learn that the thief was a friend of his. He dropped the charges to protect his friend without explaining his reasons.

This same friend repaid Fox's kindness by warning him, in May 1942, that as he was an escaped prisoner of war the police were looking for him. This news prompted Fox to make his way to Britain through Spain and Portugal. Because of this somewhat unusual set of circumstances Fox's credentials were carefully checked when he applied to officially join the SOE – and passed – by both MI5 and Scotland Yard.

Fox began his SOE training on 14 September 1942, and he soon proved to be 'an excellent example, and great influence upon the others [of the training party]; morale very high'.

He was parachuted back into France on 8 March 1943, to organise his own circuit in the Meaux region along with Marcel Rousset. The drop did not go well and they lost all their baggage, including Rousset's wireless set. Messages were relayed through the PROSPER circuit in Paris and new sets and crystals were sent out from the UK.

The PUBLICAN circuit was instructed to block or disable the railways in its area, particularly between Lagny and Meaux, and to attack a number of locomotive sheds at Vaires, Noisy-le-Sec and Faremoutiers. He was also tasked with encouraging local workers to resist being sent to Germany and, if they were forced to go, to slow down any work they were engaged upon.

Little is known of his achievements in this mission before he was arrested the following autumn. The arrest took place at the supposed safe-house of Mme Blanchard in Paris. Fox, Rousset and Jean Bouguennec were having lunch when the Gestapo arrived.

The prisoners were taken separately to Avenue Foch, as was Mme Blanchard's sister-in-law. Later the three agents were sent to Frèsnes prison. There was some suspicion that the men had been betrayed by another agent, Donald Dunton (Code name *Cypress*), but this was never proved. Rousset managed to escape on 8 June 1944, but not the other two. Fox was transferred to Germany and executed at Flossenbürg.

Because he had volunteered to go back into France despite being on the authorities' wanted list, he was awarded a posthumous Mention in Desptaches.

FRAGER, Henri Jaques Paul

Date of death:	12 October 1944	
Place of death:	Buchenwald, Germany	
Rank:	Major	
Parent unit:	General List	
Service number:	305088	
Decorations:	Mentioned in Despatches, *Médaille de la Résistance Française*	
Date joined SOE:	25 November 1943	
Code names:	Louba/Architect/Henri Dupre	
Nationality:	French	
Age at time of death:	Forty-seven	
Date of birth:	3 March 1897	
Place of birth:	Paris, France	

Location of memorial: Brookwood, UK

From the very earliest days of the German occupation of France Henri Frager, an architect in Nice in civilian life, was actively plotting against the enemy. On 25 November 1940, he dined with André Girard in a restaurant in Antibes. Girard wanted to develop a local resistance network, whereas Frager was then preparing to get to London via Algeria.

The two men went their separate ways. Girard developed the CARTE circuit whereas Frager went on to Algeria. After several failed attempts to get from Algeria to London he returned to Antibes in April 1941 and joined Girard's team, becoming his second in command.

Girard and Frager recruited others into their growing network, and on 19 September 1941, Girard had his first meeting with an SOE agent, François Basin (Code name *Olive*). Exploring the possibilities for CARTE–SOE co-operation, Buckmaster summoned Girard or any other officer of CARTE to come to London. Not wanting to go himself, Girard sent Frager. On 30 June 1942, the Polish trawler *Tarana* took Frager to Gibraltar, from where he flew to Britain by plane.

After detailed discussions Frager returned to France with F Section staff officer Nicholas Bodington. They landed at Cap d'Antibes on the night of 29/30 July 1942, from the boat *Seadog*. Two other agents, one of whom was Yvonne Rudellat, were present. On 12 September Bodington returned to England with a highly favourable report on the CARTE organisation.

However, in November 1942, a list of names and addresses of hundreds of potential CARTE members, drawn up by Girard, fell into the hands of the *Abwehr*. An assistant of Girard named André Marsac was carrying the list by train from Marseilles to Paris. While Marsac slept on the train, an *Abwehr* agent stole the briefcase that contained the list.

SOE agent Peter Churchill had also arrived in 1942 to evaluate the usefulness of the CARTE network. He was impressed by the people he met but disagreements between Girard and Frager made it necessary for SOE to choose between them. Peter Churchill, having chosen Frager as preferable, took him to London in March 1943 to be briefed by SOE on his future role. There was no need. CARTE was already doomed.

André Marsac, from whom the CARTE list had been stolen by the *Abwehr*, was arrested near the Champs Élyseé by Hugo Bleicher, a sergeant in the *Abwehr*, and incarcerated in Frèsnes prison. Bleicher, posing as an anti-Nazi colonel, convinced Marsac that he wished to defect, and the pair concocted an elaborate scheme involving the co-operation of Marsac's assistant Roger Bardet, who was persuaded by letter to visit Marsac in prison. Through the gullible Marsac, Bleicher was able to infiltrate the CARTE organisation, the sad outcome of which was the arrest, on 16 April 1943, of Peter Churchill and Odette Sansom. A bonus was provided by Marsac, who supplied Bleicher with the addresses of some twenty circuits in Bordeaux, Strasbourg and Marseilles.

Meanwhile, Henri Frager had returned to France a third time on 29 February 1944, again by sea, to organise attacks on targets for D-Day in the Vallée de l'Yonne. He received thirty-five drops of arms and equipment and was able to report considerable success harassing the enemy including damage done to the cellophane factory at Mantes. He raised and armed 700 fighters in the Yonne, 300 in the Joigny area and a further 746 in other nearby localities.

On 2 July 1944, Frager attended a rendezvous with Bleicher (again posing as the anti-Nazi colonel), and was arrested. The meeting had been arranged by Bardet. Frager was imprisoned at Frèsnes before being sent to Buchenwald where he was shot.

GAILLOT, Henri Hubert

Date of death:	1 March 1944
Place of death:	Gross-Rosen, Poland
Rank:	Lieutenant
Parent unit:	General List
Service number:	282433
Decorations:	*Croix de Guerre, Médaille Militaire, Ordre de Leopold*
Date joined SOE:	26 June 1943
Code names:	Ignace/Deacon/Jean Femand Masson
Nationality:	Belgian
Age at time of death:	Forty-seven
Date of birth:	20 April 1896
Place of birth:	Liège, Belgium

Location of memorial: Brookwood, UK

Henri Gaillot had worked for a decorating company in his home town of Liège before moving to Paris where he stated his own business. He had become so successful that he even was involved in the 1937 Paris Exposition (effectively the World Trade Fair).

Henri Gaillot had joined the French Army and was fighting with the 75th Group Divisional Recognition unit along with his friend François Vallée when captured by the Germans on 17 June 1940. Both men were decorated for their bravery in this engagement.

The two friends were imprisoned in Germany for some eighteen months when they volunteered to do farm work. This gave them their opportunity and they escaped, making their way back to France. They tried unsuccessfully to find a way to reach Britain and in the end they travelled to Tunisia from where they were able to find a ship that took them to Gibraltar.

The two men were obvious candidates for the SOE with Gaillot in particular receiving glowing reports from his assessors – he was described as a 'most remarkable character' and a 'shrewd, worldly man'. Being older than most SOE recruits (he was affectionately known in Baker Street as 'grandpere'), Gaillot was seen as being 'strong-willed, honest and a good man in any eventuality'.

Nevertheless, as Vallée had been his sergeant in the French Army, Gaillot deferred to the senior man. It was therefore Vallée who was to be the organiser of the PARSON circuit based around Rennes with Gaillot as his lieutenant. They were parachuted into France on 24 July 1943.

The objectives given to PARSON included the destruction of railways, factories, petrol stores and transformer stations. This was not enough for this hugely ambitious pair and together they devised a plan to isolate the whole of Brittany on D-Day by putting out of action all the railway lines. They raised a large number of groups of Resistance fighters and planned to train them in sabotage and guerrilla warfare. For this they waited for drops of arms and equipment but circumstances did not work in their favour as the weather was very poor and the deliveries were held up.

It was decided that because of these delays it would be safer if the two agents returned to Britain. The pick-up could not be immediately arranged as they became separated from their wireless operator. They tried to find a means of getting out of France but by this time their circuit and their letter boxes had been compromised.

Eventually they were told a Lysander would pick them up on the night of 4/5 April 1944. They were arrested whilst leaving Paris on their way to the landing ground.

It is known that Gaillot spent some time at 3 bis Place des États Unis before being moved to Germany. He was executed at Gross-Rosen.

GARDNER, Denis

Date of death:	9 June 1944
Place of death:	Beaurepaire, France
Rank:	Sergeant
Parent unit:	2 Northamptonshire Yeomanry, Royal Armoured Corps
Service number:	14290042
Decorations:	Mentioned in Despatches
Date joined SOE:	October 1944
Code names:	Ernest
Nationality:	British
Age at time of death:	Twenty
Date of birth:	23 November 1923
Place of birth:	Preston, UK
Location of grave:	Beaurepaire, France

Dennis Gardner, from Kirby Stephen near Penrith, was assigned to join the Jedburgh Operation *Veganin* (also referred to as 'Beck') in southern France as a radio operator. He was described by his training officer as being 'all that could be desired in a radio operator, an excellent worker, cheerful and keen'.

The Jedburghs were three-man teams comprised of an officer of the country into which the team was being sent, with a British or American officer plus a British, French or American wireless operator. The Jedburghs were sent into France (and later the Low Countries and further afield), usually in uniform, on or after D-Day to help local resistance networks to co-ordinate their efforts with the operations of the Allied armies.

The Jedburghs were specifically ordered neither to take command of any of the Resistance groups nor to engage in any direct action against the enemy. Instead they were to arrange arms and supplies for the Resistance and train their members in the use of weapons and explosives. What they actually did was far different, as is explained by Ian Dear: 'They suggested, helped to plan, and took part in sabotage of communications, destruction of fuel and ammunition dumps, attacks on enemy pockets cut off by the advance of the Allied armies and the procurement of intelligence.'

As part of such a team, Gardner was sent to North Africa from where the trio would be flown across the Mediterranean to be dropped by parachute at 01.30 hours on the morning of 9 June 1944. Major Harry Marten provided the following explanation of exactly what happened that night:

'I was the leader of a mission being dropped by parachute into France on the night of 8/9 June 1944. We put on our parachutes, which had previously been fitted at Bilda [in Algeria], when we crossed the French coast. We were advised that we were twelve minutes from the target and again that we were four minutes from the target area. On the second warning we were told to move up to the hole and were hitched up to the static line.

'I was hitched up first and checked my strong point; then I noticed Comdt. Noir being hitched up. I did not look to see whether Sgt. Gardner was hitched up because he was on the other side of the hole jumping No.3.

'I then asked for the pin to be put into the buckle, and this was done, and I saw it done for Comdt. Noir, but again I did not see Sgt. Gardner's being put in for the same reason. I heard Comdt. Noir ask for his pin to be bent apart, as this had not been done.

'We then jumped, and after two hours came across the body of Sgt. Gardner. The parachute was still on his back and was completely packed with the exception of the wire line, which was pulled out of the bag, except for about 2 feet, which remained folded inside. The buckle on the wire line was intact, but the binding was frayed for about half an inch on the top.'

Dennis Gardner was recommended for a posthumous Mention in Despatches.

GARRY, Emile August Henri

Date of death:	14 September 1944
Place of death:	Buchenwald, Germany
Rank:	Lieutenant
Parent unit:	General List
Service number:	309242
Decorations:	Mentioned in Despatches, *Croix de Guerre*, *Chevalier de la Legion d'Honneur*, *Médaille de la Résistance Française*
Date joined SOE:	1942
Code names:	Cinema/Phono
Nationality:	French
Age at time of death:	Thirty-five
Date of birth:	2 April 1909
Place of birth:	Paris, France

Location of memorial: Brookwood, UK

Emile Garry, a former French officer, was recruited into the SOE in the field and never went to Britain for training. He was regarded as a handsome man who bore a slight resemblance to Garry Cooper, hence his circuit was called CINEMA. He set up a small sub-circuit in the Chatres-Etampes district south of Paris within Francis Suttill's *PROSPER* network. It was tasked with undertaking acts of sabotage on railway and telephone targets in the area bounded by Chartres-Etampes-Orléans.

Garry's radio operator was Noor Inayat-Khan who joined him on 16 June 1943, meeting him at his apartment in Rue Erlanger in Auteuil. Just days later Suttill was captured by the Germans but Garry and Inayat-Khan managed to survive the initial rush of arrests that followed.

It soon became apparent that the Gestapo were aware of Garry's and Inayat-Khan's existence and they were advised by Baker Street staff officer Nicholas Bodington to get out of France as quickly as possible. Garry, and his wife Marguerite, went into hiding in Le Mans until he could be safely evacuated. Inayat-Khan approached some of her pre-war friends (completely against her training) who put her up for short periods of time. She wandered from one part of Paris to the other with her transmitter in her suitcase.

Garry eventually returned to Paris, with his Code name now changed to *Phono*. His role was to look after agents passing through Paris. Garry, however, was not content with a passive role and he undertook a number of sabotage operations, almost single-handedly. He was joined on occasion in these missions by Inayat-Khan and his wife.

Towards the end of September 1943, however, an informer gave the trio away and Inayat-Khan was arrested on 13 October at the apartment of one of Garry's friends called Solange. Garry was at Nantes when Inayat-Khan was seized. He returned to Paris with his wife, unaware of the arrest of Inayat-Khan, on 16 October, staying at the home of his sister-in-law.

A courier from Guy Bieler, the MUSICIAN organiser, brought Garry the welcome news that a Lysander pick up had been arranged for him and his wireless operator. Garry then went to Solange's apartment (which of course was being watched by the Gestapo) to see Inayat-Khan. Not finding her there Garry stayed overnight and the following morning a Frenchman called, claiming to be a SOE courier with a message from Inayat-Khan. The caller said that she had gone into hiding and needed Solange to put together a parcel of clothes for her. The man said that he would return for the parcel in thirty minutes. He did, with three SD men.

On 22 October 1943, Mr and Mrs Garry (who was heavily pregnant) were taken to the Gestapo prison at 3 bis Place des États Unis. From here they were transferred to Frèsnes where Marguerite Garry gave birth. The baby died ten days later.

The couple were treated as French terrorists rather than SOE. Nevertheless, Garry was sent to Buchenwald and executed in September 1944. His wife ended up at Ravensbrück and, after being forced to work in a German aircraft factory near Weimar for some time, survived the war. She returned to France in 1945 in very poor health. Emile Garry was recommended for a Mention in Despatches.

GEELEN, Pierre Albert Hubert

Date of death:	14 September 1944
Place of death:	Buchenwald, Germany
Rank:	Lieutenant
Parent unit:	General List
Service number:	313547
Decorations:	None recorded
Date joined SOE:	November 1943
Code names:	Serge/Grinder/Pierre Garde
Nationality:	Belgian
Age at time of death:	Twenty-eight
Date of birth:	24 June 1916
Place of birth:	Rothe, Belgium

Location of memorial: Brookwood, UK

There was real doubt about Pierre Geelen's background when he arrived in London in November 1943 and initially it was decided that he was not suitable for employment with the SOE. His story was that he was a school teacher in Belgium and that in 1942 he chose to try and reach Britain so that he could join the Belgian Army, which had reformed in the UK. He travelled through France, aiming for Spain, eventually joining a Resistance group in Marseilles.

Here Geelen was instructed in how to organise parachute drops and he took part in five operations. He was then given the mission of returning to Belgium with a colleague, Andre Heyermans, to recruit sub-agents and identify suitable landing grounds. On the way he stopped at Paris where Heyermans was arrested.

Geelen returned to the South of France and continued his work, but disagreements with the circuit chief led to him returning to Paris to join the PROSPER network. Here Geelen operated until 15 July 1943, when he and another agent were arrested by the *Feldgendarmerie* in the street near his house. Whilst they were being taken back to Geelen's house for it to be searched, the two men escaped. The pair then decided to try and reach Britain, which they did two months later.

Why this story seemed so improbable to the staff at Baker Street is not clear. Geelen was very thoroughly interrogated on his arrival, during which time he detailed his achievements in the field and talked about all the SOE agents with whom he had been in contact. He even told the tale of one agent who had landed at Chiny in Belgium and been captured with two Colt revolvers and a radio set. The man had been released when a 'tip' of 20,000 Francs had been handed over.

Despite the doubts about his story, further checks were conducted by MI5 and 'nothing adverse' was unearthed. This eventually led to the decision not to re-employ him being reversed and he began his official SOE training in November 1943.

At first he proved a poor student. On his first tests Geelen failed his Morse examination, but he persevered and before the end of the month he had mastered the communications aspects of the work to such an extent that his assessors believed that he would make a good wireless operator. In due course he was allocated to the LABOURER circuit in Angers to assist Marcel Leccia.

Geelen, Leccia and Allard were parachuted into France on 5/6 April 1944. Landing near Châteauroux, they were delivered to a safe-house nearby. The group duly began to set up their circuit but one of Leccia's friends was working for the Gestapo and all three men were arrested.

It is known that Geelen was taken to Avenue Foch and was still there as late as June 1944. All three agents were later transferred to the Cherche-Midi prison in Paris.

Geelen was executed at Buchenwald. Though listed by the CWGC under the name of Garde, this agent's real name was Geelen – Pierre Garde was the cover name he used in the field. Oddly, he was commissioned into the SOE under his cover name and it is the name Garde that appears on the Brookwood Memorial.

GOUGH, Victor Albert

Date of death:	25 November 1944
Place of death:	Schirmeck La Braque, France
Rank:	Captain
Parent unit:	Somerset Light Infantry
Service number:	148884
Decorations:	Mentioned in Despatches; *Croix de Guerre*
Date joined SOE:	23 April 1944
Code names:	Arran
Nationality:	British
Age at time of death:	Twenty-six
Date of birth:	11 September 1918
Place of birth:	Hereford, UK
Location of grave:	Durnbach, Germany

Victor Gough, a mechanical engineer in Bristol for the Imperial Tobacco Company before the war, was also something of a cartoonist and he created the Special Forces winged emblem that the Jedburghs wore on their uniforms.

He was regarded as 'a quiet, serious party' and he was trained to form part of the Jedburgh team Code named JACOB. On the night of 12 August 1944, this unit, comprising of Gough, a Frenchman, Captain Maurice Boissarie, and Sergeant Ken Seymour, was parachuted into the Vosges north of Épinal. They landed at about 01.00 hours on 13 August near the village of La Petite-Raon. Team JACOB was to assist both the local *maquis* and an SAS team that was also operating in the area.

On 15 August 1944, Team JACOB radioed Special Forces Head Quarters (SFHQ), which was co-ordinating operations behind enemy lines, to confirm that they had landed safely. Sergeant Seymour (whose Code name was *Skye*) injured his ankle in the jump, but they expected him to be mobile again in seven days.

The trio had also joined up with a *maquis* unit based in the countryside to the south of Vexaincourt. Of the 800 French volunteers in the area, only fifty were armed, the rest had to remain inactive in their homes. In two messages on 26 August, the team requested a large supply drop and indicated that their radio set was not functioning and that they were using the SAS team's equipment.

On 5 September, JACOB reported that they had not yet received another radio and that several days earlier an arms drop had proved unsuccessful, resulting in numerous casualties when Axis forces attacked them on the drop zone. On the following day, JACOB cancelled that night's arms drop, reporting that Germans were waiting on the drop zone.

The next that was heard from Team JACOB was on 15 September. In a message sent to SFHQ, it was reported that Sergeant Seymour had been captured on 17 August and was rumoured to have been shot on the 20th (in fact he survived the war as a PoW).

In a skirmish on 4 September at Viambois Farm, Captain Boissarie (who served as G. Barraud and had the Code name *Connaught*) was killed along with a number of members of the Resistance. Worse still was that another 100 *maquis* had been captured and the remainder had dispersed. Despite such set-backs, on 16 September, Gough radioed SFHQ stating that he had rallied 200 and with SAS assistance he had armed them.

At 19.00 hours on 18 September, Captain Gough sent his last message in which he said he was now operating with 800 *maquis* but he indicated that he was experiencing great difficulty working on his own after the loss of Boissaire and Seymour.

Gough was captured in the days following 18 September whilst trying to get back to the Allied army lines. He was reported missing at the end of October 1944, and is known to have been sighted in the Schirmeck-Labroque concentration camp, Alsace, on 8 November 1944. He was not seen again.

GRAHAM, Harry Huntingdon

Date of death:	29 March 1945	
Place of death:	Flossenbürg, Germany	
Rank:	Sergeant	
Parent unit:	33 Field Regiment Royal Artillery	
Service number:	800964	
Decorations:	Mentioned in Despatches	
Date joined SOE:	11 April 1943	
Code names:	Henri/Henri Berneau	
Nationality:	British	
Age at time of death:	Thirty-four	
Date of birth:	13 July 1910	
Place of birth:	Carlisle, UK	

Location of memorial: Brookwood, UK

Sergeant Harry Graham could hardly be classified as a typical SOE agent. In civilian life he had been a joiner and his French was described as 'atrocious'. Yet his assessors saw that he was 'animated with a spirit of adventure because he is definitely an adventurous type of man, who likes excitement and realises what it entails'.

Despite his lack of a grasp of the French language, Graham left for the field on 16 August 1943. As a demolition expert his mission was to attempt to destroy the Les Telots shale oil refinery at Autun in a '*coup-de-main* operation', codenamed SCULLION II. Led by Hugh Dormer, the team included David Sibree, Philip Amphlett, Victor Soskice and George Demand. Graham showed 'outstanding courage and efficiency' in accomplishing his allotted task. He was one of two men that placed demolition charges on the target.

Coup-de-main operations were single-mission expeditions to attack specific targets. After the completion of the operation the team members were supposed to make their way out of the enemy-held territory back to the UK. Consequently after the attack upon the refinery the party split into three groups with Graham and Soskice making off to a pre-arranged rendezvous. Unfortunately they did not reach their destination nor did the others mentioned above. The men were captured by the Gestapo, eventually being sent to Flossenbürg. Here they were held in solitary confinement for many months. Some were starved and beaten. They were executed, probably by hanging, at Flossenbürg on 29 March 1945.

Graham's wife was told that he did not lose his life in vain: 'His work contributed in an important way to the rapid liberation of France from the enemy, with the consequent effect that the Allied armies landing in Normandy suffered far less casualties than would otherwise have been the case.'

Graham was recommended for a posthumous Mention in Despatches.

GROVER-WILLIAMS, William Charles Frederick

Date of death:	18 March 1945
Place of death:	Sachsenhausen, Germany
Rank:	Captain
Parent unit:	General List
Service number:	231189
Decorations:	Mentioned in Despatches, *Croix de Guerre*
Date joined SOE:	17 November 1941
Code names:	Sébastien/Chestnut/Charles Fréderick Lelong
Nationality:	British
Age at time of death:	Forty-two
Date of birth:	16 January 1903
Place of birth:	Montrouge, Hauts-de-Seine, France

Location of memorial: Brookwood, UK

Grover-Williams was a well-known racing driver, having won seven grand prix for Bugatti including the inaugural Monaco Grand Prix in 1929.

Following the invasion of France, Grover-Williams, born to an English father and a French mother, made his way to Britain. Here he enlisted in the Royal Army Service Corps. As a consequence of his fluency in French and English, he was soon recruited into the ranks of the SOE, training under the name Vladimir Gatacre.

He established a small network amongst his pre-war racing friends, which included Jean-Pierre Wimille and former world champion Robert Benoist. This, the CHESTNUT circuit, was based on the Benoist estates at Auffargis near Rambouillet to the south-west of Paris.

The group settled down unmolested by the Germans who apparently respected them as well-known sportsmen, never suspecting their clandestine activities. In March 1942 CHESTNUT received its wireless operator, Robert Dowlen. Through Dowlen it received a number of arms drops, which were hidden on the estate but achieved little in terms of sabotage. The group was able to pass on valuable information through its many important contacts.

Dowlen had set up his wireless post at a farmhouse on the road to Pontoise to the north-east of Paris. Grover-Williams was determined to maintain the security of his operation and kept Dowlen and the rest of the group separated and contact with Dowlen was maintained by couriers using Benoist's car.

In early August Dowlen was located by a direction-finding van of the *Funk-Horchdienst* and captured whilst transmitting. The entire Benoist family was arrested but Robert managed to escape.

Grover-Williams was captured when the Gestapo searched the Benoist estate grounds. Fifteen German police officers in plain clothes under the command of Karl Langer began searching the estate and Grover-Williams was found in the stables of the château, where they also found one of the arms dumps. Grover-Williams was attacked and badly beaten on the spot, but he gave no information to the Germans. Nevertheless, the Germans continued to search the estate and discovered fifty-one canisters full of weapons in an old well and a further forty-seven behind a false wall in the stable block.

Grover-Williams was transported to Paris and placed in a cell on the fifth floor at 84 Avenue Foch. The discovery of the arms convinced the Germans that they had captured an SOE agent and at 19.30 hours that evening his interrogation began. He still refused to talk and the interrogation continued throughout the night.

It is known that Grover-Williams was moved to Germany in January 1944 and that he spent some time in the cells at the Reich Security Office (*Reichssicherheitshauptamt*) building in Berlin at 8 Prinz Albrechstrasse, a place known for its appalling tortures which included thumb screws and racks and more advanced techniques using electricity. In early March he was taken to the concentration camp at Sachsenhausen where he was locked in the infamous *Zellenbau* (prison cells).

Following instructions from Berlin in March 1945 to give 'special treatment' to political prisoners, Grover-Williams was taken to the *Industriehof* – an area located outside the prison enclosure on the west side of the Sachsenhausen concentration camp. Here he was shot.

It has been suggested that Grover-Williams actually survived the war, joining MI6. An individual, George Tambal, who had the same date of birth as Grover-Williams, moved in with his wife at Evreux, claiming to be her cousin. This man, be it Grover-Williams or Tambal was killed in a road accident in 1983.

GYORI, Issack

Date of death:	25 December 1944
Place of death:	Deselo, Slovenia
Rank:	Corporal
Parent unit:	Royal Army Service Corps
Service number:	PAL/275
Decorations:	None recorded
Date joined SOE:	13 June 1944
Code names:	Michael Trent
Nationality:	Naturalised British
Age at time of death:	Twenty-five
Date of birth:	1 May 1919
Place of birth:	Komárno, Czechoslovakia

Location of memorial: Athens, Greece

Issack Gyori was born in Czechoslovakia to Jewish-Hungarian parents. Though a driver with the Pioneer Corps he was actually serving with No.2 Commando when taken up by the SOE Italian Section.

With the collapse of Mussolini's Fascist regime, Italy was immediately transformed from an enemy country to an occupied one. Opportunities for the SOE, in what was previously an entirely unproductive country, opened up across central and northern Italy.

Very quickly a powerful Resistance, or liberation, movement developed. By the end of October 1943 six Italian missions had gone into the field with wireless sets and over the course of the next six months eighteen more were established. Some 200-300 tons of supplies were dropped by air to these groups and an equal amount sent in by sea.

However, as in much of Italian politics, many different factions developed within the Resistance movement. This was particularly the case in north-eastern Italy. The Slovene population there owed its allegiance to Yugoslavia's Tito and opposition soon grew between the Communist 'Garibaldi Brigades' and the other Italian partisans. It was into this dangerous area, where the Germans were not the only enemy, that Gyori, a former student of journalism, was sent.

On 21 December 1944, the so-called Slovene Battalion Resia announced that it intended to disarm all Italian partisans that passed through Resia. A group of three Italians were subsequently seized and disarmed and Gyori volunteered to accompany this group to 9 Slovene Corps at Chiapovano. He marched them off into Slovenia never to be seen again.

Nothing more was heard of this party until a report was received in London on 17 January 1945 – though it had actually been sent on 27 December 1944. This announced that Gyori was killed in a skirmish with a German patrol near Deselo whilst leading his party in a crossing of the River Isonzo on 25 December.

HAMILTON, John Trevor

Date of death:	1 May 1944
Place of death:	Gross-Rosen, Germany
Rank:	Lieutenant
Parent unit:	Royal Army Service Corps
Service number:	250966
Decorations:	None recorded
Date joined SOE:	10 August 1942
Code names:	Francois/Tobaconist/Jean Charles Rochard
Nationality:	British
Age at time of death:	Thirty-six
Date of birth:	21 May 1907
Place of birth:	Swansea, UK

Location of memorial: Brookwood, UK

Though born in Wales, John Hamilton spent many years working in Paris as a ship-broker. In this he was clearly very successful, as he is described in his SOE personal file as being 'a rich man; well-known in French shipping circles'.

With the fall of France Hamilton made his way to Britain and joined the army, leaving his wife and two children in Paris. He was able to communicate with them via Switzerland. He was highly regarded by his assessors who recorded that he was 'very shrewd ... has great powers of thinking and co-ordination'. He was earmarked for a prominent role.

It was a role that led to Hamilton being sent into the field on the night of 29/30 December 1942. He arrived in the Rhône region where he was to make contact with the GREENHEART and ALMOND circuits and give them the latest directives from London. Such was his standing within F Section Hamilton was also tasked with reporting back to Baker Street on the state of these circuits. He was also expected to raise his own group, SPRUCE, and attack a number of railways in the area around Lyons. Hamilton's remit was very wide-ranging with instruction to also attack the Creney electrical transformer station and Rennes Naval Depot in Brittany.

Hamilton was arrested at the house of another agent, Captain Joseph Marchand DSO, just a day or so after his arrival in France. The Germans were searching for an agent from the VIC escape line and instead caught the SOE man. Marchand was lucky enough to be out at the time.

Hamilton disappeared and it was not until 19 April 1943 that a report was received stating that he had been seen in Frèsnes. It is known that he was tortured and on at least two occasions electric treatment was used. He did not talk.

Hope that he might still be alive at the end of the war in Europe was raised in June 1945. A French prisoner who had returned from Russia went to the place in Marseilles where Hamilton's brother-in-law was working and said that a Lieutenant Hamilton was a patient at a hospital in Odessa.

Sadly, no further information came to light. As far as the SOE records are concerned Hamilton was taken to Ravitsch on 18 April 1945, and was later killed at Gross-Rosen.

Buchmaster wrote just these words at the end of Hamilton's casualty report: 'Very promising. What bad luck.'

HANAU, Julius

Date of death:	12 May 1943
Place of death:	Cairo, Egypt
Rank:	Colonel
Parent unit:	Intelligence Corps
Service number:	Not recorded
Decorations:	OBE
Date joined SOE:	1940
Code names:	Caesar
Nationality:	British
Age at time of death:	Fifty-eight
Date of birth:	25 April 1885
Place of birth:	South Africa
Location of grave:	Heliopolis

A South African who had spent some years in South America, Julius Hanau was a member of the Royal Army Service Corps in Salonika during the First World War. After the Armistice he remained in the Balkans becoming a member of the Secret Intelligence Service operating in Yugoslavia in the 1930s.

Hanau was part of the SOE from its inception; in fact it has been said that he was the first agent the SOE ever employed. For the first eighteen months he set up Resistance movements across the Balkans but he was withdrawn from Yugoslavia because of pressure put upon the Yugoslav authorities by the German minister in Belgrade, where Hanau was working as the representative of the Vickers Company. It was also known that the Gestapo had plans to kill him as soon as they invaded Yugoslavia.

Hanau was viewed in Baker Street as being 'courageous, loyal and charming – a good leader and organiser ... liked and admired by all who came into contact with him'. Back in London Hanau was put in charge of SOE's West African mission, where he was responsible for Operation *Postmaster*, the cutting out of ships from Santa Isabel in Fernando Po, and the acquisition of the ship *Gascon* and its cargo, both notable coups at a time when SOE was not enjoying much success.

Hanau was instrumental in the establishment of the South African mission and was crucial in planning the successful British invasion of Madagascar in May 1942 (see James Mayer). He landed with the British troops at Diego Suarez and played a key part in negotiating a surrender of the Vichy forces for which he received the OBE.

He returned to the United Kingdom on 23 June 1942. On 30 July he was appointed Director in Charge of the SOE's Iberian Sector and the North, East and West African sectors.

In October 1942, it was decided that with his twenty-five years knowledge of the Balkans, Hanau would be better employed organizing the Resistance forces in that region following the recent German occupation of Yugoslavia. He therefore relinquished his other commands and travelled to Cairo (after a period of sick leave having contracted malignant malaria in West Africa) to plan actions in the Balkans.

After spending some weeks in Cairo Hanau continued on to Istanbul in the first week of May. Just a few days after returning to Cairo he died of a heart attack. He was pronounced dead in 15 (Scottish) General Hospital.

When Hanau's wife was told of his death, she was convinced that he had been poisoned by a German agent. The Gestapo, she reasoned, knew him well and they would have been anxious to see him disposed of. She demanded a post mortem but he had already been buried, his funeral having taken place, with full military honours, at 17.00 hours on 13 May 1943, in the Heliopolis cemetery. Hanau is believed to be the oldest of the SOE casualties commemorated as such by the Commonwealth War Graves Commission.

HAYES, Victor Charles

Date of death:	1 August 1944
Place of death:	Gross-Rosen, Poland
Rank:	Captain
Parent unit:	General List
Service number:	211716
Decorations:	MBE, *Croix de Guerre avec Palme*
Date joined SOE:	1 August 1941
Code names:	Yves/Printer/Victor Charles
Nationality:	British
Age at time of death:	Thirty-six
Date of birth:	29 April 1908
Place of birth:	Paris, France

Location of memorial: Brookwood, UK

Charles Hayes first mission began when he was landed in France by felucca on 14 May 1942, to join Philippe de Vomécourt's VENTRILOQUIST circuit. Hayes had been a dental mechanic before the war and he considered himself to be a technical advisor and consequently above being a mere saboteur. He was therefore given the task of investigating potential sabotage targets.

It was not long before his activities became known to the Gestapo but he was able to escape through the Pyrénées before the Germans could track him down. He reached Britain in August 1942.

Hayes was dropped into France for his second mission on 26 November 1942, this time to support the organiser of the SCIENTIST circuit. The group's activities were expanding so rapidly that its organiser, Claude de Baissac, needed someone to assist him.

The group had some significant successes. It blew up the huge German radio sender at Quatre-Pavillons, which provided the communication between Admiral Doenitz's headquarters at Lorient and the German U–boats that were raiding Allied shipping in the Atlantic. It destroyed the power station that fed the installations at the *Luftwaffe* airfields near Mérignac some 6 miles west of Bordeaux, and the Belin-Béliet power station, which supplied the German anti-aircraft batteries and radar installation at Deux Potteaux. What E. H. Cooksbridge describes as 'innumerable' successful attacks were made against railway, road and telephone communications, in which the German Group 'G' (consisting of 1st and 19th Armies) was isolated, often for days at a time, from the German High Command.

The circuit remained immune from the widespread arrests that had affected many other groups in France until, quite suddenly, several of its members were arrested and arms dumps uncovered. Hayes' arrest came in the early hours of 14 October 1943.

That night he was staying in the house of friends of de Baissac, the Duboué family, at Lestiac, 15 miles inland from Bordeaux on the banks of the Garonne when the Gestapo came raiding. Hayes had been staying there for some time, having fallen for their eighteen-year-old daughter Suzanne.

Hayes was a widower, his wife having died two years earlier. Yet the diminutive and balding Hayes seems an unlikely match for a girl virtually half his age but he was so smitten with the young girl that he had refused an order from London to relocate and take over SCIENTIST's northern region.

Hayes and the son of the household held the Germans at bay for three hours, firing from the windows with Sten guns, pistols and grenades, even forcing the Germans to send for reinforcements. It was only when Madame Duboué was wounded in the stomach and the two men were so badly wounded that they could no longer keep fighting that they surrendered. Everyone in the house was taken prisoner.

Hayes, having been shot in the arm and leg, was taken to the Robert Piquet military hospital in Bordeaux. It was said that in recognition of his brave battle Hayes would be treated as a prisoner of war not a terrorist. In the end this made little difference as he was sent to Frèsnes where his exploits were soon forgotten.

Suzanne Duboué was sent to Ravensbrück but survived the war. Charles Hayes was executed at Gross-Rosen.

HILL, William Arthur

Date of death:	7 November 1943
Place of death:	Petrela, Albania
Rank:	Bombardier
Parent unit:	Royal Artillery
Service number:	940696
Decorations:	BEM
Date joined SOE:	1942
Code names:	None recorded
Nationality:	British
Age at time of death:	Twenty-four
Date of birth:	15 March 1919
Place of birth:	UK

Location of memorial: Athens, Greece

The first of the SOE's missions into Albania (Force 133), led by Major McLean and Major David Smiley, took place in the spring of 1943. More agents were parachuted into Albania in July and August of 1943, creating a full headquarters team and four military missions, amongst which was William Hill who was the wireless operator for the SCONCE team led by Major George Seymour. Their operational instructions were somewhat loose, as George Seymour recalled: 'Our briefing in Cairo had been, as its name implies, brief and we went in knowing very few facts. We were told shortly that our task was to organise the local populations for purposes of sabotage, subversion and guerrilla operations against the Axis occupying troops.'

Despite the fraught and complex political situation in the Balkans, the Germans were viewed as the only real enemy and the agents' final instruction was that the population was to be armed and organised 'irrespective of political or religious creed'.

The various teams attached themselves to large mixed bands of partisans that ambushed enemy patrols and attacked isolated garrisons. This constant harrying eventually drove the Germans onto the offensive. They attacked the partisans to the south of Tirana where the SCONCE team was based. Supported by tanks, artillery and Albanian collaborators, the Germans launched a set-piece attack. Two days of heavy fighting ensued culminating in the partisan's camp being attacked at dawn on 7 November 1943.

The partisans were roused by a pistol shot fired at close range; thirty seconds later German machine-guns opened up. As the British tried to get away, Hill was hit in the torso and head. Another member of the team, a former RAF rear-gunner called James Smith, tried to reach Hill to help him but it was too late – Hill was already dead. For this act of courage Smith was awarded the Military Medal.

The first that London knew of this was when his commanding officer, Brigadier Edmund Frank Davies (who was nicknamed 'Trotsky'), sent a signal from the field saying that he had been seen dead. On 11 December a further signal was sent to London stating that Hill had been buried by the Germans at Petrela.

Bombardier William Hill was recommended for the Military Medal but was awarded the British Empire Medal (Military Division), which was gazetted on 2 January 1945.

HOFFMAN, Ernst

Date of death:	Sometime after 10 October 1944
Place of death:	Graslitz, Czechoslovakia
Rank:	Lieutenant
Parent unit:	General List
Service number:	318481
Decorations:	None recorded
Date joined SOE:	8 March 1944
Code names:	Ernst Helmich/Holzer/Kraus
Nationality:	Czech
Age at time of death:	Thirty-two
Date of birth:	4 September 1912
Place of birth:	Abertham, Czechoslovakia

Location of memorial: Brookwood, UK

A Sudeten German, Hoffman was recruited for SOE's X Section, the country division for Germany, in Sweden. He duly arrived in London from Stockholm on 2 February 1942.

Hoffman began his training at the beginning of March. Hoffman had very little formal education or academic ability and at first his assessors found him so quiet and uncommunicative that they were unable to gauge his intelligence. He proved to be enthusiastic and hard working and, despite his shy and retiring manner, his assessors soon realised that he was not without self-confidence.

Hoffman was parachuted into the Sudetenland on 8 May with Otto Pichl. Hoffman's mission was to report on possible safe houses and to assess the state of the existing underground movement in the area (Bodenbach and Graslitz). His cover story was that he was a member of *Luftwaffe* ground staff. Part of his training therefore included learning about the *Luftwaffe* organisation and protocols such as saluting.

He was expected to stay in the Sudetenland for approximately three weeks. After this he would then withdraw, either through Denmark and Sweden or through France and Spain depending on the situation as it developed.

On 12 February 1945, information on the fate of both Hoffman and Pichl was received in London from the Vice Consul at Karlovy Vary in Czechoslovakia. It stated that they had been infiltrated on 9 May and both had subsequently disappeared. It was thought that Pichl had been arrested by the German Police and Hoffman appeared in the German Police list as a wanted person on 10 October 1944.

How he was discovered by the German Police is not recorded but it is known that he was tried by Court Martial and shot.

HUBBLE, Desmond Elis

Date of death:	11 September 1944
Place of death:	Buchenwald, Germany

Rank:	Captain
Parent unit:	Intelligence Corps
Service number:	109634
Decorations:	Mentioned in Despatches, *Croix de Chevalier de L'Ordre Royal du Lion avec Palme* (Belgium), *Croix de Guerre* (Belgium)

Date joined SOE:	August 1942
Code names:	Denys/Bissectrice

Nationality:	British
Age at time of death:	Thirty-four
Date of birth:	29 January 1910
Place of birth:	Barnes, Middlesex, UK

Location of memorial: Bayeux, France

Company director Desmond Hubble joined the Royal Artillery as a gunner on the very day before the declaration of war in September 1939. He quickly rose through the ranks and before the end of the year he had been commissioned. On 10 May, the day upon which Hitler launched his *Blitzkrieg* into France, Hubble became a liaison officer with one of the military missions in France.

Hubble continued in a liaison role after the fall of France, joining the 9th British Liaison Staff in the Belgian Congo. He returned to the UK on 17 June 1942. During his time in Africa Hubble had displayed, amongst his other qualities, 'initiative and discretion'. Such attributes made him an ideal candidate for the SOE.

In October 1942 Hubble went to work with SOE's West African mission in Bathurst, eventually transferring to Sierra Leone to take charge of the Freetown station. In November 1943, Hubble returned to the UK and he volunteered to help the Resistance in France.

Hubble joined the staff at Baker Street, which would usually preclude him from being exposed to the risk of capture by going into the field. Nevertheless, he was parachuted into the Ardennes on 5 June 1944. He was soon able to arrange a number of supply drops to the local Resistance group and relay important information back to Baker Street.

On 12 June he went out on a reconnaissance party that ran into a German patrol. A skirmish ensued during which Hubble, with one or two others, became separated from the main group and was captured.

Initially Hubble was imprisoned at Saint-Quentin jail, later being moved to Frèsnes and then Compiègne. According to unnamed witnesses he was badly beaten and tortured; these same people spoke of the 'admirable fortitude with which he faced these trials'.

He was eventually sent to Buchenwald during which journey he was chained to four other men. The chains were in the shape of an X, in the centre of which was a ring fitted to a pair of handcuffs that were fixed round Hubble's ankles so that he could only shuffle along. At the extremities of the chains were more handcuffs that were fastened to the ankles of the other four men of the group.

Soon after his arrival at Buchenwald, Hubble was executed. This was reported by Professor Balachowski, a PROSPER agent, who worked in the camp's Hygiene section.

A letter was compiled by the War Office that was to be sent to Hubble's mother stating that he was to be officially declared 'missing, believed killed'.

However, in the letter was the following paragraph: 'As you are aware, your son was taken prisoner by the Germans in June 1944, and we had reason shortly afterwards to hope that he was being treated as a prisoner of war. Survivors of his prison camp, however, report that he was killed by the Germans immediately after his arrival in Germany.'

This caused great security concerns at Baker Street. Why would an ordinary army officer not be treated as a prisoner of war and be shot? Such a statement would surely prompt his mother to start asking some awkward questions. At first it was recommended that the wording of the letter should be changed but then it was decided that a staff member would visit Mrs Hubble and explain to her the nature of her son's 'special employment'.

INAYAT-KHAN, Noor

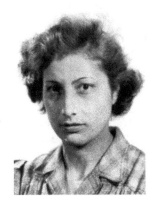

Date of death:	13 September 1944
Place of death:	Dachau, Germany
Rank:	Section Officer
Parent unit:	Women's Auxiliary Air Force (seconded to the Women's Transport Service)
Service number:	9901
Decorations:	George Cross, Mentioned in Despatches, *Croix de Guerre*
Date joined SOE:	February 1943
Code names:	Nora Baker/Madeleine/Nurse/ Jeanne-Marie Regnier
Nationality:	Indian
Age at time of death:	Thirty
Date of birth:	1 January 1914
Place of birth:	Moscow, Russia
Location of memorial:	Runnymede, UK

The story of Noor Inayat-Khan is certainly a remarkable one. A descendant of the last Mogul Emperor of southern India, she could quite legitimately claim to be an Indian princess – yet she was born in the Kremlin in 1914 where her father was teaching. Her mother was Anglo-American.

After spending some time in London, the family settled down in Paris where Inayat-Khan spent most of her childhood. She was educated at the Sorbonne and later worked on children's programmes for Radio Paris. Her French was therefore excellent.

When the Germans invaded France the family escaped to Britain by sea, arriving at Falmouth on 22 June 1940. On 19 November 1940, she joined the Women's Auxiliary Air Force (WAAF), and, as an Aircraftwoman 2nd Class, she was sent to be trained as a wireless operator. She was accepted into the SOE in February 1943.

On advice from her Conducting Officer, Flight Officer Vera Atkins, Noor took the name of Nora Baker (her mother's maiden name) to disguise her Indian origins. Yet her character could not be concealed. Noor was 'very feminine ... kind hearted, emotional, imaginative'. She was very attractive and petite and could run well but was otherwise 'clumsy' and was scared of weapons. Hardly the characteristics demanded of a secret agent. In fact the final report issued on Noor by the commander of 'B' Group Special Training School stated that 'it is very doubtful whether she is really suited to the work in the field'. How wrong he was.

Using the Code name *Madeleine*, this 'splendid, vague, dreamy creature – twice seen, never forgotten' was the first female wireless operator sent into France on 16 June 1943. *Madeline* was another recruit for one of the PROSPER sub-circuits (CINEMA). Soon after her arrival the PROSPER network was in trouble, and *Madeleine* was almost caught by the Gestapo.

However, after the PROSPER organiser, Francis Suttill, had been arrested and scores of his group had been rounded-up, *Madeleine* remained free. The Gestapo were clearly closing in upon the SOE operation in Paris yet, despite her perilous position, she continued to transmit to London. Her chances of being detected were very high. When all the other PROSPER radios had been discovered, only *Madeleine*'s remained on air.

Buckmaster told *Madeleine* to get out of Paris but she refused as without her all communication would be lost. With so many of the PROSPER leaders in captivity, the little Indian princess became the most important SOE asset in the region. She dyed her hair and was constantly on the move from apartment to apartment from where she could conduct her radio transmissions.

Predictably, her luck ran out in early October when the supposedly 'safe' house at 98 Rue de la Faisanderie was found by the Gestapo. It is alleged that she was betrayed by someone called 'Renée' who gave her away for a reward of 100,000 Francs. *Madeleine* was taken to the top floor of 84 Avenue Foch where cells were reserved for important agents.

During her confinement at the five-story Avenue Foch, *Madeleine* made two attempts at escape. The first time occurred within an hour of her arrival. She demanded a bath, which the Germans granted. As soon as she was inside the bathroom she climbed out of the window but was spotted on the window ledge and taken back inside. On the second occasion, along with two other agents held by the Gestapo, she succeeded in breaking out of the top of the old building and jumped onto the flat roofs below. Unfortunately an air raid coincided with their escape and when the Germans checked the cells the escape was uncovered. All three were quickly recaptured.

The German counter-intelligence chief in Paris, SS *Sturmbannführer* Hans Joseph Kieffer, considered *Madeleine* to be 'too dangerous' to be housed safely at Avenue Foch. She was therefore transferred to Karlsruhe prison but the place was full and she was moved on to Pforzheim prison. Here she was treated with appalling brutality. She was kept in solitary confinement, handcuffed and chained night and day in a crouching position so that she depended upon male jailers to deal with her sanitary and feeding needs. She was kept like this for almost ten months.

On 11 September 1944, *Madeleine* was moved to Karlsruhe where, along with three other female SOE agents Madeleine Damerment, Eliane Plewman and Yolande Unternahrer (see individual entries for details), she was taken that same day on to Dachau. The following day she was killed. After the war, an unnamed Dachau guard gave an account of *Madeleine*'s death to Lieutenant Colonel Wickey, a Canadian Intelligence officer, which was passed onto Vera Atkins: 'He said they did receive a group of four women, three typical French and one looking more of a Creole type.' The Creole was clearly *Madeleine*. The former camp guard continued:

'The three French women were taken, after some two or three hours of their arrival, near the crematorium where they were partially undressed, they were in rags anyway, and shot with pistols. They were handled very roughly, one of them had her face several times slapped, they were all kicked several times before being shot.

'The Creole was kept outside, chained and almost naked. She was subjected to ridicule, was slapped and kicked several times, apparently by this same man who was very fond of this type of sport. She was left all night long lying on the floor in a cell and the next day, rather than drag her along to the crematorium, they gave her some more rough handling. Finally in a cell they shot her with a small pistol and dead or half dead she was carried by some other inmates and thrown into the furnace.'

In 1947, after much endeavour on the part of Vera Atkins, Noor Inayat-Khan was awarded the George Cross.

JOHANSEN, Hans Robert Filip

Date of death:	25 July 1944
Place of death:	Copenhagen, Denmark
Rank:	Lieutenant
Parent unit:	General List
Service number:	274876
Decorations:	None recorded
Date joined SOE:	12 May 1943
Code names:	Brawn/Stump/Artichoke
Nationality:	Danish
Age at time of death:	Twenty-three
Date of birth:	7 July 1921
Place of birth:	Copenhagen, Denmark
Location of grave:	Copenhagen, Denmark

Born in Copenhagen on 7 July 1921, Johansen joined the 8th Battalion The Buffs (Royal East Kent Regiment) in 1941 before being recruited by the SOE six months later. Small and slim, his instructors regarded him as 'very quick in mind and body – he should prove a great asset'. He was therefore released from the Buffs and commissioned on 12 May 1943.

Johansen was a sabotage expert and instructor, and like almost all the fifty-seven SOE agents sent into Denmark (all of whom were Danish nationals) he was parachuted into the country. Denmark was still nominally neutral when the SOE first began to build up its organisation in the country. Eventually Denmark's status changed and it became indistinguishable from any of the other German-occupied countries.

The main purpose of the SOE in Denmark was to build up a secret Resistance group that would be activated on an eventual Allied invasion – thus the need for people such as Johansen to instruct these groups in sabotage techniques. Until the deployment of SOE agents there was effectively no Resistance organisation in Denmark.

Throughout 1943 it was predominantly explosives and other sabotage material that was dropped into the country. This changed in 1944. As the Resistance groups increased in number thousands of weapons were sent by sea to Denmark and the fifty-seven agents sent by the SOE were to support these groups.

What began as just a few hundred resisters in 1943 developed into some 10,000 by late 1944, reaching an impressive organisation of 50,000 men and women (around one percent of the population) by the end of the war. In the lead-up to D-Day these groups conducted widespread acts of sabotage, which helped to tie down German troops that otherwise might have been deployed in northern France.

The SOE was also instrumental in bringing the various political groups together thus ensuring a safe transition to peace-time conditions after the country was liberated.

Johansen was the only officially recognised Danish SOE agent to die on active service. He was captured in Copenhagen on 25 July 1944, by the Gestapo – one account stating that he was surprised during a raid on an apartment in the Nyhavn district (the oldest part of Copenhagen Harbour). He was carrying his 'L' tablet, which he ingested immediately. He died on the spot.

JONES, Sidney Charles

Date of death:	6 September 1944
Place of death:	Mauthausen, Austria
Rank:	Captain
Parent unit:	Royal Engineers
Service number:	125265
Decorations:	MBE, *Croix de Guerre avec Palme, Médaille de la Résistance Française*
Entered joined SOE:	8 July 1942
Code names:	Elie/Inventor/Jean-Marie Terbonne/ Sylvain Charles Lejeune
Nationality:	British
Age at time of death:	Forty-one
Date of birth:	25 November 1902
Place of birth:	Paris, France
Location of memorial:	Brookwood, UK

'An excellent man in every way,' is how the SOE assessors regarded Sidney Jones. He was involved in espionage for the British secret services in Paris with his cover being the representative of the Elizabeth Arden cosmetics company for France and the French colonies. His wife, an Austrian woman called Rosemary, was arrested 'for propaganda work' by the Germans, sent to a concentration camp and eventually executed.

Jones made his way to the United Kingdom and joined the SOE in the summer of 1942. After training Jones left on a specially arranged plane for Gibraltar on 16 September 1942, from where he was sent to Marseilles by felucca. He set up and operated a number of sabotage groups in the Marseilles area as the INVENTOR circuit. These groups successfully attacked railways and harbour installations in Marseilles port. In November his circuit destroyed fifty goods wagons destined for Germany.

Despite its successes the INVENTOR circuit was too distant to be re-supplied from the UK. Jones consequently made his way back to Britain by Hudson on 6 February 1943.

In the following May he was returned to France by Lysander as an organiser in the Troyes-Nancy area and to report on the Resistance movement there. He organised attacks against railways and locomotives in running sheds and marshalling yards in June and July, and planned a raid against the Vitry power station.

He was arrested in Paris some time between 19 and 22 November 1943, having been betrayed, as were many others, by local sub-agent Roger Bardet. Jones had been concerned about Bardet and had warned Henri Frager, Bardet's friend, that Bardet 'might be playing a double game'. His concerns were raised when Bardet had asked him to reveal where some of the dropping zones were. Jones refused to tell him anything. From that moment on Bardet was determined to get rid of Jones.

Jones was in bed when the Germans arrived. 'He was a brave man,' Bleicher (a sergeant in the *Abwehr*) said. 'He took his arrest calmly and only said "It's a pity, it's such a nice day today."'

Jones was put in Frèsnes, being transferred from there to Germany in May 1944. It is said he was seen in a camp at Breslau in the summer of 1944 and later reported to have been at Ravitsch. How accurate these reports were is uncertain, but what is reasonably certain is that he ended up at Mauthausen.

Whilst it was known that a large number of agents, both British and Dutch, had been executed at Mauthausen over the course of two days in September 1944, Jones was not amongst them. Investigations by Vera Atkins in 1946 led to information being supplied by a Czech national who revealed that Jones was not killed with the other agents but instead was the only Englishman who, along with a group of thirty or so other prisoners – mostly Poles and Russians – was executed at Mauthausen in the autumn of 1944.

Jones' citation for the award of the MBE, states that 'His courage and devotion to duty were outstanding'.

JUMEAU, Clement Marc

Date of death:	26 March 1944
Place of death:	Buch, Berlin Germany
Rank:	Captain
Parent unit:	Intelligence Corps
Service number:	202272
Decorations:	Mentioned in Despatches, *Croix de Guerre avec Palme*
Date joined SOE:	19 May 1941
Code names:	Robert/Reporter/André Chambon
Nationality:	British
Age at time of death:	Twenty-nine
Date of birth:	14 September 1914
Place of birth:	Mahé, Seychelles

Location of memorial: Brookwood, UK

Clement Jumeau's father was a planter in the Seychelles. After completing his secondary education in the islands the younger Jumeau travelled to the UK to further his education at Cambridge and Glasgow Universities, eventually securing his MA. On 15 December 1939, he enlisted in the Intelligence Corps.

In May 1941 he was accepted for SOE training and he immediately impressed the assessors. 'Very intelligent and keen. A really hard worker who thinks things out for himself,' were some of the comments made. However, he was also seen as being 'rather stolid and almost entirely lacking in sense of humour'.

He undertook his first mission on 11 October 1941, to the unoccupied zone of France. Whilst he was trying to organise a resistance group he was captured by the French police. He was interred in the Béleyme prison at Périgueux, a place described by Jumeau as: 'degrading and humiliating to the last degree ... hygiene and sanitation ... were non-existent. Food was unspeakably bad. In addition we were plagued with vermin and disease'. Nevertheless, after six months he escaped and made his way back to Britain through Spain.

Jumeau left for his second mission on 12 April 1943, with another agent Louis Lee-Graham. He was to be an organiser in Lyons and the surrounding area (CORSICAN circuit). The plane they were in was hit by flak about four minutes after it had crossed the French coast just east of Cabourg. The aircraft crashed in flames but both men were able to bale out. Jumeau was hurt on landing and never fully recovered.

The two men were wearing civilian clothes but when they baled out they had no documents, arms or money with them. They were picked up by a German patrol and were eventually taken by the Gestapo to a civilian prison in Frankfurt. The Germans announced their capture, which was reported by the London *Evening Standard* on 31 April. They had given the Germans the names of Captain Lee (Jumeau) and Captain Graham (Lee-Graham).

Jumeau and Lee-Graham were forced to wear civilian prisoners' clothes and were placed in solitary confinement. They were given one German book a week to read, allowed very little exercise, and put to work making envelopes.

During the winter of 1943-44 they suffered severely from cold and hunger. Their cells were not heated and both of them became ill.

In March 1944, they were sent, on foot, to the military prison at Torgau. Jumeau was by this time so ill he could not walk and on several marches during the journey had to be carried by Lee-Graham who was also very ill.

They were both removed from Torgau to a military prison-hospital in the northern Berlin suburb of Buch. Here Jumeau soon died of pulmonary tuberculosis. He received little or no medical treatment, and when he became so weak that he could not leave his bed, he was just left there to die. He received no help either to eat or perform any of his natural functions.

Incredibly, despite the trials and deprivations he endured, Lee-Graham survived the war.

KASAP, Jechel Usher

Date of death:	21 November 1943
Place of death:	Yugoslavia
Rank:	Sergeant
Parent unit:	Palestine Regiment
Service number:	PAL 12300
Decorations:	DCM, MM
Date joined SOE:	1943
Code names:	None Recorded
Nationality:	Palestinian
Age at time of death:	Twenty-two
Date of birth:	23 September 1921
Place of birth:	Not recorded

Location of memorial: Athens Memorial, Athens

The Palestinian Arab village of Sarafand al-Amar was situated on the coastal plain of Palestine, about 3 miles north-west of the town of Ramla. During the British Mandate period, which began soon after the First World War and ended in 1948, the British Army established its largest military base in the Middle East at Sarafand, as it was commonly referred to, utilising a camp originally built by Empire, predominantly Australian and New Zealand, troops during 1917.

It was at this Army base that Jechel Usher Kasap volunteered for service with the British Army on 10 September 1940 – one of 30,000 men and women who voluntarily enlisted in the British Forces in Palestine. Drafted into the Pioneer Corps, Kasap found himself in one of the Corps' ten Palestinian Companies.

Within weeks of Kasap's enlistment, on 28 October 1940, Italian forces invaded Greece. Once the decision had been made to support the Greek government, elements of a British/Commonwealth expeditionary force began to arrive in the country. This included Kasap's Pioneer Company. However, the intervention of German forces in the light of Allied successes against the Italians irrevocably altered the course of the Greek Campaign.

Finally, on 21 April 1941, the decision was taken to evacuate the British and Commonwealth forces to Crete and Egypt.

The rearguard action became a withdrawal to the southern coast. Under heavy fire the Royal Navy rescued over 40,000 troops from the south-eastern ports, despite the loss of a number of ships in face of the German aerial supremacy. However, at least 14,000 men were left behind. Private Kasap was one of this number.

At some stage during the retreat and evacuation (which was not completed until the end of April), Kasap became isolated and separated from his unit in the very south of Greece. He took to the mountains to evade capture – the start of a remarkable sequence of events.

Those Allied troops left behind could not have remained at large for long without the help of the local population and the embryonic Greek Resistance. These people fed the evaders such as Kasap from their own increasingly scanty food supplies, fitted them out with civilian clothes and, when the bitterly cold winter of 1940/41 reached its peak, either sheltered them temporarily in their own homes or provided them with blankets and other necessities to enable them to live in a cave or an improvised hut.

It was under such conditions that Kasap was able to remain at large in the mountains north of Cape Matapan (also known as Cape Tainaron), the southern-most point of mainland Greece for more than a month. Then disaster struck. Betrayed by a Greek civilian, he was captured by German soldiers on 27 May 1941.

Treated as a prisoner of war, at the end of June 1941, Kasap was being transferred by rail from Athens to Salonika. Roughly a third of the way into the journey, he succeeded in 'slipping off the train near Gravire'. One account states that as he spoke German, Kasap was able to persuade the German guard to turn a blind eye and not open fire.

Once again Kasap was at large. For three months he evaded capture in the rural Lania region, before he headed for Athens. At this stage of the war, it was here that the Greek Resistance was at its strongest.

Having learnt Greek, Kasap frequently acted as interpreter for several Greeks helping Allied evaders and escapers. He then found himself part of a party trying to escape from Greece by caique across the Aegean Sea to Turkey. Yet again, betrayal intervened and the escapers' long, narrow boat was intercepted by a German patrol vessel almost at the start of its journey off Piraeus.

Returned to Athens, Kasap was imprisoned in the city's notorious Averoff civil prison – probably because he was wearing civilian clothes he was therefore not recognised by the Italian and German authorities as a legitimate prisoner of war. This vast prison, run by the Italians (though equipped with a German-controlled wing) sported conditions that were 'universally bad'.

Following his arrival, accused of being a spy by the Germans, Kasap was sentenced to fifteen days solitary confinement, a term that was served out in the prison's dungeons. These, as their name implies, were below ground, dark, filthy and wet. There was no semblance of a latrine, and once in a dungeon a prisoner was allowed out only at the caprice of his guard until his sentence was up. Many of the British evaders and escapers who passed through Averoff were interrogated, often to the accompaniment of beatings by the *Carabinieri*, to persuade them to disclose the names of Greeks who had assisted them or the whereabouts of other hiding Allied servicemen. It is not known if Kasap avoided such treatment.

Soon after, with about twenty others, Private Kasap was put aboard a ship transporting recaptured prisoners of war from Crete to Salonika. On arrival he was held in the barracks of the Germann 50th Infantry Division. Here, his ability to speak German helped him win the confidence of an Intelligence Officer who took him out of the camp for short excursions. Taking advantage of these trips, on 6 February 1942, Kasap again made a bid for freedom and slipped away from his escort.

Kasap remained in the district surrounding Salonika for much of that year. Then, in October 1942, he made contact with an organisation working to extricate men such as him from Greece. It is possible that the people he was put in touch with were part of 'A' Force, a unit that operated in conjunction with the Middle East branch of MI9. Whichever body helped him, Kasap arrived in Turkey on 25 October 1942. His remarkable journey had all but come to an end.

Back in the Middle East, Kasap's adventures soon came to the notice of the authorities. Colonel Dudley Wrangel Clarke, GS(1) GHQ Middle East (who was involved in the formation of the Commandos, responsible for the name and concept of the US Rangers and the name of the Special Air Service) wrote: '[Kasap] evaded capture for a month and subsequently escaped no less than three times. He succeeded in spite of hardship and betrayal due to sheer determination and perseverance.'

It was, concluded Clarke, 'an excellent performance'. For his actions, Kasap was awarded the Military Medal.

Undaunted by what he had experienced, Kasap readily volunteered to return. Indeed, as Clarke had also noted in his recommendation for an award for Kasap, 'he ... will go back shortly to rescue others.'

At this point in the war, SOE was deploying Palestine Jewish volunteers, amongst many others, as wireless operators and instructors on their liaison missions to the partisans in the Balkan theatre, while MI9 intended to use them to locate and rescue Allied evaders and escapees. Both organisations consented to the volunteers' dual role.

The candidates for these tasks were selected from the ranks of the Jewish military underground, Zionist youth movement activists and Palestinian Jews already serving in the British Army (as was the case with Kasap). Of the 240 men and women who volunteered, 110 underwent the training program that commenced in Cairo in March 1943.

To facilitate his role within SOE, Kasap was transferred from the ranks of the Pioneer Corps to the Palestine Regiment on 1 August 1943. Promoted to sergeant, he was soon sent back into Axis territory. Because of certain operational difficulties, only thirty-two of the trained volunteers (including three women) were deployed on missions. Twelve of this number would not return.

The fact that Kasap is commemorated on the Athens Memorial would suggest that he was one of ten of the Palestinian Jewish SOE operatives sent to Yugoslavia. It has not been possible to establish the circumstances surrounding his death, though it is known that he died on 21 November 1943.

Four months after Kasap's death, it was announced that he had been awarded the Distinguished Conduct Medal in 'recognition of gallant and distinguished services in the field'. Kasap was one of 694 Palestinian Jews who gave their lives in the Second World War whilst serving in the British forces.

KEUN, Gerald Philip George

Date of death:	9 September 1944
Place of death:	Buchenwald, Germany

Rank:	Captain
Parent unit:	General List
Service number:	282881
Decorations:	*Legion d'Honneur, Croix de Guerre, Médaille de la Résistance Française*

Date joined SOE:	1 June 1942
Code names:	Gerald George Philip Kane

Nationality:	Dutch
Age at time of death:	Thirty-three
Date of birth:	10 August 1911
Place of birth:	Holland

Location of memorial: Brookwood, UK

Dutch-born Gerald Keun was educated at Blundell's School in Devon. Following the outbreak of war in 1939 he joined the French Army and fought with the 2nd Company 12th Regiment *Etranger d'Infanterie*. He was captured in 1940 but escaped from a camp at Cambrai in January 1941.

Keun started working for the Resistance movement and became known to British Secret Intelligence by the end of 1941. By the middle of 1942 his contacts had developed to such an extent that he moved to Paris where he set up his own organisation with direct communications with London and he then came under the auspices of the SOE.

During the following twelve months Keun made two return trips to the UK, once by air and once by sea. Subsidiary sections of his organisation were established in Lyons, Bordeaux, the Loire region and the north of France. For six months of this period, he was also in charge of a pick-up operations group, which maintained a monthly courier service with London.

Two days after he arrived in the UK for the second time, Keun learned by telegram that his co-organiser in France had been seriously wounded during an engagement with the Gestapo and had been forced into hiding. Fearing that the flow of information to Britain would suffer as a result of the incident, and in spite of very real physical fatigue after his journey to the UK, Keun insisted on returning to France immediately.

His parachute landing, however, was not successful and his spinal vertebrae were severely damaged. This did not stop Keun. Even though his doctor advised him that unless he remained on his back for some months he would be crippled for life, on at least three occasions he removed his plaster cast, and in spite of what his recommendation for the George Cross called 'great suffering', he cycled 70 miles to ensure the delivery of a courier to an agent due to leave for Britain.

He was eventually arrested on 29 June 1944. He was deported to Buchenwald, where he was hanged.

After the war the French lavished Keun with medals. All he received from HM Government was a Certificate of Commendation; the George Cross was denied him.

LANGARD, Raymond

Date of death:	3 February 1945
Place of death:	Buchenwald, Germany
Rank:	Lieutenant
Parent unit:	General List
Service number:	197049
Decorations:	None recorded
Date joined SOE:	Not recorded
Code names:	Jules Dumas/Dimu
Nationality:	French
Age at time of death:	Twenty-nine
Date of birth:	1916
Place of birth:	France

Location of memorial: Brookwood, UK

Langard was the wireless operator for Erwin Deman who was sent into France by Hudson on 19 August 1943, to start the MANGO circuit. Deman settled in Rennes in the east of Brittany as an insurance agent. This guise provided him with plausible reasons for travelling and he secured a pass to visit the forbidden coastal zone. Langard meanwhile established himself firstly at Redon and then at Quimper near the south-west Breton coast.

Deman went to a villa near Saint-Cast-le-Guildo, which belonged to another SOE agent, Cicely Lefort. Near the villa he found a secluded beach that would be ideal for clandestine movement of agents and equipment. He soon located another suitable stretch of coast further west near Morlaix. This site, though, had the disadvantage of being close to a German defensive bunker. Undeterred, his circuit came to an understanding with the German sergeant in charge, who did not want to be sent to the eastern front.

Deman went back to the UK, returning to France on 29 October 1943. Upon his return he started his operation, which was to run a sea escape line called VAR between Brittany and Cornwall, using the Royal Navy's 15th Motor Gun Boat Flotilla, which was based at Falmouth.

Deman and Langard turned the VAR line into an efficient escape route and over the winter of 1943-44 the VAR ran sixteen successful missions, carrying between them seventy men and women to and fro. They never lost a passenger but as the VAR network spread ever further to help as many escapers as possible, the pressure became too much for Deman and he was withdrawn, following another trip to the UK.

On 26 June 1944, Langard was arrested whilst transmitting. Langard was severely tortured in captivity but kept silent throughout, thus saving the lives of his companions. He died in Buchenwald eight months later.

LANSDELL, Armand Richard

Date of death:	3 July 1944
Place of death:	Saint-Aubin-Château-Neuf, France
Rank:	Lieutenant
Parent unit:	General List
Service number:	309880
Decorations:	None recorded
Date joined SOE:	2 February 1944
Code names:	Oscar/Pilgrim
Nationality:	British
Age at time of death:	Thirty-nine
Date of birth:	11 July 1904
Place of birth:	Marseilles, France
Location of grave:	Seine-et-Marne, France

Born in France to a British father and French mother, Lansdell offered his services to the British in November 1942 after the Allied forces had occupied North Africa. He went for SOE training and assessment on 7 September 1943, at the end of which was submitted the following verdict: 'A man of low practical intelligence and of slow reaction. He has shown a lot of determination in the physical tests and throughout has been keen and hard working. His limitations, however, are so considerable that the Board is unable to see in what capacity he could be usefully employed in the field.'

Nevertheless, Lansdell was an expert in telecommunications. From 1919 to 1932 he worked for the Eastern Telegraph Company in Marseilles. He left this company to work in his own workshop until the German occupation of his country in 1940, when he moved to Algiers. His Morse skills made him an ideal candidate as a wireless operator.

With the rank of second lieutenant, Lansdell was sent to France on 30 April 1944 to join the DONKEYMAN circuit. He soon became friendly with one of the regional chiefs of the *reseaux* and the pair's behaviour began to become a cause for concern. On 6 July 1944, a message was received in London from Major Henri Frager (see previous entries) via Berne in Switzerland. It read as follows:

'After last tour of inspection took up action stations on June 3rd. Regret to inform you on same day had to order execution of ORESTE and regional chief ALAIN. My decision was well considered. Both were guilty of negligence of duty, terrorism for personal ends, would-be assassination of one of my collaborators, general debauchery and permanent drunkenness. Final decision taken inevitable for restoration of discipline.' It was also alleged that they were working for the Germans.

The two men were executed by a Resistance firing squad behind the farmhouse of a Monsieur Carre, the former Mayor of Saint-Aubin-Château-Neuf where the two bodies were buried. They were later exhumed and placed in the local cemetery in a communal grave. Though he was actually killed on 3 June 1944, i.e. just three days before D-Day, it was decided in London that it would seem better if the date of his death was after the Normandy landings. The official date of his death was put exactly one month later, on 3 July.

His wife, who was still living in Algiers, was not told the truth about Lansdell's death until after the war. Originally, she was merely informed that he was 'killed in action in France'. In due course, she was told that her husband was shot on the orders of the circuit head, who was later killed in Germany.

Yet the matter did not end there. The parents of Alain, the other man shot with Lansdell, sought to have the people that killed their son prosecuted. As Henri Frager, the man who ordered the execution was himself captured by the Germans and executed, and the ones that actually pulled the triggers were merely following their commandant's orders, little came of the case.

Lansdell's body was later exhumed and reinterred in the Perreuse Château Franco British National Cemetery, not far from La Ferte Sous Jouarre, Seine-et-Marne.

LARCHER, Maurice Louis Marie Aristide

Date of death:	8 July 1944
Place of death:	St Clair, France
Rank:	Lieutenant
Parent unit:	General List
Service number:	306766
Decorations:	Mentioned in Despatches, *Croix de Legion d'Honneur*
Date joined SOE:	1 July 1943
Code names:	Vladimir/Linesman/Maurice Louis Langlade
Nationality:	British
Age at time of death:	Twenty-two
Date of birth:	23 January 1922
Place of birth:	Mauritius
Location of grave:	Bretteville-sur-Laize, France

Maurice Larcher was killed during the fight that led to the capture of Jean Renaud-Danicolle (see separate entry) and the death of Henry Joseph Cleary.

This retiring, young Mauritian left for the field on 10 February 1944, being parachuted into France to act as the wireless operator for the SCIENTIST circuit in Calvados, Normandy. This key coastal area was densely-populated by the Germans and undercover operations here were highly dangerous.

He was a strong, powerfully-built man who, his SOE assessor believed, showed courage and determination, but who was sometimes slow and rather clumsy. During his training it was thought that Larcher found difficulty in adjusting to unexpected situations and that in a difficult situation he might 'lose his head'. Yet when the unexpected happened, far from panicking, he responded well and killed one of the Germans with a knife before he himself was killed.

The incident in question occurred at a house that they were using in Saint Clair, Pierrefitte-en-Cinglais, Calvados. A neighbour had reported suspicious activity to the Germans and soldiers were sent round to investigate. Larcher died in the ensuing fight.

He was buried at Saint Clair along with twenty-five-year-old Flight Lieutenant Henry Joseph Cleary. Cleary was a Canadian fighter pilot who, serving with 602 (City of Glasgow) Squadron, had baled out when his aircraft, Supermarine Spitfire Mk.IX MH512, had been hit by anti-aircraft fire whilst attacking German transport during an 'armed reconnaissance' in the Argentan area on 1 July 1944.

So strong were the feelings of the local people concerning the betrayal of the SOE agents by one of their own men, after the area had been liberated, the bodies of Larcher and Cleary were exhumed so that they could be given a proper funeral service and to allow the locals to pay their respects. They were placed into two fine oak coffins made by a local undertaker for which he refused any payment.

The service took place on 8 October 1944, at the church of Pierrefitte-en-Cinglais a village in the hills of the Bass-Normandie. The service was conducted by Reverend Lynch, the British Roman Catholic Padre in Caen and the local parish priest. Representing the British and Commonwealth forces was Lieutenant Colonel H.N. Sissons, who left an account of the funeral, which he described as both moving and simple.

'Seated in the choir,' he wrote, 'were the representatives of the French Resistance numbering about eighty. The nave of the church, which would seat about 200, was crowded with people who overflowed into the aisle and around the West door many more were standing. In all there was a congregation of about 350 to 400 souls from Pierrefitte, a small village of not more than 200 inhabitants, and the surrounding countryside.

'At the head of the coffins were two chairs, one for an elderly Frenchman, and I was asked to occupy the other. Between us stood a member of the Resistance with the French Tricolour.'

The main theme of the service was the 'infinite gratitude' of the French people towards the men who had helped liberate their country. With the ending of the service the coffins were carried outside with the whole of the congregation following behind.

'The cemetery is very like any to be found by small English village churches,' concluded Sissons. 'They now lie in a place of honour in the centre of the churchyard, surrounded by the simple graves of the villagers.'

Maurice Larcher was Mentioned in Despatches for his 'outstanding gallantry during his mission in France'. A further exhumation of his remains, and those of Cleary, followed after the end of the fighting in Europe. Both men now lie close to each other in the Canadian War Cemetery at Bretteville-sur-Laize.

LAYZELL, Gordon Edward

Date of death:	2 February 1944
Place of death:	Staravecke, Albania
Rank:	Major
Parent unit:	South Lancashire Regiment
Service number:	130712
Decorations:	None recorded
Date joined SOE:	1943
Code names:	None recorded
Nationality:	British
Age at time of death:	Thirty-one
Date of birth:	1 June 1912
Place of birth:	Beckenham, UK

Location of memorial: Tirana, Albania

Gordon Layzell was commissioned into the British Army on 4 May 1940. In June 1941 he became Adjutant of the 1st Battalion South Lancashire Regiment (The Prince of Wales's Volunteers) with the rank of temporary captain.

Before joining the SOE in 1943 he had been employed as a staff captain with the 9th Infantry Brigade. Sent out to Cairo, Layzell, who was described by one of his colleagues, Captain Marcus Lyon, as 'a quiet and very likeable man', was then parachuted into Albania on the night of 15/16 December 1943. He was one of six men dropped that night into the mountains west of Korça.

The Germans had conducted a vigorous offensive against the Partisans during the winter of 1943-44 and Gordon Layzell's team found itself having to escape into the mountains. Believing that the Germans were no longer on their heels, they stopped on 1 February 1944, at the village of Staravecke high up on the slopes of Mount Ostravica.

The men occupied two of the houses in the village and started to prepare the area as a new base and as a dropping ground for the receipt of supplies. That afternoon Gordon Layzell and Marcus Lyon were sitting upstairs in one of the houses.

Lyon later recounted the tragic event that followed: 'Suddenly Gordon said: "My God, I think the house is on fire." Smoke was coming through the cracks in the mud wall. I got up and ran downstairs to find that Antonio and Pepini had lit a large fire ... Gordon had been hurriedly collecting his kit and had slung his Schmeisser [MP40] submachine-gun on his shoulder. I yelled up to him: "Crisis over Gordon, it's only the chimney on fire!" Then I heard a gun go off upstairs and ran up.

'Gordon was lying on the floor, a bullet wound through the back of his head ... The back of his head was shattered and I doubt if the greatest brain surgeon could have done anything for him.'

It transpired that Layzell had picked up his gun first and slung it over his right shoulder. Then, as he threw his haversack over his left shoulder it struck the cocking handle of the Schmeisser, causing it to fire.

He died from his wound at 02.20 hours on the morning of 2 February 1944. He was buried in the afternoon of the same day at Staravecke.

Layzell's wife was informed that he had been accidently killed whilst on duty but given few of the details. A letter to her on 8 March simply read: 'The operation on which Major Layzell was engaged is still going on, and for the protection of those with whom he is serving, no information can be given at the present time.' They had been married for just a year.

LECCIA, Marcel Mathieu René

Date of death:	14 September 1944
Place of death:	Buchenwald, Germany
Rank:	Lieutenant
Parent unit:	General List
Service number:	309883
Decorations:	*Croix de Guerre, Médaille de la Résistance Française*
Date joined SOE:	December 1943
Code names:	Baudouin/Labourer/Georges Louis
Nationality:	French
Age at time of death:	Thirty-three
Date of birth:	1 January 1911
Place of birth:	Ajaccio, Corsica

Location of memorial: Brookwood, UK

Marcel Leccia is recorded incorrectly by the CWGC under his documentary cover name of Georges Louis; at the same time, no biographical detail is provided by them. However, his SOE personal file reveals that he was born in Corsica and brought up in France. His father was a colonel in the French Army and when he was ordered to serve in the Army of Occupation in Germany, Marcel went with him.

In 1939, Leccia joined the French Army, becoming a second lieutenant. He fought in the Battle of France and was taken prisoner on 2 June 1940. He escaped from Germany in April 1942 and crossed the demarcation line into Vichy France on 12 June 1942. He was awarded the *Croix de Guerre* and made director of the *Maison des Prisonnier de Guerre* at Limoges; this was an organisation that helped with the repatriation of prisoners of war returning from Germany. He also helped some British officers escape into Spain.

When the Germans invaded Vichy in November 1942 Leccia's position was untenable and he escaped to the UK with his secretary Elisée Allard (see separate entry) and in December 1943 they both joined the SOE. Leccia, who was described as 'the "salesman" type; never lost for words, cheerful, entertaining and sociable', was very much the senior of the two men and when they were dropped into France on the night of 5/6 April 1944, it was Leccia who was to be the organiser of a new circuit with Allard as his second in command.

The two agents, along with their wireless operator, Pierre Geelen, landed at a place called Acre near the village of Néret, to the south-east of Châteauroux in the Indre. They were to set up the LABOURER circuit with specific objectives relating to the D-Day landings. Firstly they were to organise, train and arm a sabotage group that would go into action immediately before and on the day of the landings. The group was to blow-up the German General Staff HQ at Saint-Barthélemy-d'Anjou on the eve of the Allied invasion. Then it was to destroy the rail wagons in the goods yards of Saint-Pierre-des-Corps, a suburb to the east of Tours.

Before any of these plans could be put into place, Leccia, Geelen and Allard were betrayed by one of their sub-agents in the LABOURER circuit. It is said that the traitor was a taxi-driver and when he had the three men in his cab he actually drove them to the Gestapo HQ.

Leccia was initially taken to Avenue Foch, spending fifty-two days under interrogation there before being moved to Frèsnes. On 9 August 1944, he was sent to Compiègne and then to Buchenwald. Leccia, Allard and Geelen were amongst the agents executed by hanging at Buchenwald on 14 September 1944.

In 1946 a monument was erected at Acre, Néret, in commemoration of the landing of the three agents.

LEDOUX, Jacques Paul Henri

Date of death:	1 June 1944
Place of death:	Gross-Rosen, Poland
Rank:	Captain
Parent unit:	Highland Light Infantry (City of Glasgow Regiment)
Service number:	197049
Decorations:	None recorded
Date joined SOE:	8 April 1943
Code names:	Homere/Orator/Jacques Lelong
Nationality:	British
Age at time of death:	Twenty-three
Date of birth:	27 June 1921
Place of birth:	London, UK

Location of memorial: Brookwood, UK

'An intelligent, alert and resourceful man of undoubted loyalty to France,' was how Jacques Ledoux's SOE trainers viewed this young Englishman who had been born in London to French parents.

In spite of the qualities he was easily led. This was demonstrated when, in his fourth week of training, he was encouraged by another student to negotiate an extremely difficult obstacle 'out of sheer bravado'. The result was a fall of about 15 feet that put him in hospital.

It was decided that Ledoux would make a good organiser and he was given the task of forming a new circuit, ORATOR, in the Le Mans area. He would do this through contacts provided for him by France Antelme. He was to investigate the importance to the German war effort of the Amédée Bollée piston-ring works. If he found the production to be of value to the enemy then he was to persuade the factory manager to sabotage the works rather than be subjected to Allied air attacks. He was also to build up stocks of weapons and prepare the groups in his circuit for 'armed action' on D-Day.

Jacques Ledoux was one seven agents parachuted into two German-controlled receptions in February 1944. Also in Ledoux's particular drop were François Deniset (a Canadian), Robert Byerly (an American), and Frenchman Roland Alexandre.

Ledoux was arrested upon landing on the night of 8 February and was taken to 84 Avenue Marechal Foch where records show that he stayed there from that date until 2 March 1944 under interrogation. He was then transferred to 3 bis Place des États Unis.

'Mission a tragedy,' wrote Maurice Buckmaster. 'He showed great promise.' Buckmaster believed that Ledoux had been executed at Gross-Rosen, however, in a war crimes trial conducted in Paris after the war a different story emerged. It was revealed that a French Gestapo officer, Georges Ledanseur, took on Ledoux's identity to infiltrate the Resistance. This was discovered when a new wireless operator for Ledoux landed in France and immediately realised that the supposed Ledoux had never been in Britain. When the SOE agent challenged the fake Ledoux he was shot by the Gestapo operative with a small gun disguised as a fountain pen.

In the war crimes trial the punishment meted out to Ledoux at Avenue Foch was uncovered. It is said he was stripped, plunged into ice-cold water, wrapped in a wet sheet, beaten and subjected to other 'sadistic tortures'. Ledoux was then transported east by train but managed to escape by leaping from the train. He later died, however, because of the treatment he had received.

Ledoux was a friend of Diana Rowden who was later executed at Natzweiler and the twin brother to Georges Ledoux (Code name *Tir*) who was a wireless operator for de Gaulle's RF Section.

LEE, Lionel

Date of death:	27 June 1944
Place of death:	Gross-Rosen, Poland
Rank:	Captain
Parent unit:	Royal Armoured Corps
Service number:	235209
Decorations:	Military Cross, *Croix de Guerre avec Palme*
Date joined SOE:	Spring of 1943
Code names:	Rene/Daks/Thilbaud/ Mechanic/Jacques Heriat
Nationality:	British
Age at time of death:	Twenty-seven

Date of birth: 24 June 1917
Place of birth: London, UK

Location of memorial: Brookwood, UK

Lionel Lee's first mission, Code named SARMENT, took place in February 1943 when he was taken from North Africa by submarine to Corsica. There he worked as the wireless operator to an RF Section team whose objective was to prepare groups to receive and guide armed parties in advance of an Allied landing on the island.

Within this role, Lee took part in a number of guerrilla actions and kept in regular touch with headquarters in Algiers from Ajaccio. The Germans eventually forced the group to disperse but a second organiser was sent to Corsica and Lee remained to become his wireless operator. It is said that he never missed a transmission and that he helped arrange two successful deliveries of weapons. With time, he helped put together a group of 400 armed men in the north-west of the island. He remained active in Corsica until the island was liberated in November 1943. He then returned to Britain. Lee was awarded the Military Cross 'in recognition of gallant and distinguished services in the field', an award that was announced in a supplement to *The London Gazette* on 9 December 1943.

For his next mission, to France, Lee was to join Major Joseph Antoine France Antelme as his wireless operator. Madeleine Damerment was to be the courier. Their main objective was to start a new circuit in Brittany with, as a secondary objective, the organisation of a number of armed mobile groups that would operate in the Seine-et-Oise area to the south of Paris.

On 28 February 1944, all three took off from RAF Tempsford in Bedforsdhire to be parachuted into the Rambouillet park near the village of Sainville (in the Eure-et-Loir department), 40 or so miles east of Chartres. Not only were the Germans aware of the proposed arrival of the agents, they had even arranged the landing spot and had chosen a place suitably close to Paris (little more than an hour's drive away) because SS *Sturmbannführer* Hans Kieffer, the senior German intelligence officer in Paris during the occupation, had invited along Dr Helmuth Knochen, the chief of the *Sicherheitsdienst*, to watch the capture of Antelme who he described as a high 'British Military Intelligence officer'.

The aircraft, a Handley Page Halifax (almost certainly of 138 (Special Duties) Squadron), was scheduled to arrive over Rambouillet at 22.45 hours. By 21.15 hours the drop zone was cordoned off to make sure that local Resistance members were kept out of the way. SS units encircled the whole area and the park of Rambouillet swarmed with SS squad cars.

The Halifax announced its arrival by dropping eight large containers and six packages, including three radio transmitters and a quantity of arms. Then came the agents, with France Antelme dropping first. Waiting for them were Kieffer, his interpreter Vogt and several of his collaborators posing as Resistance men.

When all three agents were safely on the ground Kieffer threw aside all pretence and arrested the trio at gunpoint. They were taken to Avenue Foch where the men remained until 12 May 1944, before their transfer to the notorious torture cellars of the Gestapo headquarters at Rue des Saussaies. Lee was then held at 3 bis Place des États Unis.

Though it was rumoured that the three men had been executed at Mauthausen they were in fact killed at Gross-Rosen.

LEFORT, Cicely Margot

Date of death:	1 May 1945
Place of death:	Ravensbrück, Germany
Rank:	Section Officer
Parent unit:	Women's Auxiliary Air Force
Service number:	9900
Decorations:	Mentioned in Despatches, *Croix de Guerre*
Date joined SOE:	15 February 1943
Code names:	Alice/Teacher/Cécile M. Legrand
Nationality:	British
Age at time of death:	Forty-five
Date of birth:	30 April 1900
Place of birth:	London, UK

Location of memorial: Runnymede, UK

Cicely Lefort (often incorrectly given as Cecily), with the fieldname 'Alice', was a courier for the JOCKEY circuit in the south-east of France. Though she was born in London, Cicely had married a Frenchmen in 1925 and had lived in his villa in Brittany. Cicely joined the SOE towards the end of 1942 and was described by her instructors as being 'very lady-like and very English, in spite of her French background'. She was landed near Tours in France on 16 June 1943, by a Westland Lysander of 161 (Special Duties) Squadron.

Lefort was arrested by the Gestapo whilst at the house of Raymond Daujat, the leader of a local resistance group in Montélimar on 15 September 1943. She had gone to Daujat's house with Pierre Reynaud a sabotage instructor who had been sent to the JOCKEY circuit that June. Reynaud and Daujat were talking in the garden when the Gestapo raided the property. The two men managed to run away but Lefort tried to hide in the cellar. Inevitably she was found and arrested.

It is said that the only incriminating evidence found on her was a piece of paper that she could not explain. As a result she was taken to the Gestapo prison at Lyon before being sent to Frèsnes prison and finally onto Ravensbrück in January 1944. 'Although severely interrogated and ill-treated,' wrote Maurice Buckmaster in September 1945, 'she gave no vital information away.' Buckman requested that Lefort should be granted a military OBE.

Ravensbrück was a concentration camp used primarily to house women. The inmates were forced to undertake heavy manual and industrial work and any women considered unfit for such work were taken to a sub-camp called the *Jugendlager*. Originally a youth camp, the *Jugendlager* became a place where the sick and the elderly waited until they were selected to be killed.

After almost a year working in these terrible conditions, Cicely Lefort became very ill. She was operated on by a German doctor in the autumn of 1944 for cancer of the stomach. Nevertheless, she eventually became so weak that she could no longer stand during the daily roll-call, the *Appel*, and she actually volunteered to go to the *Jugendlager*. But conditions were even worse in the sub-camp. The women were forced to stand for the roll-call for seven hours each day from 03.00 in the morning and dozens collapsed and died from exhaustion. It has been stated that more than 100 women a day died or were executed.

Lefort was so frail when she was moved to the *Jugendlager* that she was selected for execution almost immediately. It was reported that just before she died she received a letter from her husband stating that he wanted a divorce.

She was forty-five years old when she died. There are two views on how she died. One is that she died as the result of an overdose of the sleeping powder frequently administered by a senior prisoner. The second is that she was gassed to death as so many were in the *Jugendlager*. The camp overseer provided this description of the gassing of the women prisoners at Ravensbrück:

'They were ordered to be undressed as if to be deloused and taken into the gas chamber. Then the door was locked. A male prisoner with a gas mask then climbed on to the roof and threw a gas container into the room through a window, which he closed. I heard groaning and whimpering in the room. After two or three minutes it grew quiet. Whether the women were dead or just senseless I cannot say.' The women, be they senseless or dead, were then burned.

LEIGH, Vera Eugenie

Date of death:	6 July 1944
Place of death:	Natzweiler-Struthof, France
Rank:	Ensign
Parent unit:	Women's Transport Service (FANY)
Service number:	F/15
Decorations:	King's Commendation for Brave Conduct
Date joined SOE:	February 1942
Code names:	Simone/Almoner/Suzanne Chavanne
Nationality:	British
Age at time of death:	Forty-one
Date of birth:	17 March 1903
Place of birth:	Leeds, UK

Location of memorial: Brookwood, UK

Vera Leigh was one of the women executed along with Andrée Borrel, Diana Rowden and Sonia Olschanezky at Natzweiler on that terrible night in July 1944. Like Borrel, she too joined the PROSPER network, having worked in a shop in Paris before the war. She was described by her trainers as 'dead keen' and as being the best shot in the group.

Born with the surname Glass, Vera was abandoned by her parents soon after birth and adopted by an American racehorse trainer, H. Eugene Leigh, whose name she took. Eugene Leigh, who raced horses in the United States, also owned stables in France. Vera had an early ambition to become a jockey, but after completing her education she worked as a dress designer. In 1927 she went into partnership with two friends to establish a fashion house in Paris.

Fleeing Paris in the face of the advancing German army, Leigh headed to Lyons to join her fiancé. Here, she soon found herself being drawn into aiding Allied escapers and evaders.

Eventually, using the alias of 'Simone', Vera Leigh worked as a courier in one of the PROSPER sub-circuits (INVENTOR). When the PROSPER group was compromised, Leigh was captured (at the Café Mas near the Place des Ternes in Paris). She was imprisoned at Frèsnes and later sent to Karlsruhe prison along with the other three girls. She was seen leaving the prison for Natzweiler with the others and was described by an eyewitness as being older and more 'stocky' than the other girls.

The *Konzentratsionslager* Natzweiler-Struthof was the only concentration camp built by the Nazis on French soil. It was built by the slave labour of those who would become its internees. Only selected members of the SS, who could be depended on not to reveal what happened inside its gates, were chosen to work at Natzweiler.

The arrival of the four girls on 6 July 1944 aroused much interest at the camp. 'It was the first time we saw women in Natzweiler,' recalled Major Van Lanschot, a Dutch Resistance leader, 'and everybody was interested in the reason for which they were brought in.'

It was thought that they might be 'comfort' women for the SS guards but when they walked down the *Lagerstrasse* to the crematorium, and could be seen clearly by the other prisoners, it was universally agreed that they were too well dressed to be girls for a brothel. And when the girls were taken down the steps of the crematorium everyone knew that the women were to be killed – that very night.

This was confirmed towards evening when the usual preparations for an execution could be seen, including the lighting of the crematorium furnace. As night fell, the prisoners strained through curtains and shutters to watch what was happening.

The statement given by Walter Schultz, from executioner Peter Straub's observations, varies somewhat from other versions of events. Recounted in Sarah Helm's excellent book *A Life in Secrets*, Straub allegedly gave this account: 'When the four women were brought from the cells they were first made to sit on a bench in the corridor which led from the oven to the dissecting room. They were told by Ganninger, who spoke a little French, to undress for medical examination. This they refused to do unless a woman doctor was called. They were also told they would be given injections against illness.'

Straub also claimed that the first woman was taken by him into the room where she was injected in the upper arm. Straub then escorted the woman back to the corridor and sat her on the bench whilst he took away the second woman. Straub said that when he returned with the second woman, the first one was already sitting 'stiff and stupefied'. He said that this shocking procedure happened with all four girls before they were taken down to the room next to the crematorium to be stripped.

It is possible that Vera Leigh was the last of the four girls to be executed. Franz Berg, an habitual criminal, was the oven stoker and his cell was in the crematorium block. He gave this statement: 'Women undressed as ready for bed. No words spoken and no resistance from three but fourth woman resisted loudly and was shut up and forcibly dragged into the room.' This fourth woman was described by Berg as 'the stout one'.

The bodies of the four brave women were left in the oven all night whilst the SS officers and some of their helpers went and got drunk at Dr Plaza's leaving party.

LEVENE, Eugène Francis

Date of death:	29 March 1945
Place of death:	Flossenbürg, Germany
Rank:	Lieutenant
Parent unit:	Royal Artillery
Service number:	235918
Decorations:	Mentioned in Despatches
Date joined SOE:	1 January 1943
Code names:	Boniface/Lawyer/Jacquot/Eugene André Nizet
Nationality:	British
Age at time of death:	Thirty-two
Date of birth:	4 June 1912
Place of birth:	Liège, Belgium

Location of memorial: Brookwood, UK

A worker in the Civil Service communications branch before the war, Eugène Levene joined the British Army becoming something of a crack shot. He took part in the King's Shooting Prize at Bisley (known as the King's Hundred as the target range was 100 yards).

Levene received only average reports from his SOE assessors and showed a worrying lack of security if it inconvenienced him. His knowledge of communications and weapons, nevertheless, made him ideal for inclusion in a *coup-de-main* party.

He was therefore parachuted into France in April 1943 as a member of the *coup-de-main* party SCULLION but he injured his leg on landing. He made his way to Paris and then to Lyon, returning to the UK after being in France for one month.

Despite his pronounced Belgian accent, Levene was sent into France for a long-term mission as an arms instructor to Henri Frager's DONKEYMAN circuit in the Vallée de l'Yonne. He was dropped by Lockheed Hudson on 15 November 1943.

He was arrested just a few days later on 20 November at a safe-house belonging to a Mr Hewitt in Paris. Hewitt himself was arrested nine days later by the Gestapo accompanied by Levene. The only conclusion that can be drawn from this is that Levene, who himself had been betrayed by Henri Déricourt, broke down under interrogation and assisted the Germans.

Levene was known to have been sent to 3 bis Place des États Unis and was interrogated at Avenue Foch. It also seems possible that he was in Frèsnes prison, later being transferred to Flossenbürg where he was executed.

LORD, Christopher James

Date of death:	15 May 1943
Place of death:	Carmaux, France
Rank:	Captain
Parent unit:	General List
Service number:	256042
Decorations:	None recorded
Date joined SOE:	3 July 1942
Code names:	Vole/Limont/Henry Hounslow/
	Jean Marie Brunet/Ferand-Jacques
Nationality:	British
Age at time of death:	Forty-two
Date of birth:	27 October 1900
Place of birth:	Birmingham, UK
Location of grave:	Laissac, Aveyron, France

Christopher Lord was recruited from the Guaranty Trust Company of New York, having previously worked for American Express in Paris. His wife was a second lieutenant with the Free French forces in London.

He went into the south of France on 15 April 1943, to form a link in a courier chain passing men and mail between Belgium and Britain. Three days after his arrival, Lord made contact with two other men who were to form part of his group at a hotel in Laissac. According to a report later received at Baker Street, Lord had 'completely lost his nerve and was suffering from a nervous breakdown. He hid in the hotel for twenty-four hours, unable to bring himself to start work.'

It was inferred that one reason for his breakdown was that he doubted the accuracy of the identification papers he had been furnished with in London. So the two sub-agents went to obtain some rather more authentic-looking papers, arranging to meet Lord at the Café de la Gare in Carmaux on 14 May 1943. The meeting duly took place but Lord was never seen again.

In December 1943, Mrs Lord was informed of the circumstances surrounding the disappearance of her husband but she was told not to worry as he had been given enough money to last until the end of the war (as no-one in 1943 could know how long the war would continue, such a comment suggests that he had a fairly large sum with him).

The war came to an end but Lord did not reappear. His wife was posted to Paris in November 1945, still anxious to discover what had happened to her husband.

She published a photograph of Lord in the local Carmaux newspapers without result. Then, in March 1946, she learned through firends that an unidentified body had been found in the spring of 1943 in a well in a small village near Carmaux. At the time the police, at the request of the Germans, had not undertaken an investigation into the death. He was buried locally.

At Mrs Lord's insistence, the body was exhumed and identified as that of Christopher Lord. He had been shot four times with a Colt revolver, which was found in 1943 at the murder scene and then dumped in the same well as his body. With the matter now becoming a murder investigation, a witness was found. This was the local mayor, who testified that two sub-agents, Albert Lefevre and Jean Chudeau, had asked him to recommend a quiet place where they could conduct an unspecified 'grand coup'.

The mayor suggested an uninhabited house; the two men went there, taking with them old newspapers to cover the windows and electrical cable. The building was identified as being the one where the body in the well was found.

The two men were pursued by the French police, but what became of them is not revealed in Lord's personal file. The motive for the murder, however, was clear – it was the large amount of cash Lord was carrying as all that was found on the body when it was pulled from the well in 1943 was a 100 Franc note that had been left in Lord's trouser pocket.

MACALISTER, John Kenneth

Date of death:	14 September 1944
Place of death:	Buchenwald, Germany
Rank:	Captain
Parent unit:	Intelligence Corps
Service number:	257470
Decorations:	Mentioned in Despatches
Date joined SOE:	30 December 1942
Code names:	Valentin/Plumber/Jean Charles Maulnier
Nationality:	Canadian
Age at time of death:	Thirty
Date of birth:	9 July 1914
Place of birth:	Guelph, Ontario, Canada

Location of memorial: Brookwood, UK

Macalister was parachuted into France on 15 June 1943, with fellow Canadian Frank Pickersgill. They landed in the Cher valley north of Valençay. Macalister was to be Pickersgill's wireless operator in a circuit (ARCHDEACON) they were to establish in the Ardennes.

Macalister had been given glowing commendations by his various SOE assessors. 'He looks upon his work as a mission from which he will allow nothing to divert him,' ran the report of 12 February 1943, on his progress. 'He has a particularly tough scholar's mind, logical and uncompromising,' ran the words of his final assessment, 'and he sees the German menace as a cancer which calls for drastic surgery.' Unfortunately his French accent was 'horrifying'.

Three days after they had landed in France, Macalister and Pickersgill, along with Yvonne Rudellat and Pierre Culioli, set off by car for Beaugency in the Loire, from where they were going to take the train to Paris. They drove into the village of Dhuizon in the Sologne only to find it full of troops. They were stopped at a control point and the two

Canadians were held for questioning. The other two agents tried to escape but were shortly captured.

At first Macalister was taken to the Gestapo HQ at Blois. From here he was transported to Frèsnes prison where he was brutally treated but showed great courage and endurance and gave no information away.

When he was captured he had his wireless plan and codes on him (all helpfully labelled by Baker Street) and these were used by the Gestapo to send messages back to London. Though it has been said that despite being savagely tortured he refused to reveal his security checks the reality is that the Germans found his security checks amongst the captured papers. It seems possible that Macalister had written them down so that he would not forget them.

From Frèsnes, Macalister was moved to 3 bis Place des États Unis. He was at this location until at least 18 April 1944, after when he was transferred to Ravitsch. On 19 May 1944, along with four others, including Frank Pickersgill, Macalister was taken from his cell and driven to Berlin. From there they were all flown back to Paris for further interrogation and housed once again in the Place des États Unis. He was later removed to Buchenwald where he was hanged.

For his 'great bravery and self-sacrifice' Macalister was recommended for a posthumous Mention in Despatches: 'A very good officer indeed – determined, reliable, full of knowledge and very serious. It was a tragedy that his invaluable services were lost so quickly.'

MAITLAND-MAKGILL-CRICHTON, David

Date of death:	24 February 1941
Place of death:	North Atlantic Ocean
Rank:	Lieutenant
Parent unit:	Royal Northumberland Fusiliers
Service number:	121526
Decorations:	None recorded
Date joined SOE:	January 1941
Code names:	None recorded
Nationality:	British
Age at time of death:	Twenty-six
Date of birth:	12 July 1914
Place of birth:	Poona, India

Location of memorial: Brookwood, UK

David Maitland-Makgill-Crichton was educated at Worcester College, Oxford, where he read history, obtaining a Third Class degree. He became a freelance journalist and travelled to Albania to write a biography of King Zog I. He was there for twelve months.

In January 1941 Colonel Oakely Hill, operating in Belgrade, asked London if Maitland-Makgill-Crichton could be seconded to his mission in Yugoslavia for operations in Albania.

This was quickly agreed upon and he was transferred from his parent unit, the Royal Northumberland Fusiliers.

On the evening of 18 February 1941, he left London for Liverpool where he was to catch a ship for Cairo. He travelled in the guise of a civil servant.

His ship, the SS *Jonathan Holt*, formed part of Convoy OB289 (OB meaning outward from Liverpool). At 02.12 hours on 24 February 1941, the convoy was to the south-west of the Faröe Islands when two torpedoes were fired from the German submarine *U-97*. One of the torpedoes hit the steamer SS *Mansepool* and the other struck the *Jonathan Holt*. From the latter there were only three survivors. The master, thirty-eight crewmembers, two gunners and ten passengers, including Maitland-Makgill-Crichton, were lost.

MAKOWSKI, Stanisław

Date of death:	23 August 1944
Place of death:	Neung-sur-Beuvron, France
Rank:	Captain
Parent unit:	General List
Service number:	204697
Decorations:	Mentioned in Despatches, *Croix de Guerre avec Palme*
Date joined SOE:	4 November 1943
Code names:	Dimitri/Machinist/Jean Romieu/ Maurice
Nationality:	French
Age at time of death:	Thirty
Date of birth:	10 May 1914
Place of birth:	Korbul, Poland

Location of memorial: Pornic, France

This young Pole had previously studied viniculture in France before taking over his father's wine business. Stanisław Makowski had joined the emigrant Polish Army in France in 1939 and had escaped from Dunkirk to England with the British Expeditionary Force in May 1940. He married a Scottish girl in Edinburgh and joined the Gambia Regiment, the Royal West African Frontier Force. He then served in Africa and he was enlisted in the SOE in 1943.

He was sent back into France to work within Philippe de Vomécourt's VENTRILOQUIST circuit on 5 April 1944. His mission was to organise the Resistance groups in Loir-et-Cher for attacks on German troops moving to support the forces fighting the Allies. On 17 June 1944, Makowski's units, using only Sten guns and a few machine-guns, fought a battle with 700 Germans at Souesmes near Salbris. The battle lasted for hours and when the resistors withdrew the German column had been scattered, leaving behind many casualties. It is said that there were 121 dead and sixty-five seriously wounded. The French had nine men killed. Four other resisters were taken prisoner and bayoneted to death.

Makowski continued to operate successfully until 17 August, on which day he was driving from Romorantin-Lanthenay towards Neung-sur-Beuvron with two FFI (*Forces Françaises de l'Interieur*) officers when they met a German troop transport. He was carrying incriminating papers and could not risk being searched. Seeing no alternative he tried to accelerate past the Germans, who opened fire.

There was a bend ahead, which he took very quickly and a door on the old car swung open, throwing one of the French men (called Rohmer) out onto the road. Makowski stopped the car and looking back he saw several German cars drive up towards where their friend lay. The two men jumped out and began to shoot at the Germans, hoping to hold them back until they could rescue Rohmer. But more German armoured cars, equipped with mounted machine-guns, arrived.

Rohmer got up, fired at the Germans and then tried to escape across a nearby river. He was killed by hand grenades in midstream. Makowski and the other Frenchman hid behind the car and continued the gunfight, but the odds were against them. Makowski was hit in the shoulders, stomach and legs. The other man was killed.

Makowski was taken to the Gestapo office at Romorantin-Lanthenay. Though mortally wounded, he was beaten for hours until he died. His body was then thrown onto a rubbish heap in the town.

The mutilated body was secretly recovered and buried in the town's cemetery. Every bone had been broken, his face was lacerated with knife or bayonet cuts and his skull had been smashed in.

Today at the bridge in Neung-sur-Beuvron stands a marble monument. Carved upon its smooth surface is the name of a British officer of Polish descent who gave his life for France.

MALRAUX, Claude Raymond

Date of death:	18 April 1944
Place of death:	Ravitsch, Germany
Rank:	Lieutenant
Parent unit:	General List
Service number:	316119
Decorations:	None recorded
Date joined SOE:	18 February 1944
Code names:	Cicero/Beaupere
Nationality:	French
Age at time of death:	Twenty-four
Date of birth:	6 April 1920
Place of birth:	Paris, France
Location of memorial:	Brookwood, UK

Little is revealed in Claude Malraux's file about his life before the war other than that he was employed as an agricultural engineer.

He went into the field in April 1943 and built up an effective sabotage network (SALESMAN) in the Rouen and Le Havre districts. Malraux claimed to have 350 men in his circuit, all of whom were armed with the many drops he had successfully received. Almost all of his men, he reported, 'have been tried or tested on either a real or fake operation.'

On 3 October 1943, Malraux led a party of eight men on the Cie. Française de Métraux, a factory making aluminium parts for the *Luftwaffe*. As a result of this attack, output from the factory was reduced by 90 percent for four months.

The circuit had experienced no security leaks and a report on the SALESMAN circuit stated that 'generally speaking, the security of the circuit is excellent'. Something, however, went disastrously wrong.

Malraux was accompanying some of the stores recently received to a secret dump in Rouen, which was in a garage. Next door to the garage was a café that was occasionally used by members of the circuit as a meeting place and as a letter box ('boite aux lettres'). It was thought that 'some mishap' occurred when Malraux was putting the goods into the garage, which alerted the Germans as a little later, on 8 March, an undercover Gestapo agent turned up at the café. He said that he was a 'refactaire' (literally meaning a person who refused an order) wanted by the Germans, and that he would like to join a Resistance group. He gave the correct password. He was told to come back in the afternoon.

Shortly afterwards, Malraux looked in at the café and was told about the visitor. Malraux told the proprietor to ask the man to meet him that evening at 19.00 hours in the Place de la Cathédrale. The man would be able to identify him because he would be wearing a grey raincoat and would be carrying a scarf in his hand.

Malraux went to the rendezvous, only to be arrested by the Gestapo. Bizarrely he was carrying two suitcases full of documents containing lists of names and details of sabotage. That same night some thirty to forty members of his circuit were also arrested including all the heads of the Le Havre groups and all the reception committees except one.

The arrests were the subject, understandably, of an intense investigation. It was known that Malraux was beaten up and it was believed that he had succumbed and revealed full details of his circuit. The main problem for Malraux was that he was carrying so many incriminating documents, which probably made any denial on his part completely pointless. It was also reported that the German officer interrogating Malraux said that if he co-operated with him, none of his circuit would be shot. The German, it seems, kept his word. Though these people were arrested, they were not executed.

On 18 April 1944, Malraux was taken by the Gestapo to Frèsnes by bus. From there he was removed to Breslau in Poland and then Ravitsch. It is believed that he was badly treated at Ravitsch, and that it was there that he was shot.

The summary of Malraux's performance as an agent was summarised by his Section Chief, who wrote: 'Dashing and brilliant. Did good work but broke down under torture.'

MARTIN-LEAKE, Stephen Philip

Date of death:	7 June 1944
Place of death:	Sheper, Albania
Rank:	Major
Parent unit:	Intelligence Corps
Service number:	146448
Decorations:	None Recorded
Date joined SOE:	1941
Code names:	None recorded
Nationality:	British
Age at time of death:	Thirty-eight
Date of birth:	6 May 1906
Place of birth:	London, UK

Location of memorial: Tirana, Albania

Stephen Philip Martin-Leake, who served as simply Leake, was educated at Dulwich College and Corpus Christie, Oxford, where he achieved an honours degree in history. He was involved with the SOE from an early date, playing a part in Operation *Postmaster*, the daring capture of two Italian ships off the West African coast in January 1942. He also had a hand in the capture of Diego Suarez in Madagascar (see entry for James Mayer) and was given charge of SOE's headquarters in Madagascar.

Martin-Leake subsequently took charge of SOE's Albanian Section, based then in Cairo, in May 1943. How he perceived his new role is revealed in an internal questionnaire:

Question 1: 'What is your military objective?' Answer: 'The military object of Allied Military Mission, Albania ... is to kill Germans.'

Question 2: 'What political assumptions are you at present working on?' Answer: 'HMG is not interested in Albanian internal politics and that the Mission is free to afford assistance to whatever elements it considers are resisting or are likely to resist the Germans.'

The Albanian's Mission' HQ moved to Bari in Italy to be nearer its theatre of operations and Martin-Leake decided to go into Albania from there to experience the situation in the country for himself. He is reported to have said: 'For a year now I've been sitting on my bottom, sending other people into the field. Now I feel I must go myself.'

His true motive was to meet with and encourage the Resistance leaders who had been severely pressed by the Germans during the winter of 1943-4 and to explain Britain's determinedly neutral policy.

Martin-Leake, who was described by David Smiley as 'a charming officer', parachuted into Albania on the night of 10/11 May 1944, with the acting rank of lieutenant colonel. Martin-Leake soon found that the partisans were stronger than had previous been thought – numbering between 10,000 and 20,000 under arms – and that they, not the Albanian Government, were the only ones opposing the Germans.

After discussions with key Resistance leaders who were to form the new provisional government, Martin-Leake set off for the coast where he was to return to Bari by boat. The party reached Sheper (also known as Sherper or Shepr) on the first evening. They pitched

their tents just outside the village and settled down for the night. A little af.
on the morning of 7 June, two German fighter-bombers attacked the little
Martin-Leake, anxious to be off on the next leg of his journey, was already aw.
the only person out of bed at the time.

The report on what happened was relayed to the War Office in Curzon Street, ⌐ondon: 'Allied Mission Camp in Shepr area dive-bombed and machine-gunned from 05.10 to 05.40 hours local time. Major Leake was killed instantly by first bomb. Burial with pan military honours 8/6/44 in SHEPR Orthodox Churchyard.'

Further details came to light in July 1946 when it was learnt from 'another of the chaps in the field' that the ceremony had taken place at 10.00 hours and had been attended by around fifty partisans and members of the Mission. Martin-Leake's coffin was draped in black cloth. A cross was placed on the grave and a wreath laid that was inscribed: 'English Colonel Philip Leake martyred for the common cause.'

Martin-Leake's remains still lie in the rural community of Sheper in southern Albania, though the exact location of his grave has been lost. Consequently, he is commemorated on a special memorial in Tirana Park Memorial Cemetery.

MAYER, James Andrew John

Date of death:	14 September 1944
Place of death:	Buchenwald, Germany
Rank:	Lieutenant
Parent unit:	General List
Service number:	301337
Decorations:	Mentioned in Despatches, *Croix de Guerre avec Palme*
Date joined SOE:	23 December 1943
Code names:	Frank/Sexton/Jacques Mallet
Nationality:	French
Age at time of death:	Twenty-four
Date of birth:	19 April 1920
Place of birth:	Tananarive, Madagascar

Location of memorial: Brookwood, UK

In November 1940, the representative of the Ford Motor Company in the Vichy-French colony of Madagascar, Percy Mayer, the brother of James Mayer, made contact with the UK High Commissioner in South Africa. Mayer, born a British Subject in Mauritius but later naturalised a French citizen, offered to provide information on Madagascar and to help persuade the colonists to detach themselves from their allegiance to Vichy.

This message was passed onto London and in January 1941 the SOE agreed to take control of Percy Mayer's activities. Percy Mayer's supervising officer was Lieutenant F. Wedlake RNVR who set up a Madagascar Mission in Cape Town. Percy was presented with a wireless set, which he subsequently hid inside a false ceiling over his bathroom at his home in the Madagascar capital of Tananarive (now Antananarivo).

Percy Mayer was instructed to 'influence Madagascar and Réunion in favour of the Free French, away from Vichy', either by 'large scale bribery' of the senior personnel or by assassinating the Governor-General. Percy Mayer built up an extensive organisation across Madagascar, which James Mayer joined and when Britain decided to mount an operation to capture the island's main naval base of Diego Suarez in the spring of 1942, his mission played a pivotal role in the operation's success.

Percy Mayer's team managed to guide the British invasion fleet at night through waters considered impassable in the dark. They also cut the telephone line between the coastal artillery battery and its headquarters. These actions allowed the British troops to land unopposed and capture the batteries before the French gunners could fire a single shot. Percy Mayer went on to become one of the SOE's most successful agents, eventually rising to the rank of Major.

Like Percy Mayer, James Mayer travelled to the UK in May 1943 to join the SOE as a fully-fledged agent. Described by his instructors as 'pleasant and well-disciplined' he was trained as a radio operator and sent into France on 11 February 1944, with the fieldname of 'Franc'. He operated in the Angoulême area for the ROVER circuit for three and a half months organising parachute receptions and instructing local Resistance groups in the use of arms and explosives. According to his SOE file, he played a large part in sabotaging communications ahead of D-Day.

He was arrested by the Gestapo towards the end of May when he and Charles Rechenmann were drawn into a trap by a local sub-agent working for the Germans. The two agents were surrounded and arrested in a café at Pont-à-Brac, near Angoulême. They both spent some months in Frèsnes prison before being transferred to Buchenwald concentration camp.

They were hanged there on 14 September 1944. James Mayer was recommended for a Mention in Despatches for 'undertaking hazardous clandestine missions'.

McBAIN, George Basil

Date of death:	August–September 1944
Place of death:	Gross-Rosen, Poland
Rank:	Pilot Officer
Parent unit:	Royal Air Force Volunteer Reserve
Service number:	71102
Decorations:	*Croix de Guerre avec Palme*
Date joined SOE:	August 1943
Code names:	Cecil/Rhymer/Georges B. Buissonnier
Nationality:	British
Age at time of death:	Twenty-seven
Date of birth:	30 August 1917
Place of birth:	Taplow, Buckinghamshire, UK
Location of memorial:	Runnymede, UK

One of 161 (Special Duties) Squadron's Lysanders with air and ground crews of 'A' Flight at RAF Tangmere. The Lysanders were hidden away in the south-east corner of the airfield, as far from the main station and prying eyes as possible. (Courtesy of the Andy Saunders Collection)

Tangmere Cottage, just opposite the main gate of RAF Tangmere, became the operational HQ for 161 (Special Duties) Squadron's wartime Lysander operations. A number of the agents featured in this book would have passed through this building at some point. (Courtesy of the Andy Saunders Collection)

Seeing the lighter side of things! This wartime cartoon by Goyet depicts the confusion of a hurried Lysander turn-around at a landing site in France and is captioned: 'Advice to operators: To avoid a Rugby scrum separate arrivals and departures!' (Courtesy of the Andy Saunders Collection)

The dangers of delivering agents to their destinations. Although the casualty rate of the RAF aircraft operating in and out of Occupied Europe was not especially high, there were losses. This was Westland Lysander T1508 of 161 (Special Duties) Squadron, which had a landing mishap in France, near Châteauroux, on 28 January 1942. Squadron Leader J. Nesbitt-Dufort DSO escaped unhurt and was later extracted by an Avro Anson. Meanwhile, Lysander T1508 was trundled onto a railway crossing to be destroyed by a passing train. (Courtesy of the Andy Saunders Collection)

The grave of agent Jaques Tayar in the French plot at Brookwood Military Cemetery, Surrey. Tayar was killed when the 161 (Special Duties) Squadron Westland Lysander he was in crashed in dense fog whilst attempting to land at RAF Tangmere, after returning from France, on 17 December 1944. The other two men on board, agent Lieutenant Colonel Albert Berthaud and the pilot, Flight Lieutenant Stephen Alers Hankey, were killed outright. Tayar was still alive when rescuers reached the scene but died in the Royal West Sussex Hospital, Chichester the next day. (Courtesy of the Andy Saunders Collection)

Not a Commonwealth War Graves Commission memorial, the Valençay SOE Memorial is a monument to the members of SOE's F Section who lost their lives during the Second World War. The memorial, designed by Elizabeth Lucas Harrison, was unveiled on 6 May 1991, by Queen Elizabeth, the Queen Mother. This event marked the fiftieth anniversary of the despatch of F Section's first agent to France. The memorial's Roll of Honour lists the names of the ninety-one male and thirteen female members of the SOE who 'gave their lives for France's freedom'. (Courtesy of Peter Holmes)

The original grave marker on the last resting place of Francisque Eugene Bec.

A photograph of Fransique Euuuguene Bec in the field.

The funeral of Francisque Eugene Bec (whose coffin can be seen in the middle) at Le Mans West Cemetery.

The memorial to Francisque Eugene Bec that was erected at the end of the Second World War.

The crematorium at Mauthausen concentration camp, where at least nine of the SOE agents who feature on the CWGC registers were killed. (Courtesy of Faigl Ladislav)

A surviving building at the site of Sachsenhausen concentration camp, the location where SOE agents such as William Grover-Williams and Francis Suttill were killed. (Courtesy of Maurice Laarman)

The memorial to those prisoners held in Montluc prison between 1942 and 1944 – one of whom was SOE agent Alcide Beauregard.

The memorial at Fort Mont-Valérien in the Paris suburb of Suresnes. Used by the Germans between 1940 and 1944 as a prison and site for executions, the fort is now a French national monument and was first consecrated as such by Charles de Gualle on 18 June 1945. The area in front of the *Mémorial de la France Combattante* (seen here) has been named the Square Abbe Franz Stock. During the German occupation, Stock looked after the condemned prisoners held in the fort, and he mentioned some 863 executions at Mont-Valérien in his diary. It is recorded that SOE agent Guy Joseph Vivian was one of those shot at this site.

The bust of Violette Szarbo GC which tops the memorial to those who served in the SOE that can be seen overlooking the Thames on Albert Embankment, London. (Courtesy of Malcolm Edwards)

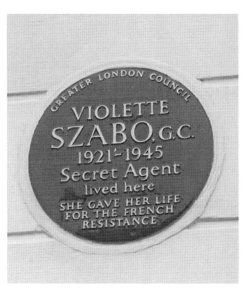

The blue wall plaque, remembering the sacrifice of Violette Szabo GC, which can be seen at 18 Burnley Road, Stockwell, London. (Courtesy Malcolm Rogers)

The plaque at the site of the former concentration camp at Natzweiler-Struthof, which commemorates three SOE agents, and one member of the French Resistence, executed on 6 July 1944. (Courtesy Dominique Bresson)

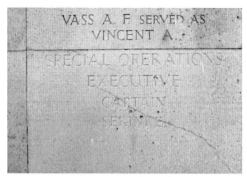

Despite all the SOE personnel who lost their lives in the Second World War, only one is listed by the Commonwealth War Graves Commission under the regiment or service name of Special Operations Executive – that of Captain Enzo Serini. This is his name carved on the Brookwood Memorial.

One of the authors, John Grehan, points out some of the names of the SOE agents killed during the Second World War who are commemorated on the Brookwood Memorial in Surrey. (HMP)

A number of the names on Panel 22 of the Brookwood Memorial in Surrey. Note the names of André Adrian Jules Maugenet and Louis Klement, two SOE agents who are recorded as having lost their lives during the war but who, research suggests, actually survived. (HMP)

Another view of the Brookwood Memorial in Surrey. Situated in Brookwood Military Cemetery, the memorial commemorates nearly 3,500 men and women of the land forces of the Commonwealth who died during the Second World War and have no known grave, the circumstances of their death being such that they could not appropriately be commemorated on any of the campaign memorials in the various theatres of war. (HMP)

George McBain worked in Paris before the war for a cotton importer. He joined the SOE and was sent into France on 3 March 1944, to join the ARCHDEACON circuit, with the *nom de guerre* of 'Cecil'. His role was to be the second in command of the circuit and to act as an arms instructor to the local recruits. It seems that his impending arrival was known by the Gestapo and he, along with three other agents intended for the LIONTAMER circuit (Lepage, Lesout and Finlayson), was arrested on arrival.

McBain was initially taken to 3 bis Place des États Unis in Paris where he remained until 18 April. He was transferred to Ravitsch 9 April 1944, to Berlin on 8 May 1944, and then back to Place des États Unis for further questioning.

Here McBain attempted to escape and as a result he was kept in manacles twenty-four hours a day. He was put in a cell with another British officer, Captain P.R. Tessier (see separate entry), who was already planning an escape attempt. Because he was handcuffed there was no chance of McBain escaping but this did not stop him helping Tessier, even though he would be left behind to face the wrath of the Gestapo. With McBain's assistance Tessier made a successful break in June 1944. After reaching Britain he reported into Baker Street to tell of McBain's bravery. As a result McBain was posthumously awarded the *Croix de Guerre*.

During the last days of June 1944 the Place des États Unis was evacuated as the Allies continued to consolidate their positions in Normandy. The prisoners were taken to Frèsnes and then dispersed to camps across Germany and Poland.

George McBain was sent to Gross-Rosen concentration camp, a satellite of Sachsenhausen, near Rogoznica in Poland. McBain was killed here.

A plaque commemorating the nineteen SOE agents murdered during August and September 1944 includes his name. The plaque is carved in local granite from a quarry where the prisoners were forced to work.

MELLOWS, Thomas Anthony

Date of death:	21 August 1944
Place of death:	Mont-de-Marsan, France
Rank:	Captain
Parent unit:	27th Royal Lancers, Royal Armoured Corps
Service number:	166686
Decorations:	None recorded
Date joined SOE:	9 August 1943
Code names:	Blase
Nationality:	British
Age at time of death:	Twenty-four
Date of birth:	8 March 1920
Place of birth:	Peterborough, UK
Location of grave:	Mont-de-Marsan, Landes, France

After his first mission in Cairo, Mellows returned to the UK in January 1944. For his second mission he left for France, via Algiers, on 27 June 1944. He was part of the Jedburgh team MARTIN, which also included Lieutenant Fourcade and Sergeant Gruen. On landing, Mellows severely injured his ankle yet he was determined to continue with his mission.

Towards the end of August the Germans had decided to evacuate the south-western part of France around Auch and the Resistance forces were determined to cause them as much trouble as possible as they withdrew. On the night of 20/21 August the Germans left Auch, after having destroyed all their munitions, field guns and a good part of the airport.

The German move was spotted and the information passed onto the Resistance at Mont-de-Marson. A tribute to Tony Mellows, found in his personal file, explains what happened next:

'... News arrived that a column of German armoured cars was approaching. Tony [and another] entered a motor car and made a tour of the town to organise its defences as Mont-de-Marsan was then quite unfortified. They arranged for the construction of road barricades and then went on to reconnoitre the enemy on the road to Bayonne.

'A column of about twenty enemy armoured trucks appeared on the southern outskirts of town and opened fire with anti-tank guns. During the course of the engagement Tony was wounded in the shoulder. It was suggested that he should be evacuated but he refused to withdraw and stood his ground, encouraging his comrades by his example.

'Suffering from his wound and from his injured foot, Tony was taken prisoner by the Germans, who stripped him of his uniform and shot him in the head four times with his own revolver, and also in his chest with a Tommy Gun, and then threw his body into a ditch. The Germans afterwards retired and proceeded to Bordeaux by another road.'

The battle at Mont-de-Marsan, between some 400 or 500 Germans and 600 partisans, lasted for five hours. At around 22.30 hours both sides, thinking they had been defeated, withdrew. During the course of the fight seventeen German trucks were captured and six or seven others were destroyed by mortar fire. Between forty and fifty Germans were killed or captured. The Resistance groups lost just three men, with another fifteen wounded.

Next day a search party was sent out. Captain Mellows' body was recovered from the ditch in a small lane. It was brought into Mont-de-Marsan, where it was placed in a metal casket in the turret of the church. Today, the lone Commonwealth War Graves Commission headstone in the town's cemetery can be found to the north-east of the entrance.

MENESSON, James Francis George

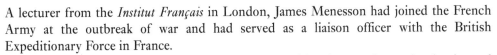

Date of death:	29 March 1945
Place of death:	Flossenbürg, Germany
Rank:	Captain
Parent unit:	General List
Service number:	183054
Decorations:	MBE, *Croix de Guerre avec Palme,* *Médaille de la Défense Nationale*
Date joined SOE:	11 February 1941
Code names:	Henri/Birch/Jean François Martinet/ James Francis Menzies
Nationality:	French, naturalised British
Age at time of death:	Twenty-eight
Date of birth:	27 April 1916
Place of birth:	Abbeville, France

Location of memorial: Brookwood, UK

A lecturer from the *Institut Français* in London, James Menesson had joined the French Army at the outbreak of war and had served as a liaison officer with the British Expeditionary Force in France.

When he joined the SOE it was thought that he would make a good organiser but instead James Menesson's academic talents were put to use helping produce a clandestine newspaper called *Le Coq Enchaniné*. The newspaper was produced in Lyons under the auspices of Emile Douboudin the area organiser.

Menesson was sent to France by felucca on 21/22 April 1942, accompanied by Maurice Pertschuk and Henri Paul Chêne. After a while, the editor of the newspaper was captured and *Le Coq Enchaniné* was closed down.

Through an acquaintance Menesson then obtained work with the Délegation du Rhône pour Secours National, which provided him with a cover story and gave him a reason to travel around by car. This enabled him to make further contacts amongst politicians, businessmen and Resistance groups 'of every colour'. In June 1943 his activities became known to the police and his secretary was arrested. Realising that his cover was blown he escaped back to the UK through Spain, though he would return.

For his second mission Menesson was given a number of tasks relating to the welfare needs of the civilian population following the Allied invasion. These were:

1. To go to the Secours National in Paris and obtain detailed information on its food stocks, clothing stores and their locations, and the measures in place to prevent the Germans from requisitioning these items.
2. To submit to the Secours National plans for co-ordinating civilian requirements in France. If agreed upon this information to be passed back to the Allies.
3. To work on undermining the morale of the German troops.

He was to return to the UK after three months.

Menesson landed by Hudson on the night of 15/16 November 1943, at the same time as André Maugenet and Paul Pardi. The Germans were well aware of the arrival of these three men and they were tailed from the landing place to the train station as the group were making their way to Paris.

As per their training, the men split up on the train, going into two separate compartments. The Gestapo followed them onto the train but could not make a move whilst the agents were separated. When they arrived at the Gare Montparnasse the three agents joined up again, only to be instantly arrested.

They were taken to Frèsnes. They were seen alive there on 17 January 1944, by a sub-agent, Pierre Pery, who had been released from Buchenwald. Pery stressed that the men had not been sent to Buchenwald whilst he was there. However, he reported that the Germans had said that 'the absence of rank markings on their uniforms labelled them as terrorists' and therefore liable to be executed. This is exactly what happened to Menesson after he had been sent to Flossenbürg, one of twenty-nine agents hanged on the same day.

MICHEL, François Gérard

Date of death:	1-15 June 1944
Place of death:	Gross-Rosen, Poland
Rank:	Lieutenant
Parent unit:	General List
Service number:	294434
Decorations:	*Chevalier de la Legion d'Honneur*
Date joined SOE:	17 July 1941
Code names:	Jacques/Dispenser/François Gérard
Nationality:	French
Age at time of death:	Twenty-nine
Date of birth:	19 December 1914
Place of birth:	France

Location of memorial: Bayeux, France.

François Michel, who served with the SOE as Frank Mitchell, was a former French Reserve officer with the equivalent rank of lieutenant colonel. He was a 'well-to-do' owner of a coal mine in Polish Silesia. Michel was involved with the SOE as a sub-agent from June 1941 and went to the UK for training in July 1941.

What happened after this is unclear until 1943. What is recorded then is that Michel was sent into France as a sabotage instructor for Frank Pickergill's ARCHDEACON circuit in Lorraine. He was sent there via an RF Section pickup operation in Burgundy in September 1943. After arriving in France he was to make his way to a contact house in Paris from where he would be passed onto ARCHDEACON. But Pickersgill had been arrested three months earlier and after landing Michel simply 'vanished' into the hands of the Gestapo. It was later found that he had been arrested in Paris the day after his arrival, on 23 September.

Incredible though it may seem, Baker Street did not know that ARCHDEACON was in German hands and stores and agents were sent to its reception committees for ten months. During that time fifteen large drops of weapons and equipment as well as six agents fell straight into the hands of the enemy.

The Germans played what became known as 'the radio game' (*funkspiel*) very skilfully. This was thanks to Joseph Placke, the assistant to the head of the wireless section at 84 Avenue Foch, who spoke good French and a little English. He impersonated Pickersgill and took over control of the circuit.

As Pickergill's wireless operator, John Macalister, had also been captured complete with his codes and security checks, Placke was able to convince London that the ARCHDEACON circuit was up and running satisfactorily. As one of F Section's officers subsequently explained: 'We had reason to believe in that circuit as an existing circuit because it did in fact exist.'

Placke arranged the receptions with the genuine French members of the circuit and he even organised trucks to take away the stores when they landed. The resisters had no idea that the trucks were driven by Germans in plain clothes or that the containers were being taken away to the Satory barracks near Versailles.

Michel was taken to Frèsnes and later sent to Gross-Rosen where he was murdered. Most of the weapons stored at the Satory barracks were recovered intact when France was liberated by the Allies.

DE MONTALEMBERT, Arthur Franz,

Date of death:	17 December 1944
Place of death:	Mauthausen, Austria
Rank:	Lieutenant
Parent unit:	General List
Service number:	309241
Decorations:	*Chevalier de la Legion d'Honneur*
Date joined SOE:	Already in the field, officially SOE 23 December 1943
Code names:	Bistouri/Satirist/Scalpel
Nationality:	French
Age at time of death:	Thirty-three
Date of birth:	31 July 1911
Place of birth:	Wezembeek-Oppem, Belgium

Location of memorial: Brookwood, UK

A local landowner, Comte Arthur de Montalembert, was recruited by France Antelme to form a circuit at Ancinnes on the edge of the Forêt de Perseigne in lower Normandy. De Montalembert lived on his family property and farm called Vaubezon, which lies to the east of Ancinnes.

The Resistance group that de Montalembert put together in early 1943, the SATIRIST circuit, gives some indication of not only the diversity of the people that joined the

Resistance but also the ordinary nature of these individuals. The group comprised de Montalembert himself, Paul Lottin, who was the local mechanic and farrier, André Malo, a simple farm hand, Paul Drecq, the village postmaster, and Abbé Luçon, who had recently arrived at Ancinnes to take over the post of village priest.

The group's first operation was the reception of a parachute drop arranged by Octave Simon through PROPSER's radio operator, Gilbert Norman. The drop was organised for the night of 14-15 June 1943. The radio code message transmitted by the BBC to alert the Ancinnes group of the impending drop was '*Elle est bleue aux fleurs rouge*', meaning 'It is blue with red flowers'.

The drop zone was arranged on a parcel of land close to a local farm and at 23.00 hours on that warm, clear summer's night two tons of arms and explosives and a radio transmitter were dropped by parachute. Ten containers were dropped in total and collected by de Montalembert, Lottin, Drecq and Malo, assisted by Cellier, the head of another resistance group based at la Quinte near Le Mans.

Some of the drop was immediately transported to a plot of land in a wood close by while the rest was hidden in a ditch to be moved over the following night, taking the men until 25 June to complete the job. The containers were transported using a cow wagon owned by a local farmer and drawn by a horse owned by the mayor of the nearby town of Livet. These men and the Resistance members were rewarded by sweets, coffee and cigarettes – precious things in time of rationing – included in the parachute containers. The radio transmitter was set up in a tower at de Montalembert's château.

The weapons and material dropped at Ancinnes were destined for a Resistance group in the Falaise area, not for use in or near Ancinnes itself. Some 300kg of supplies from the drop were collected by two Falaise Resistance members on the night of 25-26 June. But by this time Gilbert Norman was in the hands of the *Abwehr* and the mass arrests of the PROSPER circuit and those other groups associated with it had begun, including the Falaise members.

On 9 July 1943, a week after the arrest of the Falaise Resistance members, the *Feldgendarmerie* raided the homes of Lottin, Malo and Drecq. The house and workplace of Paul Lottin was the first to be visited and he was arrested in his garage workshop. A search of his premises revealed the three containers from the supply drop hidden in his woodshed. He was subsequently deported to Buchenwald on 29 October 1943, later being killed in a gas chamber in Lublin in March 1944. Malo and Drecq managed to escape.

André Malo heard a car pull up outside the building where he was lodging and took the chance to escape. He was spotted by the *Feldgendarmerie*, who had Lottin with them, and ordered to surrender. As he fled across fields they opened fire on him. He escaped uninjured and hid in a ditch, successfully evading capture.

Paul Drecq, meanwhile, was able to escape out of the back of his house whilst his wife delayed the Germans at the front door. He then hid in the bell tower of St Pierre, St Paul church with the help of Abbé Luçon for several days.

Arthur de Montalembert was not at home at Vaubezon on the day of the raid, being away in Paris on business. He was subsequently arrested at a friend's home in Le Mans on 5 October 1943. Both de Montalembert and his friend were deported to Mauthausen where de Montalembert died on 17 December 1944.

MULSANT, Pierre Louis

Date of death:	5 October 1944
Place of death:	Buchenwald, Germany
Rank:	Captain
Parent unit:	General List
Service number:	309473
Decorations:	Military Cross, *Chevalier de la Legion d'Honneur, Médaille de la Résistance Française*
Date joined SOE:	24 November 1943
Code names:	Paul/Minister/Paul Henri Maupas
Nationality:	French
Age at time of death:	Thirty
Date of birth:	13 July 1914
Place of birth:	Villefranche-sur-Saône, France

Location of memorial: Brookwood, UK

Recruited in the field by his close friend Octave Simon, former timber merchant Pierre Mulsant was actively involved in sabotage operations that included the destruction of twelve locomotives in the railway sheds at Troyes. Though he had held a responsible position in the field, becoming Simon's right-hand man, he went to Britain by Hudson on the night of 15/16 November 1943, for revisionary training and re-briefing for a further mission. In particular Baker Street wanted Mulsant to be brought up to date with developments in sabotage materials.

At the end of his training he received the following appraisal: 'A first class man – keen, interested and enthusiastic ... Fit for leadership and organisation. The best student on the course.'

Mulsant returned to France, being parachuted to the south of Blois on 3/4 March 1944. With Dennis Barrett (see his entry) as his wireless operator, he set about organising the MINISTER circuit near Troyes. Their operational area was the region between Meaux and Provins in the east/south-east of Paris in the Seine-et-Marne. He was given a range of targets including railway lines running out of Paris, telephone lines, roads between Paris and Châlons-sur-Marne, and a number of fuel dumps.

The MINISTER circuit successfully received five arms drops totalling nearly sixty containers and they safely welcomed two other groups of agents. Their sabotage operations started after D-Day. By the end of June Mulsant could count on 500 armed resisters and he declared he was strong enough to be able to hold the area bounded by Rozay-en-Brie, Nangis-St Juste and Vaudoy-en-Brie.

Led by Mulsant in person, his group attacked German communications creating real difficulties for the enemy trying to support his forces defending Normandy. They destroyed twenty-five locomotives, derailed one train, wrecked two railway turntables, destroyed one aircraft, demolished a bridge and destroyed large quantities of petrol and oil. The MINISTER group also ambushed a number of enemy patrols in which 'many' Germans were killed and wounded. The success of his circuit's actions led to Mulsant's award of the Military Cross.

Mulsant and Barrett were captured together when they went to extricate an SAS party that had got into difficulties in the Forêt de Fontainebleau. The SAS had landed in an area heavily patrolled by the SS. Ironically, the SAS team had managed to reach a position of safety by the time the two SOE men arrived to help them – the only people Mulsant and Barrett found were the Germans.

The pair was taken to Paris and a friendly French jailer in Frèsnes passed on the news that they were still alive there as late as 8 August 1944, but they were later moved to Germany. Both men were killed at Buchenwald in the second group of eleven prisoners called forward on 4 October and killed in the crematorium overnight.

MUVRIN, Nick

Date of death:	18 May 1944
Place of death:	Bulgaria
Rank:	Sergeant
Parent unit:	366 Company, Pioneer Corps
Service number:	ME 14500130
Decorations:	None recorded
Date joined SOE:	23 February 1943
Code names:	Nick Munroe
Nationality:	Canadian (formerly Yugoslavian)
Age at time of death:	Thirty-nine
Date of birth:	4 December 1904
Place of birth:	Delnice, Gorski Kotar, Yugoslavia
Location of memorial:	Brookwood, UK

Born in 1904, Nick Muvrin's first military experience came in 1925 when he served in a Searchlight Battery, part of the Yugoslav Army's Engineer Corps, near the city of Karlovac in central Croatia. Having completed his eighteen-month period with this unit, Muvrin returned to his home town of Delnice in western Croatia, the largest settlement in the mountainous region of Gorski Kotar, and took up his original job as a blacksmith.

In 1929, Muvrin emigrated to Canada, leaving his wife and son behind in Yugoslavia. For the first three years he worked as a labourer in a mine at Creighton, Ontario, before finding employment once again as a blacksmith.

Following the outbreak of the Second World War, Muvrin, by now a naturalised Canadian, enlisted in the Canadian Army. Soon after his unit arrived in the United Kingdom, Muvrin's fluency in English and Serbo-Croat brought him to the attention of the authorities. Seconded to the Pioneer Corps, he left for Cairo on 16 July 1942.

By 1943, Muvrin was part of the SOE machine, and on 1 March that year began his training at Sarafand in Palestine – his course was completed on 17 April 1943. The following comment made by the training centre's Commandant, was entered in Muvrin's file: 'Of general average with physical qualities somewhat above normal run.' The 5.7' tall, brown-haired operative had, it was noted, 'good discipline'.

Late in 1943, SOE established a base at Bari in southern Italy, from which it operated the various networks and agents in the Balkans. This organisation had the codename *Force 133* (later changed to *Force 266*). It was from here in December 1943 that Muvrin, operating with the name Munroe, was despatched to Albania as part of the so-called *Mulligatawny* Party. Under the command of thirty-three-year-old Major Mostyn Llewellyn Davies DSO, the group was parachuted into the country to make contact with a group of Bulgarian Partisans.

Bulgaria was regarded by the Allies as of considerable strategic importance in their efforts to contain German expansion towards the Middle East. Part of the remit of the SOE teams was to arrange air-drops for the partisans to assist in their fight against German units and the Pro-German Royal Bulgarian Army.

After their successful drop, the *Mulligatawny* team marched across Serbia to Crna Trava, a small village in the Jablanica District in south-eastern Serbia. On arrival the group linked up with Bulgarian Partisans of the Bulgarian Fatherland Front on the Yugoslav-Bulgarian border in December 1943.

Early in 1944, Major Mostyn Davies moved his unit across the border into Bulgaria itself, the intention being to help the Partisans establish a 'liberated zone' in south-central Bulgaria – and to act as a 'preliminary expedition' into the country. But that scheme collapsed when Mostyn Davies was killed in March.

On 12 May 1944, following a British arms drop, the Bulgarian partisans in Serbia decided to move into their homeland with immediate effect. But they were ill-equipped, unprepared and, as it turned out, over-optimistic about local support. They were assisted by a second British Military Mission (known as the *Claridge* Party) led by Major William Frank Thompson, which had absorbed some of the survivors of the *Mulligatawny* team.

It was planned that the partisans would penetrate into Bulgaria and, passing to the north of Sofia, eventually meet up with a number of partisan detachments in the Sredna Gora Mountains on the far side of the capital. Six days into the move, on 18 May 1944, elements of the partisan forces were ambushed by Bulgarian army units at the village of Litakovo.

The chaotic nature of the events at this time has meant that it has not been possible to establish a full picture of Muvrin's fate during this engagement. What is known is that Muvrin was last seen alive on 18 May by a fellow SOE volunteer, Sergeant Kenneth Scott. Scott, who survived his subsequent capture (and indeed the war) was the *Claridge* Mission's radio operator.

Scott later reported that during an interrogation on 1 June 1944, following his capture, a Gestapo agent informed him that Muvrin had been found with his radio set (it is probable that he had initially been Major Davies' radio operator before the latter's death) at the place of the ambush. From the manner in which the Gestapo agents referred to the incident, Scott was led to believe that Muvrin had already been shot and killed when he was found by the Axis forces. In his post-release account, Scott also added that as late as mid-June 1944 a Bulgarian Army NCO was 'asking casual questions' regarding Muvrin.

NEWMAN, Isidore

Date of death:	7 September 1944
Place of death:	Mauthausen, Germany
Rank:	Captain
Parent unit:	General List
Service number:	216306
Decorations:	MBE, Mentioned in Despatches, *Croix de Guerre, Médaille de la Résistance Française*
Date joined SOE:	11 July 1941
Code names:	Pépe Athlete/Pierre Jacques Nerault/Dividend/Joseph Nemourin/Julien

Nationality:	British
Age at time of death:	Twenty-eight
Date of birth:	26 January 1916
Place of birth:	Leeds, UK

Location of memorial: Brookwood, UK

A former school teacher from Hull, Isidore Newman enlisted in the army on 29 August 1940, training as a radio telegraphist with the Royal Corps of Signals at Catterick for six months. On 1 August 1941, Newman was sent for wireless officer training with the SOE. He appears to have been a successful student.

A report dated 7 August 1941, written by one of his trainers Lance Corporal MacAlister, stated that 'he was in good physical condition ... standing 1.8 metres tall, dark, with black hair, brown eyes and good looking; above average intelligence ... and after only two weeks had a good knowledge of French and French customs; he enjoys the training but has written some indiscreet letters'. Then on 14 August 1941, it was noted that Newman was 'self-assured and thinks with precision'; on 28 August that he 'sometimes seems depressed ... he went for a long walk yesterday saying he was suffering from nostalgia. His French vocabulary is improving and he does excellent work instructing other students in Morse code. Colloquial French not good but he is a patient and excellent teacher of wireless and Morse'.

Isidore Newman arrived in Antibes by canoe from a submarine in April 1942 to act as the wireless operator of François Basin's URCHIN circuit. Basin set him up with René Casale who worked as a croupier at the Cannes casino. The German officers and Gestapo men who spent their money at the casino had no idea that the roulette wheel was being spun by 'a dangerous spy and terrorist'. Casale was always pleased to declare that he made sure the Germans never won.

Newman's services were taken over by Peter Churchill when Basin was arrested on 18 August 1942. Churchill had been sent by Baker Street to act as a liaison officer between London and Girard's locally-developed CARTE group.

Newman therefore had to deal with Girard and they soon quarrelled. Girard, showing no appreciation of the difficulty and danger under which Newman operated, insisted on his exceptionally long messages being transmitted verbatim. This Newman complained, 'leaves me no initiative concerning any necessary abbreviations.' Newman was forced to work into the early hours of the morning to clear all the outgoing messages. It was, as Foot records, more than Newman's professional integrity, and his nerves, could stand, especially as Girard called Newman's complaints 'insubordination'.

Churchill saw that the growing enmity between the two was likely to cause a breach in relationships between CARTE and London. Therefore, to avoid any deepening of the rift he sent Newman back to the UK in November.

Newman returned to France by Lysander in July 1943 as the wireless operator to Philippe Liewer's SALESMAN circuit. This circuit soon built up a force of 350 men all well armed from numerous supply drops. Newman kept himself entirely apart from the group, his location being known only to Liewer and his second in charge Claude Malraux. Newman was thus able to state that the security of the circuit was 'excellent'.

The circuit was able to claim a major success when it destroyed a minesweeper at the Ateleirs et Chantiers de Normandie shipyards near Rouen. The ship had just completed a full refit when it was sunk by charges placed low down inside the hull.

On 9 or 10 March 1944, Newman was arrested by the Germans following the capture of Claude Malraux. As well as these two, a total of some eighty members of the SALESMAN circuit were taken by the Germans. In the round up of the circuit, eighteen tons of arms were also seized. Newman was executed at Mauthausen.

The SOE agent George Starr has stated that he saw Newman over a two or three day period at 84 Avenue Foch, where he was put in Starr's cell while Starr himself was kept in the guard room. Newman had apparently recognised a tie Starr was wearing, that he himself had bought in Selfridge's in London.

Newman is believed to have been transferred, possibly via the transit camp at Compiègne, to Ravitsch. From here he may well have been taken in August 1944 to Gusen, near Linz in Austria, one of many satellite camps of Mauthausen, and then to Mauthausen itself at the beginning of September. Here he was shot 'trying to escape' – as the Germans described it.

In November 1946, Buckmaster wrote the following acknowledgement of Newman's work: 'At great personal risk he continued for many months to transmit and receive Morse messages to and from Supreme Allied HQ ... essential to the successful execution of our part of the war effort. This consisted of supplying liaison officers, arms and ammunition and explosives to French patriots who would thus be able to co-ordinate their efforts to liberate their country. Having successfully completed his first mission in the south-east of France, he returned to London and volunteered to return again to another part of France. ... After carrying out invaluable work in reconstituting a previously decimated resistance group in Normandy, he was arrested by the German forces and executed. Never did he betray any secret information despite intense pressure on him to do so. His colleagues have spoken in glowing terms of his readiness to help at all times and of imperturbable sangfroid. I am happy to record this tribute to a very brave man of whom the French Resistance chiefs, as well as his British compatriots, are and always will be proud.'

'Poor Julien,' Basin later wrote, 'he was an excellent radio operator, cheerful, hard-working and courageous.'

NICHOLLS, Arthur Frederick Crane

Date of death:	11 February 1944
Place of death:	Valijas, Albania
Rank:	Major, Temporary Colonel, Acting Brigadier
Parent unit:	Coldstream Guards
Service number:	62269
Decorations:	George Cross, ERD (Emergency Reserve Decoration)
Date joined SOE:	March 1942
Code names:	None recorded
Nationality:	British
Age at time of death:	Thirty-three
Date of birth:	6 February 1911
Place of birth:	Bexhill-on-Sea, UK

Location of memorial: Tirana, Albania

The story of Arthur Nicholls is outstanding even amongst the numerous tales of courage and heroism with which the annals of the SOE abound.

It was in August 1933 that Nicholls, who had previously studied law, was commissioned as a second lieutenant in the 86th (East Anglian) (Hertfordshire Yeomanry) Field Brigade, Royal Artillery, TA. Promotion to lieutenant followed three years later – on 3 August 1936. In May 1937 he was transferred to the Coldstream Guards (Supplementary Reserve).

On the outbreak of war, Nicholls was mobilised and sent to France with the 2nd Battalion, Coldstream Guards. His knowledge of foreign languages, a skill which no doubt helped lead to his involvement with the SOE, saw him being posted as an Intelligence Officer to Headquarters of the British First Division.

Nicholls joined the SOE in March 1942 as a staff officer. He was sent into Albania as the GSO1 (General Staff Officer (Grade 1)) of the Force 133 Military Mission in October 1943. Nicholls was dropped along with a number of other officers and men to join the small team already in place. David Smiley recalled that he was 'flabbergasted' with the amount of kit that was dropped with the newcomers. This included camp furniture, two containers of stationery and a clerk complete with typewriter.

Nicholls was described as being a typical Foot Guards officer – tall, slim with a dark moustache. Smiley saw Nicholls' military bearing as being 'wholly admirable in the regular army, but not entirely suited to guerrilla warfare'. The size of the new headquarters that had arrived was also unsuited for the kind of activities the mission was engaged in, requiring more than 100 mules to move all the equipment.

In December 1943, the mission was attacked by German forces and forced to disperse. Nicholls took over command of the remains of the dispersed mission when the commanding officer, Brigadier 'Trotsky' Davis, was shot in close combat with the enemy and taken prisoner. The citation for Nicholls' award of the George Cross takes up the story as this point:

'... From then on Brigadier Nicholls lived as a fugitive in the open mountains in freezing weather. He continued leading the remnants of the Mission but was suffering from frostbite so severely that he ordered an inexperienced man to amputate both his legs without anaesthetic. He was pulled over the mountains lying upon his greatcoat by two members of his party. He was determined to reach a British Mission to make his report upon which the course of the war in Albania would depend. He succeeded in this but had gone beyond the limits of endurance and died from gangrene and heart failure.'

Major George Seymour explained exactly what happened to Nicholls as he made his valiant attempt to reach Seymour's Mission across the mountains:

'He crossed a large expanse of mountainous territory that was continually patrolled by hostile bands. He had been compelled to move by night only. He had no money, change of clothing or medical equipment. He was forced to hide in verminous sheep-folds by day and any food he had managed to obtain was almost exclusively rye-bread ... His means of progression in the first place was to sit on his overcoat and to be pulled down the snow-covered and rocky mountainside by his escort of two partisans. He later succeeded in obtaining a small mule which, although it carried him, was extremely painful since, owing to his height, his mutilated feet were continually dragging in the snow...

'When I located him he was more than half-starved, verminous, exhausted, and gangrene had obtained a firm grip on his feet. He had also had an accident having fallen down a mountain side and his shoulder was dislocated. His feet were in an almost unbelievable condition. Both were festering masses and the only indication of where his toes were was where bare bones showed through the gangrened flesh.'

Seymour took Nicholls back with him and over the course of the next few days, despite being fatally ill, he was able to make his report. He died suddenly on 11 February. Septicaemia was thought to be the cause.

Seymour recommended Nicholls for the Victoria Cross, declaring that he had: 'set an example of heroism, fortitude, courage, leadership, the will to win, and devotion to duty, which has seldom been equalled and never surpassed. He carried on far longer than could normally be considered humanly possible and this undoubtedly caused his death.'

Subsequent research by Lance Corporal Ian Tindall suggested that Nicholls was also entitled to receive the Emergency Reserve Decoration (ERD). Nicholls' daughter duly applied for the award, which was gazetted in November 1991 – forty-seven years after his death.

NORMAN, Gilbert Maurice

Date of death:	6 September 1944
Place of death:	Mauthausen, Germany
Rank:	Major
Parent unit:	Durham Light Infantry
Service number:	156759
Decorations:	Mentioned in Despatches
Date joined SOE:	15 March 1942
Code names:	Archambaud/Butcher/Gilbert Aubin
Nationality:	British
Age at time of death:	Twenty-nine
Date of birth:	7 May 1915
Place of birth:	Saint-Cloud, France

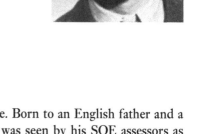

Location of memorial: Brookwood, UK

Gilbert Norman's story is a particularly unfortunate one. Born to an English father and a French mother in the Paris suburb of Saint-Cloud, he was seen by his SOE assessors as being 'perfect in all ways, has got great qualities of leadership and physical endurance'. On 31 October 1942, he was sent into France to join Francis Suttill's PROSPER circuit as its principal radio operator.

Things went very well for almost eight months. Norman acted as Suttill's second in command and helped in arranging a number of parachute drops and the dangerous job of transporting and distributing the arms received. He also took part in sabotage operations against railways.

Then, in June 1943, disaster struck the PROSPER network when two Canadian agents, Pickersgill and Macalister, who parachuted into France on the night of 10/11 June, were arrested. On them was found the addresses of Andrée Borrel and Gilbert Norman who were both arrested a little after midnight on 23 June. Norman was sleeping in the house of a locally-recruited sub-agent, Nicholas Laurent, when a man knocked at the door asking for 'Archambaud'. As he only knew his guest by his cover name of Aubin, Laurent woke Gilbert and told him about the visitor. Assuming that someone who knew his field name must be another agent, Norman went to see the man, only for fifteen men to leap out of the shadows and grab him. The Germans found not only Norman's radio set but also his back messages.

To make matters worse Pickersgill and Macalister had been carrying a package for Norman – a new set of radio crystals with details of the frequencies to be used – all neatly labelled up by Baker Street. With all this Dr Josef Goetz, the Gestapo's radio expert, was able to figure out Norman's codes, transmission times and security check.

Goetz had all the information he needed to be able to transmit to London. It was the big breakthrough that the Gestapo had long dreamed of and he did not want to make any mistakes that might jeopardise the wonderful opportunity they had been presented. So Goetz tried to persuade Norman to co-operate, but the British agent refused.

So Goetz went ahead himself, using Norman's call-sign 'Butcher'. In his first message he informed London that PROSPER had been captured. Dr Goetz himself described what happened next: 'The reply I got from the first message was quite unexpected. The message I got back said: "You have forgotten your 'true' security check. Be more careful next time."'

This second, 'true' security check was put in place so that if an agent had been captured by the Germans and forced into transmitting a message, the staff at HQ would know that if the agent did not include the second check then the call had been made under duress. It was put in place for exactly the kind of circumstance that occurred with the seizure of Norman's radio set. This was the first time that Goetz had heard of such a check.

As soon as Goetz's message was received without the security check the staff at Baker Street was alarmed but, incredible as it may seem, Maurice Buckmaster dismissed their concerns. It was Buckmaster's words that were sent back to Goetz at the next scheduled transmission telling him that he had forgotten his double security check.

Norman was shown London's reply and, naturally, he was not just shocked at this terrible blunder but absolutely furious. Norman was also shown copies of all the mail sent to London from the agents in France, making it quite clear that the Gestapo knew everything about the PROSPER circuit. At this point Norman gave in.

Though he made a 'full statement' to the counter-intelligence chief at Avenue Foch, SS *Sturmbannführer* Hans Josef Kieffer, he did try to protect as many people as he could. Certainly, there was increasing concern in London over the nature and sequencing of the messages from Norman's radio and it is clear that Norman had not revealed everything to Goetz and had possibly duped the Gestapo man. It was not Norman's fault that Baker Street failed to heed the obvious warnings. Indeed, when other agents had told Baker Street that Norman was under arrest, the reply from London was 'You must be mistaken because Archambaud is still transmitting to us'.

Gilbert Norman's apparent co-operation did him little good, however, as he was hanged at Mauthausen in September 1944.

OGDEN-SMITH, Colin Malcolm

Date of death:	29 July 1944	
Place of death:	Querrien, Finistère, France	
Rank:	Major	
Parent unit:	Royal Artillery	
Service number:	91977	
Decorations:	Mentioned in Despatches, Territorial Efficiency Decoration	
Date joined SOE:	1 April 1942	
Code names:	Dorset	
Nationality:	British	
Age at time of death:	Thirty-three	
Date of birth:	30 August 1910	
Place of birth:	Croydon, UK	
Location of grave:	Guiscriff, Morbihan, France	

The Company Director and Factory Manager of Ogden-Smith Fishing Tackle manufacturers, Temporary Captain Ogden-Smith, was sent to Algiers to act as liaison officer on behalf of SOE's Cairo Advance Base at Ringlet. Smith was familiar with North Africa as he had previously served with No.7 Commando in Egypt from where he was involved in the raids upon Bardia and Crete. At the beginning of June 1942 he had been seconded to the Small Scale Raiding Force until his selection for this new role in the Middle East.

Smith arrived in Cairo to be told that he was surplus to requirements and after just a few weeks he returned to the UK, arriving back in London on 11 October 1943. He was then ordered to undergo parachute training in preparation for his participation in a Jedburgh operation in the Finistère region of France.

The Jedburgh team of 'Francis' consisted of Ogden-Smith, *Capitaine* Le Zachmeur (an alias of Guy Le Borgne) and Sergeant Arthur Dallow. They were dropped into France on 10 July 1944, and soon put together a team of six, which included Maurice Myodon of the SAS who had become separated from his unit. This team visited all the local Resistance groups to check on how well each one was organised and to see what they might require in terms of weapons.

On 29 July 1944, Ogden-Smith's team was betrayed at their hide-out at a farm in the hamlet of Querrien. The Germans had been searching for the men for the previous two or three days but they had managed to elude their pursuers, hiding in a ditch covered with bushes some 100 yards from the farm during daylight hours. But at 21.10 hours on the evening of the 29th, approximately 100 *Feldgendarmerie* surrounded the farm and a gun battle started. Ogden-Smith killed or wounded four Germans before he himself was severely wound in the stomach by a burst of automatic fire. Unable to move, he injected himself with morphia.

Myodon was wounded by a grenade that broke a leg and an arm but to help his comrades escape, he dragged himself out into the open and emptied four magazines into the Germans, killing many of them. When he was out of ammunition he called out to the Germans 'You need not be afraid, I've got no more ammunition'. The Germans then walked up to Myodon and ordered him to put up his hands. They dragged him round and fired a burst from a sub-machine-gun into his body and then finished him off with a bullet to the head. The Germans then found the helpless Ogden-Smith and shot him. Both men were in uniform, bearing the insignia of their ranks.

Myodon's selfless actions enabled both Dallow and Zachmeur to escape. One of the Resistance fighters, though wounded, also got away. He had to hide in a stream for four hours with only his nose above the water whilst the Germans searched the area. He then walked about 7 miles before collapsing at another farm where he was taken in.

The Germans burnt down the farm at Querrien, killed the farmer, seventy-two-year-old M. Fiche, by bayoneting him in the back. They drove away all the cattle and stole anything of value from the farm. The bodies of the two British soldiers were stripped of all valuables such as jewellery, money and boots.

The group had been betrayed by a Belgian collaborator who lived a few miles from the farm. Whilst out walking one day he spotted the Allied servicemen. He sent his wife into the nearby town of Quimperlé to inform the German authorities and it was she who was in the car that led the Germans to the farm. Two days later the Belgian woman, her husband and their eldest son were killed by the Resistance.

There was an investigation into the murder of Ogden-Smith and Myodon by the War Crimes Investigation Unit in Germany after the war and the papers were handed to the French authorities for trial.

OPOCZYNSKI, Abraham

Date of death:	12 April 1945
Place of death:	Germany
Rank:	Sergeant
Parent unit:	The Queen's Own Royal West Kent Regiment
Service number:	6387010
Decorations:	None recorded
Date joined SOE:	26 June 1941
Code names:	Adam Alfred Orr/Sergeant Adam Orr
Nationality:	British
Age at time of death:	Thirty
Date of birth:	6 November 1914
Place of birth:	Łódź, Poland
Location of grave:	Durnbach, Germany

The Commonwealth War Graves Commission gives the age of Abraham Opoczynski when he died as being twenty-three, but this is incorrect. He was born in Poland to a Polish mother and a British father. He worked as a journalist in both Warsaw and London before the war and he joined the British Army in 1940.

When he started training with the SOE in the summer of 1941 he was placed in a group that consisted of Sudeten Germans, which caused some difficulty and it was recommended that he was moved to another training group. In time, though, he won everyone around with his pleasant personality and he proved to be an excellent student.

As there was no immediate prospect of being able to conduct any subversive action in Poland in the early years of the war, Opoczynski was 'loaned' to the Combined Operations HQ and took part in a raid against the French coast in 1942.

The objective of the raid was to land a small party on the beach at Sainte-Honorine-des-Pertes, a small coastal village to the north of Bayeux in Normandy. Here the raiding party was to record information of military value and capture a German soldier who was to be taken back to Britain for interrogation. The raid, known as Operation *Aquatint*, was to be conducted by the Small Scale Raiding Force (SSRF).

Aquatint was to be led by Major Gus March-Philips with Captain Geoffrey Appleyard as second in command. Amongst the other ten Commandos was an English Lord, Captain Lord Howard of Penrith, the Frenchman André Desgrange, Dutchman Jan Hellings, Opoczynki (operating as Private Adam Orr), and Private Leonard (real name Lehniger) who was a German Czech from the Sudetenland.

A little after midnight on 13 September 1942, the raiding party made landfall but in the dark they landed at the wrong part of the coast and were spotted by a German patrol. The enemy opened fire. The Commandos managed to get back to their little rowing boat with the sole exception of Lieutenant Hall who was left for dead on the beach. They pushed off and were about 100 yards from the beach when they were spotted from the shore. Three machine-guns opened up on the flimsy boat.

None of the raiding party made it back to the MTB that had taken them to the French coast. Captain Appleyard had remained on the MTB.

Three of the men had been killed, the others, including Jan Hellings and Opoczynski, were taken prisoner. Both Hellings (who served as Private Jan Hollings) and Opoczynski men were known to have spent some time *Stalag* VIIIB at Lamsdorf (now Lambinowice) south-western Poland, but they were moved around between POW camps including *Stalag* 133 and *Luft Dulag*.

On 29 November 1942, a note from Opoczynski was received in London via the Red Cross stating that he had been captured unhurt. His main concern was that the War Office should confirm his rank of sergeant as he was being treated by his captors as a mere private.

A prisoner who was repatriated to the UK stated that he had seen the two men in *Stalag* 344 (as *Stalag* VIIIB had been renumbered in 1943) as late as June 1944 when it was reported that they were both fit and well.

All that is known about the eventual fate of these two is that they were killed close to the end of the war. A number of those buried at Durnbach, where graves can be found, are known to have come from men who died or were killed at surrounding POW camps or Flossenbürg concentration camp.

PALMER, Sir Anthony Frederick Mark

Date of death:	18 May 1941
Place of death:	Uncertain, possibly the Aegean Sea
Rank:	Major
Parent unit:	Royal Artillery
Service number:	63572
Decorations:	None recorded
Date joined SOE:	19 February 1941
Code names:	None recorded
Nationality:	British
Age at time of death:	Twenty-six
Date of birth:	29 August 1914
Place of birth:	Staffordshire, UK
Location of memorial:	Brookwood, UK

Sir Anthony Palmer was educated at Marlborough College, passing as top of his term into Sandhurst Military Academy as a King's Cadet. He went on to join the 5th Fusiliers and served with them in Palestine in 1934. In 1935, Anthony Palmer succeeded his father Sir Alfred Molyneux Palmer as the fourth baronet Palmer.

He left the regiment in 1937 but with the outbreak of war he returned to service with the Royal Artillery. He was with the BEF in France and was involved in the Dunkirk evacuation. Palmer agreed to serve with the SOE in the Middle East and set off for Cairo on 7 March 1941.

On Friday, 18 May 1941, Major Anthony Palmer and twenty-three Jewish volunteers from Palestine, all members of Palestine Infantry Companies attached to The Buffs (Royal East Kent Regiment), embarked from Haifa Port upon the Commando boat *Sea Lion* (in Hebrew *Ari Hayam*). They were to undertake Operation *Boatswain*, which was the destruction of the oil refineries near Tripoli in Lebanon. They never reached their destination.

There is much mystery surrounding the fate of the *Sea Lion*. It is not impossible that it was accidentally hit, or attacked, by a British submarine as a French naval radio operator (based in Lebanon) intercepted a transmission in English at 07.55 hours on the morning of 19 May referring to an incident that had occurred the previous evening.

According to a Jewish agent in Lebanon a number of bodies were later washed ashore, one of which appeared to be that of Palmer. The clothing on the bodies was recognised as being that worn by Palmer's party. Equally, on 6 June, there was a German broadcast that stated that a British officer and a number of men in a motor boat had been picked up by the Germans off Bardia, Libya.

There then followed all manner of rumours. It has been said that survivors from the raiding party were summarily executed and, by contrast, there were reports that Palmer and some of his men were alive and that they had been taken prisoner and were being held on an island off the coast of Syria. It was said that from there Palmer was shipped to either Alexandretta or Antioch before being moved to Germany. Another report claimed that he was in France and that he had been transported there through Turkey. It was said that some members of Palmer's raiding party were in prison in Paris.

Because of the special nature of Palmer's activities, SOE did not want to press too hard with their enquiries in case the Germans learnt of their interest, as this might have placed him in even greater danger, possibly of torture. Baker Street did not even notify the Red Cross of his disappearance.

The other twenty-three men are listed in the final chapter of this book.

PARDI, Paul Baptiste

Date of death:	19 May 1944	
Place of death:	Gross-Rosen, Poland	
Rank:	Lieutenant	
Parent unit:	General List	
Service number:	297148	
Decorations:	King's Medal for Courage in the Cause of Freedom, *Médaille de la Résistance Française*	
Date joined SOE:	10 July 1943	
Code names:	Philibert/Pawnbroker/ Paul B. Giacommetti	

Nationality:	French
Age at time of death:	Twenty-four
Date of birth:	19 April 1920
Place of birth:	Sotta, Corsica

Location of memorial: Brookwood, UK

Paul Pardi was a civilian pilot before the war, operating out of Ajaccio, Corsica. In 1939 he joined the French air force as a volunteer sergeant pilot, being demobilised following the Armistice in the summer of 1940.

Pardi was one of a number of Corsicans recruited by a British officer who went to the island to establish a Resistance network. The French authorities soon learnt of this group and all the Corsican leaders were captured. The other members of the group, which included Pardi, hid the British officer at great risk to themselves.

Eventually Pardi was able to get to Britain, escaping in the French submarine *Casabianca*, where he was selected for training with the SOE. His role was to be that of a Lysander receiver for Claude de Baissac's SCIENTIST network in Normandy, a position that was described as being urgently required.

His assessors considered Pardi to be: 'A tough, sturdy Corsican with plenty of self-assurance and native cunning born of experience in the field ... He should be capable of acting as a leader of a small active band of young men like himself. The work for which he has been selected seems very suitable.'

He landed in France on the night of 15/16 November 1943, on the same Hudson flight as André Maugenet and James Menesson. The Germans had been informed by the double agent Henri Déricourt, the SOE's main aircraft movements' officer in northern France, of the planned arrival of the three agents and the men were followed and captured when they reached Paris.

Though all three were interrogated, and unquestionably tortured, Pardi and Menesson did not reveal any sensitive information. It is known that Pardi was in 3 bis Place des États Unis and it was thought that he was later transferred to Ravitsch, occupying cell number 3.

At some point in time he was transferred to Gross-Rosen where he was executed. His name is amongst nineteen agents carved with pride on a memorial plaque in the well-preserved grounds of the former concentration camp.

Prior to being sent to France, Pardi had married an English woman and fathered a son, Jacques. In September 1946, Pardi's widow received a letter from the British authorities outlining what little was known at the time of her husband's death. The letter stated that he was last seen alive at Ravitsch on 19 May 1944.

PERTSCHUK, Maurice

Date of death:	29 March 1945
Place of death:	Buchenwald, Germany
Rank:	Lieutenant
Parent unit:	General List
Service number:	216751
Decorations:	MBE, Mentioned in Despatches, *Croix de Guerre, Chevalier de la Legion d'Honneur*
Date joined SOE:	3 September 1941
Code names:	Eugène/Prunus/Gerard Henri Perreau
Nationality:	British
Age at time of death:	Twenty-three
Date of birth:	31 July 1921
Place of birth:	Paris, France

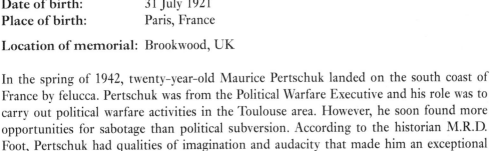

Location of memorial: Brookwood, UK

In the spring of 1942, twenty-year-old Maurice Pertschuk landed on the south coast of France by felucca. Pertschuk was from the Political Warfare Executive and his role was to carry out political warfare activities in the Toulouse area. However, he soon found more opportunities for sabotage than political subversion. According to the historian M.R.D. Foot, Pertschuk had qualities of imagination and audacity that made him an exceptional organiser: 'He was brave and quick-witted as well as diplomatic.' He was soon taken over by SOE and his circuit was named PRUNUS. His wireless operator was Marcus Bloom.

PRUNUS received a number of supply drops and Pertschuk began to prepare for an ambitious attack upon the Toulouse powder explosive factory. The success of this operation led to his award of the MBE. Further attacks were made against telecommunications targets in October 1942 and January 1943 with the help of telephone and telegraph workers that had joined his groups. He also helped protect the Allied escape routes across the Pyrénées. Altogether he built up fifteen Resistance groups.

Pertschuk and Bloom were captured together on 12 April 1943, in the house in which they were staying, the Château d'Equerre, which was surrounded by Germans. They had been betrayed by a sub-agent called Meggle who had been arrested earlier that day.

In January 1944 Pertschuk was transported to Buchenwald concentration camp. Here he used the name Martin Perkins in the hope that with a British-sounding name he might stand a greater chance of survival. The SOE agents were certainly treated better than prisoners in other parts of the camp where, as another agent, Alfred Newton, declared that it was 'impossible to describe the dirt, the muck, and the maddening scenes of brutality'. There were so many prisoners dying, or being killed, that the crematoria could not keep up with the burning of the bodies and often the corpses would simply be thrown out of the blocks into the compound and left to rot on the ground.

After surviving for more than a year in the terrible conditions of Buchenwald, Pertschuk must have thought that he would see the end of the war. But just two weeks before the camp was liberated by American troops, he was located by the SS and hanged.

One of his co-prisoners, Christopher Burney, dedicated his book *Dungeon Democracy* to his friend: 'To the memory of Maurice Pertschuk, hanged in Buchenwald crematorium on March 29, 1945, who fought more gallantly than any of us and died more sadly.'

PICHL, Otto

Date of death:	31 August 1944
Place of death:	Ústí nad Labem (Aussig an der Elbe), Czech Republic
Rank:	Lieutenant
Parent unit:	General List
Service number:	318482
Decorations:	None recorded
Date joined SOE:	24 January 1944
Code names:	Paul Dunsch/Paul Presisinger
Nationality:	Czechoslovakian
Age at time of death:	Forty-seven
Date of birth:	20 November 1896
Place of birth:	Neusattel, Bohemia
Location of memorial:	Brookwood, UK

A former District Secretary of the Sudeten Social Democratic Party, Otto Pichl was a Sudeten German with a Czech passport. At the age of eighteen, Pichl was conscripted into the Austrian Army and served on the Russian front. He was wounded on 6 October 1915. After recovering from his wounds he was sent to the Italian front where he was wounded yet again. At the end of the war he served in the Czech Army for fourteen weeks before being placed on the reserve list. He undertook further reserve training in 1924. He found work as a miner and a glass-blower.

Over the following years, Pichl became actively involved in politics until the German occupation of the Sudetenland in 1938. He moved to Denmark (via Poland), eventually ending up in Sweden working in a glass-blowing factory.

Pichl travelled from Stockholm to the UK on 7 January 1944, to undergo 'special' training. Though he had trouble with map reading and understanding Morse, Pichl was 'good and keen on demolitions' and his energy and motivation, despite his age, was described as being 100 percent. Certainly he made his strong anti-Fascist views plain and was described as being 'fanatically and lyrically democratic in his outlook'.

For his mission Pichl was to be sent into his home district (Bodenbach and Graslitz) of what was at that time Eastern Germany as a political organiser with the intention of forming anti-Nazi cells to conduct sabotage and propaganda work. He was to maintain contact with London by coded letter. He was also to find safe houses where the partisans could meet and hide. His cover was to be that of a war-worker, probably a miner.

On 1 May 1944, his training having finished, Pichl was commissioned as a second lieutenant in the British Army and along with Ernst Hoffman (see previous entry) he was infiltrated into eastern Germany, by parachute, on 9 May 1944. Little is known of their mission but it was soon learnt that both of them were dead. It is understood that Hoffman was shot by the Gestapo and that Pichl committed suicide rather than face capture. He was last seen alive at Graslitz. His body was found at Aussig an der Elbe (now Ústí nad Labem).

It is believed that Pichl had swallowed one of the cyanide tablets with which he had been issued. Next to his body was a note that read: 'I have Jacksch's mission [?]. Long live freedom!' He was buried by the Germans without being identified.

PICKERSGILL, Frank Herbert Dedrick

Date of death:	On or after 14 September 1944
Place of death:	Buchenwald, Germany
Rank:	Captain
Parent unit:	Canadian Intelligence Corps
Service number:	Not recorded
Decorations:	Mentioned in Despatches, *Chevalier de la Legion d'Honneur*, *Croix de Guerre*
Date joined SOE:	9 November 1942
Code names:	Bertrand/Archdeacon/ François Marie Picard
Nationality:	Canadian
Age at time of death:	Twenty-six
Date of birth:	28 May 1918
Place of birth:	Winnipeg, Manitoba, Canada
Location of memorial:	Groesbeek, Netherlands

The Canadian, Frank Pickersgill, who, according to the SOE agent Wing Commander Forest Frederick Edward Yeo-Thomas could barely complete a sentence in French, was sent into France on 15 June 1943. He was selected to act as organiser for the ARCHDEACON circuit in the Ardennes, a sub-circuit of PHYSICIAN.

Some idea of the scope of the proposed operation can be gauged by the targets that he was given, some of which were beyond the Ardennes – the railway lines leading from Bazancourt and Pont Maudit; the engine sheds, marshalling yards and wagon works at Mohon and Lunes; and the textile works at Sedan.

Pickersgill's career, unfortunately, was all too brief. He was arrested just three days after his arrival in France along with another Canadian agent John Macalister (see previous entry) who was to be his radio operator. They were being driven to Paris by Yvonne Ruddelat and a local resister, Pierre Culioli, when they were stopped by the SD at Dhuizon. A search found two of the latest SOE miniature radio receiving sets. The two Canadians were arrested and beaten throughout the night by men under the command of SS *Sturmführer* Ludwig Bauer.

They were taken to the Gestapo headquarters at Blois and later on to Frèsnes prison – Pickersgill's name was subsequently found inscribed on a wall at Frèsnes along with the date 26.6.43. He spent more than a year at Frèsnes, where he was very badly treated. 'He showed great courage and self-sacrifice in refusing to divulge, under torture, the names of his accomplices,' Major-General Gubbins wrote in September 1945 when recommending Pickersgill for a posthumous Mention in Despatches. He was then removed to 3 bis Place des États Unis.

On 18 April 1944, Pickersgill was sent to Ravitsch on the Polish-Silesian border, north-east of Breslau (now Wrocław). A month later he was flown back to Paris with a number of others and taken to Avenue Foch. By then he was in very poor physical condition.

Here he was subject to further interrogations. During one of these sessions he grabbed a bottle, broke the neck and stabbed it into the neck of an SS guard, severing the man's jugular vein. Pickersgill leapt from the second-floor window and was making off down the avenue towards the Bois de Boulogne when he was brought down by a hail of bullets. Pickersgill was hit twice; he had also broken his arm when he jumped down from the window. The SS guard died.

Pickersgill was taken to La Petit hospital where he received an injection. Exactly what he was injected with is not clear but it is said that after receiving the injection he 'may' have talked. Not every source supports this view. Oddly, Baker Street only became aware that Pickersgill had been arrested in June 1944 as the pre-prepared 'good news letters' had continued to be sent to his relatives by the SOE staff. When his brother was finally informed of Pickersgill's incarceration he was warned that 'he must not attempt to send any message to his brother, or institute any enquiries, that might draw the particular attention of the German authorities to his brother's case'.

Nevertheless, Frank Pickersgill was driven to Buchenwald in August 1944. Little more than a fortnight after his arrival at the concentration camp he was summarily executed, one of thirty-five men killed that day. Though there are conflicting reports about how the men died, it is often stated that the men were hung on meat hooks and strangled with piano wire.

Frank Pickersgill was the younger brother of John Whitney 'Jack' Pickersgill, PC, CC, a post-war MP and Cabinet Minister in the Canadian House of Commons.

PLEWMAN, Eliane Sophie

Date of death:	13 September 1944
Place of death:	Dachau, Germany
Rank:	Ensign
Parent unit:	Women's Transport Service (FANY)
Service number:	F/23
Decorations:	*Croix de Guerre avec étoile de vermeil*
Date joined SOE:	25 February 1943
Code names:	Gaby/Dean/Eliane J. Prunier
Nationality:	French
Age at time of death:	Twenty-six

Date of birth: 6 December 1917
Place of birth: Marseilles, France

Location of memorial: Brookwood, UK

Eliane Browne-Bartroli was born in Marseilles in 1917. Her father was English but her mother was Spanish and Eliane was educated in both England and Spain. After college Eliane went to work in an importing company in Leicester.

After the outbreak of the Second World War, Eliane worked for the British Embassies in Madrid and Lisbon. In 1942 she returned to Britain to work for the Spanish Section of the Ministry of Information. That same summer she married British Army officer Tom Plewman.

Now Eliane Plewman, she joined the SOE later that year and was parachuted into France on the night of 13/14 August 1943, near Lons-le-Saunier. Described by M.R.D. Foot as being 'conspicuously attractive' Plewman was a courier for Charles Skepper's MONK circuit, which operated around Marseilles. One of her main tasks was to maintain communications between Skepper in Marseilles and fellow agent Arthur Steele (see separate entry) who transmitted from locations outside the city.

In the spring of 1944 a Frenchman in the pay of the Gestapo, Jean Bousquet, infiltrated the circuit. The intelligence he provided ultimately led to the capture of Skepper. Hearing that there had been a German raid at Skepper's residence, Plewman and Steele made their way there to see if they could help. When they arrived they found the entrance to the flat guarded by two Germans. Believing that Skepper was still in the apartment the two agents, Plewman with a pistol in her hand, tried to force their way in to rescue their comrade. They were both overwhelmed and captured.

Eliane Plewman was interrogated by the Gestapo in March 1944 before being taken with seven other female SOE agents to Karlsruhe prison in May the same year. Amongst those agents sent to Karlsruhe were Andrée Borrel, Vera Leigh, Diana Rowden, Yolande Beekman (real name Yolande Unternahrer), Noor Inayat-Khan and Madeleine Damerment. It is known that Plewman occupied cell number 16 as she use to tap Morse messages to the occupant of cell 17, a German political prisoner who survived the war.

On 11 September the Karlsruhe Gestapo took Plewman, Beekman, Inayat-Khan and Damerment to Dachau, where Inayat-Khan was separated from the others. According to the information given to a Lieutenant-Colonel H. J. Wickey who was the Officer Commanding Canadian Intelligence and Military Governor of Wuppertal-Eberfeld after the war, the remaining three women were 'handled very roughly, one of them had her face slapped several times; they were all kicked several times'.

Eliane Plewman was executed by a single shot in the back of the head just a few hours after her arrival at the concentration camp.

The traitor Bousquet was found after the war by French intelligence officers in the US zone of Germany, working for the Americans. He was taken to Marseilles, tried and executed.

PRASSINOS, Mario Lambros Achilles

Date of death:	4 March 1945
Place of death:	Schwerin, Germany
Rank:	Lieutenant
Parenet unit:	General List
Service number:	294435
Decorations:	OBE
Date joined SOE:	Not recorded
Code names:	Captain Forbes
Nationality:	Greek
Age at time of death:	Forty-seven
Date of birth:	1898
Place of birth:	Egypt

Location of memorial: Brookwood, UK

One of the most famous of the Allied escape and evasion lines established in France during the Second World War was the so-called 'Pat-Line'. Based in the southern French port of Marseilles, the organisation had been named after one its founders, Belgian Major-General Comte Albert-Marie Edmond Guérisse GC, KBE, DSO, who operated under the nom de guerre of Patrick Albert 'Pat' O'Leary, the name of a Canadian friend.

Mario Prassinos was one of those who became involved in the Pat-Line at an early stage. A Greek citizen, Prassinos had married a French woman, Marguerite, and the couple chose to settle in her home town. Through his involvement in the Pat-Line, much of Prassinos' early work in the war had been under the auspices of the MI9 – the Directorate of Military Intelligence's department charged with aiding Resistance organisations in the occupied countries, particularly in respect of escape and evasion.

Initially the Pat-Line helped men left behind after Dunkirk, though it later assisted many Allied airman escape the clutches of the Germans and Vichy French. Those involved in the organisation, including, amongst others, the Australian Bruce Dowding, continually received, examined, equipped and prepared the escapers and evaders for their return to Britain, usually by crossing over the Pyrénées or by submarine off the coast.

The first British officer to make a 'home run' after an escape from Colditz in the Second World War, army officer and future MP Airey Neave DSO, OBE, MC, recalled meeting Mario Prassinos for the first time during his journey along the Pat-Line: '... A short, middle-aged man in the smartest business clothes, carrying a black hat and cane, like a character from some pre-war film set on the French Riviera, entered ... and introduced himself with care and elegance.'

At one point, Prassinos, described as a *Convoyeur* in the Marseille network, was almost caught by the Vichy *gendarmerie* whilst recovering parachute containers from a supply drop. Whilst the two men he was with were caught, Prassinos slipped through the net and escaped back to Marseilles.

By the end of 1942, his work in the then unoccupied part of France had not gone unnoticed by the Vichy authorities, and Prassinos was forced to leave France. Like so many of those he had previously helped, his journey would take him over the Pyrénées into Spain.

On 13 December 1942, the group he was to travel with gathered at an address in Toulouse. The unlikely collection of travelling companions, seven in number, included two American pilots from 133 (Eagle) Squadron RAF. Led by their guide, Paul Ulmann, the group journeyed to Perpignan by train, continuing from there along the branch line to Céret. Before they reached the station here, all eight men jumped from the train and set off into the foothills of the Pyrénées.

After the first night, it soon became apparent that things were not going according to plan. Ulmann was missing, and one of the evaders had set off alone, never to be seen again. Prassinos had also injured his leg and was in no condition to continue at the same pace as the others. As a result, one party went on ahead, leaving Prassinos to struggle on in the company of Sergeant Ralph Forster RAF and one of the Americans, Flying Officer Eric Doorly.

The three men eventually crossed the border into Spain near the village of Espolla, in Catalonia. Here, they were turned back by the Spanish Police who hinted that they could try and enter Spain again if they did so in an 'orthodox manner'. Exceedingly cold and hungry, the three men spent the night in the mountains in an isolated barn on the French side of the border. The next morning, 15 December 1942, they headed to the custom's post in the village of Rabós where they were finally permitted entry.

Initially arrested and imprisoned, Forster was able to persuade the Spanish authorities that all three men 'were genuine service evaders'. Prassinos, for his part, had made the journey under the alias 'Captain Forbes'. Seen by a representative from the British Consulate at Barcelona on 30 January 1943, Prassinos was freed on 2 February – two days before his companions. He soon reached the United Kingdom.

Once in Britain, Prassinos switched allegiance from MI9 and was recruited by the SOE. After he had completed his training he returned to France, eventually being captured by the Germans. It has not been possible to establish the date and circumstances of his arrest.

Prassinos died of typhus at the SS penalty (or punishment) camp near Schwerin some 50 miles east of Hamburg. In March and April 1945, the camp at Schwerin was used as a reception centre for increasing numbers of concentration camp prisoners – a situation that led to a Typhoid-epidemic in the area. These unfortunate individuals, from locations such as Sachsenhausen and Ravensbrück, had been ordered out of the camps in the face of the advancing Soviet forces and sent west on a number of forced marches. It is not known if Prassinos had been held at another camp prior to his arrival at Schwerin.

Prassinos was once described by Pat O'Leary as 'the bravest man I ever knew'. On the same day that Mario Prassinos's widow accepted his posthumous OBE, his co-worker on the Pat-Line, Louis Nouveau (who had survived incarceration in Buchenwald), was decorated with the George Medal by King George VI.

RABINOVITCH, Adolphe

Date of death:	2/3 March 1944
Place of death:	Gross-Rosen, Poland
Rank:	Captain
Parent unit:	General List
Service number:	234268
Decorations:	Mentioned in Despatches, *Croix de Guerre avec Étoile de Vermeil*
Date joined SOE:	11 February 1942
Code names:	Arnaud/Aatalpha/Guy Dieudonne/Denis Joseph Rocher/Achilie Richards
Nationality:	Naturalised Egyptian
Age at time of death:	Twenty-five
Date of birth:	27 May 1918
Place of birth:	Moscow, Russia

Location of memorial: Brookwood, UK

Described as a 'giant of a man', 'Alex' Rabinovitch, the son of a Jewish-Russian family, had grown up in Egypt. Having also studied in Paris, been a junior wrestling and boxing champion, Rabinovitch settled in the United States of America before the Second World War.

In 1939 he volunteered for service in the French Foreign Legion, but was taken prisoner by the Germans in June 1940. Three months later he escaped but was not pursued by the Germans as he was formally demobbed on 22 October 1940. He escaped to Britain through Spain in September 1941, joining the SOE in February 1942.

At the end of his training, Rabinovitch was described by his instructor as 'an enigma' – he was apparently seen as being argumentative with no sense of humour. However, he was a trained soldier with experience of guerrilla warfare and it was acknowledged that he had a fine brain and was highly educated.

As a trained wireless operator, twenty-four-year-old Rabinovitch was parachuted into France, to the north of Grenoble, on the night of 27/28 August 1942. His instructions were to make his way to Paris. However, the pilot of the RAF Hudson missed the intended drop zone and Rabinovitch found himself entirely alone.

Not knowing where he was, he set off south – in the wrong direction – and was extremely fortunate to be picked up by a sub-agent of the CARTE group and was taken to Cannes. As a much-sought-after wireless operator, he proved extremely valuable and organiser Peter Churchill gained permission from Baker Street to keep him down in the South of France.

When the Germans moved into the unoccupied zone of France in November 1942 a great many members of the Resistance movement were rounded up. Churchill, for example, was in Paris when he learnt that his flat in Cannes had been raided by the Germans and some of his friends arrested. He managed to get a message through to Rabinovitch who joined Churchill at his new base in a little village in the mountains of the Haute-Savoie called Saint-Jorioz. Rabinovitch set up his radio at a nearby village of Faverges. At this point Churchill and Rabinovitch changed their identities, with Rabinovitch becoming Guy Dieudonne. Their circuit was SPINDLE.

Secure in its mountain retreat, Churchill's group set up some forty drop zones, each with a well-organised reception committee. At the same time, contact was re-established with the PROSPER network in Paris. All was going well until André Marsac, one of the PROSPER agents, was captured by the Germans and tricked into helping them.

In the unfolding disaster that followed, numerous arrests were made. Somehow, Rabinovitch remained free and along with Victor Hazan (codename *Gervais*), he got back in contact with the networks around Annecy and on the Côte d'Azur and was eventually able to escape back to Britain via Spain.

Undeterred, on his second mission Rabinovitch (who had by this time had been promoted from lieutenant to captain) was dropped into France, on 2 March 1944, with Roger Sabourin. His mission was to start a new circuit (BARGEE) at Nancy. The reception by the ARCHDEACON circuit was in fact organised by the Gestapo and both men were wounded when they tried to run from the Germans' reception committee. They were captured after attempting to escape through the surrounding woods.

Peter Churchill DSO, *Croix de Guerre*, dedicated his book *Duel of Wits* to his 'beloved' Arnaud, 'a violent, difficult and heroic radio operator, and through him to all underground men and women of his supreme calibre who died, as they lived, in solitude.'

RAFFERTY, Brian Dominic

Date of death:	29 March 1945
Place of death:	Flossenbürg, Germany
Rank:	Captain
Parent unit:	Royal Berkshire Regiment
Service number:	129641
Decorations:	Military Cross, *Croix de Guerre avec Etoile de Vermeil*
Date joined SOE:	3 March 1943
Code names:	Dominique/Aubretia/Bertrand Dominic Remy/Michel Dominic
Nationality:	British
Age at time of death:	Twenty-five
Date of birth:	1 September 1919
Place of birth:	Hull, UK

Location of memorial: Brookwood, UK

Brian Rafferty, a Christ Church undergraduate who had been earmarked for a career in the Consular Service, was sent to help run a circuit in the Bourbonnaise not far from Vichy, in the then unoccupied zone. He dropped on 24 September 1942, with Christian Hudson, the circuit organiser, and George Jones, the wireless operator. Rafferty was to be in charge of receptions and training. Upon landing it was found that one of the suitcases, which held Rafferty's and Hudson's documents, was missing. The suitcase eventually fell into the hands of the French police and Hudson was soon arrested.

With the arrest of Hudson, Rafferty took control of the HEADMASTER 1 circuit. As well as sabotage, the main objective of the circuit was the accumulation of large stocks of equipment in the Massif Central in preparation for operations on D-Day.

Of Irish descent, Rafferty had, according to M.R.D. Foot, all the charm, vivacity and most importantly, all the fighting spirit of his race, and his group achieved a notable success when they burnt 300 tons of tyres at the Michelin factory at Clermont-Ferrand at a time when Germany's rubber shortage was particularly acute. Yet it was this natural exuberance that ultimately led to his downfall.

On 6 June 1943, Rafferty and Jones had been at a meeting in a café on the outskirts of Clermont-Ferrand to organise the escape of a Commandant Bourgeois who was in a nearby prison. There was also a supply drop planned for that night and, as Rafferty was leaving, he was heard to remark, 'Yes, it's a fine moonlight night, we shall have great fun.' Unbeknown to the SOE men, a waiter in the café who overheard this flippant remark was a German informant.

Rafferty and Jones were followed by the Gestapo and arrested that night on their way to the reception area. Jones managed to escape but Rafferty was not so fortunate.

Rafferty was taken to Dijon prison where he managed to conceal his true identity for many weeks, despite being brutally tortured, thus giving his comrades chance to get away. Rafferty behaved with 'exemplary courage' and revealed nothing – even though it was reported that he had his arm broken and that he was 'unrecognisably bruised and in a lamentable condition'.

When the Germans eventually discovered that he was a British agent Rafferty was sent to Frèsnes. He was taken to Flossenbürg on 9 April 1944, where he was treated reasonably well and, along with other agents there, was not expected to work as the other prisoners were. Their morale therefore remained high and they were hopeful of being liberated by the advancing Allied armies. Then, on 28 March 1945, an order was received from Berlin to execute some of the prisoners and remove the rest to a camp further inland. The SOE agents were those that were executed. This was accomplished by hanging during the course of the night.

Because Rafferty had given nothing away under torture his group survived more or less intact and it went on to be highly successful during the liberation of France. As Buckmaster later wrote, Rafferty was immensely popular in France, where his personal charm was greatly loved. 'Rather inclined to act the wild Irishman ... He did a good, if unorthodox, job.'

RECHENMANN, Charles Théophile

Date of death:	14 September 1944
Place of death:	Buchenwald, Germany
Rank:	Captain
Parent unit:	General List
Service number:	309474
Decorations:	MBE , *Croix de Guerre*
Date joined SOE:	23 November 1943
Code names:	Julien/Rover/Claude Roland
Nationality:	French
Age at time of death:	Thirty-two
Date of birth:	24 August 1912
Place of birth:	Saint-Louis, Moselle, France

Location of memorial: Brookwood, UK

An engineer working in Paris in an electrical instrument manufacturing company until the outbreak of war, Charles Rechenmann was taken prisoner by the Germans during the fall of France. He was released in August 1940 on the proviso that he remained in Germany or in Lorraine.

However, as soon as he was released he made an unsuccessful attempt to make his way to the UK via the Pyrénées and Spain. Following this he started working with the Resistance in June 1941. Early in 1942 he was contacted by an SOE officer, Captain Ben Cowburn, and together they built up an effective circuit in the area around the town of Tarbes in the Hautes-Pyrénées department in south-western France.

In December 1942 Rechenmann again tried to get to Britain but he was arrested and interrogated by the *Feldgendarmerie* and the Gestapo. Again he was released, maintaining that he was merely going on holiday. Cowburn, meanwhile, had gone back to the UK, returning on 11 April to establish the TINKER circuit round Troyes. For this work, Cowburn intended to make use of Rechenmann's services. The latter's role in TINKER was to organise railway sabotage groups for action on D-Day and to plan industrial sabotage when the opportunity arose. In addition, he had to arrange his own reception facilities for parachute drops.

Hunted by the Gestapo, Rechenmann left France in November 1943 by Hudson (it is believed that one of the other passengers on the flight, a member of the Resistance, was the future French President François Mitterrand). In the UK he undertook 'revisionary' training with an emphasis on sabotage. As he had been working in the field for some time he was treated with respect by the SOE trainers who had nothing but praise for his efforts. He became a proficient wireless operator. 'Very keen hard worker ... active and intelligent ... very keen ... worked hard,' were the kinds of phrases used by all of those that came into contact with him at the Special Training Schools. Buchmaster described him as 'courageous and gallant'.

Rechenmann returned to France by sea on Wednesday, 21 March 1944. This time his mission was to start the ROVER circuit amongst his friends in and around Tarbes. Instead of using a false identity as agents generally did, he actually operated under his own true name (though later he did return to using a cover name for security reasons).

The objectives he had been set were to sabotage factories and railroads in the Tarbes region and on 23 March 1944, he organised and led an attack on the Hispano Suiza works at Tarbes. The attack was successful and the factory was completely 'immobilised'. It is said that the ROVER circuit also sabotaged other local factories and a weapons or munitions store in the Hautes-Pyrénées.

On 12 May the same year, Rechenmann had a meeting with a sub-agent called Rene Bochereau at the Cheval de Bronze café in Angoulême. They were both sitting there when they were suddenly surrounded by seven Gestapo men with drawn weapons. Some accounts state that it may have been the case that Bochereau, having been bribed by the Gestapo, had drawn him into a trap.

Rechenann was initially taken to Angoulême prison and from there to Frèsnes. He was still at Frèsnes on 6 August 1944 (his wife received a letter from him on that day asking her to send him some clothes). Very soon after this he was deported to Buchenwald where he was executed later that same month.

REIK, Chaviva

Date of death:	20 November 1944
Place of death:	Banská Bystrica, Slovakia
Rank:	Sergeant
Parent unit:	Women's Auxiliary Air Force
Service number:	2992503
Decorations:	None Recorded
Date joined SOE:	1943
Code names:	Ada Robinson/Martha Martinovic
Nationality:	Slovakian
Age at time of death:	Thirty
Date of birth:	1914
Place of birth:	Nadabula, Slovakia

Location of memorial: Jerusalem, Israel

Born Marta Reik (or possibly Emma Reik) in the Slovakian village of Nadabula, this future SOE agent grew up in Banská Bystrica in the Carpathian Mountains. In 1939 she emigrated to Palestine, later joining the Palmach, which was the elite strike force branch of the Haganah, the Jewish underground paramilitary organisation.

The SOE approached the Palmach in 1943 to enquire whether it would supply people with the right qualities for special operations and with a prior knowledge of Central Europe. The call was open to women as well as men. Reik was one of the young women accepted.

She joined the Women's Auxiliary Air Force as Ada Robinson. After training, Reik (whose first name is also referred to as Haviva) and three others, including Stephan Reiss (see next entry), were due to be parachuted into Slovakia from Bari in Italy. For reasons that are not entirely clear Reik, being a woman, was not permitted to go on this mission.

It was not until a week later that she persuaded a group of US pilots who were flying to Banská Bystrica (which had just been liberated from the Germans by Slovakian partisans) to take her along with them. She finally met up with the other three members of her group on 21 September 1944. At the end of the month, a fifth parachutist, Abba Berdiczew, joined them, bringing radio equipment.

In Banská Bystrica, Reik and the others engaged in relief and rescue activities, particularly helping recover Allied POWs. Late in September the Germans moved to suppress the partisan rebellion, re-taking Banská Bystrica on 27 October.

Reik and the others escaped with about forty Jewish partisans. They established an armed camp in the mountains, but they were captured after a few days by Ukrainian *Waffen* SS troops of the Galicia Division.

On 20 November 1944, the Germans shot most of the captive Jews, including Reik and Reiss, the rest being transported to Mauthausen.

On 10 September 1952, Chaviva Reik's remains were exhumed and taken to Israel where they were reburied in Mount Herzl military cemetery in Jerusalem (along with those of Reiss and Hannah Szenes). In memory of her sacrifice the Kibbutz Lehavot Haviva, the Givat Haviva institute, and numerous streets in Israel are named after Haviva Reik.

REISZ (REISS), Stephan Rafael

Date of death:	20 November 1944
Place of death:	Banská Bystrica, Slovakia
Rank:	Sergeant
Parent unit:	159 G.H.Q. (Middle East) Royal Air Force Volunteer Reserve
Service number:	769472
Decorations:	None recorded
Date joiend SOE:	1943
Code names:	Stephen Rice
Nationality:	Slovakian
Age at time of death:	Thirty
Date of birth:	1914
Place of birth:	

Location of memorial: Jerusalem, Israel

Of Jewish extraction, Stephan Reiss served with the SOE as Stephen Rice. Like Chaviva Reik he joined the Palmach and volunteered to be part of its new parachute unit. His opportunity for action against the pro-German government in Slovakia came following an uprising by dissident groups headed by the Agrarian party and the Slovak Communists. These groups formed themselves into a single body to consolidate their opposition. This was the Slovenska Narodna Rada (SNR) or Slovak National Council. Its objective was to overthrow the government and detach Slovakia from the Axis.

The revolt against the puppet regime of the Slovak People's Party took shape in December 1943. Reiss and his comrades were sent to contact this group at Banská Bystrica in September 1944.

Over 2,000 Jews fought in the uprising, and about 500 fell in battle. The uprising was timed to coincide with Allied advances, particularly those of the Soviet Army. However, the Red Army held back. Nevertheless the partisans made considerable gains, and on 28 August the Germans decided to occupy Slovakia and eliminate the uprising.

As part of this offensive, on 27 October 1944, the Germans occupied Banská Bystrica. Reiss and the other parachutists escaped with about forty Jewish partisans. They built a camp in the mountains, but they were captured after a few days. On November 20 the Germans shot most of the Jews that they had captured, including Reiss.

His remains were also recovered in 1952 and reburied in the Mount Herzl military cemetery in Jerusalem.

RENAUD, Jean

Date of death:	After 10 June 1944	
Place of death:	Pierrefitte-en-Cinglais, France	

Rank:	Lieutenant
Parent unit:	General List
Service number:	325124
Decorations:	Military Cross, *Croix de Guerre*, *Chevalier de la Legion d'Honneur*, *Médaille de la Résistance Française*

Date joined SOE:	2 June 1944
Code names:	Jean/John Fox

Nationality:	French
Age at time of death:	Forty-one
Date of birth:	4 December 1903
Place of birth:	Cluny, Saône-et-Loire, France

Location of memorial: Brookwood, UK

From almost as soon as the Germans occupied France in 1940, Jean Renaud was active in the Resistance movement in the region around the Saône-et-Loire. In 1942 he set up his own group in the Cluny area where he and his family lived.

In August 1943 he was arrested by the Gestapo for distributing anti-German leaflets and was sentenced to three months imprisonment in a concentration camp. Following his release, in the autumn of 1943, he was joined by Albert Browne-Bartroli who formalised the group under the auspices of the SOE as the DITCHER circuit. Renaud took on the role of Browne-Bartroli's lieutenant.

From January 1944 Renaud was again being hunted by the Gestapo; the following month Renaud went to Britain to be fully indoctrinated into the SOE, returning to France in the same month. It was at that time that Renaud's wife was arrested by the Germans and was transported to a concentration camp in Germany. The Renaud's three children were also arrested.

It was largely through Renaud's efforts over a long period of time that the resistance groups in the Cluny region were turned into a highly effective force, initially in sabotage operations and, after D-Day, as strong fighting units. He organised more than 100 supply drops and trained the local groups.

In his SOE personal file it is recorded that on 11 June 1944, he led a party against a German post, drawing the enemy's fire upon himself to allow the others in the party to overrun the position. The following day he was again in command of a group that conducted a successful attack upon a German convoy. In both these operations 'much booty' was seized and several prisoners taken.

Shortly after this he was surprised by the Germans at Cluny station where he was unloading food seized from the Germans that was being 'diverted' to the Resistance. He was shot in the leg, which was broken, as he tried to run away. Renaud was, of course, well known to the Germans and he was very severely tortured by them. It is thought that because of his past record he would have been shot by the Gestapo soon after they had finished torturing him, whereas Buckmaster believed that Renaud had been transported to Germany before he died but there is no evidence for this. All that can be stated for certain is that he died whilst in the hands of the Gestapo. That said, the date of his death given by the Commonwealth War Graves Commission of 10 June 1944, does not correspond to the details in his file.

After the war Browne-Bartroli said this about his colleague: 'Jean Renard [*sic*] worked with me from the very first day [October 1943] in organising and caring for the *maquis* of Cluny. This most honest and un-ambitious man never stopped a minute fighting in every possible way against the Germans ... When people were talking of resistance in Cluny, they were thinking of Jean Renard.'

It was because of Renaud's 'magnificent services to the Allied cause and his great courage and self-sacrifice and devotion to duty' that Buckmaster recommended Renaud for the Military Cross.

Jean Renaud's wife survived the war and returned to France.

RENAUD-DANDICOLLE, Jean Marie

Date of death:	17 July 1944
Place of death:	St Clair, France
Rank:	Captain
Parent unit:	General List
Service number:	297762
Decorations:	Military Cross, *Croix de Guerre, Chevalier de la Legion d'Honneur, Médaille de la Résistance Française*
Date joined SOE:	1 September 1943
Code names:	Rene/Verger/Jean Marie Demirmont/John Danby
Nationality:	French
Age at time of death:	Twenty

Date of birth: 8 November 1923
Place of birth: Bordeaux, France

Location of memorial: Bayeux, France

Still a student at the time of the fall of France in 1940, Jean Renaud-Dandicolle graduated as a lawyer in Bordeaux on 11 July 1942. Despite this achievement, he had joined the French Resistance in the early part of that year. By 1943 he had become the assistant of a British SOE organiser in the south-west of France. By August 1943 his work or presence had not gone unnoticed and he was being sought by the Gestapo. His only option was to escape to Britain – he flew out in a Lysander from a field near Villefranche-sur-Saône on the night of 19/20 August.

Once in Britain, Renaud-Dandicolle was quickly put into training for a rapid return to France. He was trained specifically in how to attack railways and rolling stock, including engine sheds and wagon sidings. Though his assessor noted that Renaud-Dandicolle was 'very intelligent, keen and enterprising' he lamented the fact that there had not been sufficient time to train him fully.

After training, Renaud-Dandicolle was commissioned as Captain John Danby and sent back into France, this time to Normandy, on 28 January 1944. His personal file details some of his achievements:

'On one occasion, pursued by the Gestapo, he led to safety two W/T operators and their sets, saved the major part of the parachuted material, and destroyed what could not be moved, to prevent it falling into enemy hands.

'On the eve of D-Day Capt. Danby organised a successful reception [of air-dropped supplies] 600 yards from a German watch post. On another occasion, surrounded by a German patrol with forty of his men, he kept the enemy at bay for forty-eight hours, and made a completely successful withdrawal, taking the wounded with him.

'After D-Day he carried out harassing activities against the enemy, and inspired his men by his fearless leadership in every attack.'

Renaud-Dandicolle's capture by the Germans was an unfortunate affair. Along with a fellow Resistance member, Maurice Larcher, and a Canadian airman evader, Flight Lieutenant Henry Cleary, Renaud-Dandicolle was staying in a farmhouse at Saint Clair near Pierrefitte-en-Cinglais, Calvados. Sadly, a neighbour held a grudge against the owners of the farm, Georges and Eugenia Grosclaude, and it is believed that this man had informed the Gestapo of suspicious goings-on at the house.

On 10 July 1944, a German officer and an NCO of the SS Panzer-Division *Leibstandarte Adolf Hitler* visited the house under the pretext of wishing to commandeer a room. They asked to be shown round the building. A subsequent account of what happened next states that Renaud-Dandicolle, 'seeing that they were making for the room containing arms, shot and killed the officer, but the NCO managed to get away and raise the alarm. More Germans came and a fight ensued.'

Larcher killed one of the Germans with a knife but he himself was killed. In one of the reports it is stated that Renaud-Dandicolle killed three German officers before he was finally disarmed. Incredibly, Renaud-Dandicolle then managed to escape after 'fighting bare-fisted with the sentry guarding him' but he was pursued and shot in the jaw. He was finally taken prisoner only after he had fallen exhausted by the roadside. That was the last that any of the group ever saw of Renaud-Dandicolle.

It is thought that he was shot in the vicinity of his arrest and buried close by. Having lost both their leaders, the circuit members went into hiding until the arrival of the Allied forces a few weeks later. The Germans burnt down the farmhouse.

Renaud-Dandicolle's organiser, Major de Baissac DSO, submitted the following report: 'I want to place on record that he was a perfect lieutenant, and that without his assistance I should not have been able to achieve my mission or organise my circuit.

'I hope that in any case, alive or dead, a suitable reward for his bravery and competence will be given to him, as he was undoubtedly one of the best men as well as one of the most capable agents I have ever come across.'

Renaud-Dandicolle was awarded the Military Cross. A memorial, built from stones recovered from the destroyed farmhouse, was erected in 1946 at St Clair in memory of the three men.

ROBERTS, Sidney George

Date of death:	22 December 1943
Place of death:	Albania
Rank:	Corporal
Parent unit:	Durham Light Infantry
Service number:	5443791
Decorations:	Military Medal
Date joined SOE:	1943
Code names:	None recorded
Nationality:	British
Age at time of death:	Twenty-nine
Date of birth:	3 October 1914
Place of birth:	Plymouth, UK
Location of memorial:	Tirana, Albania

Sidney Roberts was sent into Albania on 17 July 1943, as Major Peter Kempt's wireless operator. Kempt described Roberts as 'a quiet young man, brave and intelligent.'

In the engagement with the Germans near Petrela in which Arthur Hill was killed (see previous entry) Roberts, Major George Seymour and Sergeant James Smith escaped. They were ambushed again by the Germans. Seymour and Smith got away but Roberts was captured.

Roberts did not stay a prisoner for long. When he was captured he had managed to keep his pistol hidden from the Germans. He waited for his moment and then pulled out his gun, shot one of the guards and pushed another over a cliff. He then jumped over the cliff and managed to escape.

Roberts went on the run but he had damaged his leg when he jumped from the cliff. He was eventually found in the care of a partisan in November 1943 but he was in a terrible condition due to exposure, lack of food and a 'violent' attack of dysentery. He died of pneumonia on 22 December 1943.

By the end of the war the Communists had gained control of most of Albania thanks entirely to arms sent to them by the SOE.

ROCKINGHAM, David William

Date of death:	20 October 1943
Place of death:	Tragjas, Albania

Rank:	Signalman
Parent unit:	Royal Corps of Signals
Service number:	2390796
Decorations:	None recorded

Date joined SOE:	30 July 1943
Code names:	None recorded

Nationality:	British
Age at time of death:	Twenty-one
Date of birth:	27 July 1922
Place of birth:	London, UK

Location of memorial: Tirana, Albania

As the wireless operator for the STORAGE Mission, Rockingham, a former assistant surveyor and estate agent, was sent into Albania on Operation SAPLING 7 on the night of 19/20 October 1943.

The aircraft crashed into the side of Mount Mrite near Tragjas. Everyone on board was killed, including Captain Alfred Careless. Details of the crash are given in the entry relating to Alfred Careless.

ROLFE, Lilian Verna

Date of death:	5 February 1945
Place of death:	Ravensbrück, Germany

Rank:	Section Officer
Parent unit:	Women's Auxiliary Air Force
Service number:	9907
Decorations:	*Croix de Guerre avec Palme*

Date joined SOE:	26 November 1943
Code names:	Nadine/Recluse/Claudine Irene Rodier

Nationality:	British
Age at time of death:	Thirty
Date of birth:	26 April 1914
Place of birth:	Paris, France

Location of memorial: Runnymede, UK

Like so many of the SOE agents, Lilian Rolfe had a complicated background. One of a pair of twin sisters born in Paris of British parents, her family moved to Brazil in the early 1930s.

Lilian Rolfe made her way to Britain in 1943, leaving employment in the British Embassy in Rio de Janeiro, and, fluent in French, she volunteered to join the SOE. She was accepted into the service on 26 November of that year.

Rolfe trained as a wireless operator for the HISTORIAN circuit and duly landed by a Lysander operating from RAF Tangmere on 5 April 1944, near Bléré. Strapped to her body were her tiny transmitter and receiver.

Under her fieldname of Nadine, Rolfe transmitted the messages that enabled substantial quantities of arms to be delivered to the local Resistance groups. She was even engaged in combat with German troops near the small town of Olivet.

Then, quite by chance, Rolfe was arrested on 31 July 1944. The Germans raided a house at Nangis looking for a suspected member of the Resistance. The man they were after was not there but they found a woman lodging in the house whose papers appeared suspect. This woman was taken to the Gestapo headquarters in Orléans where they soon discovered they had caught a much bigger fish than they had imagined – the wireless operator of the local SOE circuit.

As a result, Rolfe was taken to Paris and moved on to Frèsnes prison before being transferred to Ravensbrück concentration camp around 8 August. Also at Ravensbrück were Violette Szabo and Denise Bloch.

The women at Ravensbrück were used as cheap labour in a large textile and leather supply factory that was adjacent to the camp. Many were also sent out to work at such well-known companies as BMW, Heinkel, Krupp and Siemens. These companies were charged an average of six marks per prisoner per day. From this the camp authorities spent less than one mark on food and clothing for each prisoner, producing a handsome profit. The only other expense for the camp authorities was the two marks that it cost to cremate the women after they had been worked to death.

Rolfe, Szabo and Bloch were sent to work in the fields at Torgau where they were involved in a failed escape attempt. Because of this, they were returned to Ravensbrück and sent to the punishment block; here they were given almost no food. They were released on 19 October 1944, and sent to join a working party that was building a new airfield at Königsberg. Here they had to fell trees, pull cartloads of rocks and dig ditches up to their waists in near-freezing water.

The three women agents eventually arrived back at Ravensbrück, their deaths following soon after.

It was not until 13 March 1946, when Ravensbrück's former second in command, SS-*Obersturmführer* Johann Schwarzhüber (who had previously served at Dachau, Sachsenhausen and Auschwitz II, better known as Birkenau), was interviewed by Vera Atkins, by this time Squadron Officer, that the first news concerning the fate of Rolfe, Szabo and Bloch since August 1944 was uncovered.

In his confession, which was repeated in the British Military Court at Hamburg (where sixteen members of staff from Ravensbrück were put on trial between 5 December 1946 and 3 February 1947), Schwarzhüber recalled clearly the killing of the three women, an act that was conducted differently than the usual method of gassing:

'One evening towards 19.00 hours they were called out [of the punishment block] and taken to the courtyard by the crematorium ... Camp *Kommandant* [SS-*Hauptsturmführer* Fritz] Suhren made these arrangements. He read out the order for their shooting ... I accompanied the three women to the crematorium yard. A female camp overseer was also present and sent back when we reached the crematorium. [SS Sergeant] Zappe stood guard over them while they were waiting to be shot.'

One witness described all three women as being 'emaciated, dirty and weak'. Indeed Lilian Rolfe, who had been in hospital before being recalled to Ravensbrück, was so ill and weak by this stage of her captivity that she had to be carried to the yard.

'All three were very brave and I was deeply moved,' added Schwarzhüber. 'Suhren was also impressed by the bearing of these women. He was annoyed that the Gestapo did not themselves carry out these shootings.'

The three SOE women were brought forward individually. Held by an SS corporal known as Schenk, they were shot through the back of the neck by SS-*Scharführer* Schulte, a block leader from the mens' camp, using a small-calibre gun.

The camp doctor, SS-*Sturmbannführer* Trommer, certified the deaths and the clothed bodies were removed singly by internees and stripped of all clothing. After Ravensbrück's dentist, Dr Martin Hellinger, had removed any gold teeth, the bodies of the three women were then cremated.

ROWDEN, Diana Hope

Date of death:	6 July 1944
Place of death:	Natzweiler, France
Rank:	Section Officer
Parent unit:	Women's Auxiliary Air Force
Service number:	4193
Decorations:	Mentioned in Despatches, *Croix de Guerre*
Date joined SOE:	18 March 1943
Code names:	Paulette/Chaplain/Juliette Thérèse Rondeau
Nationality:	British
Age at time of death:	Twenty-nine
Date of birth:	31 January 1915
Place of birth:	London, UK

Location of memorial: Runnymede, UK

Diana Rowden had grown up in the South of France where her father, Major A.C. Rowden, had a villa and a yacht. She was completely bilingual but with a bow in her fair, wavy hair she looked quintessentially English.

Having been educated in Britain, in 1933 Rowden returned to France, enrolled at the Sorbonne, and finally found employment as a journalist in the French capital. Following the outbreak of war in 1939, she volunteered to serve with the French Red Cross, being assigned to the Anglo-American Ambulance Corps.

Unable to escape following the French surrender, Rowden remained in France until the summer of 1941 when she managed to reach Britain via the Pyrénées.

In September 1941 Rowden enlisted in the Women's Auxiliary Air Force, at one point working as Assistant Section Officer for Intelligence Duties in the department of the Chief of Air Staff. In July 1942, she was promoted to Section Officer. In early March 1943, Rowden received an invitation to a preliminary interview with an officer of SOE F Section, and on 18 March began her training.

Rowden's operational service with the organisation started on 16 June 1943, when she was sent to be a courier to Captain John Renshaw Starr's ACROBAT circuit in the Jura area in the east of France. She also helped agent Harry Rée plan an attack on the Peugeot plant at Sochaux, a factory where tank turrets and aircraft engines were manufactured.

However, a month after she arrived, Starr was arrested. Rowden and wireless operator John Young took refuge with a French family in their saw-mill at the village of Clairvaux-les-Lacs, near Lons-le-Saunier. The mill complex comprised an isolated group of houses in the woods. Here, the Janier-Dubry family allowed the two agents to carry on their work and they soon built up a number of strong teams in the area.

They operated successfully until November 1943 when another agent who had been sent from London, André Maugenet, was captured by the Gestapo on his arrival in France. Maugenet, as is documented previously, carried with him a letter from Young's wife to her husband, readily agreed to aid the Germans.

Shortly after his capture a French collaborator put on Maugenet's leather jacket with its fur collar, took his imitation crocodile-skin suitcase containing his personal belongings, a large sum of money and the SOE agents forged identity papers and went alone to the saw-mill. When he had made certain that Young was using the property he returned that evening with three cars packed with twenty members of the *Geheime Feldpolizei*. Young and Rowden were taken away in handcuffs.

The two agents were held at Avenue Foch before being taken to Frèsnes on 5 December 1943. Rowden was removed to Karlsruhe on 5 May 1944. From there she joined Vera Leigh and Andrée Borrel on that fateful journey to Natzweiler-Struthof in July 1944.

When the women arrived at Natzweiler, the camp's SS political officer, Magnus Wochner (who would subsequently be implicated in the murders of fifty Allied POWs following the Great Escape), had objected when told verbally that the women should be executed. This, he remarked, was highly 'unorthodox'. The normal procedure was for execution orders to be received on a secret teleprinter or by a direct letter from Berlin to the *Kommandant*. But it was not out of humanity that Wochner raised his objections, merely because it breached procedure. When he was told by the Karlsruhe Gestapo man that the women's names were not to be entered in any records, the political officer ceased his objections.

Unknown to the girls there were two other SOE agents already in Natzweiler – Brian Stonehouse and Robert Sheppard, both of F Section. Stonehouse saw the women marched down to the crematorium. In civilian life he had been an artist for *Vogue* magazine and he had drawn sketches of them. He portrayed them 'stepping out, looking ahead, holding their heads high as they carried their little cases and packages down the *Lagerstrasse*, almost as if they had come to stay just for the night'.

Indeed, Diana Rowden and the three other girls would have no need for any other belongings. Within four or five hours of their arrival at Natzweiler they were murdered.

The fourth woman killed at Natzweiler was Sonia Olschanezky. A member of a Russian-Jewish family that fled to Paris in the 1930s, she was recruited in the spring of 1942 for the Robin (JUGGLER) sub-circuit of the PROSPER network, where she operated as courier. A former ballet dancer, she was betrayed and arrested in January 1944 when she was meeting what she believed was an agent just arrived from Britain.

Waiting for her instead was the Gestapo. Olschanezky was transported to Karlsruhe and, as we now know, on to Natzweiler. As Sonia Olschanezky was recruited in France and not the UK she was unknown to the British authorities and her name does not feature on the Commonwealth War Graves Commission list of SOE agents, despite considerable efforts to bring her the recognition she unquestionably deserved.

RUDDELAT, Yvonne Claire

Date of death:	23 or 24 April 1945
Place of death:	Bergen-Belsen, Germany
Rank:	Ensign
Parent unit:	Women's Transport Service (FANY)
Service number:	F/2
Decorations:	MBE
Date joined SOE:	1942
Code names:	Jacqueline/Soaptree/Jacqueline Viallet
Nationality:	French
Age at time of death:	Forty-eight
Date of birth:	January 1897
Place of birth:	Maisons-Laffitte, France.

Location of memorial: Brookwood, UK

Yvonne Ruddelat (also spelt Rudelatt) was older than many of the women recruited into the SOE. Born in Maisons-Laffitte, in the north-western suburbs of Paris, the youngest of ten children, she was forty-five years old when she was spotted working as a receptionist in a London hotel. She had left France following the death of her father and difficulties with her mother.

After her training, Ruddelat was infiltrated into southern France via Gibraltar on 30 July 1942, to become the first female SOE agent to be sent abroad. In terrible weather, she landed by small boat on the Riviera coast and travelled to Tours, close to the border of the occupied zone.

In time, Ruddelat travelled north to join the PROSPER circuit in Paris as a courier where her 'air of innocence and anxiety to please', her instructors observed, 'should prove a most valuable cover asset'.

She did indeed prove most valuable as by March 1943 Ruddelat had bicycled hundreds of miles across the Loire region delivering her messages. Her work, Buckmaster later wrote, 'involved widespread travelling and dangerous liaison activity between the various groups of her circuit. She had to pass numerous enemy controls, some on a bicycle with explosives hidden in a basket fixed to the handlebars.'

Ruddelat specialised in organising parachute drops and became something of an expert in sabotage. She took part in the blowing up of the Chaigny power station south of Orléans and was personally responsible for sabotaging two locomotives in the goods station at Le Mans in March 1943.

Ruddelat was arrested on 21 March 1943, following the capture of Francis Suttill. She and sub-agent Pierre Culioli were taking two recently arrived Canadian agents (Macalister and Pickersgill) to the railway station at Beaugency by car when they were stopped at a German checkpoint at Dhuizon. Though Ruddelat's and Culioli's papers were in order there was some doubt about those of the other two and they were taken into the town hall for interrogation. Believing that the two Canadians were certain to be arrested, Ruddelat and Culioli tried to escape in the car when a bullet hit her in the back of her head as they drove away, knocking her unconscious.

Culioli saw the amount of blood coming from his colleagues wound, and since Ruddelat was unresponsive, he decided to kill himself rather than be taken and tortured. He drove the vehicle at speed into a ditch and then the wall of a building.

However, the two woke up in a hospital at Blois a few hours later. Ruddelat was told that her injury was not life threatening and that the bullet had not pierced her brain, but that it would be unsafe to remove it. After a period in hospital at Blois she was transferred to Frèsnes prison and then, on 21 April 1944, she was taken to Ravensbrück.

In February 1945, 2,500 elderly and ill women were sent from Ravensbrück to what they thought would be a 'convalescent camp' but which was actually Bergen-Belsen. Ruddelat, who had not given the German authorities her real name, possibly suffering from amnesia, was recorded as 'Jacqueline Gautier'. Yvonne Ruddelat never fully recovered from her head wound, suffering repeated periods of amnesia. She was described by one eye-witness at Belsen as being in an 'awful condition' and by 10 April 1945, she knew she was dying after contracting Typhus.

Though Allied forces liberated Belsen on 15 April, conditions at the camp were utterly chaotic (it was reported that at the time the camp was handed over to the British there were some 10,000 bodies lying unburied) and she died towards the end of the month. She never revealed her true name and so was not recognised at the time of her death as an SOE agent. She was therefore buried in a mass grave.

Yvonne Ruddelat was recommended for the Military Cross, which is normally awarded to men. As this decoration cannot be awarded posthumously, it was not approved.

SABOURIN, Roméo Roger

Date of death:	14 September 1944
Place of death:	Buchenwald, Germany
Rank:	Lieutenant
Parent unit:	Canadian Intelligence Corps
Service number:	Not recorded
Decorations:	None recorded
Date joined SOE:	2 January 1944
Code names:	Leonard/Sorcerer/Guy Robert Desjardin
Nationality:	Canadian
Age at time of death:	Twenty-one

Date of birth:	1 January 1923
Place of birth:	Montréal, Canada

Location of memorial: Groesbeek, Netherlands

A lieutenant in the Canadian Army, French-speaking Sabourin was sent for an assessment of his suitability for employment with the SOE at the beginning of August 1943. After twenty days, his assessor wrote: 'He is very immature, irresponsible and vain, and it is doubtful whether he will acquire in a few months training enough stability and concentration to make him worth employing.' The final comment from the assessor was that Sabourin should not be taken on by the SOE.

However, his 'sincere desire to help France, and a pressing ambition to get there at the first opportunity' eventually resulted in Sabourin being trained as a wireless operator.

Sadly Sabourin was another agent who landed in France straight into the arms of the Gestapo. He was sent on 2 March 1944, to join the SORCERER circuit, which had already been 'blown'.

Along with Adolphe Rabinovitch he landed on time at the drop zone. The two agents removed their flying kit before the German reception committee came up to them. The field in which they had landed was on the edge of a wood and, upon hearing German words being spoken, they slipped into the trees and opened fire on the speakers.

A gunfight ensued in which two Germans were killed – but the two agents were also wounded. Sabourin was arrested and taken to 3 bis Place des États Unis. His radio was never heard in London. Whether this was because of his wounds or his refusal to transmit is not clear.

Sabourin was later transferred to Buchenwald and was one of thirty-seven Allied officers murdered on 14 September 1944, a number that included fellow agents Frank Pickersgill and George Wilkinson. According to witnesses, they displayed great courage at their execution.

DE SAINT-GENIÈS, Baron Marie Joseph Gonzagues

Date of death:	26 June 1944
Place of death:	Faubourg de Chalon, France.
Rank:	Captain
Parent unit:	General List
Service number:	309904
Decorations:	Mentioned in Despatches, *Croix de Guerre avec palm*
Date joined SOE:	2 February 1944
Code names:	Lucien/Scholar/George Henri Holleneau
Nationality:	French, naturalised British in 1944
Age at time of death:	Twenty-seven
Date of birth:	11 February 1917
Place of birth:	Fondettas, France
Location of grave:	Choloy, France

De Saint-Geniès became involved in the Resistance movement in October 1941 in Vichy. He became the liaison man between the French General de la Laurencie and the US Military Attaché at Vichy. In this capacity he knew the man who sealed the French diplomatic bag when it went to Lisbon. This enabled De Saint-Geniès to smuggle out information about the local Resistance movement. In Lisbon, this information was passed on by the French Embassy to the British authorities.

In June 1942, De Saint-Geniès decided to try and escape to Britain. After two unsuccessful attempts by boat (one of which nearly resulted in his capture) he reached the United Kingdom on 19 June 1943, and joined the SOE. After training he was parachuted into the Jura on 18 March 1944.

His mission was to take over control of the DIRECTOR circuit, which had lost its leader and was on the point of breaking up. He was to recruit and train wireless operators for each of the groups that constituted the circuit and had instructions to attack the Salon-de-Provence aerodrome as well as the fortifications in the Alps that ran between Col de Mont Genèvre and the Col de Larche.

De Saint-Geniès quickly got the circuit back up and running (under the name of SCHOLAR) and he was able to report back on the situation in the Jura and describe what equipment was needed for the planned operations for D-Day. By the time the Allies landed in Normandy on 6 June he had developed four significant groups. Two of these numbered 300 men each; the others totalling 200 and 100. These groups successfully attacked railway lines in the region, destroying locomotives and sabotaging turntables and signal boxes. De Saint-Geniès also led a number of guerrilla attacks upon German garrisons and road convoys. He also arranged the reception of thirteen drops of arms and other supplies, amounting to 409 containers. It was following the last of these that he was killed.

His death was a truly unfortunate affair. His circuit had participated in Operation *Cadillac*, the first mass daylight drop of supplies by the USAAF, and after hiding away an astonishing thirty-six B-17 loads of arms, the team was going to celebrate.

A dinner was arranged in their best safe-house – a cheese factory – at Faubourg de Chalon, Dole. The team settled down to their meal but a sub-agent had been caught by the Germans close by carrying a transmitter and they decided to raid the factory. They burst into the building to find the caretaker's wife sat alone at a table set for eight.

Not getting a satisfactory response from the poor, clearly agitated woman, an NCO fired a threatening burst of automatic fire through the ceiling and into the loft where De Saint-Geniès was hiding. He was hit in the head (right in the middle of his forehead) and his blood seeped through the ceiling. This was seen by the Germans who then searched the building and seized the rest of De Saint-Geniès' team.

There are two slightly different versions of this incident in his personal file, both received from the field. One is that De Saint-Geniès was looking out of an attic window when he was shot in the forehead, the other is that he was shot whilst trying to escape from the building he was hiding in and died shortly afterwards.

His Section Head in London described De Saint-Geniès as 'an outstandingly fine officer. He would undoubtedly have made his mark on history if he had lived.'

SARRETTE, Paul François Marie Charles William

Date of death:	5 September 1944
Place of death:	Chiddes, France
Rank:	Captain
Parent unit:	General List
Service number:	294479
Decorations:	Mentioned in Despatches, *Croix de Guerre, Chevalier de la Legion d'Honneur*
Date joined SOE:	30 June 1943
Code names:	Louis/Gondolier/Paul Saulieux/ Contrand/Amede/Paul Sawyer
Nationality:	Canadian
Age at time of death:	Twenty-one
Date of birth:	1 January 1923
Place of birth:	Montréal, Canada
Location of grave:	Chiddes, France

Paul Sarrette was recruited in the field and worked as an unofficial lieutenant of the SOE organiser of the RODOLPHE circuit in the region between Marseilles and Lyon, under the code name of 'Contrand'.

He decided to go to London to train to become a fully-fledged member of the SOE. However, when he reached London on 30 May 1943, via Gibraltar, he was treated with considerable suspicion, arousing fears that he might be a German plant. Another agent who had known Sarrette in France (in fact had gone to the same school as Sarrette) stated that Sarrette previously had pro-Vichy sentiments. Though there was some criticism levelled at Baker Street for not checking his background thoroughly and too readily assuming he was 'one of us', it was eventually decided that nothing could be found to not warrant using him in the field.

In training he impressed his assessors with his 'exceptional qualities', which displayed themselves in a 'maturity and balance unusual for his age'. Considered to have 'ample courage and determination', Sarrette made it quite clear to his handlers that he was not interested in passive work such as operating a wireless – he wanted to be involved in sabotage. He showed a particular aptitude during his training for climbing ropes. His only weakness, it was reported, was 'an over-interest in the opposite sex'.

Sarrette also expressed a wish to work alone or under another leader, but he displayed such a natural gift for leadership that he was sent back into France on 21 December 1943, to control a small unit (GONDOLIER) in the Nièvre area of Burgundy. He was to operate under the name of Paul Sawyer.

Quickly setting about his mission, Sarrette brought together a number of Resistance parties, eventually totalling 1,500 men. He ran this force on very strict military lines. This group worked successfully during and after D-Day, as outlined in the recommendation submitted for his award of the *Croix de Guerre*:

'Sawyer's troops concentrated on guerrilla action, attacking small groups of German troops, organising ambushes, blocking roads, etc. On one occasion, four lorry-loads of troops were blown up by mines; on another, thirty-five enemy troops were killed in an ambush.

'The German forces retreating through the Nièvre from the west of France, were so severely harassed and delayed in their retreat by Sawyer's forces that the American troops north and south of the sector were able to join up and force the surrender of 3,000 Germans.'

This remarkable SOE career came to an end on 6 September 1944. Captain K.Y.M. Mackenzie RA later explained in detail what happened:

'Captain Sawyer, on returning to our camp on his way back from an inspection of No.1 Company's emplacement for an ambush against a German armoured column, stopped a moment to watch the progress of a trial shoot with one of the 3–inch mortars sent out from Britain a few days previously.

'The first mortar bomb was fired and the spot where it fell noted. The second mortar bomb exploded upon contacting the firing-pin and plate. The mortar tube exploded from the ball, in fragments, and killed seven people, including Captain Sawyer ... [he] was wounded by a metal fragment which penetrated clean through his heart. He had no other wound.

'On realising what had happened, Captain Sawyer immediately gave the order to notify our hospital. He then fell unconscious and succumbed three-quarters-of-an-hour later while being transported to our hospital at Champlevrier.'

Sawyer, along with the other six victims of the accident, was buried in Chiddes cemetery.

SAVON, Gilbert Joseph

Date of death:	1 April 1944
Place of death:	Karlsruhe, Germany
Rank:	Lieutenant
Parent unit:	General List
Service number:	191270
Decorations:	None recorded
Date joined SOE:	Not recorded
Code names:	G.J. Strutt
Nationality:	French
Age at time of death:	Thirty-three
Date of birth:	20 June 1910
Place of birth:	Marseilles, France
Location of memorial:	Brookwood, UK

There is very little information available relating to Gilbert Savon. All that is known for certain is contained in a French Ministry of Defence report, which states the following:

'By Order of the Secretary of State for Veterans, dated 1 April 1998, the words 'Death by Deportation' are [to be] affixed to the actions and declaratory judgments of death [on the following individuals] – Savon (Gilbert), born 20 June 1910, at Marseille (Bouches-du-Rhône), died on 1 April 1944, at Karlsruhe (Germany).'

Savon was not part of F Section and may, therefore, have been a member of de Gaulle's RF Section.

SCHWATSCHKO, Alexandre

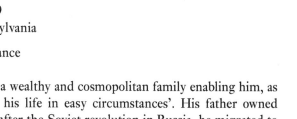

Date of death:	7 June 1944
Place of death:	Éguzon, France
Rank:	Lieutenant
Parent unit:	General List
Service number:	297765
Decorations:	Mentioned in Desptaches
Date joined SOE:	7 June 1943
Code names:	Olive/Politician/Albert Poulnot/Alexander Shaw
Nationality:	Russian
Age at time of death:	Twenty-four
Date of birth:	19 July 1919
Place of birth:	Clug, Transylvania
Location of grave:	Éguzon, France

Alexandre Schwatschko was born into a wealthy and cosmopolitan family enabling him, as his SOE report described 'to live all his life in easy circumstances'. His father owned extensive property in the Ukraine but after the Soviet revolution in Russia, he migrated to France, becoming the regional representative of the firm L'Air Liquide. Alexandre himself was born in Transylvania.

At the outbreak of war in 1939, Schwatschko applied for enlistment in the French Air Force and in October of that year was sent to the flying school at Istres-Le Tubé. There he remained until shortly before the Franco-German armistice when he was evacuated to Aix-en-Provence before being demobilised. From then on he lived a life of leisure, spending the winter of 1941-2, for example, skiing in the Pyrénées.

It was across the Pyrénées that Schwatschko made his attempt to get to Britain. He was arrested by Spanish border guards and was taken to San Sebastian. Here he was able to make contact with the British Consul. The Consul advised him to destroy his papers and pretend to be Canadian. Though he spent some time in the notorious internment camp at Miranda de Ebro in northern Spain, he was eventually released and made his way to Gibraltar. He was put aboard the troopship HMT *Letitia* and arrived in Britain on 5 March 1942.

When he arrived in London he was thoroughly interrogated, in which he made an impression of great frankness and sincerity. 'He appears to be a young man of intelligence and good education, who is anxious to engage in activity of a dangerous and adventurous type.' For his SOE activities he took the name of Alexander Shaw. His assessor saw him being 'impetuous through fearlessness'.

Schwatschko was landed in France by sea in February 1944 to work with Maurice Southgate's STATIONER circuit in the Tarbes/Châteauroux area organising Lysander 'pick-up' operations. Within a month he had identified and reported back on ten suitable sites in the region. 'The selection of grounds and transmission of the relevant information,' read the recommendation for his Mention in Despatches, 'can only be carried out by a technical expert and Shaw's success in these duties was outstanding.

'Shaw's effort enabled a large number of agents to be landed in and evacuated from France. He organised these difficult and dangerous operations with great skill and took great pains to ensure, often at the risk of his own life, the safety of all those who passed through his hands.'

Schwatschko was stopped at a German check-point whilst attempting to cross the hydro-electric dam of Barrage d'Éguzon, 50 miles north of Limoges, on the evening of 7 June 1944. He was taken to a nearby Police Station where a fight broke out and in the resulting encounter Schwatschko killed a German officer before he too was killed.

Schwatschko was buried at Éguzon the following day.

SEHMER, John

Date of death:	23 January 1945
Place of death:	Mauthausen, Austria
Rank:	Major
Parent unit:	Royal Tank Regiment, Royal Armoured Corps
Service number:	73958
Decorations:	MBE
Date joined SOE:	19 September 1943
Code names:	None Recorded
Nationality:	British
Age at time of death:	Thirty-one
Date of birth:	19 April 1913
Place of birth:	Wiggington Lodge, Staffordshire, UK

Location of memorial: Brookwood, UK

A former tank corps commander, John Sehmer had completed one mission in Serbia before being asked to undertake a second mission in Hungary, with Privates Willis and Wilson, as part of Operation *Windproof*. This was an operation run by the SOE in Slovakia and Hungary, the intention being to aid communication between London and local underground forces, support a Slovak uprising, and assist the Hungarian Government's negotiations for an armistice with the Allies.

The few personnel deployed were in a particularly unenviable position. Working at the maximum range of the Special Duties Halifax bombers based at Bari, the men were at the mercy of the weather, missed supply drops, Foreign Office duplicity, and the political turmoil between Moscow, London and the various governments in exile.

At the same time, rather than send Sehmer and his team into the field through Yugoslavia where, according to M.R.D. Foot, British officers were regarded with intense suspicion, he was routed through what was considered an easier and safer country, Slovakia. The three-man team was duly parachuted into Slovakia on 18 September 1944.

In one report, Major Sehmer indicated that his unit was dropped some 15 miles from its intended drop zone and almost on top of German forces. The men also ran the very real risk of being shot by the Slovak sentries he noted.

Whilst still in Slovakia, Sehmer joined forces with an American OSS team (the so-called 'Dawes' mission) around the Hron valley in the Lower Tatras. It was whilst they were living in a farmhouse to the north of the village of Polomka that they were caught by local Axis forces on Boxing Day 1944.

That morning, as the people in the house were getting dressed or preparing breakfast, it was surrounded by a force of some 250 men; some were locals, but led by Germans. They opened fire on the house with machine-guns. It is presumed that the German force was able to get so close to the house because the sentry fell asleep having celebrated Christmas too enthusiastically the previous evening.

The partisans held out for some three hours until the Germans brought up artillery, at which point the resisters tried to slip away. It was later learnt that the whole group had been captured.

Sehmer's team was imprisoned at Banská Bystrica in central Slovakia before being moved to Mauthausen Concentration Camp on 6 January 1945. Here they were placed in individual cells. That same day five men from the *Reichssicherheitshauptamt* (the Reich Main Security Office) in Berlin were sent to interrogate them.

On the 7th, Sehmer was interrogated by the Germans and was beaten by the Mauthausen camp commander, SS-*Standartenführer* Franz Zieries. Then another of the Germans produced his *Tibetanische Gebetsmühle*, an instrument consisting of three or four wooden sticks the size of large pencils, and put it through Sehmer's fingers. Sitting behind him, a second German pressed Sehmer's fingers, thereby producing a very sharp pain without breaking any fingers. Later on Sehmer was suspended by his arms and re-interrogated. This excruciating torture lasted for four days.

On, or about, 23 January 1945, Major Sehmer was shot by Zieries. The bullet pierced the back of his head. Prisoners took the body to the refrigerator room of the crematory. It is not known exactly what happened to his body but it is possible that it was thrown into a mass grave along with a number of Americans who had also been killed. The American victims included OSS's Lieutenant James Holt Green, who had been dropped into the field the day before Sehmer. In total, eleven Americans, along with Joseph Morton, a journalist who was attached to them, were also shot or beheaded at Mauthausen at this time.

On 24 January 1945, the German Overseas News Agency made the following announcement: 'Eighteen members of one Anglo–American group of agents, headed by an American named Green and an Englishman named Sehmer, who posed as a major, were caught on Slovakian soil in the hinterland of the German fighting sector. Investigations revealed that they had the task to carry out acts of sabotage in Anglo–American interests. The agents, who wore mufti when arrested, were sentenced to death by court martial.'

In a twist to the story of Major Sehmer, in January 2004 it was announced that the commander of the unit that had affected his capture in 1944, eighty-six-year-old Ladislav Nižňanský, had been arrested at his home in Munich. The German authorities stated that Nižňanský was being formally investigated by the police for the murder of scores of civilians – not the deaths of the SOE and OSS personnel. He was acquitted when the case went to trial.

SELBY, Neil Beauchamp

Date of death:	1 October 1943
Place of death:	Belgrade, Yugoslavia
Rank:	Major
Parent unit:	1st Royal Dragoons, Royal Armoured Corps
Service number:	117474
Decorations:	None recorded
Date joined SOE:	1941
Code names:	None recorded
Nationality:	British
Age at time of death:	Twenty-eight
Date of birth:	13 March 1915
Place of birth:	Sheffield, UK

Location of memorial: Athens, Greece

The SOE's operations in Yugoslavia were concentrated on supporting Tito's Communist partisans at the expense of the royalist Chetniks under Draža Mihailović. The first mission sent into Yugoslavia to help Tito, Code named HYDRA, was led by Major Terence Atherton with Sergeant O'Donovan as his wireless operator.

Atherton was carrying a substantial amount of gold bullion with him to fund the partisans. The two men were murdered and the gold stolen.

On 5 February 1942, a team of four (Operation DISCLAIMER) was handed over by the locals to the Germans three days after it had landed. A similar fate befell the next mission, the two men involved, Captain Morgan and Corporal Small, being captured on landing.

The run of failures continued throughout April and May and when Major Neil Selby arrived in Yugoslavia with twenty-six-year-old Sergeant John William Rochester (Royal Corps of Signals and of Yugoslavian extraction whose family name was Yovanovic). Under the mission name of REPARTEE, the pair was to join the Mihailović forces of Major Dragutin Keserović.

Selby had previously served for twelve months with No.11 Commando and the objective of his mission was to equip and train a Yugoslav 'commando', not to exercise actual leadership of this formation. Selby found his relations with these forces impossible due to political disagreements and questions of leadership of the commando – and he decided on his own initiative to attempt to reach partisan territory.

On 13 August the two men set out on their journey in plain (peasant's) clothes. Unfortunately they were captured by pro-German troops in the village of Juline on 18 August. Handed over to the German authorities, Selby and Rochester were transported to Belgrade. They were found to be carrying a wireless set and a quantity of 'English' gold.

There was much contradictory evidence concerning Selby's fate. Initially it was reported that he had been killed in action but gradually it became apparent that he had been taken prisoner. There are three versions of his death, all of which are reported in his SOE personal file.

The first version came from the cousin of an SOE sub-agent (a courier): 'During a visit to the Gestapo offices in Ratnicki Dom in Belgrade, he heard German personnel discussing Major Selby's death, which had occurred during an interrogation. He had apparently lost his temper, struck a nearby German guard with a paperweight or other heavy instrument and was immediately shot by a German guard.'

The second version came from a Serb who was a prisoner at Ratnicki Dom. On one occasion he was cleaning out a cell opening off a passage in which Selby was allowed to take exercise. He heard a shot and looking round saw that Selby had been shot in the back of the head whilst walking away from the prison guard. He also stated that there was no furniture or other objects in the passage so Selby could not have hit the guard with anything as had been rumoured.

The final possible explanation that has been given is that Selby was killed in an attempt to escape after having disarmed and killed his own escort.

Nigel West gives his date of death as August 1943, the Commonwealth War Graves Commission as 1 October 1943. Sergeant Rochester also did not survive Operation REPARTEE. Commemorated on the Athens Memorial like Selby, his official date of death is recorded as being 18 August 1943.

SERINI, Enzo

Date of death:	18 November 1944
Place of death:	Dachau, Germany
Rank:	Captain
Parent unit:	Palestinian Regiment
Service number:	PAL/2639580
Decorations:	None recorded
Date joined SOE:	Not recorded
Code names:	Shmel Barda/Samuel Barda
Nationality:	Italian
Age at time of death:	Thirty-nine
Date of birth:	17 April 1905
Place of birth:	Rome, Italy
Location of memorial:	Brookwood, UK

Enzo Sereni was born in Rome where his father was physician to the King of Italy. He grew up in an assimilated household but became a Zionist as a teenager and was one of the first Italian Zionists. After obtaining his PhD from the University of Rome, he travelled to British-controlled Palestine in 1927. He worked in the orange groves in Rehovot and soon helped found kibbutz Givat Brenner. He was a pacifist who advocated co-existence with the Arabs and integration of Jewish and Arab society.

With the outbreak of war, he joined the British Army, and was involved in disseminating anti-fascist propaganda in Egypt on behalf of the SOE. He was one of the editors of the newspaper *Corriere d'Italia*, which was sponsored by the SOE and distributed in the Italian prisoner of war camps in the hope of encouraging some of the detainees to join the Allied cause as undercover saboteurs.

Before long it was noticed by John de Salis, the officer in charge of the Italian desk in SOE's psychological warfare division, that the newspaper was carrying pro-Communist articles. This led to the dismissal of the editorial board and the arrest of Serini. In protest, Serini went on hunger strike and after eleven days he was released.

The SOE sent him to Baghdad to continue his activities but Sereni got in trouble with his British superior officers for his Zionist views. He was also imprisoned briefly for forging passports to enable Jews to escape Egypt for Palestine.

Despite his relatively advanced age Serini was selected for further employment with the SOE and on 15 May 1944, he was parachuted into Northern Italy but was captured immediately. According to records, he was shot in Dachau concentration camp on 18 November 1944. A kibbutz in Israel, the Netzer Serini, is named after him, as is a street in Haifa (Enzo Sireni).

SEVENET, Henri Paul

Date of death:	20 July 1944
Place of death:	La Galaube, France
Rank:	Captain
Parent unit:	General List
Service number:	241689
Decorations:	Mentioned in Despatches, *Legion d'Honneur*; *Croix de Guerre*
Date joined SOE:	2 August 1942
Code names:	Rodolphe/Detective/Henri Dagobert/Henry Thomas/Mathieu
Nationality:	French
Age at time of death:	Twenty-nine
Date of birth:	3 November 1914
Place of birth:	Chédigny, France
Location of grave:	Laprade, Aude, France

Henri Sevenet, a former worker at Citroën in Lyons, was recruited into the SOE by Phillipe de Vomécourt, who was an old family friend, in April 1941. He then helped the

HISTORIAN operation as a 'letter box' through which messages could be sent. He also assisted with the deployment of the first ever SOE wireless set to operate in France at Châteauroux.

When Vomécourt's brother Pierre was captured by the Germans a notebook was seized, which gave Sevenet's name and address. He therefore left France and made his way over the Pyrénées and to Britain via Gibraltar.

After a month's training Sevenet was commissioned a captain under the name of Henry Thomas and went back to France on 27 August 1942. He was dropped near Chédigny, some 2 miles north-east of Chambourg-sur-Indre. His instructions were to sabotage the railway line between Tours and Poitiers and to find suitable places for the dropping of supplies.

Sevenet identified a point along the railway line where he could block the line by causing a landslide. He then found three good landing grounds and sent a message asking for the explosives, but received no reply. He sent, in all, fifty-three messages but failed to get a response from London.

Despite the disappointment of being unable to contact Baker Street, Sevenet began to organise his own circuit. He remained in touch with Vomécourt who advised him of a series of arrests. The fact that there was a degree of overlap amongst a number of the circuits meant that the arrests became widespread. In February 1943 Sevenet was told that a warrant for his arrest had been seen at the Toulouse Gestapo offices and he decided to escape to Britain once again.

He was parachuted blind on his third mission on 15 September 1943. He was told, for security reasons, to sever all contact with Vomécourt's circuit. By 28 June 1944, he had put together a group of 600 well-armed men and this group fought a battle with a large number of Germans, killing six of the enemy and wounding two others.

On 20 July Sevenet's little army was attacked by a strong column of German infantry (said to number 4,000 men) with tanks, artillery and even aircraft.

Sevenet's group suffered heavy losses in the engagement and had to disperse, leaving arms and equipment behind. What happened next was detailed on 30 November 1944:

'It appears that two reconnaissance planes flew over La Galaube, where Sevenet was preparing to go back to HQ. He got into the car, when one of the planes let go some red smoke. Everybody got out to find cover and warn the camps by telephone.

'Sevenet went up under some big trees towards a hut, the others down towards the road. A heavy bomb of the gliding type flew down, razed most of the trees, cut Sevenet's head, pulled off an arm, and cut a few fingers of the other hand. This was at 7 pm.'

Four days later his body was found thrown by the Germans under a manure heap. His ring and rosary were removed (the only things left) to be sent to his mother. He was buried in Laprade cemetery.

SIBREE, David Whytehead

Date of death:	29 March 1945
Place of death:	Flossenbürg, Germany
Rank:	Lieutenant
Parent unit:	General List
Service number:	28245
Decorations:	None recorded
Date joined SOE:	April 1943
Code names:	David Morand
Nationality:	British
Age at time of death:	Thirty-two
Date of birth:	28 June 1912
Place of birth:	Hull, UK

Location of memorial: Brookwood, UK

David Sibree arrived in the UK on 5 December 1942 from North Africa, where he had been serving (since 1937) with the French Foreign Legion. On his arrival he declared his interest in joining a commando unit.

As with all foreign nationals arriving in Britain, and especially those who were potential SOE recruits, he was investigated by MI5. In the investigation into Sibree's background it was discovered that he was 'a phoney officer of British nationality'. Why he ran away to join the Foreign Legion is not disclosed in his personal file and his dubious background did not prevent him being recruited by F Section.

On 20 April 1943, just a few days before he was due to start his SOE training, he was involved in a drunken brawl in London and arrested by the police. This was viewed as a serious breach of discipline in a potential secret service operative and he was warned that any repetition would result in his dismissal from the SOE.

Though it was fairly evident that his temperament made him unsuitable for a long-term undercover mission, he was likely to be useful in *coup-de-main* operations. In this role, Sibree left on 16 August 1943, as part of the six-man strong sabotage team SCULLION II. Its objective was to destroy the Les Telots shale oil refinery near Autun.

This, as the Code name implies, was the second attempt to sabotage the factory, SCULLION I having failed. The first mission was led by Captain Hugh Dormer and he was to lead the second attack. In advance of this second operation another agent, George Demand (see separate entry), had landed four days earlier to prepare the ground. They managed to lay their explosives and some damage was done to the plant. There are differing views on just how effective the operation had been.

Only Captain Dormer and Sergeant Birch managed to return to the UK. The others were captured by the Germans in a villa at Ville D'Avray. Sent to Paris, it is known that all of these men were in Frèsnes as late as November 1943, later being transferred to Flossenbürg.

Here a total of fifteen SOE agents were held in solitary confinement. They were starved and some were beaten. Finally all were executed without trial. Two were shot in 1944. The remaining thirteen were hanged, one by one, on 29 March 1945, less than six weeks before the end of the war. In accordance with the German policy that their fates should never be known, their bodies were immediately cremated.

In 2007 a memorial commemorating these men (nine of whom were British, four were French, one was American and one was Canadian) was unveiled at the site of the camp. 'I am glad David is being remembered,' said his cousin, Roger Wood, in an interview in *The Times*. 'He was evidently ready to take the difficult path whenever it seemed to him appropriate, whatever the consequence.'

SIMON, Jean Alexandre Robert

Date of death:	27 January 1944
Place of death:	Sochaux, France
Rank:	Second Lieutenant
Parent unit:	General List
Service number:	313421
Decorations:	*Croix de Guerre, Grand Croix de la Legion d'honneur, Médaille de la Résistance Française*
Date joined SOE:	28 March 1944
Code names:	Claude
Nationality:	French
Age at time of death:	Twenty-six
Date of birth:	22 January 1918
Place of birth:	Saint-Claude, Jura, France
Location of memorial:	Brookwood, UK

Jean Simon was recruited into the SOE by Captain Harry Rée who established the STOCKBROKER circuit in the Jura in 1943 and he worked as Rée's lieutenant. This circuit achieved some remarkable successes.

The Peugeot motor factory in the Montbéliard suburb of the French town of Sochaux, near the Swiss border, had been converted to make tank turrets for the German forces and Focke-Wulf engine parts for the *Luftwaffe*. The factory was high on the RAF's target list but it was situated close to a railway station in a densely populated part of the town and high-level bombing would inevitably result in heavy civilian casualties. This is exactly what happened when it was attacked by the RAF on the night of 14 July 1943, by a force of 165 Handley Page Halifax bombers.

The attack had no effect upon production at the factory but large numbers of local people were killed. Some of the bombs dropped fell almost as much as a mile away.

Harry Rée made contact with one of the directors of the Peugeot Company, whom it was understood was sympathetic to the Allied cause, and asked him if he would agree to sabotage his own factory. Such a move would prevent the indiscriminate damage done by bombing and would ensure that there were no civilian deaths. The director saw the wisdom of such collaboration but he wanted to be certain that Reé could prevent his factory being bombed if he agreed to the sabotage. Reé invited the director to compose a message that would be broadcast by the BBC to confirm the arrangement. A few nights later the message was given out by the BBC and the Peugeot boss was convinced.

The foreman of the tank turret plant also agreed to the plan and the result was that the plant was out of action for much of the rest of the war. This must rate as one of the most effective SOE operations of the entire conflict as it cost nothing in terms of resources or lives, yet was completely successful.

Rée had to leave France when he became involved in a fist fight with a *Feldgendarme* who was trying to arrest him. His circuit, meanwhile, continued to operate successfully under Jean Simon's leadership – until Simon was betrayed on 5 February 1944, that is.

In what was described as 'an ambush' German *Feldgendarmes* encircled the Café Grangier in Sochaux where Simon, Eric Cauchi and a sub-agent were meeting. The Germans attacked the café with firearms. The agents fought back and a number of Germans were hit in the engagement. Though the attack upon the café was immediately reported, it was not known at the time what had happened to Jean Simon.

Then, on 16 February 1944, Baker Street was informed that Simon had been killed in the gunfight at the Café Grangier as had Eric Cauchi.

As Jean Simon had been recruited in the field no details of his background were ever passed onto London. Baker Street therefore had no knowledge of any surviving next of kin and it was left to the new French Government after the war to try and notify his relatives.

SIMON, Octave Anne Guillaume

Date of death:	1 August 1944
Place of death:	Gross-Rosen, Poland
Rank:	Lieutenant
Parent unit:	General List
Service number:	306642
Decorations:	Military Cross, *Croix de Guerre avec Palme, Chevalier de la Legion d'Honneur, Medaille de la Resistance Français*
Date joined SOE:	3 September 1943
Code names:	Badois/Satirist/Guillaume Octave Sabatier
Nationality:	French
Age at time of death:	Thirty
Date of birth:	10 April 1914
Place of birth:	Lyons, France
Location of memorial:	Brookwood, UK

A notable sculptor before the war, Octave Simon had been involved in Resistance work of one sort or another since 1940. He first became involved with the SOE when he undertook work with Philippe de Vomécourt's VENTRILOQUIST circuit in 1942. When de Vomécourt was arrested Simon managed to get in touch with Francis Suttill who asked him to try and organise a circuit in the Sarthe.

Simon was well known in the Sarthe and had many influential contacts in the region. The area was relatively free of German troops, which enabled Simon to receive arms drops and many of the weapons that reached Suttill came through Simon's SATIRIST circuit.

When Suttill was arrested in June 1942 all the sub-circuits of his PROSPER network were endangered, none more so than SATIRIST. Within weeks the arrests began and the entire circuit was quickly broken up. Simon had to run for his life, eventually making his way down to Angers after three or four 'hair's-breadth' escapes from the Gestapo. He was picked up from Angers by Hudson on the night of 19/20 August 1942, and taken to London.

He returned to France on 7 March the following year. He was accompanied by his radio operator Marcel Defence. They were to restart the SATIRIST circuit. However, they were dropped by Hudson to a reception arranged by Francis Garel's BUTLER circuit. Garel, along with his wireless operator Marcel Rousset and Marcel Fox, had been captured by the Germans in Paris and Simon and Defence were seized upon landing.

Rousset had been forced to use his wireless to send messages back to London but, as was the case far too often, Rousset followed the correct procedures for falsifying his security checks only for Baker Street to disregard them. Rousset even persuaded the Germans that he transmitted in French for Gustave Biéler and Fox and in English for Garel when in fact in normal circumstances the opposite was the case. When the first message purporting to come from Garel was sent to London in English, the only observation that Baker Street made was to ask why Rousset had changed language.

The Germans continued to use Rousset's machine for nine months, receiving in that time numerous supply drops as well as capturing agents such as Detal, Duclos and, of course, Simon and Defence.

It is recorded that he died at Gross-Rosen.

SINCLAIR, Jack Andrew Eugene Marcel

Date of death:	1 May 1944
Place of death:	Baumettes, France
Rank:	Lieutenant
Parent unit:	General List
Service number:	316615
Decorations:	None recorded
Date joined SOE:	28 October 1943
Code names:	Adalbert/Shopkeeper/Jaques André Eugéné Berthier
Nationality:	British
Age at time of death:	Twenty-two
Date of birth:	17 September 1921
Place of birth:	Rouen, France

Location of memorial: Brookwood, UK

Young Jack Sinclair was born in France to an English father and French mother. The family lived in Rouen until Jack was aged six when they moved to Marseilles, eventually settling in Bordeaux where they remained until the French capitulation of 1940.

In Britain, Jack became a trainee draughtsman before he volunteered for the Intelligence Corps, subsequently being recruited into the SOE in October 1943. His assessors found that Sinclair was a very reserved and quiet individual. He was so unobtrusive, remarked one assessor, 'that one often forgot he was there'.

Though he did not display any particular powers of leadership, he was earmarked for a position as the organiser of a small group of saboteurs within the MONK circuit.

Sinclair was duly parachuted into France on 6/7 March 1944, from Algiers, to join his allotted circuit, which was led by Charles Skepper. Due to what M.R.D. Foot calls 'a horrible staff muddle with an OSS radio game' he was dropped to the wrong reception committee. Instead of landing to an SOE group he was dropped to an OSS one that was controlled by the Germans. He was arrested upon landing.

He was initially interred in Marseilles but after that all trace of him was lost. It is not thought that Sinclair was tortured, yet around a dozen of the MONK personnel were subsequently arrested. This, however, was due to betrayal by a local Frenchman who was tracked down and executed after the war. There was simply no need to torture Sinclair, who, having been arrested upon arrival, knew little in any case. The rest of Skepper's group went into hiding and the circuit was never resurrected.

In an attempt to find out what had happened to Sinclair, his case was passed onto the French War Crimes Liaison Group after the war. On 19 March 1946, a letter was received that confirmed that Sinclair was at the notorious Baumettes Prison (also known as the Centre Pénitentiaire de Marseille) as late as April 1944. The letter ended with these words: 'I am quite unable to give any further information on what has become of him, from the day that the cell doors closed behind him.'

It is presumed that Sinclair never left Baumettes alive.

SKEPPER, Charles Milne

Date of death:	4 April 1944
Place of death:	Possibly Buchenwald, Germany
Rank:	Captain
Parent unit:	General List
Service number:	270156
Decorations:	MBE, *Croix de Guerre avec Palme*
Date joined SOE:	1942
Code names:	Bernard/Monk/Henri Truchot
Nationality:	British
Age at time of death:	Thirty-nine
Date of birth:	26 February 1905
Place of birth:	Richmond, Surrey, UK

Location of memorial: Brookwood, UK

Charles Skepper was formerly an antique dealer travelling between China and Paris. He also worked for the British Propaganda Station in Shanghai. He operated for two months with Chinese guerrillas before being wounded and taken prisoner. He spent four months under terrible conditions in a Japanese prison camp where he caught beri-beri. Described as 100 percent disabled, he was part of a prisoner exchange organised by the International Red Cross and taken to Gibraltar.

He was sent into France by Lysander on 16 June 1943, to organise a circuit in the Marseilles area. With him was Cicely Lefort and together they travelled down to the south of France where they separated, with Skepper going on to Marseilles. Three days later he was joined by Arthur Steele who was to be his wireless operator. The third member of the group that was to carry the name MONK was Elaine Plewman who was parachuted into the Jura on the 13/14 August.

Skepper lived in a small flat in Marseilles operating a small antiques business to conceal his handling of weapons. The MONK circuit, though small, was effective. One of its most notable successes was an attack on the synthetic oil plant at L'Estaque where three oil tanks were destroyed and six others damaged. Skepper's team also blocked an important railway tunnel near the Italian border by derailing a train inside and carried out a successful attack upon a cement works at Fos-sur-mer.

It is said that in the months preceding both D-Day and the Allied landings in the South of France (Operation *Dragoon*), the MONK circuit provided important information about the deployment of German forces and the coastal fortifications in the South of France. The swift success achieved by Allied forces under US General Patch in August 1944 was due in part to this information.

Skepper worked successfully for nine months but after significant achievements in cutting several power lines and destroying a number of locomotives (see Arthur Steele's previous entry) he was betrayed by a man known as 'Bousquet'. He was arrested, after something of a struggle, along with local sub-agent Julien (or possibly Marc) Villevielle at Skepper's flat on 23 March 1944.

He was taken to the Gestapo prison in Marseilles and it is known that he was tortured whilst here. Skepper was then moved, first to Frèsnes and then on to Compiegne. He was transferred to Germany on 2 July 1944, and was known to be held in the Gestapo prison in Hamburg. It is not known whether he was executed there or at Buchenwald.

'This gallant and distinguished officer merits high recognition,' wrote Colonel Craddock on behalf of Gubbins when recommending Skepper for an OBE. 'He showed great courage, endurance and devotion to duty.'

When Bousquet was arrested in 1945 and subsequently tried, Villevielle, who survived his captivity, was the principle prosecution witness.

STEELE, Arthur

Date of death:	14 September 1944
Place of death:	Buchenwald, Germany
Rank:	Captain
Parent unit:	General List
Service number:	263403
Decorations:	Mentioned in Despatches, *Médaille de la Défense Nationale, Croix de Guerre avec Palme*
Date joined SOE:	15 October 1942
Code names:	Laurent/Waiter/Arthur Saulnier/ Arthur Clermont
Nationality:	British
Age at time of death:	Twenty-three
Date of birth:	6 April 1921
Place of birth:	Noeux-les-Mines

Location of memorial: Brookwood, UK

Arthur Steele, described as 'tall, dark and gay', was a London music student and barely twenty-two-years-old when, on 19 June 1943, he went to France as the wireless operator to Charles Skepper. Eliane Plewman joined them as the circuit courier.

The trio of agents established a small but effective circuit in and around Marseilles which, after the Allied landings in North Africa, became one of the main centres of clandestine traffic between Algiers and Occupied France. Because of this the Gestapo put every effort into destroying the Resistance organisations in the city and along the south coast.

As radio reception was poor in the city centre, Steele moved to an isolated villa outside Marseilles. The Gestapo knew there was someone transmitting from the area and in December 1943 Steele had to move and he was hidden in the home of a Mme Régis in a villa above the coastal community of Saint-Raphaël.

Steele maintained constant radio communications with London for nine months, making possible the delivery of arms not only to his own MONK circuit but also to other Resistance groups in the region. In that time he handled nearly 400 messages.

In January 1944 the MONK team derailed a train in a tunnel on the main line between Marseilles and Toulon and then destroyed the breakdown train that came to clear the wreckage. The line was closed for four days.

They extended their activities and put thirty locomotives out of action that month and another thirty in March. Then, on 23 March, disaster struck; Skepper and one of his sub-agents were arrested at Skepper's flat on the Rue Merandet in Marseilles.

Steele and Elaine Plewman turned up the next day at Skepper's address and walked straight into the trap laid by the waiting Gestapo. It is not known why they went there when they did. It may have been an attempt to rescue Steele, as M.R.D. Foot had proposed, or simply as a pre-arranged meeting. According to Mme Régis, the three SOE agents were betrayed by a Frenchman who was tracked down and executed after the war by the *Départment de la Surveillance du Territoire*, which was responsible for investigating cases of suspected treason.

Steele's wireless set continued to send messages back to London until July 1944. At no time were the staff at Baker Street in any doubt that the set was either being used by a German operator or that it was Steele sending the transmissions under duress.

He was taken to the Gestapo's prison in Marseilles before being moved to Paris. He was seen at 3 bis Place des États Unis by Marcel Rousset, an agent with the BUTLER circuit who had also been arrested but escaped in June 1944. Steele was later transferred to Germany and executed at Buchenwald.

SUTTILL, Francis Alfred

Date of death:	23 March 1945
Place of death:	Sachsenhausen, Germany
Rank:	Major
Parent unit:	East Surrey Regiment
Service number:	130049
Decorations:	DSO
Date joined SOE:	16 March 1942
Code names:	Prosper/Physician/François
	Desprées
Nationality:	British
Age at time of death:	Thirty-five
Date of birth:	17 March 1910
Place of birth:	Mons-en-Barœul, France

Location of memorial: Groesbeek, Netherlands

Francis Suttill was born in France at Mons-en-Barœul to a French mother and English father who managed a textile manufacturing plant in Lille. Educated in both Britain and in France, at Lille University, he studied law and went on to become a barrister.

Married with two sons, Suttill joined the British Army at the outbreak of war in September 1939. He was eventually recruited into the SOE and chosen to establish the PROSPER circuit based in Paris.

Along with Andrée Borrel he built a very extensive network covering a large part of northern France. Its reach was such that Suttill resources included parachute reception teams in the Ardennes in Belgium, near Falaise in Normandy, three around Le Mans and two around Troyes (which were eventually absorbed by the TINKER circuit).

His most notable achievements were the sabotage of the Chaingy power station in March 1943, the destruction of 1,000 litres of petrol, and a number of successful attacks on enemy goods trains on the Orléans-Paris line. In April 1943 alone his groups conducted sixty-three sabotage operations against enemy targets. He also established one of the most important of all the safe houses. This was set up in the famous *Ecole Nationale d'Agriculture* at Grignon, north-west of Versailles. Its director, and many of the teaching staff, worked for PROSPER.

The downfall of the PROSPER circuit, when it came, was swift and dramatic. Two Canadian agents, Pickersgill and Macalister, who parachuted into France on the night of 10/11 June 1943, to start up a new circuit in Ardennes, were arrested on 21 June. On them was found the addresses of Andrée Borrel and Gilbert Norman (the PROSPER wireless operator) who were both arrested on the evening of 23 June.

Early the next morning the Gestapo tracked Suttill down to a small hotel on the Rue de Mazagran in Paris where he was arrested. He was taken to the SD headquarters at Avenue Foch along with the other agents that had been captured.

Much has been written about what may have taken place during the period of Suttill's interrogation and it has been stated that he was 'horribly tortured'. All that is known for certain is that the PROSPER circuit was hopelessly compromised and hundreds of agents and Resistance fighters were swiftly rounded up.

As for Suttill, after a few days at Avenue Foch he was deported to Berlin and then moved to Sachsenhausen concentration camp. He was placed in solitary confinement in the prison block where he remained until his execution at the end of March 1945, along with Charles Grover-Williams, who had been the organiser of the CHESTNUT circuit.

Another inmate of the prison, Wing Commander Day, reported that, despite the nature of their confinement, Suttill and Grover-Williams were still able to communicate. Both men were reasonably well fed but received no Red Cross parcels. Day saw the two men taken away from the prison block but he did not know what had happened to them.

After the war Vera Atkins, with the title of Squadron Officer, tried to uncover the details of Suttill's execution. She managed to obtain a statement from another inmate at Sachsenhausen, Paul Schroter, through an interview with Special Branch. Schroter used to work in the kitchen and when the so-called 'ambulance car' came to take away the prisoners for execution he was locked away in the scullery so that he could not be a witness to what was taking place.

Despite this, Schroter recalled Grover-Williams and Suttill being taken away, though he could not be too precise about the date – he had been able to watch through a 'chink' in the scullery door. The men left in their civilian clothing, which was returned to the prison after the executions. Schroter was certain that the men had been either hanged or gassed as the clothes showed no signs of shooting.

Unfortunately, all the Sachsenhausen camp guards were seized by the Soviets at the end of the war for their own war crimes investigations, which ended further attempts at obtaining information.

Suttill received a glowing testimonial from Major General Gubbins: 'During his nine months of clandestine work, this officer made a very great contribution to the organisation of resistance in northern France. The achievements he attained were quite unparalleled at the time. A magnificent leader ... He showed outstanding bravery and self-sacrifice, and never failed to carry out personally the most dangerous tasks.'

He was awarded the Distinguished Service Order after his death.

SZABO, Violette Reine Elizabeth

Date of death:	5 February 1945
Place of death:	Ravensbrück, Germany
Rank:	Ensign
Parent unit:	Women's Transport Service (FANY)
Service number:	F/29
Decorations:	George Cross, MBE, *Croix de Guerre*, *Médaille de la Résistance Française*
Date joined SOE:	10 September 1943
Code names:	Louise/Seamstress/Corinne Reine Leroy
Nationality:	French
Age at time of death:	Twenty-three
Date of birth:	26 June 1921
Place of birth:	Paris, France
Location of memorial:	Brookwood, UK

Arguably the most famous of all the SOE agents, and one who typified their daring and stubborn courage, is Violette Szabo. Much of this is due to the 1958 film *Carve Her Name With Pride* which still has the power to generate strong emotions.

Born in Paris to a French mother and British father (who had met in the First World War), Violette Bushell's family moved to Brixton where she grew up, eventually working on the perfume counter in the Bon Marché department store in Brixton.

In 1939, Violette Bushell married a French Foreign Legionnaire of Hungarian descent, Etienne Szabo, after a whirlwind romance. Violette was nineteen, Etienne was thirty-one. Shortly after the birth of their only child, Tania, Etienne died from chest wounds at the Battle of El Alamein in October 1942. He had never seen his daughter.

This heroine joined the SOE in July 1943. At the end of her training her instructors described her thus: 'A quiet, physically tough, self-willed girl of average intelligence. Out for excitement and adventure but not entirely frivolous. Has plenty of confidence in herself and gets on well with others. Plucky and persistent in her endeavours. Not easily rattled.' It was recommended that she would be well-suited to the role of courier.

For her first mission, Violette was dropped into France by parachute on 5 April 1944. Her cover story was that she was Corinne Reine Le Roy (using her mother's maiden name), a commercial secretary. Her job was to find out if one of the PROSPER sub-circuits had been penetrated. Szabo established beyond doubt that the cell had been blown, and was flown back to Britain at the end of April.

Having taken off from RAF Tempsford in Bedfordshire, Szabo was parachuted back into France in the early hours of 8 June 1944, just two days after the Allied landings in Normandy. Like most of the agents in France at this time, her efforts were directed at interrupting German communications to prevent them reinforcing the troops defending Normandy.

Szabo had injured her ankle during a parachute training exercise and its continuing weakness would lead to her capture just three days after landing at Sussac, some 30 miles south-east of Limoges. The incident that resulted in Szabo's capture was subsequently recounted by Jacques Dufour who was escorting Szabo and another accomplice, Jean Bariaud.

As the party drove round a bend near the village of Salon-la-Tour, they saw a roadblock manned by German soldiers who waved them down. The road block was one of a number put in place during the hunt for *Sturmbannführer* Helmut Kämpfe, the commander of the III. Battalion, 4th SS Panzer Grenadier Regiment *Der Führer*, who had been seized by the French Resistance on 9 June 1944. (Kämpfe was subsequently executed and his body set alight; he was the highest ranking officer ever to be captured by the Resistance).

As their vehicle approached the German troops, Dufour warned his friends to be prepared to jump out and run. Dufour drove up to about 30 yards from the roadblock and stopped the car.

'I jumped flat on the road surface by the car, and started shooting,' he later recalled. 'I noticed Bariaud, who was unarmed, running away, but found that Szabo had taken up a similar position to mine on the other side of the car, and was firing too.

'By that time though, one of the three Germans had been hit; the other two were spraying us generously. I ordered Szabo to retreat through a wheat field, towards a wood 400 yards away, under cover of my fire. As soon as she had reached the high wheat she resumed firing, and I took advantage of it to fall back.

'At first the going was good, as we walked, bending so as not to show our heads over the top of the wheat, but soon we heard the rumble of armoured cars, and machine-guns began spraying close to us ... So we had to continue our progress towards the wood crawling flat and cautiously on the ground, an exhausting and awfully slow process.

'Then we heard infantry running up the road and entering the wheat field while other armoured cars went driving around it. So we had to resume firing each in turn to cover the other's progress, to keep the infantrymen from running up to us.

'When we weren't more than 30 yards from the edge of the wood Szabo, who by then had her clothes all ripped to ribbons and was bleeding from numerous scratches all over her legs, told me she was exhausted and could not go an inch further.

'She insisted she wanted me to try and get away, that there was no point in my staying with her. So I went on while she kept on firing from time to time and I managed to hide under a haystack in the courtyard of a small farm.'

Szabo's previously injured ankle had given way and she limped into captivity. Dufour and Bariaud both escaped. The German soldier in charge of the roadblock said that Szabo was the bravest woman he had ever seen.

She was initially taken to the Gestapo headquarters in Limoges prior to being transferred to the town's prison. On 12 June 1944, she was moved to Frèsnes but spent some periods of time under interrogation at SD headquarters at Avenue Foch.

On 8 August 1944, Szabo was one of seven women transferred to Ravensbrück, via Saarbrücken, arriving at the female concentration camp some seventeen days later. On her journey from Frèsnes, Szabo had been put in chains that consisted of heavy bangles around her wrist and ankle. These were joined together by a very short chain, which meant that she could not stand upright. She was then chained to another prisoner. Little wonder then that the beautiful Violette was already looking 'thin and worn out'.

Along with Lilian Rolfe and Denise Bloch, she was sent to work in a munitions factory at Torgau and then to a work camp at Königsberg in eastern Germany. This remained the case until the middle of January 1945 when the trio were returned to Ravensbrück.

Just a few days after their return to the concentration camp the three girls were murdered. Though Denise and Lilian had to be assisted or carried out to their place of execution, Violette Szabo walked unaided to her death.

On 17 December 1946, it was announced that Szabo had been awarded the George Cross – only the second woman ever to be bestowed with this honour. The citation, which differs somewhat from Defour's account, stated:

'Madame Szabo volunteered to undertake a particularly dangerous mission in France. She was parachuted into France in April 1944, and undertook the task with enthusiasm. In her execution of the delicate researches entailed she showed great presence of mind and astuteness. She was twice arrested by the German security authorities, but each time managed to get away. Eventually, however, with other members of her group, she was surrounded by the Gestapo in a house in the south-west of France.

'Resistance appeared hopeless, but Madame Szabo, seizing a Sten gun and as much ammunition as she could carry, barricaded herself in part of the house, and, exchanging shot for shot with the enemy, killed or wounded several of them. By constant movement she avoided being cornered and fought until she dropped exhausted. She was arrested and had to undergo solitary confinement. She was then continuously and atrociously tortured, but never by word or deed gave away any of her aquaintances, or told the enemy anything of value. She was ultimately executed. Madame Szabo gave a magnificent example of courage and steadfastness.'

Fellow SOE agent Odette Churchill GC, MBE, *Chevalier de la Legion d'Honneur*, who herself had survived incarceration in Ravensbrück, once described Szabo as 'the bravest of us all'.

SZENES, Hannah

Date of death:	16 May 1944	
Place of death:	Budapest, Hungary	

Rank:	Aircraftwoman 2nd Class	
Parent unit:	Women's Auxiliary Air Force	
Service number:	2992382	
Decorations:	None recorded	
Date joined SOE:	Not recorded	
Code names:	Georg	
Nationality:	Hungarian	
Age at time of death:	Twenty-three	
Date of birth:	1921	
Place of birth:	Budapest, Hungary	

Location of memorial: Jerusalem, Israel

Hannah (or Anna) Szenes was born to an assimilated Jewish family in Hungary. With the situation in that country becoming ever more difficult for Jews in the late 1930s, she emigrated to the British Mandate of Palestine in 1939. After living in a kibbutz and serving in a paramilitary group called the Haganah, Szenes asked to join the British forces. For much of her life, she had kept a diary (which was published in Hebrew in 1946). On 8 January 1943, she gave the following explanation for this decision: 'Suddenly, the idea grabbed me that I must go to Hungary, and be there during these days. To lend a hand … and I decided to rise and act.'

Soon after this, Szenes was accepted for SOE training. The latter was undertaken in Egypt.

In March 1944 she was parachuted into Yugoslavia to conduct operations in Hungary along with two other agents, Yoel Palgi and Peretz Goldstein. Their mission was to serve as one of more than thirty agents who would be airdropped behind enemy lines to rendezvous with partisan fighters.

The timing of their insertion was unfortunate as it coincided with the German occupation of Hungary. Szenes' two colleagues considered that it was now too dangerous to continue with their operation and they aborted the mission. Szenes, though, was made of sterner stuff and, after a period of time helping the partisans in the Balkans, she continued into Hungary.

At the border she was stopped and searched, and as she was carrying her SOE wireless transmitter with her, she was arrested. Szenes was taken to the Hungarian Intelligence headquarters in Budapest where she was tied to a chair, stripped and whipped, clubbed and beaten for several hours. This punishment continued for several months.

In her file is a paper that quotes an unidentified man who was in prison at the same time as Szenes: 'Source says that her treatment was appalling even judged by the standard of that usually accorded to spies, but that she managed always to keep absolutely silent. Her spirit had, however, been broken and she was not interested in any possible ways of saving herself … and asked him to try and smuggle something to her to enable her to commit suicide. This source refused to do so, saying that while there was life there was hope.'

This same source confirmed that Szenes was subsequently shot. He stated that he had seen her body lying in the courtyard off Margit Körút – a road not far from the River Danube in the centre of Budapest. This source added that he believed that she had been executed because she had refused to talk.

In an interview with *The People* newspaper on 22 August 1971, Hannah's mother, Katherina Senesh, revealed further details of her daughter's treatment.

One day she was taken to the Hungarian Intelligence headquarters in Budapest. 'The door opened and I went rigid,' the old woman recalled. 'Four men led in my Hannah, her face [was] bruised and swollen, her hair in a filthy tangle, eyes blackened. I was shattered, all my hopes for her collapsed like a house of cards … The Nazis watched us like hawks. Hannah tore herself away from them and threw herself into my arms sobbing. She asked me to forgive her. What for? One of the Nazis ordered me to talk to her, to persuade her to tell "everything", otherwise this would be the last time I saw her.'

Hannah, as we now know, did not talk. She was tried for treason; her hearing began on 28 October 1944. This was a problematic case for the Hungarian judiciary. Twice the trial was delayed to allow the judges to reach a satisfactory verdict. Whilst in custody, Szenes wrote the following in her diary: '… I played a number in a game. The dice have rolled. I have lost.'

However, before the Hungarian judges arrived at a verdict, Szenes was taken from her cell and executed by a German firing squad. Though the date of her death is listed by the Commonwealth War Graves Commission as being in May, her execution took place much later, on 7 November 1944. It is said that she refused to wear a blindfold so that she could look her killers in the eye.

TESSIER, Paul Raymond Elie

Date of death:	26 August 1944
Place of death:	Clichy-sous-Bois, France
Rank:	Captain
Parent unit:	Reconnaissance Corps, Royal Armoured Corps
Service number:	262994
Decorations:	Mentioned in Despatches
Date joined SOE:	5 March 1943
Code names:	Théodore/ Comedian/Paul Terrier
Nationality:	British
Age at time of death:	Twenty-seven
Date of birth:	15 October 1916
Place of birth:	London, UK

Location of memorial: Lagny-sur-Marne, France

In May 1940, Paul Tessier, a trained diamond setter, enlisted with the Royal Fusiliers, joining the Royal Armoured Corps in July 1942. Having been born to French parents and fluent in French, but of British nationality, eight months later he was accepted into the SOE.

Described as 'tough and enthusiastic', and anxious to finish his training so that he could 'get down to the real thing', his first mission to France was in August 1943 as part of the DRESSMAKER sabotage team. They were parachuted north of Escoussens, with their objective being the tanneries at Mazamet in the Tarn that were reported as working for the Germans. Their intelligence turned out to be faulty as the tanneries were already disused. The men became ill after drinking contaminated water and the party had to return to the UK.

Tessier, married with two children, was sent back into the field on 10 January 1944, this time to act as the lieutenant to Gustave Biéler (MUSICIAN circuit). Nothing more was heard about him at Baker Street and it was assumed that he had been arrested on landing or very shortly afterwards as it was later known that the circuit that arranged his reception had been infiltrated.

Then, on 27 June 1944, a message was received from the wireless operator of Dumont-Guillemet's SPIRITUALIST circuit that Tessier was now working for them. Tessier had been arrested on 25 January and taken to 3 bis Place des États Unis from where he had managed to escape, thanks to the assistance of George McBain (see previous entry).

Tessier broke through an outside wall with a stolen iron bar and tied his bedding together to form a rope by which he was able to climb down to freedom. What makes this escape even more remarkable is that he did this even though the Germans had broken his hand during a recent interrogation.

By rights, Tessier should have left France. His face was familiar to the Germans and the Gestapo were intent on recapturing him. As by this time the Allies had landed in Normandy, instead he took the decision to remain in Paris – an extremely dangerous location for him – to help with the liberation of France. He sought shelter with Bertie Cane, an English woman living in Lagny-sur-Marne.

During his time with the SPIRITUALIST circuit he identified three locations for air drops and helped organise twelve drops of weapons. As sabotage was his forté he was involved in attacks upon the railways running from Paris to Strasbourg and Metz. His decision to remain in Paris would prove a fatal one for he was killed in the fighting in the eastern suburbs of the city on the morning of 27 August 1944. At the time he and three other members of the Resistance had been trying to cross the German lines at Clichy-sous-Bois to recover some weapons when his vehicle was fired on by the Germans. He was wounded, captured, then shot to the ground. He was left there to die.

Paul Tessier was buried at Lagny-sur-Marne, a town some 18 miles by road east of Paris. A road in the town has since been dedicated to his memory.

TROTOBAS, Michael Alfred Raymond

Date of death:	27 November 1943
Place of death:	Lille, France
Rank:	Captain
Parent unit:	Manchester Regiment
Service number:	167302
Decorations:	Mentioned in Despatches, *Médaille de la Résistance Français*
Date joined SOE:	2 April 1941
Code names:	Sylvestre/Farmer/Joseph Rampal
Nationality:	British
Age at time of death:	Twenty-nine
Date of birth:	30 May 1914
Place of birth:	Brighton, UK
Location of grave:	Lille, France

Born to a British mother (some accounts say Irish) and a French father (who had served in the French Army in the First World War and became a German prisoner of war), at the age of sixteen Michael Trotobas trained as a chef at Stoke Poges Golf Club. However, after just four months he ran away to Paris. After a variety of jobs he returned to the UK in 1933 and joined the British Army.

Trotobas returned to France with the Middlesex Regiment in 1939 and was involved in the Battle of France, being wounded in the retreat and evacuated from Dunkirk. He was later commissioned as a Second Lieutenant in a machine-gun company of the Manchester Regiment.

By virtue of his language skills, Trotobas was recruited into the SOE in April 1941 where he displayed 'guts and determination'. Trotobas was one of six agents dropped into France, to the south of Châteauroux, on the night of 6/7 September 1941. The mission was not a success and he was arrested on 27 October the same year.

Trotobas was imprisoned at Limoges prior to being transferred to Mauzac internment camp in March 1942.

In July 1942 Trotobas escaped from Mauzac with ten others, all of whom established important circuits the following year. Two women helped in this escape, one of them being Virginia Hall, an American citizen and correspondent of the *New York Post*. She helped Trotobas and his friends by smuggling duplicate keys to them. According to one source SOE paid a million francs in bribes to enable Trotobas and others to make their escape. Trotobas led a party of escapers towards the Pyrénées and the Spanish border, arriving back in the UK in November 1942.

This agent's second mission in France was to establish a sabotage circuit based around Lille. Because there was a large *Luftwaffe* airbase at Merville west of Lille it was not possible to drop Trotobas and his wireless operator, Arthur Staggs, directly into their area. Instead the two agents were parachuted into the country to the south-west of Paris. Nevertheless, the FARMER circuit soon became firmly established in this area, which had been occupied by the Germans in the First World War and whose people still retained bitter memories of those days.

This area was also one through which the main railway lines ran, which would be of vital importance in the movement of supplies from Germany when the reinvasion of north-west Europe began. The railways would be FARMER's main targets.

At the end of February 1943, Trotobas, known locally as Captain Michel, destroyed forty railway trucks in a derailment on the Lens-Béthune line. The line was also closed for two days to clear the track. FARMER continued to hit the railways and, by the middle of the year, it was achieving between fifteen and twenty derailments a week.

Trotobas's first real setback was when Staggs was arrested in December 1942. Though his SOE affiliation was not established by the Germans and he was later released, he could no longer operate. This meant that Trotobas could only make contact with London through operators with other circuits. From April 1943 he used Dubois of the DONKEYMAN circuit in the Loire. Through Dubois, Trotobas was able to secure a replacement for Staggs, Lieutenant Olivier (Lieutenant Michael Reeve).

Olivier, however, was not the wireless operator Trotobas has wished for but a sabotage instructor. Though disappointed, Trotobas returned to Lille to mount a major operation against the locomotive works at Fives in the eastern suburbs of the city. This was one of the largest and most important in France.

Disguised in *gendarmerie* uniforms borrowed from a friendly police station, the group of twenty walked up to the main gate and convinced the guards that they were there to carry out an inspection of the premises. Once inside, the group laid charges in the transformer house. The resulting explosion destroyed 4,000,000 litres of oil and twenty-two transformers were damaged. The plant was out of operation for some two months.

It is stated that following this action Trotobas had the simple message 'Operation performed' sent to London. The answer was almost as blunt: 'Well done. Stop. Please send pictures.'

Undeterred, Trotobas returned to the works and, posing as a member of staff, set about obtaining the required images – with the assistance of a number of Germans present. These pictures were duly sent to Baker Street with a short note: 'With greetings; Resistance.'

Over the following weeks, FARMER continued its remarkable attacks against the French railways. According to M.R.D. Foot, one report in November stated that on the Amiens-

Arras line there were four derailments in just five days, all of which caused major disruptions to the railroad timetables. Both sides of the line, it was said, were 'absolutely littered' with damaged trucks, carriages and material.

Trotobas's success, and the popularity that he enjoyed amongst the locals, would lead to his downfall; his fame meant that he was well known by large numbers of people. It was perhaps inevitable that this would eventually offer the Gestapo an opportunity to penetrate his circuit.

This happened after Lieutenant Olivier had been arrested on the morning of 27 November. A sub-agent, who was attempting to escape from France into Spain after he had shot a German soldier, was captured trying to cross the Pyrénées. Under torture the sub-agent disclosed the name of the person, a local baker called Dewispelaere, who had helped him get away from Lille. The Germans raided Dewispelaere's house at 01.00 hours on the morning of 27 November 1943, and as well as the baker, they discovered Lieutenant Olivier.

The Gestapo wanted to know where Trotobas was hiding and Olivier was roughly treated. To save himself further pain he gave the address of a place he believed Trotobas had recently left.

Olivier went with the Germans to show them the house. The place was raided at 06.45 hours that same morning and a senior German was killed. So too was Trotobas.

Inspired, rather than discouraged by his death, Trotobas's circuit redoubled its activities and continued to create chaos on the railway network in north-eastern France. By the time of the liberation, the FARMER circuit had lost fifty members shot by the enemy, eighty-five deported and assumed dead, and 200 killed in action out of a total membership of around 8,000.

Trotobas was so highly regarded by the French people that the road in which he was killed in Lille was renamed after the war Rue du Capitaine Michel.

UNTERNAHRER, Yolande Elsa Maria

Date of death:	13 September 1944
Place of death:	Dachau, Germany
Rank:	Section Officer
Parent unit:	Women's Auxiliary Air Force
Service number:	9902
Decorations:	Mentioned in Despatches, *Croix de Guerre*
Date joined SOE:	15 February 1943
Code names:	Mariette/Palmist/Yvonne de Chauvigny/Yolande Elsa Maria Beekman
Nationality:	French
Age at time of death:	Thirty-two
Date of birth:	7 November 1911
Place of birth:	Paris, France
Location of memorial:	Runnymede, UK

Born in Paris to a Swiss family in 1911, Unternahrer moved as a child to London. This background was noted by the SOE instructors: 'Although her childhood was spent in Paris and she knows Switzerland only as a place for holidays, there is, nevertheless, a lot of the sterling Swiss quality in her quiet self-confidence and serenely cheerful outlook on life. She has a ready sense of humour without being witty; more common sense than intellect; more reliability than initiative. She shows any amount of determination in mastering the intricacies of W/T and gives the impression that although she expects to learn slowly and with pains, it never occurs to her that she will not get there in the end.'

When war broke out she enlisted in the WAAF where she was trained as a wireless operator. However, her language skills – she would grow up fluent in English, German, Italian and French – and radio expertise made her an ideal candidate for the SOE, and she was transferred in early 1943. She also married Sergeant Jaap Beekman of the Dutch Army and served with the SOE as Yolande Beekman, by which name she is more generally known.

Shortly after the marriage, on the night of 17–18 September 1943, she was flown into France by an aircraft piloted by Squadron Leader Austin of 624 (Special Duties) Squadron. Her SOE trainers viewed her as: 'feminine enough, alive and intuitive ... her motive is idealism 'the good of the cause' and devotion to duty.' Her job in France was to act as the wireless operator to Gustave Biéler's MUSICIAN circuit at Saint-Quentin in the *département* of Aisne.

Unternahrer helped organise the delivery of a great deal of munitions and actually participated in over twenty parachute drops before being arrested in Saint-Quentin on 13 January 1944 at the Café Moulin Brulé along with Biéler.

Unfortunately, Unternahrer had made the fatal mistake of repeatedly transmitting messages from the same location, on the same wavelength, at the same hour, on the same three days of the week. It was not too difficult for the German direction-finders to track her down. It seems that she and Biéler had decided, contrary to their training, that it was safer to send messages from a well-hidden wireless than risk continually changing location.

At the Gestapo headquarters in Saint-Quentin the two were tortured repeatedly but they did not break their silence and they were taken to Avenue Foch before being transferred to Frèsnes prison near Paris. Here Unternahrer shared a cell with a Hedwig Müller, a nurse that had been arrested by the Gestapo in 1944, who after the war reported that Unternahrer rarely left her cell as her legs had became very weak – possibly due to the brutal treatment she had received at the hands of her captors.

Frèsnes was a civilian prison and it appears that when a chief wardress realised that Unternahrer and the other SOE girls held there were classified as 'political prisoners' she objected and as a result Unternahrer, Damerment, Plewman and Inayat-Khan were moved to Karlsruhe.

At the prison here, at 01.30 hours on the morning of 10 September 1944, she was woken and taken with the three other girls in handcuffs down to the local railway station. The train was taking them to Dachau. They arrived at the concentration camp late at night and the women were woken very early the next morning. They were marched out to a sandy courtyard along one side of which was a building with a large chimney. According to the evidence given by a Karlsruhe Gestapo officer, Max Wassmer, the girls were told 'to kneel down with their faces towards a small mound of earth and were then each shot through the back of the neck as they held hands'.

This, though, was not the truth. The girls were badly beaten and 'cruelly murdered'. What form this took has never been established.

VASS, Alexander Francis

Date of death:	23 December 1944
Place of death:	Limburg, Germany
Rank:	Second Lieutenant
Parent unit:	General List
Service number:	83995
Decorations:	None recorded
Date joined SOE:	7 October 1943
Code names:	Alexander Vincent/Sergeant Victor
Nationality:	Hungarian, naturalised Canadian
Age at time of death:	Thirty-two
Date of birth:	25 October 1912
Place of birth:	Komló, Hungary

Location of memorial: Brookwood, UK

Described as being of slight build, dark-haired Alexander Vass had enlisted in the Royal Canadian Army Medical Corps early in 1943, leaving his job as a linotype operator in Toronto. Within a few months, the SOE's hunt for volunteers to serve in Hungary had yielded results. Fluent in English and Hungarian (he had been twelve-years-old when his family settled in Canada), Vass had answered the call and was duly released from the Canadian Army in October 1943 whilst serving in Italy.

In training in Scotland it was noted that 'his standard of moral is very high and his loyalty to the Allied cause is indisputable. He is very patriotic.' Despite one author referring to him as highly strung, Vass was highly praised throughout his training, becoming one of the best radio operators and proving to be very fit and capable. It was recorded that he had 'excelled in his parachute training at Ringway'.

On the night of 3/4 July 1944, Vass, serving under the name Alexander Vincent, was one of four passengers on a 148 (Special Duties) Squadron Handley Page Halifax Mk.II (serial number JP286, coded 'FS-S'), which had taken off from Brindisi in Italy.

The destination, for the Halifax's passengers at least, was the town of Bakony, north of Lake Balaton in western Hungary. A member of the DEERHURST mission, Vass was to be dropped by parachute. (He was replacing Lieutenant Stephen Mate – a former sergeant in the Canadian Army – who was killed in an air crash off Cornwall on 17 April 1944.)

The Halifax did not return and nothing was heard of Vass until a report was received through French sources that all four men (erroneously described as American airmen) had been in the Gestapo prison in Budapest since 29 July 1944.

Post-war research has revealed that the Halifax, flown by twenty-four-year-old Squadron Leader Surry Philip Victor Bird, was almost certainly intercepted and shot down by the night-fighter flown by *Hauptmann* Leopold Fellerer of StabIII/*NJG6*. He submitted a claim for a 'kill' made at 01.50 hours on the 4th whilst some 7 miles north-east of Kaposvár, Hungary. The 'plane crashed and exploded, all eight crew being killed. This indicates that the aircraft's human cargo, Vass included, must have already made their jump. The crew of JP286 had succeeded in their mission, but it cost them their lives.

It was later revealed in a Hungarian newspaper, and confirmed by a signal from Istanbul, that the men had landed next to a Jewish labour camp close to the porcelain manufacturing centre of Herend, near the city of Veszprém (and therefore some miles from their intended drop zone). They had been quickly arrested.

One of the other passengers in the aircraft, Lieutenant-Colonel E.P.E. Broughay, later described how the small team had, after one abortive pass, been dropped in the wrong place, landing in the middle of a forest and split into two pairs:

'Our parachutes were draped over tree-tops and I for one was left hanging about 30 feet up a tree ... There was no hope of concealing our whereabouts.

'At dawn the [Hungarian] Army, assisted by the Home Guard, were soon out in force. Despite this, both Vincent [Vass] and I – Vincent found himself with me on our side of the hill – managed to conceal ourselves for about twenty-four hours, escaping detection by only feet from the lines of troops who were combing the area. On a subsequent drag, a soldier came right upon our hideout. We were lucky that he did not shoot us in his fright.

'We were captured and taken down the hill to join our other companions [Major R.J.M. 'Dickie' Wright and Sergeant A.S. Manley] at the Staff HQ set up in the woods.'

After being strip-searched and a brief interrogation, the four men were taken by truck to Veszprém where Broughay recalled that they were informed that the whole team was going to be shot the following day. Thankfully this threat never materialised, and all four instead found themselves being taken to the 'secret Police HQ in Budapest'.

It was known that the men were subsequently transferred to the German *Durchgangslager der Luftwaffe* (Dulag Luft – a transit camp for air force prisoners of war) at Limburg. Whilst still in captivity at Limburg, Vass was killed by an Allied air raid in December 1944.

VIVIAN, Guy Joseph

Date of death:	9 November 1943
Place of death:	Paris, France
Rank:	Captain
Parent unit:	General List
Service number:	241054
Decorations:	None recorded
Date joined SOE:	23 April 1942
Code names:	Schellens/Goat/Jean Choudon
Nationality:	Naturalised British
Age at time of death:	Thirty-two
Date of birth:	18 January 1911
Place of birth:	Antwerp, Belgium
Location of memorial:	Brookwood, UK

Born to a British father and Belgian mother in Antwerp, Guy Vivian left Belgium in 1935 to work for the General Post Office in Britain as a linguist switchboard operator. He joined the Royal Corps of Signals in September 1939, operating with the BEF in Cherbourg until June 1940.

He married his Belgian wife at an early age and against his parent's wishes. This did not trouble his SOE assessors but his extra-marital activities certainly did. These are the words of Lance Corporal Ashley: 'My impression is that he is cynical, hypocritical and subservient to his superiors. I believe these characteristics to be due more to his conjugal infidelities than to any other cause. He says that he has had nearly 1,000 mistresses in his life, mostly young ones. At Cherbourg he had a flat where he gave English lessons to young girls and, to quote him, 'My flat was a real brothel'.'

Others saw a different side to him. One regarded him as 'careful in his conversations and guarded in his behaviour. His manner in public was always most commendable.'

Having joined the SOE on 23 April 1942, Vivian was sent into the field by Lysander on 13 April 1943. He was instructed to organise a courier line for passing men and mail back and forwards between Belgium and Britain. He was landed in France, as this was easier than attempting to land in Belgium.

Little is revealed in his personal file about his subsequent activities but the last contact London received from Vivian was a report sent through the diplomatic bag from Berne, Switzerland on 13 November 1943. He was arrested at 48 bis Rue des Belles-Feuilles in Paris and the Gestapo seized his papers, which gave away the nature of his activities.

It transpired that Lance Corporal Ashley was correct in being concerned about Vivian's philandering as it was his intense interest in women that was his undoing. The reason why the Gestapo had visited him was because they were investigating his alleged murder of a 'girl spy' to whom he had talked too much.

It has been said that Vivian was shot by the Germans at the Fort du Mont-Valérien in November 1943. Located in Suresnes, a western suburb of Paris, this fortress was used by the Germans as a place of execution between 1940 and 1944. Prisoners were brought to the fort by vehicle from other locations around the capital. On arrival they were held in a disused chapel before being walked the short distance to a prepared clearing. The bodies of those shot by firing squad were then buried in a variety of cemeteries in the Paris area. For some unexplained reason, Vivian's body was not buried in the Père-Lachaise cemetery until 4 December 1943.

WALLACE, David John

Date of death:	17 August 1944
Place of death:	Menina, Greece
Rank:	Major
Parent unit:	King's Royal Rifle Corps
Service number:	240118
Decorations:	None recorded
Date joined SOE:	7 May 1943
Code names:	None recorded
Nationality:	British
Age at time of death:	Twenty-nine
Date of birth:	3 October 1914
Place of birth:	London
Location of grave:	Paramythia, Greece

The son of Captain the Rt. Hon. Euan Wallace, MC, PC, and of Lady Idina Wallace (née Sackville), David Wallace worked as a Press Attaché to the British Legation in Athens before the German invasion of Greece in 1941. In this capacity he was well known to Lord Ridley who recommended Wallace to the staff at Baker Street in glowing terms.

Wallace was, according to the peer, 'absolutely and entirely first class in every respect – clever, brave and an excellent mixer.' With such a recommendation Wallace was taken on by the SOE for training on 7 May 1943.

On 3 June 1943, Wallace left for Cairo, returning on 3 September. He went back to Cairo on 11 October from where he was dropped into Greece on 18 July 1944.

At this time the Greek Resistance groups were on the offensive against the Germans, but they were also fighting each other for control of Greece after the war.

One of those groups, which had received considerable support from the Allies, was the right-wing *Ethnikos Dimokratikos Ellinikos Syndesmos* (EDES – National Republican Greek League), which was led by Napoleon Zervas. Wallace was sent into the area controlled by Zervas as an 'observer'. He sought permission from the Senior British Liaison Officer in the Epirus region, Lieutenant-Colonel Barnes, to visit the whole area, including the fighting units of Zervas's forces. Barnes agreed but he stipulated that on grounds of safety Wallace must remain with HQ units.

On 17 August 1944, Zervas's forces attacked the German positions at Menina on the road running inland from Igoumenitsa to Yannina. Wallace wanted to watch the fighting and he went to one of the forward posts, which was commanded by the American Captain J.A. Rogers. It was this officer who submitted the report on Wallace's death:

'Major Wallace came to my station near Paramythia ... being in charge of this station and knowing his position in this country, solely as an observer, we talked of his taking part in the affair. He asked me if he could come along just to watch. I placed him with a competent officer and told him if he would please follow at a safe distance, which he consented to do.

'At a phase of the battle he evidently showed himself and was fired on by a heavy machine-gun. He went into a prone position and one bullet hit him in the top of his left shoulder coming out about half-way down his spine. He lived a few minutes only.'

Hard fighting continued all day and through the night. By the time the Germans withdrew thirty-five men had been wounded and ten, including Wallace, had been killed.

He was buried at Paramythia the following day. His grave, the single Commonwealth burial in the cemetery, is marked by a memorial raised by the 10th Greek Division, the strongest national Resistance force fighting against the Germans. The inscription is in Greek. The translation reads: 'Here rests amongst his guerrilla comrades an Englishman, Major David Wallace, killed on 17th August, 1944, in the Battle of Menina. The soil of Greece is honoured to give shelter to this hero.'

WHITTY, Valentine Edward

Date of death:	12 July 1945	
Place of death:	London, UK	
Rank:	Major	
Parent unit:	5th Royal Tank Regiment, Royal Armoured Corps	
Service number:	171993	
Decorations:	Mentioned in Despatches, *Croix de Guerre avec Palme*	
Date joined SOE:	3 April 1944	
Code names:	Ross	
Nationality:	British	
Age at time of death:	Forty-two	
Date of birth:	May 1903	
Place of birth:	Vancouver, Canada	

Location of memorial: Golders Green, UK

Canadian-born Valentine Whitty was with the 7th Armoured Division in Italy when he was invited to join the SOE expressly for employment with a Jedburgh team.

Having accepted, he began his training in April 1944 during which time there was an investigation into his background that revealed discrepancies in the information which he had provided on joining. It transpired that Whitty had lied about his age; he had given a birth date in May 1909, by which point he was, in reality, already six years old. When confronted over this he said that he did not give his true age as he feared that the SOE would consider him too old to be taken on (which was actually true). According to his personal file, there was also some suspicion that he had more than one wife.

Other concerns were that in the course of the background checks he was identified as actually being Valentine Edward Corrado. This individual had been found guilty of embezzlement at Worthing Police Court in West Sussex in 1933, and of stealing a blank cheque and obtaining £7 10s 0d by false pretences. In this case the offender was bound over for twelve months and ordered to pay 12 guineas in costs. Whitty eventually admitted to the Judge Advocate General's office he had indeed been born Corrado, and that he had changed his name by deed poll in about 1934.

Whilst Whitty had claimed to have been a gold mining engineer before the war, it transpired that he was an advertising representative until his conviction, following which he went to work in a preparatory school. He also had two other aliases. Nothing about Valentine Whitty was as it seemed.

When he was challenged about his deception he stated that he hid his true identity as he did not want his past to damage his future. 'Major Whitty asserts that he had no other reason for the deception,' states one report, 'than to live down his past and he endeavours to explain that his education claims were merely put in because he thought that the more he 'wrote himself up' the better chance he had of obtaining some employment ...'

Though he was considered by some to be 'a rogue and a liar', others felt differently. On 19 December 1944, Lieutenant Colonel L. Carleton-Smith gave the following description: 'A remarkable personality, forceful character but pleasant at the same time. A good organiser and leader.'

His training went well and he was parachuted into France to lead the HAROLD Jedburgh. The rest of his team was Sergeant Harry Verlander (reputedly the youngest of the Jedburgh personnel) and the Frenchman Lieutenant Pierre Rimbaut.

Despite his dubious past, Whitty conducted his mission in France, though there are different opinions on his performance in the field. The team jumped from their aircraft at the lowest possible altitude (300 feet) and Whitty later claimed that instead of landing in a field he landed on the roof of a bakery, rolled off and fell onto the cobbled street below, damaging his back. Though he later claimed to have been badly hurt in his fall, he made no mention of this fact at the time. In a letter to the authors, Harry Verlander described exactly what happened: 'Pierre was given the honour of jumping first into his homeland, followed by myself and finally Major Whitty who landed within 15 to 20 feet of myself just outside a village. However, he did overshoot the field and landed on a country pathway between the field and the village. As Pierre started to bury the 'chutes, Whitty joined me to signal to the plane to drop our equipment on three parachutes. The first (Pierre's) arrived safely, the second, mine, 'candled' and bounced on impact, damaging my rucksack and spare radio receiver and the third overshot the field and we could not find it. In fact, we took the risk of walking round the village, which happened to be occupied by German troops, for a couple of hours looking for it. As it was getting light, we were forced to leave the area and at this point we knew nothing about a bakery. It was only after three nights' walking to our designated mission area of L'Absie that we heard that the third 'chute had fallen at the back of the bakery.' This was Whitty's 'chute containing his kit and radio set.

It was said that he performed well in the field and no derogatory reports were received in London about his conduct, though his team members found him to be very temperamental. During his time in France he did not consult a doctor or discuss any back or neck problems with the rest of his team, though they did notice that he wore a corset.

Upon his return to the UK in December 1944, he complained that because of his bad landing in France he could not move his neck and when he was examined by a Harley Street doctor it was found that he had broken two of his vertebrae. Incredible though it may seem, it appears that Whitty had continued to operate behind enemy lines with a broken neck.

Whitty urgently needed an operation but this he refused as he 'detested' anaesthetic. He threatened to kill himself a number of times. Then, on 12 July 1945, he shot himself in an hotel on Oxford Street, London. He left a suicide note to his wife.

The Coroner at the St Pancras inquest pronounced that Whitty had taken his life 'while of unsound mind'. Officially, Whitty was the last SOE agent to give his or her life in the Second World War.

WILKINSON, Edward Mountford

Date of death:	7 September 1944
Place of death:	Mauthausen, Austria
Rank:	Flying Officer
Parent unit:	Royal Air Force Volunteer Reserve
Service number:	71123
Decorations:	Mentioned in Despatches, *Croix de Guerre*
Date joined SOE:	1942
Code names:	Alexandre/Privet/Edmund Paul Montfort
Nationality:	American
Age at time of death:	Forty-two
Date of birth:	27 June 1902
Place of birth:	St Louis, Missouri, USA

Location of memorial: Runnymede, UK

Though born in Missouri, Edward Wilkinson spoke better French than he did English. He parachuted into a prepared dropping zone near Grand Bourg north of the Limoges on the night of 1/2 June 1942 along with his organiser Benjamin Cowburn to start the TINKER circuit in the unoccupied zone.

The group needed a wireless operator and were able to enlist the services of Denis Rake who had reached France by felucca two weeks earlier. To get hold of a transmitter Wilkinson and Rake travelled to Lyons, meeting up with another agent, Richard Heslop, who had recently arrived in France.

There are two versions of the arrest of these men. One is that they stopped off at Limoges overnight on 15 August. That evening Rake was in the hotel alone when two French police inspectors entered to carry out a spot check. Rake's unease at the sight of these two officials did not pass unnoticed and he was detained on suspicion. When Wilkinson and Heslop went into the hotel to meet Rake, they too were arrested.

The other version, the one given out by Denis Rake, is that he was due to meet the other two agents at the Hotel des Faisans and he was waiting in his room when the door was pushed in by Gendarmes dragging with them Heslop and Wilkinson. With horror Rake saw that they were handcuffed. What shocked him even more was the look on the other two agent's faces – they believed that Rake had betrayed them.

Rake and Wilkinson claimed to have only just met each other but they had on them large quantities of mint-new 1,000-franc notes numbered consecutively and their identity cards, supposedly issued in different towns, were made out in the same handwriting!

The three men were taken to Castres prison and then moved to Chambaran prisoner of war camp, but they were not held there for long. When the Germans walked into Vichy and took over the previously unoccupied zone, the prison governor, either because of his disgust with the Germans or because of pro–Allied sentiments, released the SOE men whom he had been ordered to shoot.

Wilkinson wanted to have nothing further to do with what he perceived as being the traitor Rake and went onto Angers alone, establishing the PRIVET network with a small number of his personal friends. He was arrested for a second time on 6 June 1943, when he walked into a German trap in Paris. With his capture the PRIVET circuit ceased its activities. After being interned in Layfayette prison, he was moved to Germany and executed at Mauthausen.

In his recommendation for Wilkinson to be awarded a Mention in Despatches, Buckmaster described Edward Wilkinson as being 'as hard as they come'.

WILKINSON, George Alfred

Date of death:	5 October 1944
Place of death:	Buchenwald, Germany
Rank:	Captain
Parent unit:	General List
Service number:	294481
Decorations:	Mentioned in Despatches, *Croix de Guerre*
Date joined SOE:	6 July 1943
Code names:	Etienne/Historian/Georges Alfred Verdia
Nationality:	Dual British & French
Age at time of death:	Thirty-one
Date of birth:	31 August 1913
Place of birth:	Paris, France

Location of memorial: Brookwood, UK

Born in Paris on 31 August 1913 with dual British and French nationality, Wilkinson left his wife and child in France when he joined the British Army. He was regarded very highly by his instructors who considered him to be, 'of very high intelligence ... quick, alert, imaginative and very resourceful in action. He has qualities of leadership and at once inspires confidence in others.'

He was parachuted into France on 5 April 1944 as an organiser for the HISTORIAN circuit in the Orléans area – where his wife was still residing. It was an area where, to quote the SOE file, German 'repressive measures' had effectively checked all previous attempts to develop a Resistance network.

He soon developed a strong organisation and was able to arrange substantial arms drops that enabled them to prepare for large-scale action on D-Day. The measure of his achievements was shown on 6 June 1944 when all the railway and telecommunications targets he had been set were successfully attacked.

Wilkinson was arrested towards the end of June at Olivet and for the first fortnight he was kept at the Eugéne Vignat prison in Orléans. He was then taken to Frèsnes prison where he was seen by other agents and was at that stage looking well. He was part of a large batch of SOE and Resistance operatives taken from Frèsnes to Buchenwald via Reims and Saarbrücken, which they reached on 14 August. On their arrival at Buchenwald the men were put to work on different jobs.

On 24 August 1944, Allied aircraft bombed the Gustloff armaments factory outside the camp, where many prisoners worked. Several bombs fell on the SS barracks, killing eighty and injuring 300 SS men and many more prisoners. It is said that in retaliation for the Allied raid the camp commandant, SS *Obersturmbann-Führer* Pfister ordered the execution of all the British and French 'terrorists'.

The first executions took place on 14 September (initially reported to be seventeen in total) and those that were not called out thought that they might be safe. However, on 5 October a further number, including George Wilkinson, were called out and shot that day. Because those that were called out did not know whether they were being selected for a transfer or to be placed on some other work detail, there was no opportunity for them to give any final instructions or messages to comrades or loved-ones.

Those left behind were only aware of the fate of the ones taken away when they saw the lists showing that the others had been shot (though initial investigations indicated that they had been hanged). It was reported that the men had died bravely, 'standing rigidly to attention and saying: 'Long live France, long live England'.'

WORMS, Jean Alexandre

Date of death:	29 March 1945
Place of death:	Flossenbürg, Germany
Rank:	Lieutenant
Parent unit:	General List
Service number:	260903
Decorations:	Military Cross, *Croix de Guerre avec Palme*, *Médaille de la Résistance Française*
Date joined SOE:	Not recorded
Code names:	Robin/Juggler/Jules Warrens/Jean de Verieux
Nationality:	French
Age at time of death:	Thirty-six
Date of birth:	February 1909
Place of birth:	Paris, France

Location of memorial: Brookwood, UK

As early as September 1940, Jean Worms, a Swiss businessman, had been actively involved in the Resistance movement in Paris and inevitably this resulted in him joining the PROSPER circuit. In April 1942 Francis Suttill asked Worms to help him secure the release of two of his sub-agents, the sisters Tambour, who had been arrested by the *Abwehr*. Worms was given a million francs (around £70,000 at today's values) to bribe their captors into releasing them.

The Germans saw this as a great opportunity to have some fun with the Resistance. They agreed to meet Worms who handed over the cash. The *Abwehr* responded by sending two women to Worms – the women were a pair of middle-aged prostitutes.

In October 1942 he left France by felucca to go to Britain for training, returning as a fully-fledged SOE agent on 22 January 1943, landing not far from Châtres. Serving as Jean de Verieux, he became the second in command of the JUGGLER circuit, organising sabotage groups on the upper Marne round Châlons. It is said that he had put together ten, ten-man-strong teams in and around Châlons, and these achieved some early successes against the local railway network.

The JUGGLER *réseaux* was a sub-circuit of the PROSPER network and it was completely disrupted by the mass arrests in the summer of 1943. Worms suggested to Baker Street that he should take over the remnants of PROSPER to try and stabilise affairs but Buckmaster did not want to take that risk in such an unpredictable situation.

Despite the arrests, Worms continued to eat at the same black market restaurant, the *Chez Tutulle*, in the Rue Perglèse as he had previously. He was arrested there on 1 July 1943. One of his colleagues, Jean Weil, was going to join Worms and he arrived to see his colleague being led to a car in handcuffs. Weil left France as quickly as he could, escaping through Switzerland. The circuit was taken over by his second in command, Sonia Olschanezky.

Worms was killed at Flossenbürg in March 1945. It is estimated that between April of 1944 and April of 1945, more than 1,500 executions were carried out here. To this end, six new gallows hooks were installed. In the last months the rate of daily executions overtook the capacity of the crematorium. As a solution, the SS began stacking the bodies in piles, drenching them with gasoline, and setting them alight.

YOUNG, John Cuthbert

Date of death:	6 September 1944
Place of death:	Mauthausen, Austria
Rank:	Lieutenant
Parent unit:	General List
Service number:	241152
Decorations:	MBE, *Croix de Guerre avec Palme*
Date joined SOE:	27 April 1942
Code names:	Gabriel/Judge/Charles Camus
Nationality:	British
Age at time of death:	Thirty-six
Date of birth:	25 September 1907
Place of birth:	Newcastle, UK

Location of memorial: Brookwood, UK

John Young, a fire insurance surveyor before military service, married a French girl but, having been born in Newcastle of British parents, his French speech was undeniably English.

Young struggled to keep up with the other students in physical activities during his SOE training. There were also security issues. A letter was seen during his time under assessment in which not only did a naval officer discuss Young's possible future secret employment but also his wife stated that she wanted to join FANY and be a wireless operator so that she could be near him when he took off on his mission.

Having been 'grilled' about these indiscretions it was considered that he now had 'an excellent understanding of the importance of being security minded'. As a result he was gazetted a Second Lieutenant and became effective with the SOE on 16 June 1942.

Young was parachuted into France on 19 May 1943, as a wireless operator to a circuit (ACROBAT) near Saint-Étienne in eastern France. A month after his arrival his circuit chief, John Starr, was arrested by the Germans and the organisation was in danger of being broken up. Young took over command and kept it operating, maintaining regular contact with London and organising sabotage missions under perilous conditions. Assisted by Diana Rowden, he eventually could count on a body of 3,500 armed fighters.

The local Gestapo knew all about Young. They had his description and direction-finding teams had detected his set – they were on the alert for his every transmission. By August he had become so seriously compromised he was advised to leave France. However, Young was determined to remain at his post until his successor was in the field. Two days before his replacement arrived, on the evening of 18 November 1943, a thirty-five-man-strong Gestapo team finally tracked him down.

This came about, according to more than one source, because of the capture of André Maugenet following his arrival in France in November 1943. He was carrying with him a personal letter from John Young's wife to her husband at Clairvaux.

A French collaborator adopted Maugenet's identity and, carrying Mrs Young's letter, turned up at the Janier-Dubry saw-mill where Young was staying and asked for 'Gabriel'. He handed the letter to Young who immediately recognised his wife's handwriting and warmly welcomed the newcomer. After some discussion the man left. That evening a German vehicle drove into the yard of the saw-mill. Eighteen soldiers and SS men jumped out and wildly opened fire. They then smashed down the door and dragged out Young and Diana Rowden.

Young seems to have been moved around a great deal during the time he was in captivity. At first he was taken to Lyon and the following day sent to the Cherche-Midi prison in Paris. Whilst he certainly spent some time at 3 bis Place des États Unis, this message was found on the wall at 84 Avenue Foch: 'Lt J.C. Young, arrived 20.11.43.'

At the beginning of 1944 he was at prison in Troyes. On 18 April 1944, he was moved to Ravitsch. Young was eventually transported to Mauthausen where he was executed.

References and Endnotes

G. Adler: TNA HS9/9/3.

J. Agazarian: TNA HS9/11/1; TNA HS8/100/2; TNA HS8/895; information about Flossenbürg in TNA HS9/324/4; Fuller, *Penetration*, pp.47, 99-102 and 149; Tickell, *Odette*, p.199; Foot, *SOE in France*, pp. 261, 266, 263, 286-7; L. Jones, *Quiet Courage*, pp. 147, 148, 155, 330.

R. Alexandre: TNA HS9/21/4; Foot, *France*, pp. 302; Fuller, *Penetration*, p. 134; West, *Secret War*, pp.153, 162.

E. Allard: TNA HS9/23/2; Foot, *France*, p.335: Perrin, *Spirit of Resistance*, p.151.

P. Amphlett: TNA HS9/30/1; Foot, *France*, pp.224 & 263.

J. Amps: TNA HS9/30/2; Foot, *France*, pp.178 &2 75; L. Jones, p.55; Fuller, *Penetration*, p.46.

F. Antelme: TNA HS9/42-44; TNA HS8/100/2; L. Jones, pp.217-8, 224, 232; Nicholas, *Death be not Proud*, pp.240, 278, 283, 285; Foot, *France*, pp.302-3, 304-7.

J. Austin: TNA HS9/65/6; TNA HS9/1121/1.

D. Barrett: TNA HS9/94/7; TNA HS8/100/2; Foot, *France*, pp.263, 360 & 375; Perrin, pp.158, 195; West, p. 291.

A. Beauregard: TNA HS9/111/1: Foot, *France*, pp.329-30; West, p.296.

F. Bec: TNA HS9/111/5.

Y. Beekman: L. Jones, pp.205, 304, 321; B. Cook *Women and War*, p.59; Nicholas, pp.110-111; Foot, *France*, pp.324, 378, 377; Escott, *Heroines of SOE*, pp.121-4.

R. Benoist: TNA HS9/127 & 128; TNA HS8/100/2; Foot, *France*, pp.336, 360, (his Operation Orders are reproduced in full on pages 447-50 of Foot); Perrin, p.151; L. Jones, pp.221-2, 260; Nicholas, pp.190, 267; Fuller, *Penetration*, pp.147, 153.

E. Berliner: TNA HS9/134/5.

L. Bertheau: TNA HS9/138/3; Perrin, pp.118-120, 176-7.

G. Bieler: TNA HS9/147/5; TNA HS8/100/2; Nicholas, pp.44, 106, 110-1, 241 & 278; L. Jones, pp.149, 205, 332; Fuller, *Penetration*, pp.47, 106; West, pp.294; Foot, *France*, pp.200, 324, 373; Ian Dear, *Escape and Evasion*, p.146.

A. Block: TNA HS9/195/4; TNA HS8/100/2; De Vomécourt, *Who Live to See the Day*, p.100. Details concerning identity cards can be found in TNA HS9/324/4; Foot, *France*, pp.156,158, 174-5.

D. Bloch: Ottaway, *Violette Szabo*, pp.143-5; TNA HS9/165/8; TNA HS8/100/2; L. Jones, pp.222-5, 274, 311, 314, 317-8; Fuller, *Penetration*, pp.137, 147, 153; Foot, *France*, pp.360, 378; Escott, pp.146-8.

M. Bloom: TNA HS9/166/7; TNA HS8/895; Le Chêne, *Mauthausen*, pp.122-3; Foot, *France*, pp.245-6; Cookridge, *Inside SOE*, pp.170; Dourlein, *Inside North Pole*, pp.170.

A. Borrell:	TNA HS9/183; S. Helm, *Life in Secrets,* pp.11, 226, 251; TNA HS8/895; L. Jones, pp.98, 138, 139, 147, 148, 320-21; Nicholas, pp.42-3, 63, 67, 68-73; Fuller, *Penetration*, pp.72, 84, 85, 87-9, 98, 178; Foot *France*, pp.283, 376.
J. Bouguennec:	TNA HS9/189/8; Foot *France*, pp.154, 157, 183, 231, 234, 283-4.
H. Button:	TNA HS9/249/4; Bailey, *The Wildest Province*, pp.95. 156, 190, 276-7, 289, 290; Smiley, *Albanian Assignment*, p.151.
M. Byck:	TNA HS9/250/2; TNA HS8/100/2; Escott, pp.176-80; L. Jones, pp.245, 248, 259; Cookridge, p.377; Foot *France*, p.337; Howarth, *Undercover*, p.185.
R. Byerly:	TNA HS9/ 251/1; Foot, *France*, p.302; West, pp.153, 163.
A Careless:	TNA HS9/268/4; Bailey, pp.195-6.
E. Cauchi:	TNA HS9/281/5; TNA HS8/895; West, pp.163; Foot *France*, pp.256, 327.
M. Clech:	TNA HS9/324/4; TNA HS8/100/2; TNA HS8/895; Foot, *France*, pp.264 & 275; L. Jones, pp.131, 151, 156; Nicholas, pp.18, 125, 226-7, 240, 285-6; Fuller, *Penetration*, pp.43, 56, 66, 122, 123, 152.
G. Clement:	TNA HS9 /325/3; TNA HS8/895; Foot, *France*, pp.233-4; West, p.163.
E. Coppin:	TNA HS9/350/9; Foot *France*, pp.194-5, 226; TNA HS8/895.
G. Demand:	Brief details of the SCULLION missions can be found in TNA HS9/30/1, TNA HS6 334 and Foot, *France*, p.224; Howarth, p.208.
M. Damerment:	TNA HS9/1654; Helm, pp.274-5; L. Jones, pp.216-8, 304; Nicholas, pp.43, 66-7, 68, 72-3, 230-5, 268, 278, 283; Fuller, *Penetration*, pp.109, 110, 134, 144; Foot *France*, pp.143, 83, 302-7, 377; Escott, pp.140-2.
M. Defence:	Foot, *France*, pp.249-51, 297; Fuller, *Penetration*, p.135; Cookridge, pp.253, 324.
P. Dareme:	TNA HS9/1483.
G. De St Geniès:	Foot, *France*, pp.360-1; TNA HS9/576/2; L. Jones, p.198; West, pp.164, 291.
J. Detal:	Fuller, *Penetration*, pp.135 & 153; Foot, *France*, p.297; Perrin, pp.138, 147-151.
A. Defendini:	TNA HS9/412/2; Fuller, *Penetration*, pp.136, 153; Foot *France*, p.104, 293-4.
F. Deniset:	TNA HS9/418/1; Foot, *France*, p.302; Fuller, *Penetration*, p.134; Perrin, *Spirit of Resistance*, pp.130-1; West, p.152.
R. Dowlen:	TNA HS9/447/2; TNA HS8/100/2; TNA HS8/895; Foot, *France*, pp.260, 286, 287-8, 299; Fuller, *Penetration*, pp.50, 85, 99; Cookridge, p.256.
E. Duboudin:	TNA HS9/452/3; TNA HS8/100/2; Fuller, *Penetration*, p.14; Cookridge, pp.246-8; Foot *France*, pp.157, 184, 190-3, 227, 329.

P. Duclos:	TNA HS9/453/7; Foot, *France*, p.297; Fuller, *Penetration*, p.135.
D. Finlayson:	TNA HS9/513/8; West, p.164; Foot *France*, pp.293-4.
M. Fox:	HS9/535/1; TNA HS8/100/2; TNA HS8/895; Foot, *France*, pp.231, 283-4 & 296.
H. Frager:	TNA HS9/536/1; TNA HS8/100/2; L. Jones, pp.149, 262, 272; Fuller, *Penetration*, pp.149, 152, 153; Foot *France*, pp.224-8, 255-5, 26-, 262-3, 367, 275, 276, 294, 326, 361, 375.
H. Gaillot:	TNA HS9/554/1; Foot *France*, pp.233, 264.
D. Gardner:	TNA HS9/563/6; Dear, pp.181-4; Foot, *France*, p.76.
H. Garry:	TNA HS8/100/2; L. Jones, pp.154-6, 158, 217,332; Nicholas, pp.66-7, 240, 267, 278, 283, 286; Fuller, *Penetration*, pp.65, 85, 134, 153, 173; TNA HS9/566/2; Cookridge, pp.208, 214, 255, 259, 266-9, 270-1, 305-6, 385-6; Foot *France*, pp.297-301, 302.
P. Geelen:	TNA HS9/570/6; Foot, *France*, p.335.
V. Gough:	THA HS9/604/5; West, p.350; Dear, pp.192 & 193.
H. Graham:	TNA HS9/606/5; HS6/364 (SCULLION operation).
C. Grover-Williams:	TNA HS9/1596/8; TNA HS8/100/2; TNA HS8/895; Foot, *France*, pp.175-6, 275, 26-8; Cookridge, pp.256-7, 266, 268; Saward, *The Grand Prix Saboteurs*, pp.310-8.
I. Gyori:	TNA HS9/640/6.
J. Hamilton:	TNA HS9/650/6; West, p.165; Foot *France*, p.193.
J. Hanau:	TNA HS9/653/2; Foot, *SOE: An outline history 1940-46*, pp.15-16, 23; West, pp.12-14, 64, 110.
C. Hayes:	TNA HS9/681/3; TNA HS8/895; Perrin, p.89; Foot, *France*, pp.180-1, 250-1; Cookridge, pp.324-5.
W. Hill:	TNA HA9/710/4; R. Bailey, pp.75, 101-2.
E. Hoffman:	TNA HS9/726/6.
D. Hubble:	TNA HS9/756/1; Foot *France*, p.28; Marshall, *White Rabbit*, pp.184 & 206.
N. Inayat-Khan:	TNA HS9/836/5; W. Stevenson, *A Man Callred Intrepid*, pp.230-2 & 217; Helm, pp.415-6; Fuller, *Madeleine*, pp.121, 156-83; Fuller, *Penetration*, pp.109, 119-21; Escott, pp.60-81; L. Jones, pp.49, 157-9, 215, 153-4, 321; Nicholas, pp.67, 68, 72, 74, 122, 223; Foot *France*, 295, 298-306, 320, 376-8; Escott, *The Heroines of SOE*, 97-102.
H. Johansen:	TNA HS9/799/8; Seaman, *Special Operations Executive*, pp.193-200.
S. Jones:	TNA HS9/809/5; Foot, *France*, pp.194-5, 261, 264, 325, 450-1; Cookridge, pp.291, 293, 297.
C. Jumeau:	TNA HS9/815/4; Cookridge, p.125; Foot *France*, pp.76, 183.
J. Kasap:	W. Mason, *Prisoners of War*, p.230; Archives of the Royal Pioneer Corps Association. Over the years, the association has built up a database of over 700,000 personnel who served in the Corps during the Second World War; Supplement to the *London Gazette*, 11 March 1943; the archives of the Royal Pioneer Corps

	Association; the website of the American–Israeli Cooperative Enterprise: www.jewishvirtuallibrary.org; Supplement to the *London Gazette*, 21 March 1944.
G. Keun:	TNA HS9/835/7.
R. Lansdell:	TNA HS9/886/5.
R. Langard:	Foot, *France*, pp.70-1; West, p.165.
M. Larcher:	TNA HS9/890/1; TNA HS8/100/2; Foot, *France*, p.359; L. Jones, pp.242, 267, 291; West, p.295.
G. Layzell:	TNA HS9/898/3; Bailey, pp.225-5, 230, 231.
M. Leccia:	TNA HS9/902/3; West, p.166.
J. Ledoux:	TNA HS9/904/1; Foot, *France*, p.302.
L. Lee:	TNA HS9/905/4; Cookridge, pp.302-3; West, p.153; Foot *France*, pp.291, 83, 302-7.
C. Lefort:	TNA HS9/908/1; TNA HS8/895; Helm, p.314; L. Jones, pp.160, 311, 317; Fuller, *Penetration*, pp.64 & 65; Foot *France*, pp.68, 228-9, 261, 377; Escott, pp.103-6.
V. Leigh:	TNA HS9/910/3; TNA HS8/895; Helm, p.259; L. Jones, pp.152, 304, 320-1; Nicholas, pp.63-4, 67-74, 105, 124-7, 220-1, 231, 244, 268, 272; Fuller, *Penetration*, pp.100, 122, 144, 152; Foot *France*, pp.261, 264, 376; Escott, pp.92-6.
E. Levene:	TNA HS9/918/1; West, p.166; Foot *France*, p.263.
H. Lord:	TNA HS9/939/8.
J. Macalister:	TNA HS9/954/2; Foot, *France*, pp.297, 281, 290, 293-4, 299, 301; West, pp.147-9.
D. Maitland-Makgill-Crichton:	TNA HS9/372.
C. Malraux:	TNA HS9/980/7; Foot, *France*, pp.100, 234; West, p.166.
S. Makowski:	TNA HS9/978/2; TNA HS8/100/2; Cookridge, pp.378-9.
S. Martin-Leake:	TNA HS9/900/1; Bailey, pp.7, 47-8, 136-9, 223, 239, 244-6; Smiley, pp.98, 120.
J. Mayer:	Grehan, *The Forgotten Invasion*, pp.39-43; TNA HS9/1011-4; Foot *France*, p.334.
G. McBain:	TNA HS9/954/6; Fuller, *Penetration*, p.136.
A. Mellows:	TNA HS9/1016/8.
J. Menesson:	TNA HS9/1021/1.
F. Michel:	TNA HS9/1029/4; Foot, *France*, p.293. Most of these stores were in fact recovered more or less intact by the Allies after the liberation of France; West, pp.148, 167, 302.
Comte de Montelembert:	TNA HS9/1052/8; Foot, *France*, p.284.
P. Mulsant:	TNA HS9/1074/4; TNA HS8/100/2; West, pp.169, 291.
N. Muvrin:	TNA HS9/1081/1; Obituary of former SOE radio operator Kenneth Scott, *The Times*, 13 November 2008.
I. Newman:	TNA HS9/1096/2; Cookridge, pp.151-2, 165; West, p.167. *Hull Daily Mail*, November 1946.

A. Nicholls:	TNA HS9/1644; Bailey, pp.95-7, 98-115, 123-6, 145-6, 155, 199; West, pp.184, 185; Smiley, pp.83-4, 103; Howarth, p.96.
G. Norman:	NA HS9/1110/5; TNA HS8/895; Helm, pp.190, 341-2, 285-8; Fuller, pp.72, 74, 79-87; L. Jones, pp.114, 138-41, 143, 147-8, 215, 218; Nicholas, pp.42, 52, 170, 178-9, 239, 278, 286.
A Opoczynski:	TNA HS9/1123/8.
C. Ogden-Smith:	TNA HS9/1377/2. The SAS member Maurice Myodon is recorded in Ogden-Smith's Personal account, though the authors were unable to verify this.
A Palmer:	TNA HS9/1138/8.
P. Pardi:	TNA HS9/1143/7; Foot, *France*, pp.263; West, 167.
M. Pertschuk:	TNA HS9/1172/7; Perrin, pp.144, 147-8, 173; Foot, *France*, pp.190, 195-6, 245-6; Cookridge, pp.169, 386.
F. Pickersgill:	TNA HS9/1186-2; Stevenson, pp.230-1; Marshall, *White Rabbit*, pp.180 & 198; L. Jones, pp.136-9, 218-20; Cookridge, pp.227-30; West, pp.147-9, 150-1, 154.
O. Pichl:	TNA HS9/1185/3.
E. Plewman:	TNA HS9/1195/1; Foot, *France*, p.229; L. Jones, pp.201, 205, 304, 321; Nicholas, pp.43, 67, 68, 72-3, 189-191, 220, 230-1, 234, 263-4, 268, 278; Escott in *Heroines of SOE*, pp.111-4, states that Steele and Plewman went to see Skepper to give him some messages and that the Gestapo were lying in wait for them.
O. Prassinos:	Airey Neave, *Saturday at MI9*, p.54; Ian Dear, *Escape and Evasion*, p.37; Clutton-Brock, *RAF Evaders*, pp.108-109; Jones, pp.53, 104, 216, 250.
A Rabinovitz:	TNA HS9/1223/4; L. Jones, pp.122, 125, 126; West, pp.150, 168.
B. Rafferty:	TNA HS9/1225/2; Foot, *History*, p.166; Foot, *France*, pp.194 & 253-4; L. Jones, pp.171 & 175; Cookridge, pp.250; West, p.292; TNA HS8/895.
C. Rechenmann:	TNA HS9/1238/1.
J. Renaud-Dandicolle:	TNA HS9/391/7; TNA HS8/100/2; L. Jones, pp.242, 267, 291.
J. Renaud:	TNA HS9/1246/2; West, p.168.
S. Roberts:	TNA HS9/1267; Bailey, pp.65, 101-2; West, p.195.
D. Rockingham:	TNA HS9/1274/6; Bailey, p.195.
L. Rolfe:	TNA HS8/100/2; Helm, pp.312-5; Escott, pp.200-8; L. Jones, pp.243, 275, 311, 314-5, 317-8; Nicholas, pp.28, 199, 216; West, pp.169, 291; Escott, pp.166-70.
D. Rowden:	TNA HS9/1287/6; TNA HS8/895; Helm, p.198; Escott, pp.82-90; L. Jones, pp.162, 304-5, 320-1; Nicholas, pp.35, 37-8, 63-4, 67-74; 90, 105, 122, 128, 136-8, 140-144, 148, 221, 230-1 241, 268, 272, 278; Cookridge, pp.280-2, 284-6, 296-7; Escott, pp.107-110.
Y. Ruddelat:	TNA HS9/895; Helm, p.11; L. Jones, pp.98, 138-9, 147-8, 218, 311, 318, 324; West, pp.143, 169; Binney, *The Women Who Lived for Danger*, pp.322-3. Escott, pp.39 43, 222-3.

R. Sabourin:	TNA HS9/1296/4; Foot, *France*, pp.293-4, 303, 307; West, p.169.
P. Sarrette:	TNA HS9/1314/3; West, pp.169, 291, 294.
G. Savon:	French Ministry of Defence, report reference DEFM9854005A, dated 14 July 1998.
A . Schwatschko:	TNA HS9/1331/1; West, p.169.
N. Selby:	TNA HS9/978/2; West, pp.189, 195; Davidson, *Special Operations Europe*, pp.168.
J. Sehmer:	Foot, *History*, p.203; West, pp.190, 312; Lees, pp.33, 34, 54-59, 65-69, 140, 146; Howarth, p.42.
E. Serini:	West, pp.66-7.
H. Sevenet:	TNA HS9/1346/2; TNA HS8/100/2; West, pp.169, 290, 293.
J. Simon:	TNA HS9/1362/4; Foot, *France*, pp.256, 327; Cookridge, pp.187, 194, 281, 285, 287-8; West, p.169.
O. Simon:	TNA HS9/1362/8; TNA HS8/100/2; Foot, *France*, pp.230, 240, 262, 284, 286, 297; West, p.169.
J. Sinclair:	TNA HS9/1365/4; West, p.169.
C. Skepper:	L. Jones, pp.136, 153, 163; Nicholas, pp.246-50, 253, 256, 261-2, 286; TNA HS9/1370/1; Cookridge, pp.214, 252, 333-6.; West, p.169.
A Steele:	Nicholas, pp.264-5; TNA HS9/1410/2; Cookridge, pp.252, 333-6, 385-6; West, p.170.
F. Suttill:	TNA HS9/1430/6; TNA HS8/100/2; Howarth, p.215; Helm, pp.11-12, 68, 110-11, 218, 280-1, 285, 344; Fuller, pp.72-6; L. Jones, pp.139, 140, 147, 148; Nicholas, pp.238-41, 243, 267, 269, 278, 287; Cookridge, pp.201-3, 207-10, 213-6, 224-8, 231-9.
V. Szabo:	This account of the fight, quoted in Ottaway, pp.106-7, differs considerably with her citation for the George Cross, which states: '... With other members of her group, she was surrounded by the Gestapo in a house in the south-west of France. Resistance appeared hopeless, but Madame Szabo, seizing a Sten gun and as much ammunition as she could carry, barricaded herself in part of the house, and, exchanging shot for shot with the enemy, killed or wounded several of them. By constant movement she avoided being cornered and fought until she dropped exhausted.' See J. Turner, *Awards of the George Cross*, pp.107-8; TNA HA9/1435; TNA HS8/100/2; L. Jones, pp.157, 274-5, 314-5, 317-8; Nicholas, pp.271-3; Cookridge, pp.317-21, 330, 387; West, pp.150, 170, 297, 307, 309; Howarth, pp.213-4.
H. Szenes:	TNA HS9/1437/5; Binney, pp.315-6.
P. Tessier:	TNA HS9/1453/2; West, p.170.
M. Trotobas:	TNA HS9/1487/1; TNA HS8/1002; Foot, *France*, pp.146, 183, 237-9, 234-4, 256; L. Jones, pp.149, 204; Nicholas, pp.203, 240-1, 278; Cookridge, pp.253, 255, 272, 275-9; West, pp.150, 170, 293; Howarth, p.213.

Y. Unternahrer: TNA HS9/114/2; Helm, pp.328-9; Nicholas, pp.43, 67, 68.

A. Vass: TNA HS9/1521/4. R. Maclean, *Canadians Behind Enemy Lines*, p164.

G. Vivian: TNA HS9/1538/1.

D. Wallace: TNA HS9/1553/1; West, pp.219, 356, 358; Howarth, pp.149-50.

V. Whitty: TNA HS9/1586/1; West, p.350; H. Verlander, *My War in SOE*, pp.76-7.

E. Wilkinson: TNA HS9/1593/1; TNA HS8/100/2; TNA HS8/895; B. Cowburn, *No Cloak, No Dagger*, pp.116-7; Foot, *France*, pp.177-8, 199-200, 231, 279; Cookridge, pp.195-6, 358-9; 147, 170.

G. Wilkinson: TNA HS9/1593/1; Foot, *France*, pp.360, 375; Cookridge, pp.330, 375, 385-6; West, 170, 291. Though there is nothing in his HS9 personal file to indicate that Edward Wilkinson was his brother, it is universally accepted that Edward and George were brothers.

J. Worms: TNA HS9/1621/4; TNA HS8/100/2; Saward, p.151; West, pp.147, 170.

J. Young: TNA HS9/1632/5; TNA HS8/895; L. Jones, pp.161-2; Nicholas, pp.154-6; 158-9, 162-3, 241, 287; Cookridge, pp.189-90, 193-4 280-5, 334, 387; West, pp.170, 302.

Chapter 3

The Missing Men

Two of the 140 agents officially recognised by the Commonwealth War Graves Commission as being killed in action whilst serving with the SOE did, in fact, survive the war. As will be seen, their fate is still either unclear or has yet to be revealed.

MAUGENET, André Adrian Jules

Date of death:	Not known
Place of death:	Not known
Rank:	Lieutenant
Parent unit:	General List
Service number:	211681
Decorations:	None recorded
Date joined SOE:	14 May 1943
Code names:	Benoit/Thatcher/André Adrien Jules Rouvray
Nationality:	French
Age at time of death:	Not known
Date of birth:	28 December 1904
Place of birth:	Châteauroux, France

Location of memorial: Brookwood, UK

'He is very intelligent indeed,' wrote an SOE assessor about André Maugenet on 3 August 1943, 'both academically and practically, and extremely quick witted. He has very considerable imagination and initiative ... He has a most pleasant personality, a very great sense of humour and is extremely popular.'

Such fulsome praise was unusual from the hard-nosed assessors. The final verdict on André Maugenet was that he was likely to be at his best 'in action'. His commitment to the Allied cause, however, was the subject of much concern.

He was the supervisor of native labour for the Shell Oil Company at Port Said but was called up by the French Government at the outbreak of war and joined the French Foreign Legion. With the fall of France he fled the Legion and joined the Fighting French. Maugenet subsequently deserted the Fighting French and went to work with the British Army in September 1941, becoming involved in commando work for G.S.I. G(R) Egypt but on an entirely unofficial basis. He was also employed by the SOE on a post-occupation plan for Egypt but it was decided on what is described as 'the highest military authority' to hand him over to the Free French as a deserter.

Maugenet was tried by the Free French and sentenced to sixty days detention after which he was handed back to the SOE who could have him if they still wanted him. The SOE's Middle East Head of Mission wanted nothing to do with Maugenet and asked for him to be removed from Cairo. MI5, however, refused to allow either Maugenet or his wife to enter the UK. Maugenet, it seems had deserted not once, but twice from the Free French.

By the time the response from MI5 had been received in Cairo, the unwanted couple had been put on a ship for the UK via South Africa. A cable was then sent to Durban to hold the Maugenets when the ship docked. They were duly arrested in Durban but as the South African authorities also wanted nothing to do with him, it was finally accepted that he would have to be allowed to continue onto Britain (his wife was Scottish).

Though initially not accepted for clandestine work with the SOE he was eventually trained and sent by Lysander into France on 15 November 1943, as the assistant to the leader of a circuit in the Saint-Étienne area. He landed safely but was soon arrested as he made his way to Paris.

On 18 November he (or someone posing as him) joined his leader, John Young, in Saint-Étienne. Within an hour the Gestapo turned up carrying submachine-guns and arrested Young and the other members of the group, actively assisted by Maugenet who was also armed. It is not known whether or not Maugenet was actually the person that was helping the Germans or someone else acting as Maugenet, but what is beyond question is that he revealed information about the circuit to the Gestapo, which led to the arrests.

Maugenet was held at 3 bis Place des État Unis and was transferred to Ravitsch where he was still reported alive in May 1944. From there he may have been moved onto Gross-Rosen where it was reported that he had been executed, even though the CWCC give his date of death as 15 November 1943 (the date he landed in France). None of this was believed by the French who were convinced that he had been protected by the Germans and that he had survived the war. It is said that in 1954 he was tracked down by the French authorities to Canada and extradition proceedings were begun in Ottawa in 1955. But before he could be extradited he escaped to South Africa. The French authorities tried to follow him but he was never found. His details are revealed in TNA HS9/1008/2.

KLEMENT, Louis

Date of death:	1 December 1943
Place of death:	Not known
Rank:	Lieutenant
Parent unit:	General List
Service number:	252416
Decorations:	Not known
Date joined SOE:	1941-1942
Code names:	Tibor/Lewis/Lajos/Vajda/Clement
Nationality:	Hungarian
Age at time of death:	Not known

Date of birth: 1920
Place of birth: Hungary

Location of memorial: Brookwood, UK

Also listed on the CWGC register as belonging to the SOE, with a date of death as 1 December 1943, is Lieutenant L. Klement, service number 252416. This is actually Louis Klement who was born in Hungary in 1920 and survived the war.

Klement joined the French Foreign Legion before making his way to the United Kingdom to work with the Free French Forces, no doubt RF Section as it is said that he trained with the French as a parachutist. At some stage, being an enemy alien, he was interred on the Isle of Man. After his release he worked as a theatre stage hand in London.

There is some doubt about the start of his SOE activities, variously being given as 1941 and 1942. He was trained as a wireless operator and became the first British agent to be sent into Hungary, arriving there through Poland (he was a fluent Polish speaker). Klement operated with the cover names of Tibor, Lewis, Lajos, Vajda and Clement.

Klement joined an existing underground cell in Budapest that was working against the Fascist regime. The cell gathered information on key installations such as airfields, factories and oil refineries, which was passed onto the British via Klement. The group also liberated a number of Allied prisoners of war from Hungarian camps and prisons and helped them reach the safety of the Allied lines at Bari via Tito's partisans in Yugoslavia.

In September 1944 the Soviets invaded Hungary and soon members of the group were rounded up. Klement was last seen in Budapest in the Geological Institute in December of that year. A report was sent to London that he had been arrested and executed on 6 December 1944.

Research indicates that Klement was arrested in Budapest as a British spy by the Soviet NKVD/SMERSH early in 1945 and transported to Russia's notorious Vladimir prison. The largest prison in Russia, Vladimir was used to hold 'dangerous' criminals. Klement was sentenced to twelve years imprisonment.

Despite attempts by the British Foreign Office, it proved impossible to obtain his release. Klement and two other Hungarians who had helped the Allies, Lazlo Pap and Karoly Schandl, were held in a special section of the prison where the cells are fitted with microphones and ultrasonic torture devices. These men were assigned numbers and were held in such severe isolation in Vladimir that not even the guards knew their real identity. Only Schandl survived to tell the story of their treatment at the hands of the Soviets. Klement's personal file is still closed to the public until 1 January 2022. However, there are details concerning his capture and imprisonment in the HS4 series files that cover SOE activities in Hungary.

Chapter 4

Known Unto Man

Of the 140 officially-recorded SOE casualties, only thirty-three have a known grave. These graves are located in twenty-one cemeteries around the world, of which fourteen, some sixty-seven percent, are in France. The remaining casualties, having no known grave, are commemorated on seven of the many memorials constructed and/or maintained by the Commonwealth War Graves Commission (CWGC).

Established by Royal Charter in 1917, the CWGC pays tribute to the 1,700,000 men and women of the Commonwealth forces who died in the two world wars. This figure includes the graves of more than 935,000 identified casualties and almost 212,000 unidentified individuals. The names of almost 760,000 people can be found on memorials to the missing. Since its inception, the Commission has constructed some 2,500 war cemeteries and plots at military and civil sites in around 150 countries.

The guiding principles of the Commission are that each casualty should be commemorated by name on a headstone or memorial, that their headstone or memorial should be permanent and uniform, and that there should be no distinction made on account of nationality, military or civil rank, race or creed.

All those men and women who gave their lives whilst serving in the SOE did so for a cause they all felt passionately about. They all knew the risks and dangers they faced, but still volunteered to undertake their missions.

To remind us of their sacrifice, the names of these SOE men and women are carved with pride on headstones or memorials at the following Commonwealth War Graves Commission sites.

THE MEMORIALS

The Bayeux Memorial
Calvados, France
Number commemorated: 4

Of the six memorials, the Bayeux Memorial, along with the Groesbeek Memorial in the Netherlands, has the fourth highest number of SOE casualties commemorated on its panels. Having died or been killed between June and September 1944, all the SOE casualties remembered here are related to the D-Day landings.

The town of Bayeux, in Normandy, lies 15 miles north-west of Caen. The memorial is situated in the south-western outskirts of the town on the appropriately named Boulevard Fabian Ware (Sir Fabian Ware was the founder of the CWGC).

The Bayeux Memorial in Normandy. It bears the name of four members of SOE. (Courtesy of CWGC)

The Allied offensive in north-western Europe began with the Normandy landings of 6 June 1944. The Bayeux Memorial stands opposite the Bayeux War Cemetery and bears the names of more than 1,800 men of the Commonwealth land forces who died in the early stages of the campaign and have no known grave. They died in operations undertaken in preparation for the invasion, during the landings themselves, in the intense fighting in Normandy itself, and as a result of the advance to the River Seine in August.

There was little actual fighting in Bayeux although it was the first French town of importance to be liberated. Interestingly, the Bayeux War Cemetery is the largest Commonwealth cemetery of the Second World War in France.

The Athens Memorial
Greece
Number commemorated: 5

Of those memorials that bare the names of SOE casualties, the Athens Memorial has the largest number outside of the United Kingdom – five in total.

The Athens Memorial stands within Phaleron War Cemetery, which can be found a few miles to the south-east of Athens on the coast road from Athens to Vouliaghmen. It commemorates nearly 3,000 members of the land forces of the Commonwealth who lost their lives during the campaigns in Greece and Crete in 1941 and 1944-1945, in the Dodecanese Islands in 1943-1945 and in Yugoslavia in 1943-1945, all of whom have no known grave.

The site of the cemetery in which the memorial stands was chosen originally by the British Fourth Division as a burial ground for Commonwealth casualties of the Greek Civil

The Athens Memorial in Greece. Located within Phaleron War Cemetery, this memorial commemorates nearly 3,000 members of the land forces of the Commonwealth who lost their lives during the campaigns in Greece and Crete in 1941 and 1944-1945, in the Dodecanese Islands in 1943-1945 and in Yugoslavia in 1943-1945, and who have no known grave. Five members of SOE are named on its panels. (Courtesy of CWGC)

War (December 1944-February 1945). Subsequently, the military authorities, in conjunction with the Greek Government and the Army Graves Service, decided that it would be the most suitable site for a Second World War cemetery for the whole mainland of Greece. The 23rd and 24th Graves Registration Units and the 21st and 22nd Australian War Graves Units worked together to bring in graves of the 1941 campaign from the battlefields, temporary military cemeteries and from various civil cemeteries. There are now 2,028 Commonwealth servicemen of the Second World War buried or commemorated in this cemetery.

The Cassino Memorial
Italy
Number commemorated: 2

Only two SOE casualties are commemorated on the Cassino Memorial – an Italian (Adler) and an Austrian (Berliner).

On 3 September 1943, the Allies invaded the Italian mainland, the landings coinciding with an armistice made with the Italians who then re-entered the war on the Allied side. Despite stiff resistance, progress through southern Italy was rapid. However, by the end of October the Allies were facing the German winter defensive position known as the Gustav Line, which stretched from the river Garigliano in the west to the Sangro in the east. Initial attempts to breach the western end of the line were unsuccessful. Operations in January

The Cassino Memorial. (Courtesy of the CWGC)

1944 landed troops behind the German lines at Anzio, but defences were well organised, and a breakthrough was not actually achieved until 18 May, when Cassino was finally taken.

The site for the memorial, and the cemetery (of the same name) in which it stands, was originally selected in January 1944, but the development of the battle during the first five months of that year made it impossible to use it until after the Germans had withdrawn from Cassino. During these early months of 1944, Cassino saw some of the fiercest fighting of the Italian campaign, the town and the dominating Monastery Hill proving the most stubborn obstacles encountered in the advance towards Rome. The majority of those buried in the war cemetery died in the battles during these months.

The memorial commemorates over 4,000 Commonwealth servicemen who took part in the Italian campaign and whose graves are not known.

The Groesbeek Memorial
Gelderland, The Netherlands
Number commemorated: 4

Of the four men commemorated on the Groesbeek Memorial – a figure that places in equal ranking with the Bayeaux Memorial in Normandy – three lost their lives within a nine day period in September 1944. The fourth, Major Francis Suttill DSO, died in March 1945.

The memorial commemorates by name 1,030 members of the Commonwealth land forces who died during the campaign in north-west Europe between the time of crossing the Seine at the end of August 1944 and the end of the war in Europe, and whose graves are not known.

As with all the other memorials, the Groesbeek Memorial was constructed within a war cemetery – Groesbeek Canadian War Cemetery. The village of Groesbeek, from which both draw their names, is located in the east of the Netherlands approximately 5 miles south-east

The Groesbeek Memorial. (Courtesy of the CWGC)

of the city of Nijmegen. Three of the four SOE casualties on the panels of this memorial are Canadian, mirroring the fact that the majority of the burials in the surrounding cemetery are from this country.

The Brookwood Memorial
Surrey, United Kingdom
Number commemorated: 81

Situated in Brookwood Military Cemetery (the UK's only open CWGC cemetery) the Brookwood Memorial commemorates nearly 3,500 men and women of the land forces of the Commonwealth who died during the Second World War and have no known grave, the circumstances of their death being such that they could not appropriately be commemorated on any of the campaign memorials in the various theatres of war.

As a direct result, because of the very nature of their work and, in many cases, their fate, a large proportion of those SOE agents who lost their lives in the Second World War are commemorated on the Brookwood Memorial. In fact, the total figure is eighty-three, representing fifty-nine percent of all of SOE's wartime casualties.

It was in 1917 that an area of land in the privately-run Brookwood Cemetery (The London Necropolis) was set aside for the burial of men and women of the forces of the Commonwealth and the United States, who had died, many of battle wounds, in the London district. On the outbreak of the Second World War, the site was further extended to accommodate casualties from this conflict. The memorial itself, standing as it does in the largest Commonwealth war cemetery in the United Kingdom (which covers approximately 37 acres) was designed by Ralph Hobday and unveiled by Queen Elizabeth II on 25 October 1958.

During the Second World War, SOE's French Section alone sent more than 400 agents behind enemy lines. At least 100 of them were listed as 'Missing Believed Dead' by May 1945

The Commonwealth War Grave Commission's Brookwood Memorial in Surrey. This memorial commemorates the largest number of SOE agents who lost their lives in the Second World War – roughly fifty-nine percent of the total, in fact. (HMP)

– many of these men and women have their names carved on the panels of the Brookwood Memorial. Some of those who died would become famous, Ensign Violette Szabo for example, whilst others remain virtually unknown. The memorial also commemorates SOE's first casualty (Lieutenant David Maitland-Makgill-Crichton) as well as, almost, its last (Lieutenant Louis Eugene Bertheau, who was the second to last to be killed).

Golders Green Crematorium
Middlesex, United Kingdom
Number commemorated: 1

It is only since the beginning of the twentieth century that the ancient custom of cremation instead of burial has been followed again to any extent in the United Kingdom. As a result, soon after the turn of the century the Cremation Society of England felt the need for the establishment of a crematorium in the vicinity of London to serve the requirements of the Metropolis. The London Cremation Company Limited was formed for this purpose, and the Crematorium was opened in 1902.

Men and women who died in the service of their country during both world wars were cremated here. After the Second World War a site was selected and made available to the Commission, through the generosity of the London Cremation Company Limited, for the erection of a memorial to the men and women who died in the two world wars and were cremated here.

The memorial, which is situated at the end of the long terrace in front of the memorial cloisters immediately behind the ornamental lily pool, was designed by the Commission's Chief Architect and Artistic Adviser, Sir Edward Maufe, to harmonise with the adjacent

Golders Green Crematorium.

buildings. It consists of a small Portland stone colonnade protecting and enshrining three bronze panels bearing the names. Inside the curved pediment are the dates 1914–1918 and 1939-1945, and carved on the frieze beneath are the words 'PRO PATRIA' (for one's country). The columns are linked at the base by wrought iron balustrades, and a sea shell, representing immortality, is engraved on the capital of each column. The memorial, which was unveiled by Lord Wigram and dedicated by the Bishop of Willesden in May 1952, is approached on either side by a curved flight of steps, and is set against a background of trees.

Golders Green itself is a large residential area about 5 miles north of London, in the municipal borough of Hendon. The crematorium is situated on the northern border of Hampstead Heath, the entrance being in Hoop Lane leading off Finchley Road on the northern side of Golders Green underground station.

The sole SOE casualty commemorated here, Major Valentine Edward Whitty, is the last to have lost his life.

The Runnymede Memorial
Surrey, United Kingdom
Number commemorated: 9

On 12 September 1944, one of SOE's most famous casualties, Section Officer Nora Inayat-Khan, was transferred to Dachau concentration camp. Soon after her arrival, in the early hours of the morning of 13 September 1944, Nora was executed by a shot to the head. But Section Officer Inayat-Khan had not been alone. Three other SOE agents had also been transferred with her from Karlsruhe prison. They were Section Officer Yolande

The Air Forces Memorial at Runnymede, Surrey, commemorates by name over 20,000 personnel who were lost in the Second World War and who have no known graves. Nine of this number were SOE agents – agents such as Section Officer Inayat-Khan who was shot at Dachau concentration camp in September 1944. (Courtesy of the CWGC)

Unternahrer (served as Yolande Beekman), Ensign Madeleine Damerment and Ensign Elaine Plewman. The other three were executed at about the same time as Inayat-Khan, the bodies of all four immediately cremated.

As members of the WAAF, both Inayat-Khan and Yolande Unternahrer are commemorated on the Runnymede Memorial (Damerment and Plewman, on the other hand, are listed on the Brookwood Memorial).

This imposing memorial, which overlooks the River Thames on Cooper's Hill at Englefield Green between Windsor and Egham, is the only one of the six memorials bearing the names of SOE casualties not located within the grounds of a war cemetery. Known as the Air Forces Memorial, the structure commemorates by name over 20,000 air force personnel who were lost in the Second World War during operations from bases in the United Kingdom and North and Western Europe, and who have no known graves. Of the nine SOE casualties whose names can be found here, five are of female agents.

THE CEMETERIES

Tirana Park Memorial Cemetery
Tirana, Albania
Number of burials: 7

With seven SOE burials, the Tirana Park Memorial Cemetery represents the largest single gathering of those SOE casualties who have a known grave, although, in some respects, it could be claimed that their last resting places are in fact unknown.

The CWGC graves in Tirana Park Memorial Cemetery in Albania – including that of SOE's Brigadier Arthur Nicholls GC. (Courtesy of the CWGC)

Following the end of the war in Europe, a British Army Graves Registration Unit entered Albania with the task of concentrating the remains of those Commonwealth servicemen lost in the struggle to secure Albania's freedom into a site chosen in the capital, Tirana. However, due to the political situation in the country, this task could not be completed, though fifty-two sets of remains were recovered in the short time available.

Eventually, in 1955, after repeated requests to enter the country were refused, the Commission took the decision to commemorate the thirty-eight identified casualties on special memorials erected in Phaleron War Cemetery in Greece. The situation remained thus until 1994, when a change in the political situation in Albania allowed a Commission representative access for the first time. He discovered that the original individual burials had been moved by the Communist authorities to an unmarked collective grave located under a path near the university buildings in Tirana. At the beginning of 1995, the thirty-eight special memorials were removed from Phaleron and re-erected as close as possible to the site of the mass grave, in an area designated the Tirana Park Memorial Cemetery.

The Cemetery itself is situated in the Great Park of Tirana, on the main boulevard, close to the Hotel Sheraton and the Main University Buildings.

Copenhagen (Hellerup) Mindelunden Memorial Park
Copenhagen, Denmark
Number of burials: 1

One of seven sites within Copenhagen containing CWGC burials, this cemetery is the location of just one Commonwealth casualty – SOE's Lieutenant Hans Johansen.

The cemetery is located in the suburb of Hellerup, which is to the north of the city centre. The entrance is on Tuborgvej at the junction with Anders Lassans Vej, next to the overhead railway bridge. To locate Johansen's headstone, follow the main path from the park's entrance, then take the second path on the right. The lone CWGC grave is on the far side of the statue in the third row from the front, and the second grave from the left.

In containing just one SOE casualty, the Mindelunden Memorial Park is representative of most cemeteries where SOE agents were buried. Of the twenty-two such sites, sixteen contain just one SOE casualty; four have two burials; and one – in Jerusalem – has three.

Heliopolis War Cemetery
Cario, Egypt
Number of burials: 1

Heliopolis, a major suburb of Cairo, lies 6 miles or so to the north-east of the main city centre, not a huge distance from the airport. Heliopolis War Cemetery, with the grave of one SOE casualty, is situated opposite El Banat (Girls') College in Nabil el Wakkard Street, and access to the cemetery is from this street.

Cairo was also a significant hospital centre during the Second World War, as well as a leave centre with many social clubs and hostels. The cemetery at Heliopolis was opened in October 1941 for burials from the many hospitals in the area coping with the wounded and sick, mainly from the Western Desert campaigns. After the war, 125 graves were moved into the cemetery from Mena Camp Military Cemetery where permanent maintenance was not possible. There are now 1,742 Commonwealth casualties of the Second World War buried or commemorated in the cemetery, and the eighty-three war graves of other nationalities reflect the diverse make up of the Middle East Command during this period.

Heliopolis War Cemetery. (Courtesy of the CWGC)

Beaurepaire (1940) Communal Cemetery. (Courtesy of the CWGC)

Beaurepaire (1940) Communal Cemetery
Isere, France
Number of burials: 1

One of the fourteen cemeteries in France containing at least one SOE casualty, the Beaurepaire (1940) Communal Cemetery can be found in the village of Beaurepaire. This, in turn, is in the Department of the Isere, 33 miles west-north-west of Grenoble. The cemetery is on the west side of the village.

The British soldier, a member of Jedburgh Team *Veganin*, is buried in the vault of the Truchet family.

Bretteville-sur-Laize Canadian War Cemetery
Calvados, France
Number of burials: 1

The Allied offensive in north-west Europe began with the Normandy landings of 6 June 1944. For the most part, those buried at Bretteville-sur-Laize Canadian War Cemetery died during the later stages of the battle of Normandy, the capture of Caen and the thrust southwards – led initially by the 4th Canadian and 1st Polish Armoured Divisions – to close the Falaise Gap (almost every unit of Canadian 2nd Corps is represented in the cemetery).

Bretteville-sur-Laize Canadian War Cemetery. (Courtesy of the CWGC)

This is certainly the case of the SOE casualty, Lieutenant Maurice Larcher, who was killed on 8 July 1944.

The cemetery lies on the west side of the main road from Caen to Falaise, about 9 miles south of Caen and just north of the village of Cintheaux. The village of Bretteville lies to the south-west of the cemetery.

Chiddes Communal Cemetery
Burgundy, France
Number of burials: 1

Chiddes is a village and commune 37 miles south-east of Nevers, and 5 miles north-west of the town of Luzy.

The cemetery is south of the village and west of the road to Avree. The single CWGC war grave – an SOE casualty – is south-east of the entrance, near the rear wall.

Choloy War Cemetery
Meurthe-et-Moselle, France
Number of burials: 1

Choloy War Cemetery. (Courtesy of the CWGC)

Choloy War Cemetery was created by the British Army's Graves Service for the re-burial of casualties recovered from isolated sites, communal cemeteries, and small churchyards in north-eastern France where permanent maintenance of the graves was not possible.

In 1950, for the same reason, the CWGC found it necessary to move in to this cemetery more than 100 graves from a number of churchyards and civil cemeteries in the same area. Those who lie in Choloy War Cemetery are mostly airmen; but there are also soldiers belonging to the forces of the United Kingdom who died in the Saar region during the first few months of the war, i.e. up to May 1940, or as prisoners of war.

Choloy is a village 17 miles west of Nancy and 3 miles west of Toul, a town on the main road from Paris to Nancy. The cemetery is 2 miles west of Toul.

Éguzon Communal Cemetery
Indre, France
Number of burials: 1

The SOE casualty buried in Éguzon Communal Cemetery represents something of an anomaly for those researching the organisation's casualties. Though there is only one CWGC headstone in the cemetery, there are in fact two names listed on the CWGC's database for this site: Lieutenant Alexandre Schwatschko and Lieutenant Alexandre Shaw. However, as explained previously these two names represent the same casualty. It is for this reason that an initial check on the Commission's casualty rolls suggests a total of 141 SOE casualties, when in fact that number is 140.

Éguzon is a village some 26 miles south of Châteauroux, and 22 miles south-west of the town of La Châtre. The cemetery lies on the southern side of the village. Schwatschko's (his true family name) lone Commonwealth burial cafn be found south-east of the entrance and south of the main path after descending the steps.

Guiscriff Communal Cemetery. (Courtesy of the CWGC)

Guiscriff Communal Cemetery
Morbihan, France
Number of burials: 1

Guiscriff is a village and commune some 10 miles north-east of Rosporden, a town on the main Paris-Le Mans-Quimper railway line. The cemetery is about 300 yards west of the village church on the southern side of the road to Scaer.

The grave of the sole SOE casualty, Major Colin Ogden-Smith, is not marked by a CWGC headstone – he was buried with two Frenchmen in a plot that was marked by a marble memorial erected by the local people. This grave is 30 feet north-east of the entrance.

Lagny Communal Cemetery
Seine-et-Marne, France
Number of burials: 1

Lagny is a town and commune 25 miles north of Melun, and 18 miles, by road, east of Paris. The cemetery is on the eastern side of the town between the River Marne and the road to Coulommiers. Near the north-east corner is the grave of the SOE casualty.

Laissac Communal Cemetery
Aveyron, France
Number of burials: 1

Laissac is a village and commune located in the Pyrénées Mountains, by the Aveyron River in the Department of Aveyron. The village lies 12 miles east of Rodez, the chief town of the department, and some 8 miles south-east of Bozouls. The village is situated at the junction of the Rodez-Severac road and the road to Gabriac. The cemetery is west of a track leading off the north side of the road from Rodez.

Captain Christopher Lord, the sole Commonwealth casualty in this cemetery, was buried in the private vault of the Solinhac family.

Laprade Churchyard
Aude, France
Number of burials: 1

Laprade is a village and commune in the Department of the Aude 16 miles north-west of Carcassonne, the chief town of the department, and about 9 miles south-west of Mazamet, a town in the Department of the Tarn.

The village is situated on the local road, which turns west off the main Carcassonne-Mazamet road. The one Commonwealth war grave in this cemetery is north-west of the entrance.

Le Mans West Cemetery
La Sarthe, France
Number of burials: 1

The large town of Le Mans is the seat of the Prefecture of the Department of La Sarthe. The cemetery is in the north-west suburb of the town, west of the River Sarthe, off a main road, the Avenue Rhin et Danube. From this road, turn into the Rue des Etamines, then left

Le Mans West Cemetery. (Courtesy of the CWGC)

into Rue de la Madelaine. The cemetery is off the Rue de la Madelaine in the Rue de le Garenne. The War Graves plot is at the far end of the cemetery on the left hand side.

In 1914, when Saint-Nazaire and Nantes were British bases, Le Mans was an Advanced Base and a hospital centre. In 1939 the British General Headquarters were concentrated here from 14 to 21 September, and in June 1940 the Headquarters of the southern portion of the British Expeditionary Force was at Château de la Blanchardiere, Le Mans.

There are sixty-one Commonwealth burials of the First World War and ninety-seven of the second. SOE's Second Lieutenant Francisque Bec lies in Plot 38, Row C, Grave 50.

Lille Southern Cemetery
Nord, France
Number of burials: 1

Of the 576 identified Commonwealth burials, of two world wars, at this site, one is of an SOE agent – Captain Michael Trotobas. The cemetery entrance can be found at the junction of the Rue du Faubourg des Postes and the Rue de l'Arbrissead.

Lille was occupied by the Germans from 27 August 1914 to 5 September 1914, and again on 12 October; and it remained in their hands, undamaged by Allied artillery, until 17 October 1918. The Southern Cemetery was used by the Germans during the greater part of the First World War, and after the Armistice by the 39th Stationary Hospital and the 1st Australian Casualty Clearing Station.

During the Second World War, at the end of March 1940, the 50th Division was near Lille; while in May the same year No.10 Casualty Clearing Station used the cemetery from 16th to 25th of the month.

Lille Southern Cemetery. (Courtesy of the CWGC)

Mont-de-Marsan Communal Cemetery
Landes, France
Number of burials: 1

The town of Mont-de-Marsan is the capital of the Landes department in Aquitaine, south-western France. There are two cemeteries in the town containing Commonwealth burials – the Communal Cemetery and the Mont-de-Marsan (L'Hopital Ste Anne) Cemetery. The latter contains three CWGC burials (a private from the African Pioneer Corps (East Africa); and two privates from the Native Military Corps, South African Forces); whilst the former is the last resting place of the SOE casualty, Captain Thomas Mellows.

Mont-de-Marsan Communal Cemetery is in the north-western part of the town, west of the Boulevard D'Haussez and north of the main road to Garein and Sarbres. Mellows' grave is north-east of the entrance.

Perreuse Château Franco British National Cemetery
Seine-et-Marne, France
Number of burials: 2

There are two SOE casualties buried in this cemetery. The cemetery itself is situated within the grounds of the Château Perreuse near the community of Signy-Signets, which is 3 miles south-west of the town of La Ferte Sous-Jouarre, and 37 miles east of Paris.

The Château was used by French medical units throughout the First World War and the site of the cemetery was presented by the owner, Mme. Dumez, to the French Government. The cemetery contains 150 Commonwealth burials of the First World War, all brought in

Perreuse Château Franco British National Cemetery. (Courtesy of the CWGC)

from the surrounding battlefields, and sixteen from the Second World War. Of the latter, all but the two SOE casualties are aircrew.

It is known that one of the two SOE casualties, Lieutenant Eric Cauchi and Lieutenant Arman Lansdell, has always been buried in the Perreuse Château Franco British National Cemetery, whilst the other was exhumed from his isolated burial site at St. Aubin Château-Neuf Communal Cemetery, at Yonne.

Pornic War Cemetery
Loire-Atlantique, France
Number of burials: 2

Pornic is on the north side of Borgneuf Bay and is 31 miles west-south-west of Nantes and 12 miles south-south-east of the port of Saint-Nazaire via the bridge over the River Loire. The cemetery is on the north-eastern outskirts of the town, less than one mile east of the church on the south side of the road to Chauve.

The majority of the CWGC burials here were soldiers washed ashore after the sinking of the troopship *Lancastria* in the Bay of Biscay on 17 June 1940. There are now two Commonwealth burials of the 1914–1918 war and 395 of the 1939–1945 war commemorated here. Of the 1939–1945 war, 160 are unidentified. The two SOE casualties, Section Officer Muriel Byck and Captain Stanislaw Makowski, lie side-by-side in the northern part of the cemetery near the Cross of Sacrifice.

Pornic War Cemetery. (Courtesy of the CWGC)

Dürnbach War Cemetery. (Courtesy of the CWGC)

Dürnbach War Cemetery
Bad Tolz, Bayern, Germany
Number of burials: 2

The small village of Dürnbach lies in the south of Germany approximately 27 miles south of Munich. The vast majority of those buried here are airmen shot down over Bavaria, Württemberg, Austria, Hessen and Thuringia, transferred from their scattered graves by the Army Graves Service. The remainder are men who were killed while escaping from prisoner of war camps in the same areas, or who died towards the end of the war on forced marches from the camps to more remote areas.

As the site of the cemetery was not chosen until after hostilities in Europe had ceased, by officers of the British Army and Royal Air Force in conjunction with officers of the American Occupation Forces (in whose zone Dürnbach lay), it is almost certain that both of the SOE casualties were brought into the site from their original burial location. These are the only two SOE personnel who lie in Germany.

Paramythia Civil Cemetery
Thesprotia, Greece
Number of burials: 1

The town of Paramythia lies some 160 miles north-west of Athens. On the outbreak of war, it was the administrative centre of the district of Thesprotia. It was the scene of the infamous Paramythia Executions (also known as the Paramythia Massacre) during which, between 19-29 September 1943, members of the German 1st Mountain Division and a Muslim Cham Albanian militia murdered some 201 Greek villagers and destroyed nineteen villages.

The cemetery itself surrounds an old church on the lower road that goes through the village. Major Wallace's grave is in the lower section of the cemetery on the left hand side.

Paramythia Civil Cemetery. (Courtesy of the CWGC)

Jerusalem Mount Hertzel Cemetery
Jerusalem, Israel
Number of burials: 3

Mount Hertzel (or Herzl) is one of the great hills of Jerusalem on the southern side of the city. The National Military Cemetery is located on the northern slope of the hill, within a large park that also contains a museum. The park is reached via Herzl Boulevard, which runs off Ruppin Road. It is the focal point of commemorative proceedings relating to the State of Israel and, consequently, a very well known area.

The three Commonwealth burials – all members of SOE – are in the top right section among a group of seven headstones (the other four are memorial headstones and contain no burials). None of the plots have standard CWGC headstones.

A check of the register for this cemetery reveals an unusual anomaly – it states that there are six identified CWGC burials here. Of the names listed, three – Sergeant Martha Martinovic, Sergeant Ada Robinson and Sergeant Chaviva Reik – all relate to the same person, her true name being the last listed here. Sergeant Rafael Reisz is also listed under an alias, Sergeant S. Rice.

Jerusalem Mount Hertzel Cemetery. (Courtesy of the CWGC)

Hattem General Cemetery
Gelderland, The Netherlands
Number of burials: 1

Hattem is a small town some 2 miles south of Zwolle, on the main Zwolle–Apeldoorn road. The cemetery is on the south-eastern side of the town, about 500 yards from the railway station. The one British (SOE) grave is in the southern half of the cemetery, near the boundary.

Chapter 5

Not Forgotten

A list of agents died on active service who are not recorded as SOE casualties in the records of the Commonwealth War Graves Commission

There are a number of reasons why the following people were not recorded as members of the SOE by the CWGC. The principle explanation was that many of them were actually members of the armed forces of a country outside the Commonwealth and therefore could not be commemorated by the CWGC (although this did not preclude some members of the French Army from being so recognised).

Others were recruited into the SOE abroad and did not undergo the usual training and assessment in the United Kingdom. Their personal files, if one was ever opened, were not, therefore, held at Baker Street. As a consequence, when they went missing or were killed the staff at Baker Street did not submit a casualty report. There are also some individuals who were seconded to other special service organisations at the time when they died. Their commemoration, therefore, refers to the unit to which they were attached, not the SOE. Additionally there were considerable numbers of individuals who were involved in SOE operations, and are recorded on commemorative sites including some of those on the internet, as being members of the SOE whose official connection with that organisation cannot be verified. Yet these people died serving with the SOE, even in some cases in exactly the same operations as officially-recognised SOE agents, and to have omitted them in this study would have been an injustice, particularly as their omission from official records may simply be because of administrative failings or because of that almost impenetrable veil of secrecy that shrouded every aspect of the SOE.

There are others, however, whose exclusion from the lists of SOE casualties supplied to the CWGC is inexplicable. This is especially the case with those members of the organisations set up in Singapore and Australia as these were officially recognised establishments of the SOE.

Many of these people were trained in Britain and sent into the field by the SOE. They were in every respect as much SOE agents as the ones recorded by the CWGC and a considerable number even have their own personal files in the HS9 series in the National Archives at Kew. What is known about the fate of these people is shown below. Because of the complications referred to above it is inevitable that this list is far from complete.

I FRANCE

Name	Field Name	Main Circuit	Fate
BERTHAUD, Albert			Killed in air accident, 17 December 1943
BISSET, Edward G.A.	Adjacent	Tilleul (M)	Killed accidentally, 24 September 1944
DARLING, George	George	Prosper/Physician	Killed in gunfight, June 1943
DEDIEU, Gerard	Jerome	Permit	Killed in air accident, 1 February 1945
DELSANTI, Louis	Frère	Arthur	Drowned, Lübeck, 3 May 1945
DORMER, Hugh E.J.	Paul	Scullion 1&2 (M)	Killed, 12 August 1944
DUBOIS, Jean R. André	Hercule	Donkeyman	Executed Buchenwald, 6 September 1944
GÜELL, Jacques.T.P.M.	Theodore	Tilleul	Air crash in UK, 7 August 1945
HAY, Alistair K.H.			Killed in action, France, 13 June 1944
LANIS, Maurice	Colin	Liontamer	Executed, Gross-Rosen, 1944/45
LAVIGNE, Madeleine	Isabelle	Silversmith	Died in Paris of embolism, February 1945
LEPAGE, Maurice	Colin	Liontamer	Executed, Gross-Rosen, September 1944
LESOUT, Edmond	Tristan	Liontamer	Executed, Gross-Rosen, September 1944
MOCH, André		Pimento	Killed by the Milice, February 1944
MATHIEU, René M.A.	Aimé	Stationer	Died
MENILGLAISE, Jean	Miguel	Bricklayer	Missing
PEARSON, D.M.		Pedagogue	Executed, Gross-Rosen, 1944/5
PTIER, Dominigue, E.			Died Rheims, 11 January 1944
SOSKICE, Victor A.	Solway	Scullion 2 (M)	Executed
TAYAR, Jaques			Died, 18 December 1943, following air accident the previous day
WYATT, David A.			Killed Dieppe, 19 August 1942
ULLMANN, Paul E.B.	Alceste	Stockbroker	Shot, April 1944
VALLEE, Francoise	Oscar	Parson	Executed, 1 March 1944

Two French agents, whose graves are at the Brookwood cemetery in Surrey, but not identified as belonging to the SOE, are Albert Berthaud and Jaques Tayar – and both of these men were killed in the UK.

In the early hours of Friday 17 December 1943, these two agents were being flown to RAF Tangmere in West Sussex by a 161 (Special Duties) Squadron Westland Lysander piloted by Flight Lieutenant Stephen Hankey. A dense bank of fog had shrouded southern England during the course of the night and already one Lysander on its return to Tangmere had crashed, killing the pilot. The same fate was to befall Hankey and the two agents he was carrying as his plane crashed into a tree at nearby Yapton – Tayar was still alive when rescuers reached the scene, but died in hospital the following day.

Though the local police submitted a report on the first Lysander disaster (as in this instance only the pilot died, the SOE agents on board having survived), no police record of Hankey's crash was allowed to survive and no mention of it appears in the local constabulary records.

The casualties had to be registered by law but to prevent any association being made between the deaths of RAF pilots and the Frenchmen, the four deaths were registered by four different people. Berthaud's and Taylor's bodies were removed to London by an SOE Conducting Officer and buried together at Brookwood.

George Darling was the PHYSICIAN organiser in east Normandy. His circuit was in fact a sub-circuit of Suttill's PROSPER network based in Paris and when that circuit was blown Darling was also compromised. He was visited at the address where he was staying at Trie-Château at the end of June 1943 by a party that he thought was a group of sub-agents. He took them to one of his arms caches only realising when it was too late that they were Germans. He opened fire on them but was shot down.

Hugh Dormer, who earned the DSO for his deeds with the SOE in the SCULLION raids upon the Les Talots synthetic oil refinery, and whose diaries were published in 1947, had returned to his regiment, the Irish Guards, when he was killed in action and so was not considered an SOE casualty.

Jean Roger André Dubois was recruited in the field by Raymond Flower (*Gaspar*) and arrived in Britain in March 1943. The following month, after a period of training, he returned to France. The wireless operator for the DONKEYMAN circuit, Dubois was sat with his transmitter on a table at a house in Montrouge (a suburb south of Paris) when two members of the SD, Auguste Scherer and Ernest Vogt, burst into his room. He immediately drew his pistol and fired. His first shot killed Scherer. Vogt drew his own gun and fired at Dubois as the agent turned his gun on the German. Both kept on firing until they had emptied their weapons. In a letter to historian Jean Fuller, Vogt wrote, 'When both our pistols were empty, we stood looking at each other, across the table, weaponless, since all our bullets were in each others' bodies. I then felt myself fainting.' Both men survived the gunfight. Incarcerated in Frèsnes prison, where his wounds were treated (some accounts state he had suffered as many as seven gunshot wounds), Dubois was subsequently transferred to Ravitch and later Gross-Rosen

Canadian Jean Paul Archambault (Code name *Chio*) completed his service with F Section but volunteered to continue after the liberation of France. He was parachuted into Burma but was fatally wounded when the explosives he was preparing accidently ignited. He died on 19 May 1945, at the age of thirty-six. He was awarded the Military Cross.

Sergeant Alfred Claude Brenton Sowden (Royal Corps of Signals) was another F Section agent who was lost in the Far East. After the liberation of France, where he had been the wireless operator for the PEDLAR circuit, he went to India where he died, aged twenty-seven. He is remembered at the Rangoon Memorial. He was awarded the Military Medal.

Louis Delsanti, aka *Frère*, a Corsican who had been dismissed from his post of Commissioner of Ussel in June 1942 after being suspected of supplying fake identity cards to the Resistance, joined Henri Peulevé's ARTHUR circuit. He was captured with Peulevé, eventually being moved via Compiègne to the Neuengamme concentration camp. From here he was evacuated with thousands of other prisoners in the final days of the war and crammed into the requisitioned former luxury liner *Cap Arcona*. On 3 May 1945, in the Bay of Lübeck, the RAF attacked it and two other ships. Approximately 7,000 people were killed, including Delsanti.

Captain Dominique Edgar Potier, a Belgian Air Force officer, parachuted into France in July 1943 to organise Lysander extractions in the Rheims area. His greatest contribution to the Allied cause was when he became involved in the 'Possum' escape network for MI9. He was betrayed and walked into a Gestapo trap. He was taken to Rheims prison where he was savagely beaten. Other inmates spoke of his terrible treatment. In the end he could not take any more torture and he threw himself over the internal gallery of the prison. Potier was taken to the American Memorial Hospital where he died of his injuries on 11 January 1944. According to Airey Neave (MI9's chief organiser), Potier was 'one of the bravest of all the agents'. He was aged forty.

Cardiff-born Major Jacques Vaillant Güell (or de Güélis) MBE MC, was an interpreter with the British Expeditionary Force at General Gort's Headquarters in France in 1940. He was taken prisoner by the Germans after their invasion but managed to escape. Güell was subsequently recommended to the SOE by Lieutenant General Alan Brooke. He became a briefing officer for F Section before being parachuted blind into France in August 1941 to investigate the Resistance groups in the unoccupied zone. After returning to London he helped establish the SOE base in Algiers (its cover-name was Inter-Service Signals Unit) called MASSINGHAM, which became an important staging post of the infiltration of agents into southern France.

Güell was next involved in the disastrous Dieppe raid of August 1942 on which he was sent by Baker Street as an observer. On 7 July 1944, he went back to France to assist with the Resistance and after the liberation of the country he was appointed to the Special Allied Airborne Reconnaissance Force. Made up of three-man teams they were parachuted in advance of the Allied armies to secure the safety of Allied troops in prisoner of war camps across Europe. On one such mission on 7 August 1945, the aircraft that Güell was in crashed whilst still over the UK and he was killed. His decorations included the MBE, MC and the *Croix de Guerre*.

Major David Alexander Wyatt (parent unit Royal Engineers) also took part in the Dieppe raid as the SOE Liaison Officer with the Combined Operations Headquarters. He was killed in action at Dieppe on 19 August 1942, and was buried at the Canadian War Cemetery in Dieppe.

Captain Alastair Kerr Hay (parent unit Royal Artillery), SOE Algiers, was part of the Inter-Allied Mission *Michel* and was killed in action near Barcelonnette, France on 13 June 1944. Hay was buried at Mazargues War Cemetery, Marsailles. He was thirty-two.

II THE NETHERLANDS

Name	Field Name	Fate
ANDRINGA, T.C.	Turnip	Killed in Mauthausen, September 1944
ARENDSE, P.A.	Seakale	Arrested on landing, killed Mauthausen September 1944
BAATSEN, A.A.	Watercress	Arrested on landing, killed Mauthausen September 1944
BAKKER, J.	Cucumber II	Arrested on landing, possibly executed in Gross-Rosen
BARMÉ	Trapping	Shot, 8 March 1945
BEUKEMA, Toe Water, K.W.	Kale	Arrested on landing, killed Mauthausen September 1944
BIALLOSTERSKI, T.	Draughts	Arrested, died of wounds, 26 February 1945
BOCKMA, J.	Halma	Shot down and killed, 6 July 1944
BOOGART, P.C.	Kohlrabi	Arrested on landing, killed Mauthausen September 1944
BRAGGAAR, C.C.	Parsley A	Arrested on landing, killed Mauthausen September 1944
BRINKGREVE, H.	Dudley	Shot, 5 March 1945
BUIZER, J.J.C.	Spinach	Arrested on landing, killed Mauthausen, September 1944
BUKKENS, J.	Marrow II	Arrested on landing, killed Mauthausen, September 1944
CELOSSE, N.J.	Faro	Shot, 5 September 1944
DANE, J.C.	Cucumber	Arrested on landing, killed Mauthausen, September 1944
DE BREY, O.W.	Croquet	Arrested on landing, killed Mauthausen, September 1944
DEKKERS, C.M.	Poker	Killed in Hudson aircraft shot down near Gilze, 1 June 1944
DE HAAS, J.H.M.	Potato	Killed in Mauthausen, September 1944
DE KYUFF, A.J.	Mustard	Arrested on landing, killed Mauthausen, September 1944
DROOGLEVER FORTUYN, C.	Mangold	Arrested on landing, killed Mauthausen, September 1944
DUBOIS, A.	Ham	Shot 9 March 1945 whilst with MI9
GREYDANUS, J.	Jingle	Parachute did not open, 12 April 1945
GROENEWOUD, J.	Claude	Killed in action, 19 September 1944
HOFSTEDE, J.	Tomato	Arrested on landing, killed Mauthausen, September 1944
HOLVOET, R.	Bacon	Shot 10 April 1945, whilst with MI9
HOOGEWERFF, W.H.	Coursing	Shot, 8 March 1945
JAMBROES, G.L.	Marrow	Arrested on landing, killed Mauthausen, September 1944
JONGELIE, R.C.	Parsley	Arrested on landing, killed Mauthausen, September 1944
JORDAAN, H.J.	Trumpet	Died in Mauthausen, 3 May 1945
KAMPHORST, P.	Tomato II	Arrested on landing, killed Mauthausen, September 1944
KIST, J.C.	Hockey	Arrested on landing, suspected killed Gross-Rosen

Name	Field Name	Fate
KLOOS, B.	Leek	Killed in Mauthausen, September 1944
KOOLSTRA, M.	Celery II	Arrested on landing, killed Mauthausen, September 1944
KROON, G.	Skating	Injured on landing, captured, died 2 May 1945
KUENEN, G.J.	Football	Killed in Hudson aircraft shot down near Gilze, 1 June 1944
KWINT, P.J.	Fives	Shot down and killed, 6 July 1944
MACARÉ H.M.	Celery III	Arrested on landing, suspected killed Gross-Rosen
MINK, A.B.	Polo	Arrested on landing, killed Mauthausen, September 1944
MOODY, A.K.	Cauliflower	Arrested on landing, possibly killed in Gross-Rosen
MOLENAAR, J.	Turnip II	Severely injured on landing, swallowed cyanide pill
OVERES, H.J.	Cress	Arrested on landing, possibly killed in Gross-Rosen
PALS, M.	Pumkin	Arrested on landing, possibly killed in Gross-Rosen
PARLEVLIET, H.	Beetroot	Missing, possibly killed in Gross-Rosen
POSTMA, S.	Sculling	Shot, 2 December 1944
POUWELS, C.C.	Tomato III	Arrested on landing, suspected killed Gross-Rosen
PUNT, L.M.	Squash	Arrested on landing, killed Mauthausen, September 1944
RAS, G.H.G.	Lettuce	Killed in Mauthausen, September 1944
REISIGER, H.G.	Turniquoits	Killed in Neuengamme, March 1945
ROUWERD, F.W.	Netball	Arrested on landing, suspected killed Gross-Rosen
RUSELER, G.L.	Broccoli	Arrested on landing, killed Mauthausen, September 1944
SANDERS, H.A.J.	Curling	Shot, 6 September 1944
SEBES, H.	Leek II	Killed in Mauthausen, September 1944
SPORRE, C.J.	Glasshouse	Presumed drowned, 13/14 November 1941
STEEKSMA, H.R.	Celery	Arrested on landing, killed Mauthausen, September 1944
STROOBANTS, H.	Operation *Roderigo*	Killed in crash of Halifax LL307 at Tholen, 3 June 1944
TACONIS, T.	Catarrh	Killed in Mauthausen, September 1944
VAN DER BOR, K.	Endive	Arrested on landing, killed Mauthausen, September 1944
VAN DER GIESSEN	Cabbage	Shot, August 1944
VAN DER WILDEN, P.	Tennis	Arrested on landing, killed Mauthausen, September 1944
VAN DER WILDEN, W.	Golf	Arrested on landing, killed Mauthausen, September 1944
VAN HEMERT, G.J.	Leek A	Arrested on landing, killed Mauthausen, September 1944
VAN HULSTEYN, C.E.	Radish	Arrested on landing, killed Mauthausen, September 1944

Name	Field Name	Fate
VAN UYTVANCK, I.	Gherkin	Arrested on landing, killed Mauthausen, September 1944
VAN OS, G.	Broadbean	Arrested on landing, killed Mauthausen, September 1944
VAN RIETSCHOTEN, J.J.	Parsnip	Shot, August 1944
VAN STEEN, A.	Beetroot II	Missing, possibly killed in Gross-Rosen
VERHOFF, P.	Racquets	Shot down and killed, 6 July 1944
WARNDORFER, Jacques A.	–	Killed, 12 January 1945
WENGER, A.J.	Lacrosse	Killed in Mauthausen, September 1944

The enormous losses in the Netherlands were the result of the same procedural failures in London that caused the downfall of the PROSPER circuit in Paris. An agent called Lauwers was unfortunate to be captured by the *Abwehr* because of the actions of a treacherous Dutchman. Once in enemy hands he was persuaded to transmit to London. In his first message he deliberately missed out the security check but this was not noticed by the staff of N Section, who considered such things as 'irritating'.

Lauwers continued to transmit using no security check at all, yet this was never questioned at Baker Street. As a consequence other agents, including many wireless operators, were captured and encouraged to transmit back to London. Almost all of them tried to warn Baker Street in their messages but in vain. Soon the Germans were able to use their own radio operators and as a consequence, they exerted virtually total control of the SOE network in the Netherlands for fifteen months from March 1942 until the summer of 1943. To the Germans, this became known as the 'English game', or *Das Englandspiel*, or more officially Operation *North Pole* (*Uternehmen Nordpol*).

Incredibly, suspicions about the situation in the Netherlands were confirmed by a simple trick. Towards the end of June 1943, the signals team in London decided to try and deceive one of the supposed Dutch agents. At the end of a message the signaller signed off with the letters HH. This was the standard, automatic Nazi signal clerks' farewell – it stood for *Heil Hitler*.

The trick worked, as the person at the other end, without thinking, responded with the HH Now N Section knew that their network had been infiltrated. The extent of the enemy's penetration of the Dutch network was not fully appreciated, however, until late 1943 when two agents managed to escape from the Haaren seminary near Tilburg, which was being used to hold the SOE prisoners.

On 27 November 1943, most of the SOE prisoners were blindfolded and sent to Assen near the German border. Five months later all of these prisoners were transported to Ravitsch in Silesia. In early September 1944 nine of them disappeared, most probably to Gross-Rosen, never to be seen again. Then, on 6 September, the remaining agents were moved to Mauthausen. In one of the most sickening incidents of the Second World War they, along with a few F Section agents, were taken to the granite quarry. Here they were beaten and tormented all day long. Half of them died or were killed. Then the next day those that had survived the first day's ordeal were subjected to the same treatment until they were all dead.

Even after the end of the war in Europe one of the Dutch agents was killed. With Japan still fighting, the future of the Dutch colonies in the Far East remained a subject of concern. A number of the surviving agents therefore volunteered to continue their secret work in Asia. One of these, Peter Charles Henry Vickery (Stanley II) was killed in a take-off crash in India on 1 April 1945 (see Jedburgh Operations below). He was the last of the Dutch SOE agents to die in service.

Such were the scale of the disasters in the Netherlands, questions were subsequently asked in its parliament that led to a parliamentary commission being appointed to investigate the whole affair. The commission questioned all the survivors and all the available Germans who had been involved. It sat for more than two years and in its conclusions exonerated many of those courageous agents over whom considerable doubt and suspicion had formed.

On the Groesbeek Memorial is the name of Frederick Benson (true name Fritz Becker) who was a German Jewish refugee who was a member of the Intelligence Corps attached to the SOE. He was killed on 29 October 1944, aged twenty-two.

III BELGIUM

Name	Field Name	Fate
AARENS, G.M.C.	Canticle	Beheaded on 2 or 9 December 1944
BAR, L.	Dormouse	Shot, 10 February 1944
BERNAERDT, W.G.H.C.	Mink	Killed, 19 April 1944
BRICHAUX, D.	Alsatian	Parachute did not open, 20 April 1943
CAMPION, A.	Periwig	Changed sides, but killed in air raid, 7 September 1943
CERF, R.	Tiger	Shot, 4 August 1942
CEYSSENS, J.J.L.	Gibbon	Died in Belsen, 15 March 1945
CLASER, C.	Bull	Died 12 December, Gross-Rosen
COPINNE, R.	Mastiff	Shot, 18 January 1943
DAVREUX, P.J.M.	Menecrates	Killed in action, 1 September 1944
DELMEIRE, A.	Canticle	Beheaded, 7 June 1944
DEFLEM, J.V.	Mule	Killed in action on landing, 1 May 1942
DELPLACE, A.J.	Nicanor	Killed, September 1944
DEPREZ, R.A.	Lucullus	Shot down en route, 31 March 1944
GIROULLE, A.	Troilus	Shot down en route, 31 March 1944
GOFFIN, H.	Fortinbras	Killed air crash 8 January 1944, Tolworth Hill, Bedford
GRUNER, M.F.	Flavius	Arrested August 1944, vanished in Germany
HOTTIA, A.	Marmoset	Shot, 30 September 1943
HOYEZ, C.A.F.	Cowdor	Arrested 25 May 1944 and vanished
HUYSMANS, L.	Buckhound	Arrested 26 September 1943, presumed killed
JOYE, L.J.J.	Sempronius	Killed early September 1944
KAANEN, L.	Sable	Killed in action on landing, 1 May 1942
LEBLICQ, A.J.	Moonshine	Killed in a parachute accident
LEMMENS, V.J.	Koala	Shot, 8 October 1942
FLOTTE, U.G.A.F.	Lynx	Arrested 15 August 1942, wounded but vanished
MAUS, J.N.L.	Outcast	Shot, 8 July 1942
MICHAUX, R.P.E.	Lucius	Killed air crash 8 January 1944, Tolworth Hill, Bedford

Name	Field Name	Fate
MOREAU, F.J.G.	Cayote	Killed, 17 December 1942
NEY, J.H.	Marcius	Died in Neuengamme early 1945
OSTERRIETH, P.R.	Platypus	Killed 13 June 1944, in Allied air raid on Bochum
PASSELECQ, V.M.	Incomparable	Executed, 7 June 1944
PICQUART, J.	Lamb	Mortally wounded on landing, 1 May 1942
SCHAEPDRYVER, A.G.	Publius	Died in Mauthausen, 1 February 1945
STERCKMANS, J.	Wallaby	Shot, 5 December 1942
STINGHLAMBER, G.	Musjid	Shot 22 May 1944, at Gorden, Brandenburg
TROMME, E.M.J.	Caesarewitch	Shot, 25 February 1942
VAN DER MEERSCHE, L.C.	Ibex	Killed in an air raid, 7 September 1943
VAN LOO, E.J.	Ocelot	Arrested on landing, 29 August 1942, presumed killed
VAN IMPE, O.M.	Arboretum	Executed, 22 May 1944
VERHAEGEN, H.P.	Thersites	Killed air crash, 8 January 1944, Tolworth Hill, Bedford
VLIEX, P.J.L.H.	Marmot	Shot 8, June 1943
WAMPACH, F.J.	Vermilion	Shot 10 December 1943, commemorated at the Tir National
WARGNIES, J.H.	Philotus	Shot, 7 July 1944
WOUTERS, A.	Antenor	Killed, 5 September 1944
WOUTERS, R.M.	Mongoose	Shot, August 1944

The Belgian disasters began in January 1942. Armand Campion, a former French Foreign Legionnaire and holder of the *Croix de Guerre*, was recruited into the SOE and parachuted into Belgium near Silly, north of Mons.

He began sending messages back to London until he was arrested whilst actually sitting at his radio set in his brother's house in Brussels. The Germans did not have to work hard on Campion. He denounced everyone he could think of – including his brother, sister-in-law, his nieces, everyone he had met in training, and all the members of the reception committee that helped him when he landed in Belgium.

From then onwards, as with the Netherlands, large numbers of agents landed straight into the hands of the enemy. By late October 1942, forty-five agents had been despatched to Belgium and of these thirty-two were either in enemy hands or dead.

When these arrests became known of at Baker Street they were put down to successful direction-finding by the Gestapo; treachery was not considered. Campion's complicity was not discovered by London for over a year. As it happened, justice of a kind was done when Campion was killed in an Allied air raid. Further arrests followed, through bad luck, more treachery and efficient work by the Gestapo.

The death of one Belgian agent caused a minor security issue in the UK. When this agent, Armand Leblicq, tried to jump from the Armstrong Whitworth Whitley over the Ardennes his static line became entangled in the aircraft's tail wheel. He hung there until the Whitley returned to base at Newmarket. By this time, of course, Leblicq was dead. 'There could be no explaining all this in a coroner's court,' explained SOE historian M.R.D. Foot, 'with all the press and public present. His body, suitably weighted, was loaded into a Whitley's bomb bay, and committed to the sea outside the 3-mile limit.'

IV GERMANY/AUSTRIA

Name	Field Name	Fate
CORBISIER, G.J.F.	—	Shot down over France, 21 March 1944
DE WINTER, L.G.	—	Shot down over France, 21 March 1944
HESKETH-PRICHARD	—	Killed in action, Yugoslavia, 3 December 1944
KONIG, K.	—	Executed, Germany, 1944
MAYR, H.M.	Bakersfield	Killed in action, Innsbruck, 1 January 1945
MOREL, J.J.L.	—	Shot down over France, 21 March 1944
TREICHL, W.	—	Lost in action, Tolmezzo, 12 December 1944

There were three Belgian agents that were killed undertaking a mission for X Section (Germany). These were L.G. De Winter, J.J.L. Morel and G.J.F. Corbisier, all of whom were killed when the 161 Squadron Lockheed Hudson (serial FH803) they were in was shot down just north of Clervaux on 21 March 1944. None of these were recognised by the CWGC as SOE.

It is often stated, incorrectly, that the SOE's only official X Section endeavour into the Greater Reich was Operation *Chowder*. This involved Major Alfred Hesketh-Prichard (Royal Fusiliers) and Peter Wilkinson crossing into Austria from Yugoslavia. Before they even reached the frontier Wilkinson was recalled but Hesketh-Prichard continued on alone. He was never seen again and was believed killed on 3 December 1944. He was awarded the MC.

Viennese Austrian William Taggart (true name Wolfgang Treichl) was a former Wehrmacht officer with General Rommel's *Afrika Korps* but he deserted with his men to the British. He joined the SOE's X Section and was inserted into Austria with three others on Operation *Seafront*. The party landed at the wrong place and Taggart was killed in a gunfight at the Wehrmacht barracks in Tolmezzo, Italy, on 12 October 1944. Two of the other men were taken prisoner but survived the war and the fourth member (Huber) managed to evade capture.

Lieutenant Hubert Mayr (aka Jean Georgeau, Josef Rimmel) was killed in action near Innsbruck, Austria, whilst engaged in Operation *Bakersfield* on 1 January 1945. He is remembered at the Cassino Memorial, Italy. He was aged thirty-two.

Kurt Konig, an anti-Nazi Sudeten German, escaped from the German Army in 1942 and made his way to Britain via Spain. He joined the SOE in 1943. He was sent into Germany to act as a saboteur and he successfully sabotaged the railway line between Cologne and Koblenz. He was arrested in January 1944 and executed in Germany in February the following year. He has no known grave.

V CZECHOSLOVAKIA

Name	Field Name	Fate
BUBLIK, J.	Bioscope	Committed suicide in Prague, 18 June 1942
BARDICEV, A.	Amsterdam	Executed Mauthausen, 15 January 1945
BARTOS, A.	Silver A	Died of wounds, 22 June 1942
CUPAL, L.	Tin	Committed suicide in Velehrad, 15 January 1943
DANIELS, A.	Operation Windproof	Executed Mauthausen, 24 January 1944
DVORAK, O.	Steel A	Shot near Krivokat, 30 June 1942
GABČÍK, J.	Anthropoid	Committed suicide in Prague, 18 June 1942
GRUHUT, J.	Amsterdam	Executed Mauthausen, 1945
HRUBY, J.	Bioscope	Committed suicide in Prague, 18 June 1942
JASINEK, L.	Antimony	Committed suicide, January 1943
KOLARIK, I.	Distance	Suicide on arrest at Zlin, 1 April 1942
KOUBA, B.	Bioscope	Suicide after capture at Kutna Hora, 3 May 1942
KUBIŠ, J.	Anthropoid	Committed suicide in Prague, 18 June 1942
LUKASTIK, V.	Intransitive	Shot, 8 January 1943
MIKS, A.	Zinc	Shot at Krivolet, 30 April 1942
OPALKA, A.	Out	Committed suicide in Prague, 18 June 1942
PECHAL, O.	Zinc	Killed in Prague, 18 June 1942
POTUCEK, J.	Silver A	Shot, 2 August 1942
SVARC, J.	Tin	Committed suicide in Prague, 18 June 1942
VALCIK, J.	Silver A	Committed suicide in Prague, 18 June 1942
ZAVORKA, F.	Antimony	Committed suicide, January 1943

Czechoslovakia was the scene of one of the SOE's most famous missions – the attempted assassination of the head of the RSHA, or *Reichssicherheitshauptamt* (Reich Main Security Office), SS-*Obergruppenführer* Reinhart Heydrich. Known as Operation *Anthropoid*, it was conducted by Jan Kubiš and Josef Gabčík. As both men were officially attached to the Czech 1st Brigade based in the UK they therefore are not listed on the CWGC register.

Though successful in its specific objective, *Anthropoid* eventually proved counter-productive. A wave of reprisals followed Heydrich's death, which resulted in thousands of Czechs being arrested and executed. Whole villages were depopulated, their residents transported to concentration camps. Consequently, there was little support for further clandestine operations in Czechoslovakia. Kubiš and Gabčík committed suicide rather than face arrest.

Aircraftman 2nd Class Aba Bardicev joined the Royal Air Force Volunteer Reserve but became involved in special operations under the name of Robert Willis with the code name of *Anticlimax*. He participated in the highly-secret Operation *Amsterdam* but was captured by the Germans on Christmas Day 1944 whilst trying to buy food dressed in British uniform. He was executed at Mauthausen on 15 January 1945.

Also part of Operation *Amsterdam*, Sergeant Jindrich Gruhut (serving as Lieutenant M. Jamay), was captured by the Germans at Banská Bystrica, also in uniform. He was executed at Mauthausen but the actual date of his death is unclear.

An English language teacher from Slovakia, Margita Kockova was attached to 'A' Force SOE as part of Operation *Windproof* being used as an interpreter at the 1st Czechoslovak Army Headquarters. She was captured by the Germans in October 1944 and executed at Mauthausen, Austria, on 24 January 1945.

VI YUGOSLAVIA

Name	Field Name	Fate
ATHERTON, Arthur T., Major	Hydra	Robbed and murdered, 15 July 1942
BLAKE, Albert H.		Died of malaria, 30 July 1944
BLACKMORE, Leslie	Roughshod	Died, 9 June 1943
DAVIES, Mostyn L.	Mulligatawny	Died of wounds, Gerdelicha, 25 March 1944
GOLDSTEIN, Peretz	Chicken	Executed Germany, 1 March 1945
KNIGHT, Donald Ewart, Captain	–	Killed in air raid, 27 November 1943
LINDSTROM, Fred J. (aka Captain Hawksworth)	Angelica	Arrested soon after landing, executed 4 June 1943
O'DONOVAN, Patrick, Sergeant	Hydra	Killed with Atherton, 15 July 1942
PAVLIC, Paul	Fungus	Killed in German ambush, 1942/43
RUSSELL, Thomas C.	–	Murdered Romania, 4 September 1943
SMITH, Sidney, Lieutenant	Fugue	Shot, 5 June 1943
STUPPEL, Rudolf, Major	–	Killed, 31 October 1945 (Buried Belgrade War Cemetery)
THOMPSON, Henry	Fugue	Shot, 6 June 1943
THOMPSON, William F., Major	Mulligatawny/Claridges	Executed Litakovo, 10 June 1944
WALKER, John M.	Claridges	Killed in action, 18 May 1944
WHETHERLY, Robin E., Major	-	Killed in air raid by machine-gun fire, 27 November 1943 (Buried Belgrade War Cemetery)

Private Peretz (or Ferenez) Goldstein, a Palestinian Jew (parent unit the Pioneer Corps), was parachuted into Yugoslavia as a wireless operator for Operation *Chicken*. He was arrested by Hungarian Fascists in Budapest and murdered on, or shortly after, 1 March 1945, at Sachsenhausen-Oranienburg, Germany. He is remembered on the Athens Memorial.

The SOE operation in pro-Axis Bulgaria (which from 1941 onwards included parts of Yugoslavia) was not set up until 1944 and it suffered its first casualties at the end of March. Major Mostyn Llewellyn Davies (ex-SOE Lagos, Nigeria, and New York) and Major William Frank Thompson, both educated at Oxford University, were caught in a watermill by a Bulgarian patrol at Novo Selo. Mostyn Davies and his sergeant wireless operator were both killed (Davies dying of his wounds that same day), though Thompson managed to escape, revolver in hand, blazing away at the enemy. Major Mostyn Davies was awarded the DSO.

In April 1944 another attempt to organise the Bulgarian partisans (Operation *Claridges*) was led by Flight Lieutenant Kenneth Sayers with Sergeants Nick Muvrin (see main entry), John McCullum Walker and Kenneth Scott ex-Royal Signals. On 18 May, Muvrin and Walker were killed in an ambush by Bulgarian troops, with the other two being captured and handed over to the Gestapo in Sofia. Scott was pressed into service by the Germans but he left out his security check on his first transmission and, unusually, this was taken note of in London and no damage resulted. Scott died in 2008.

On 23 May 1944, Thompson took part in the clash at the village of Batuliya between the Bulgarian *Gendarmerie* and the Second Brigade of National Liberation of the partisans. He was wounded by the enemy forces, captured and in the nearby village of on 10 June 1944.

Thompson was seen as great hero in Bulgaria and after the war a number of villages were amalgamated and renamed in honour of Frank Thompson. Even today there is still a railway station in Bulgaria called 'Tompson' and a day nursery in Sofia was named after him.

Also considered to be a member of SOE Bulgaria was Corporal Albert Henry Blake (parent unit No.40 Commando, Royal Marines) who was evacuated to Italy on 29 July 1944, suffering from malaria. He died, aged twenty-one, in Brindisi on 30 July and was buried at Bari War Cemetery.

Captain Thomas Charles David Russell served in the 2nd Scots Guards in Egypt alongside David Stirling with the Long Range Desert Group. He was awarded the Military Cross for his part in Operation *Ranji*, the raid on Tobruk. He was parachuted into Yugoslavia on 15/16 June 1943, and crossed over the border into Romania in August with two other operatives to make contact with the local Resistance. In September 1943 they were staying in a house in the village of Varciarove near Timişoara. While one of them was making a radio transmission in the woods nearby the other two were attacked, probably by thieves. Russell was murdered but the other agent escaped.

VI1 NORWAY/DENMARK

Name	Field Name	Fate
AALL, Christian	—	Executed in Trandum, 1942
CASPEREN, Ole	Archer and Heron	Executed, 1944
BINGHAM, Brian	Moonshine	Lost at sea in the Skaggerak, 12 May 1945
BOELSKOV, Erik		Killed in explosion, Copenhagen, 25 August 1943
BRUHN, Johan	Chilblain	Killed in parachute accident, Torpeskov, near Haslev, 27/28 December 1941
DEINBOLL, Peter	Crupper	Died at sea following the loss of a 138 Squadron Short Stirling, serial LJ993, in bad weather, 8-9 November 1943
ERIKSEN, Eivind D.	Seagull	Died when Norwegian submarine HNoMS *Uredd* struck a mine in Fuglov Fjord, 28 February 1943
GETZ, Per	Seagull	Died when Norwegian submarine HNoMS *Uredd* struck a mine in Fuglov Fjord, 28 February 1943
GJESTLAND, Arne	Crupper	Died at sea following the loss of a 138 Squadron Short Stirling, serial LJ993, in bad weather, 8-9 November 1943
GRONG, Thorlief D.	Seagull	Died when Norwegian submarine HNoMS *Uredd* struck a mine in Fuglov Fjord, 28 February 1943
HANSEN, Hans R.	Seagull	Died when Norwegian submarine HNoMS *Uredd* struck a mine in Fuglov Fjord, 28 February 1943

Name	Field Name	Fate
HODSTANGE, Gunnar	Omega	Lost at sea
HVAAL, Emile	Anchor	Executed in Trandum, 1942
JOHANSEN, Hans Robert Philip, Lieutenant	Died 27 July 1944 –	
JOHANNESSEN, Poul Herman J.	– –	Committed suicide, 5 September 1942
LARSEN, H.H.P.	–	Executed, Copenhagen, 31 April 1942
LINDBERG, Konrad	–	Executed, 11 August 1941
LINGE, Martin Jensen	Archery	Killed in action, Maaloy, 27 December 1941
MARTHINSSON, Erling	–	Executed in Trandum, 1942 with Aall
NORMAN, Frithof	–	Disappeared on mission, 1942
NYGAARD, Paul K.	Vesilon	Lost on operations
PEDERSEN, Frithof	–	Executed with Lindberg, 11 August 1941
REVIK, Per	Boreas	Died on operations
ROTTBALL, Christian M.	–	Killed in gun fight with Germans, Copenhagen, 26 September 1942
SJOBERG, Birger	Archer and Heron	Killed in action, 9 June 1944
SKOG, Tobias	Seagull	Died when Norwegian submarine HNoMS *Uredd* struck a mine in Fuglov Fjord, 28 February 1943
VAERUM, Arne	–	Betrayed and shot at Televag, 26 April 1942
VALDERHAUG, I.	–	Arrested and executed, 1941/1942

An actor in peacetime, Captain Martin Linge was the commanding officer of the Norwegian Army's Norwegian Independent Company 1, informally known as *Kompani Linge*, which was attached to the SOE. He led his men on a raid against the islands of Maaloy and Vaagso off the west coast of Norway on 27 December 1941. This raid, Operation *Archery*, was the first truly combined operation mounted by the British in which the Army, Navy and Air Force were all involved. The raid was a considerable success but Linge was killed in street fighting in Maaloy during an attack on the local German headquarters. He was forty-seven. A total of 530 Norwegians served in Norwegian Independent Company 1, of whom fifty-seven lost their lives. Following Linge's death, the name of the unit was formalised as *Lingekompaniet* in his honour.

Second Lieutenant Erik Boelskov was a member of the SOE's SD (Danish) Section. He was killed by an explosion in Copenhagen on 25 August 1943. He was aged twenty-two. Shown as being on the General List, with the service number 291081, Boelskov's is the only CWGC grave in Koge Cemetery.

Another Danish Section agent lost in action was thirty-seven-year-old Captain Carl Johan Bruhn, whose parent unit was The Buffs (Royal East Kent Regiment). Bruhn was on his way to Denmark to take over command of SOE's Danish operations but he was killed when his parachute failed to open on the night of 27/28 December 1941. His watch stopped at 02.05 hours. The CWGC incorrectly give his date of death as 17 December.

Second Lieutenant Poul Herman Johannes Johannessen was another member of the SOE's Danish Section. He was seized by the Germans but immediately committed suicide to avoid internment at 8 Vinkelager, Copenhagen, on 5 September 1942. He was buried at Copenhagen (Bronshoj) Cemetery.

Captain Christian Michael Rottball, SOE Danish Section, was killed in a shoot-out with the police on 26 September 1942. He was aged twenty-five. Thirty-one-year-old Second Lieutenant Hans Henrik Pay Larsen (General List), codename 'Trick', was parachuted into Denmark in February 1942. It was later reported that he had become a 'dangerous liability' and was shot by a fellow agent on 30 April 1943. He is remembered at the Medjez-el-Bab Memorial, Tunisia.

Lieutenant Commander Brian Bingham MBE, DSC, RNR (true name Sylvanus Brian John Reynolds) served with the SOE on Operation *Moonshine* in supplying arms and equipment to the Danish Resistance via Sweden from September 1944 to February 1945. He died whilst participating on a special mission from Aberdeen to rescue three British merchant ships stranded at Gothenberg when, on 12 May 1945, the vessel he was on, HMMGB 2002, struck a mine in the Skaggerak.

VIII FAR EAST

Name	Field Name	Fate
ARCHAMBAULT, Jean P. Captain.	SOE Force 136	Killed in explosives accident, Burma, 19 May 1945
BAIRD, Alexander, Private	STS 101	Died in captivity, Siam, 7 October 1943
BRERETON MARTIN, William, Major	Force 136	Killed, 25 January 1945
BURTON, Henry Ronald, Corporal	Puma	Died Singapore, 4 December 1941
CAMERON, Colin, Sergeant	Rimau	Died Merapas Island, 5 November 1944
CAREY, Walter, Lieutenant	Rimau	Executed, Singapore, 7 July 1945
COLE, Sidney, Private	STS 101	Died in captivity, Siam, 4 October 1943
CRAFT, Colin, Corporal	Rimau	Killed in action, Indonesia, 21 December 1944
CROFT-MOSS, James Charles, Lieutenant	Starfish	Killed in action Indonesia, 19 August 1945
DARBY, Oliver, Lieutenant	FMS Volunteer Force	Killed, Malaya, 17 March 1944
DAVIDSON, Donald M.N., Lieutenant-Commander	Rimau	Killed in action, Tapai Island, Indonesia, 18 October 1944
FALLS, Walter G., Able Seaman	Rimau	Executed, Singapore, 7 July 1945
FLETCHER, Roland, Corporal	Rimau	Executed, Singapore, 7 July 1945
ELLIS, Henry Everard, Major	Semut 1	Killed in action, Borneo, 25 March 1945
GOOLEY, David, Sergeant	Rimau	Died, Merapas Island, 5 November 1944
GRAHAM, Ronald, Lieutenant	Oriental Mission SOE	Member of 'stay behind party', executed Kuala Lumpur, 18 September 1942
HABIB, Shah, Jemadar	SOE Celyon, Operation Bunkum	Killed in accident, Andaman Islands, 24 February 1943
HALLEY, Paul Vladimar, Captain	Force 136	Killed in car crash, India, 25 December 1944

Name	Field Name	Fate
HARDY, John, Lance Corporal	Rimau	Executed, Singapore, 7 July 1945
HOUGHTON, Robert George, Sergeant	Robin	Died as PoW, 20 April 1945
HUSTON, Andrew William George, Able Seaman	Rimau	Drowned, Indonesia, 16 December 1944
INGELTON, Reginald M., Major	Rimau	Executed, Singapore, 7 July 1945
KOK, Ngit Yin, Captain	Billow	Killed in failed SOE landing in Siam, 2 September 1944
LYON, Ivan, Lieutenant Colonel	Rimau	Died, Tapai Island 16 October 1944
MACKINTOSH, John Ali, Lieutenant Colonel	-	Died of typhoid in Turkey, 4 January 1945 Buried at Istanbul (Ferikoi) Protestant Cemetery
MACKINTOSH, Stanley McLeod, Captain.	Force 136	Died of typhoid, Siam, 16 June 1945
MARSH, Frederick, Able Seaman	Rimau	Died in captivity, Singapore, 11 January 1945
McCRINDLE, Eric John, Captain	Harlington	Executed in Rangoon, Burma, 15 February 1944
McMILLAN, Leslie Thomas, Captain.	Robin	Presumed drowned, Balikpapan Bay, 20 March 1945. Commemorated on the Laubuan Memorial, Malaysia
MYERS, Ernest Henry, Signalman	Platypus	Taken prisoner, executed in Borneo, 4 July 1945 Commemorated on the Laubuan Memorial, Malaysia
NIMMO, Major James R., DSO	Harlington	Executed Burma, 15 February 1944.
NOONE, Herbert Deane, Lieutenant	SOE Malaya	Member of 'stay behind' party, last seen 3 November 1943
POXON, Ernest, Private	Force 136	Died, 22 August 1944.
RAND, Guy Widdrington, Lieutenant	SOE Malaya	Member of 'stay behind' party, killed 17 March 1943.
PACE, Hugo Joseph, Lance-Corporal	Rimau	Died of disease in captivity, Dili, Timor 19 January 1945
PAGE, Robert, Captain	Rimau	Executed, Singapore, 7 July 1945
REID, John, Lieutenant	SOE Malaya	Member of 'stay behind' party, died in Changi prison, 12 May 1944
REYMOND, Bruno, Lieutenant	Rimau	Drowned, Cape Satai, Borneo, 21 December 1945
RIGGS, J. Gregor, Sub Lieutenant	Rimau	Died, Merapas Island, 5 November 1944
ROBINSON, Stanley R., Lieutenant	SOE Malaya	Died in guerrilla camp Perak, Malaya, 15 September 1943
ROSS, Robert, Lieutenant	Rimau	Died, Tapai Island,16 October 1944
SARGENT, Albert, Warrant Officer 2	Rimau	Executed, Singapore, 7 July 1945

Name	Field Name	Fate
SAWYER, Frederick, Corporal	SOE Burma	Drowned fording a flooded river, Burma, 12 June 1942
SEAHRIM, Hugh Paul, Major	Force 136	Executed, Rangoon, 22 September 1944
SENG, Guy L.B.S., Colonel	Force 136	Died in captivity, Malaysia, 29 June 1944
SHEARN, Charles, R., Captain	Force 136	Killed in action, Burma, 4 May 1945
SOMERSET, William Percy, Major	Carpenter	Killed in action, Malaysia, 25 January 1945
STEWART, Clair, Corporal	Rimau	Executed, Singapore, 7 July 1945
STOTT, Donald John, Major	Robin	Presumed drowned, Balikpapan Bay, 20 March 1945 Commemorated on the Laubuan Memorial, Malaysia
SMYLLIE, Thomas M., Lieutenant	SOE Malaya	Member of 'stay behind' party died 21 March 1943
SOWDEN, Alfred C.B., Sergeant, MM	Force 136	Died India, 1 September 1945
STUBINGTON, William H., Second Lieutenant	SOE Malaya	Member of 'stay behind' party, killed 17 March 1945
TREMLETT, Frederick Innes, Lieutenant Colonel	Force 136	Died Malaysia, 2 August 1945 Commemorated on the Singapore Memorial
TYSON, Brian F., Captain	SOE Malaya	Member of 'stay behind' party, killed 18 January 1943
VANRENEN, Frank Campbell, Lieutenant	Oriental Mission SOE	Member of 'stay behind' party, executed Kuala Lumpur, 18 September 1942
WARNE, Douglas, Private	Rimau	Died in captivity following a lethal tetanus injection, Soerabaya, Java, April 1945 (CWGC give the date of his death as 15 December 1945)
WARREN, Alfred, Warrant Officer 2	Rimau	Executed, Singapore, 7 July 1945
WILLERSDORF, Jeffery, Warrant Officer 2	Rimau	Died of wounds or of disease, Romang Island, Dili, Timor, 1-10 February 1945 (CWGC give the date of his death as 15 December 1945)

A number of SOE agents were killed in operations in the Far East. Falkirk-born Alexander Baird, whose parent unit was the Argyll and Sutherland Highlanders, was captured by the Japanese whilst operating out of the SOE's establishment Special Training School 101 at Tanjong Baili in Singapore. He was worked to death on the Burma-Siam Railway and died at the age of twenty-three at Kanchanaburi, Siam, on 7 October 1943.

Private Sidney Cole, also an Argyll and Sutherland Highlander from Special Training School (STS) 101, was another who lost his life on the Burma-Siam Railway. He died on 4 October 1943, and was buried at Thanbyzayat War Cemetery in modern-day Thailand.

Colonel Guy Lim Bo Seng was Force 136 Regional Chinese Agent (SOE). Seng was born in China but lived in Singapore, which he left just before the Japanese occupation. He organised the first of the Force 136 (the SOE's umbrella organisation for their activities in south-east Asia) agents to be infiltrated into Malaya in May 1942 under the Code name Operation *Gustavus*. Their objective was to set up an espionage network to gather military intelligence about the Japanese. This would allow the British Army to carefully plan the invasion of Malaya and Singapore. Seng was betrayed and captured by the Japanese in March 1944. He was later reported to be a PoW in Perak, Malaysia. He suffered terribly in prison and contracted dysentery. The Japanese refused to give him any medical help and he died in captivity aged thirty-five on 29 June 1944.

Major Henry Everard Ellis was part of the Z Special Unit raiding force arm of the Melbourne-based Services Reconnaissance Department, Australia (also known as Special Operations Australia). A member of the Leicestershire Regiment, Ellis was one of a number of SOE agents who had escaped from Singapore before its fall to the Japanese. He was lost on an insertion operation (SEMUT 1) into Borneo on 25 March 1945 when his plane, a Liberator of 200 Flight RAAF, went missing off northern Borneo.

Lieutenant Commander Donald Montague Noel Davidson was part of a twenty-three man SOE Z Special Unit raiding team sent on a mission to sink Japanese shipping in Singapore harbour by placing limpet mines on ships. Bearing the Code name Operation *Rimau*, motorised one-man semi-submersible canoes were to be used to gain access to the harbour. They travelled with all their equipment towards Singapore in a junk but on the scheduled day of the operation, 10 October 1944, disaster struck. A Japanese patrol boat challenged the *Mustika* and someone on board opened fire. Their cover blown, the commander, Lieutenant Colonel Ivan Lyon, had no option but to abort the mission.

Lyon, however, decided to try a reduced-scale operation with just six men, including Davidson. This group managed to sink (or at least damage) three ships but the Japanese caught up with the raiders on Soreh Island. A gun battle ensued and Davidson and Campbell were severely wounded. Davidson escaped to Tapai Island where he died on 18 October either through his wounds or by swallowing his cyanide pill. He was awarded the DSO and the MBE. Further losses included Lieutenant Harold Robert Ross, of the SOE Services Research Department, Australia, who died on 16 October 1944, aged twenty-seven. Also lost was Sub-Lieutenant James Riggs RNVR also of the SOE Services Research Department, and Sergeant Colin Cameron AIF and Sergeant David Gooley who were killed in a gun battle on Merapas Island in the Riouw Archipelago on 5 November 1944 when a Japanese party landed on the island.

When the rendezvous with the submarine sent to recover the team was not met, the men tried to island-hop across the 3,000 miles of enemy-held territory between Singapore and Australia. Inevitably this proved impossible. Able Seaman Andrew W.G. Huston was drowned off Boeaja Island, Lingga Archipelago, Indonesia on 15 or 16 December 1944. Lieutenant Bruno Reymond RANR was also drowned, in this case it was off Cape Satai, Borneo on 12 December 1944. Able Seaman Frederick Marsh was wounded in the operation and on 17 December he was placed in a PoW camp on Tjempa Island. He died of his wounds and fever on 1 February 1945 at Tandjung Pagar, Singapore. Colonel Lyon and nine others from Operation *Rimau* were captured and taken to Outram Road Prison in Singapore. These included Royal Marine Major Reginald Middleton Ingleton and Able Seaman Walter Gordon Falls. On 3 July 1945, they were put on trial for espionage, found guilty and executed. The ten men were beheaded at Bukit Timah, Singapore on 7 July 1945 – barely a month before the war came to an end. All twenty-three men of the operation were lost.

When the Japanese invaded Burma, Major Hugh Paul Seagrim (19th Hyderabad Regiment later seconded to the 20th Burma Rifles) was given the task of raising guerilla forces from amongst the local tribes, particularly the Karens. When the British were driven out of Burma, Seagrim's rebel band was left isolated for many months. It was not until October 1943 that Force 136 was able to drop agents behind the enemy lines and make contact with Seagrim. He continued to lead his guerillas against the Japanese but they were gradually wiped out by a concentrated Japanese manhunt.

To prevent further bloodshed to the locals, some 270 of whom had been rounded up and were being systematically slaughtered, Seagrim surrendered on 15 March 1944. Along with eight of his group, he was executed in Rangoon on 22 September 1944. Seagrim pleaded that the others were following his orders and as such they should be spared, but they were determined to die with him and were all executed. He was posthumously awarded the George Cross for 'most conspicuous gallantry in carrying out hazardous work in a very brave manner'. He had previously been awarded the DSO and been appointed an MBE.

Of interest is the fact that Seagrim's brother, Lieutenant Colonel Derek Anthony Seagrim, was awarded the Victoria Cross for his actions in March 1943 during the fighting in North Africa. The Seagrim brothers are the only siblings to have been awarded the George Cross and the Victoria Cross between them.

Captain Charles Ronald Shearn had operated successfully with F Section (PERMIT circuit) and volunteered to continue his work with the SOE after the liberation of France. He was dropped onto the Shan Plateau in eastern Burma with two others on 26 April 1945. After a successful attack upon an enemy barracks with some 300 locally-recruited troops, he led his patrol against a small group of pro-Japanese Thais in Mongton monastery on 4 May 1945. He was wounded in the wrist and stomach. Though he was carried away by his men he died of his wounds.

IX GREECE, ITALY AND THE MEDITERRANEAN

Name	Field Name	Fate
ARUEH, Gelbert	Boatswain	Missing at sea, Eastern Mediterranean, 18 May 1941
BARUCH, Jacobson	Boatswain	Missing at sea, Eastern Mediterranean, 18 May 1941
CADOGAN, C.M., Captain	Special Mission	Lost at sea, Eastern Mediterranean, 23 June 1941
COHEN, Mordehai	Boatswain	Missing at sea, Eastern Mediterranean, 18 May 1941
CUMBERLEDGE, Claude Michael Bulstrode, Lieutenant Commander	SOE Greece	Executed Flossenbürg, Germany, 10 April 1945
DAREWSKI, N.T.L., Major	Flap	Killed in motor vehicle accident, Marsaglin, Italy, 15 November 1944

Name	Field Name	Fate
DE LUCIA, John, Aircraftsman 2	Rankin	Executed, Italy, 12 May 1944
EIZEN, Arieh	Boatswain	Missing at sea, Eastern Mediterranean, 18 May 1941
GUBBINS, John McVean, Captain	No.1 Special Force	Killed in action, Anzio, Italy, 6 February 1944
HANDLEY, Thomas E., Sergeant, MM.	Locksmith	Executed, Sachsenhausen, Germany, 10 April 1945
HECKER, Issac, Warrant Officer	Boatswain	Missing at sea, Eastern Mediterranean, 18 May 1941
HOPE, Adrian A, Major	Chariton	Killed in action, Italy, 17 April 1945
HUBBARD, W.A., Lieutenant	SOE Military Mission	Shot by accident, Triklinos, Grece, 13 October 1943
JACOB, Gordon	Boatswain	Missing at sea, Eastern Mediterranean, 18 May 1941
KARAYANNI, Lela	SOE Greece	Executed, Haidari concentration camp, Athens, 8 September 1944.
KEANY, John, Captain	Chariton	Died, Italy, 8 March 1945
KESTERTON, Ian Douglas, Corporal	Force 133	Killed in air crash, Greece, 1 December 1943
KNOX, William Arthur, Warrant Officer	Force 133	Killed in action, Crete, 23 March 1944
KOPLER, Gershon, Sergeant	Boatswain	Missing at sea, Eastern Mediterranean, 18 May 1941
KURAKIM, Menaham	Boatswain	Missing at sea, Eastern Mediterranean, 18 May 1941
McKENNA, George Hughes, Gunner	Force 133	Killed in air crash, Greece, 1 December 1943
MULGAN, John A.E.	Force 133	Committed suicide from overdose of morphia, Cairo, 26 April 1945
NAFHA, David, Sergeant	Boatswain	Missing at sea, Eastern Mediterranean, 18 May 1941
NORDEN, Israel, Engineer, *Sea Lion*	Boatswain	Missing at sea, Eastern Mediterranean, 18 May 1941
NURIEL, Abraham	Boatswain	Missing at sea, Eastern Mediterranean, 18 May 1941
PAGLIN, Nerial	Boatswain	Missing at sea, Eastern Mediterranean, 18 May 1941
PERKINS, D.C., Sergeant	Force 133	Killed in action, Crete, 28 February 1944
PICCHI, Fortunato, Private	Colossus	Executed, 6 April 1941, Italy
PLONCHIK, Mordehai	Boatswain	Missing at sea, Eastern Mediterranean, 18 May 1941
ROTMAN, Zeev	Boatswain	Missing at sea, Eastern Mediterranean, 18 May 1941
SAMI, Hanovitz	Boatswain	Missing at sea, Eastern Mediterranean, 18 May 1941
SHEPPARD, L.F., Lieutenant Colonel	SOE Liaison	Killed by landmine, Greece, 30 December 1944
SHOHET, Amiram, Warrant Officer, *Sea Lion*	Boatswain	Missing at sea, Eastern Mediterranean, 18 May 1941

Name	Field Name	Fate
SMART, Ian Albert, Major	Force 133	Killed in air crash, Greece, 1 December 1943
SPECTOR, Zvi, Lieutenant	Boatswain	Missing at sea, Eastern Mediterranean, 18 May 1941
STEPHENSEN, John Cory, Captain	Force 133	Killed in air crash, Greece, 1 December 1943
TAMPLIN, Guy R. Colonel	SOE Middle East	Died, Cairo, 4 November 1943
TEMES, Ariel	Boatswain	Missing at sea, Eastern Mediterranean, 18 May 1941
TSIGANTES, John, Major	Thurgoland	Executed, Greece, January 1943
TOLEY, Alan Willoughby, Lieutenant	Force 133	Killed in air crash, Greece, 1 December 1943
UTCHITEL, Shimon	Boatswain	Missing at sea, Eastern Mediterranean, 18 May 1941
VEIMAN, Ephraim	Boatswain	Missing at sea, Eastern Mediterranean, 18 May 1941
WALLACE, D.J, Major	Force 133 (Foreign Office Representative)	Killed in action, Meninas, Greece, 17 August 1944
WEISMAN, Haim	Boatswain	Missing at sea, Eastern Mediterranean, 18 May 1941
WHITAKER, Charles F., Captain	SOE Italy	Killed in air crash near Ivren, Italy, 11 September 1944
WIGRAM, Lionel, Major	SOE Wigforce	Killed in action, Pizzoferrato, Italy, 3 February 1944
YOFEH, Katriel, Warrant Officer	Boatswain	Missing at sea, Eastern Mediterranean, 18 May 1941. (Skipper of the *Sea Lion*).
ZERNER, Yehuda	Boatswain	Missing at sea, Eastern Mediterranean, 18 May 1941

Amongst those Greeks who died in service with the SOE is Lela (or Eleni) Karayanni, some details of whom have been published. A mother of seven, five of whom worked with her, she helped gather intelligence and was engaged in sabotage and arranging the escape of British servicemen to Egypt in which she organised the first escape by caique to Cairo. She was arrested in October 1941 but released six months later.

She immediately resumed her clandestine work controlling a large network of supporters until she was betrayed and captured in March 1944. Lela was executed on 8 September 1944. She was posthumously awarded the King's Commendation for Bravery and the Award of Heroism and Self-Sacrifice by the Academy of Athens.

Warrant Officer William Arthur Knox was sent to assist the partisans in Crete on 31 October 1943. His team proved so successful that the Germans mounted a major operation to evict it from its base in the White Mountains. The partisans should have been quite safe but they were betrayed by the Cretans who had turned against them. Bill Knox was hiding in a cave that was attacked by a force of some 500 Germans on 23 March 1944. Knox was killed in the gunfight.

In the spring of 1945 the Germans were withdrawing from Greece and had prepared the bridge over the Corinth Canal for demolition. An SOE team was sent to save the bridge.

The team's wireless operator was Sergeant Thomas Edward Handley who was captured by the Germans and executed on 10 April 1945. Though some accounts state that he was killed at Flossenbürg he is remembered on the memorial at Sachsenhausen. He was awarded the Military Medal.

Staff Sergeant Dudley Churchill Perkins, New Zealand Artillery, was part of the Allied force defending Crete when the island was seized by the Germans in May 1941. He was amongst some 6,000 men taken prisoner. He and a number of others managed to escape and they hid out on the island until a SBS party managed to rescue them in June 1942 and take them to Alexandria. On 28 April 1943, he was transferred to the SOE's Force 133 and returned to Crete to help the partisans.

Becoming known as 'The Lion of Crete', Perkins led his partisan groups in many actions and in one of them he was wounded, with the bullet lodging in his body close to his kidney. A local butcher removed the bullet with his butcher's knife.

On 28 February 1944, Perkins was leading his group when they encountered a German patrol. Perkins was hit in the chest by machine-gun fire and died immediately. The CWGC gives the date of his death as 25 February but a memorial in Crete bears the date of 28 February.

The famous New Zealand novelist Lieutenant Colonel John Mulgan joined Force 133 in May 1943. Mulgan, who had studied Greek at Auckland University College, was parachuted into northern Greece where he led partisan groups in guerilla operations against the Germans. He was awarded the Military Cross for the attacks against German communications. Ill and exhausted he was flown to Cairo in October 1944 where he began his last book, *Report on Experience*, his account of his war years. It was in Cairo where, on 26 April 1945, he took an overdose of morphia from his medical kit. The reasons for his suicide remain unclear.

Lieutenant Colonel Leslie Frederick Sheppard DSO (Intelligence Corps) was also with Force 133 in service with the United Nations Relief and Rehabilitation Administration as the SOE's Liaison Officer. He was killed by a landmine on 30 December 1944.

Major David John Wallace MC, King's Royal Rifle Corps, is buried at the Paramythia Civil Cemetery in Greece and his memorial is inscribed with these words: 'Here rests amongst his guerilla comrades an Englishman, Major David Wallace, killed on 17 August, 1944, in an air attack during the battle of Merinas. The soil of Greece is honoured to give shelter to this hero.'

Lieutenant Wilfred Arthur Hubbard (parent unit, New Zealand Armoured Corps) was part of the SOE Military Mission to the Greek Resistance during the ongoing conflict between the rival Greek parties, the ELAS (*Ellinikós Laïkós Apeleftherotikós Stratós*) the military arm of the left-wing National Liberation Front, and the EDES (*Ethnikos Dimokratikos Ellinikos Syndesmos*) the right-wing National Republican Greek League, He was one of a number of men sent there in an attempt to bring the two sides together in a common opposition to the occupying German forces. He was accidentally shot by an ELAS gunman at Triklinos on 13 October 1943. He is buried at the Phaleran War Cemetery.

The Greek Army Major John (Ioannis) Tsigantes was sent into Greece on Operation *Thurgoland* and became a well known figure in the Greek Resistance movement as the leader of a group called Midas 614. He was captured by the Italians who discovered his hiding place in Athens and was executed by them in January 1943.

Aircraftsman John de Lucia (born in Italy in 1913 as Giovani di Lucia) from Niagara Falls, Ontario, was a member of the Royal Canadian Air Force. As an SOE wireless operator he was parachuted north of Verona as part of the RANKIN mission in early 1944 to help Italian partisans to protect key installations, such as bridges and hydro-electric plants from destruction by the retreating Germans. He was captured and executed in Italy. His last words before his execution were: 'This was expected and I am ready to face it. I die happily.'

Major Neville Lawrence Temple Darewski (Royal Army Ordnance Corps), having taken part in Mission *Livingston II* in Slovenia in August 1943, went on a second mission Code named *Flap* in Italy 1944. He established an airfield at Vesime in the Province of Asti for the delivery of supplies to the partisans of northern Italy. As well as Lysanders, the airfield received a C-47 Dakota and a B-25 Mitchell. Darewski was killed in a freak accident on 15 November 1944, when he was crushed against a wall by the side of a truck in the town of Marsaglia. Aged thirty-one, he was buried at Staglieno Cemetery, Genoa.

Captain John McVean Gubbins (parent unit, 5th Battalion Cameron Highlanders) was the son of Major General Gubbins, head of the SOE from September 1943 until the end of the war. John Gubbins was an instructor at STS 21 at Arisaig, Inverness-shire, which specialised in commando-style training in 1941. He was killed in action at Anzio on 6 February 1944, aged twenty-two. He is remembered at the Cassino Memorial, Italy.

Colonel Guy Richard Tamplin MC, former Director of Special Operations, Balkans, was the Head of Country Sections, Cairo. He was found slumped over his desk in Cairo having died from a heart attack or stroke on 4 November 1943. His boss, Brigadier Mervin Keble, had been experimenting with a new form of poison and rumours spread that Tamplin had met his end at Keble's hands. He was the recipient of numerous anonymous phone calls congratulating him on committing 'the perfect crime'. None of this was ever seriously investigated.

Former barrister, Captain Christopher Michael Cadogan (parent unit, Royal Berkshire Regiment and 11 Military Mission (Phantom)) joined the SOE in July 1940. He died whilst returning from a special mission to Turkey on 23 June 1941, when the Turkish vessel he was on was sunk by a German submarine near Cyprus. His last letter home ended with these words: 'Do not grieve too much about my dying. I have done a little already in this life but there is a huge amount still to be done. Remember that the world will get better if people behave in a decent Christian way to each other.'

South African born Major Adrian A. Hope went into Piedmont Northern Italy on 4 February 1945, as part of No.1 Special Force on the *Chariton* mission. He was killed behind enemy lines on 17 April 1945, and was buried at the Stalgieno Cemetery.

Captain John Keany (Royal Irish Fusiliers) was also killed on Operation *Chariton*. He died on 8 March 1945, and was buried in the Milan War Cemetery.

Also lost in Italy was Major Lionel Wigram, who was the former Chief Instructor of GHQ Home Forces Battle School at Barnard's Castle, County Durham. He went into Italy in 1943 with the SOE and was killed in action at Pizzoferrato on 3 February 1944. He was buried at the Moro River Canadian War Cemetery, Italy.

One of the earliest SOE casualties was the Italian Fortunato Picchi who was taken on Operation *Colossus*, Britain's first ever parachute raid. The operation was the destruction of the Tragino Aqueduct in south-east Italy and Picchi (who served in the guise of a Frenchman under the name of Pierre Dupont) was one of two Italian-speaking interpreters. After demolishing one of the piers of the aqueduct he and the rest of the paratroopers were captured whilst trying to reach the coast where they were due to be rescued by submarine.

Under interrogation he admitted that he was indeed Italian but declared that, 'they will soon see that I am a true lover of Italy, but at the same time a hater of the Fascist regime.' He was taken from Naples Central Prison and executed on Palm Sunday, 1941 at Bravetta, Rome.

X JEDBURGH OPERATIONS

Name	Field Name	Fate
BRINKGREVE, Hendrik	Dudley	Killed in action, Overyssel, Holland, 5 March 1945
BRITTON, David J.	Nation/Reindeer	Killed in action, Sittang Valley, Burma, 3 June 1945
COLVIN, Peter M.	Nation/Hart	Killed when aircraft he was in crashed on take-off, India, 1 April 1945
MARCHANT, Godfrey	Nation/Hart	Killed when aircraft he was in crashed on take-off, India, 1 April 1945
GROENEWOUD, J.	Claude	Killed in action, Arnhem, 18 September 1944
RADICE, Jocelyn F.D.	Bunny	Fatally wounded in combat. Died Longeau, France, 27 August 1944
VICKERY, P.C.H.	Nation/Hart	Killed when aircraft he was in crashed on take-off, India, 1 April 1945

There were SOE losses in Jedburgh operations in many theatres, some of whom appear under their original units on the CWGC list. Jedburgh teams included SOE agents but were also composed of US personnel from the Office of Strategic Services (OSS) and the Free French *Bureau Central de Renseignements et d'Action*.

Between June and September 1944, 276 Jedburgh personnel were dropped into France, Belgium and the Netherlands. Between D-Day and VE Day, Jedburghs carried out possibly 101 operations in Europe. Later they conducted similar operations with Allied Special Forces in the Far East, including the SOE's Force 136.

Jacobus Groenewoud was a member of Jedburgh team 'Claude', which took part in the famous Operation *Market Garden* to seize the bridges over the Lower Rhine in 1944. The team consisted of two Americans plus the Dutchman Groenewoud and they were tasked with liaising between Major General Urquhart and the local Dutch Resistance. They dropped with the 1st Parachute Brigade Headquarters and Groenewoud found himself involved in the battle for the Arnhem Bridge. He was killed in the fighting on 18 September 1944.

The costly 'Dudley' Jedburgh operation included Sergeant John Austin, who is recognised by the CWGC. Details of the mission are given under Austin's entry in the main SOE listing.

Jedburgh 'Bunny' operated in the Haute Marne organising stores and aiding communications for the local 'Ovale' Resistance group. In the course of its operations the team encountered a German convoy drawn up in the main street of the small town of Longeau on 20 August 1944. Rather than try and quietly withdraw, they drove on through, attacking the convoy with automatic weapons and hand grenades. Some fifteen Germans were killed but Major Radice, the team leader, was wounded in both legs. His colleagues took him back to their campsite and, after removing anything that might identify him as being a combatant, he was taken to Langres hospital. His legs had become gangrenous and they were amputated but the infection had already spread and he died at some point between 25 and 27 August.

XI OTHER SPHERES OF OPERATION

In May 1940 the French merchant ship, *Le Rhone* was sailing its route in the Mediterranean when France capitulated to the Germans. The ship's skipper, Claude Costa, steamed to Gibraltar and offered the vessel and its cargo to the British. All but six of the crew accepted Britain's offer to be repatriated back to France. The others chose to join the British forces and with their ship, re-named as the Special Service Vessel HMS *Fidelity* and the crew numbers augmented by other French and Belgian sailors, they began to participate in operations for the SOE.

Up until the end of 1941, the ship conducted two covert operations in the Mediterranean and a series of complicated landings of agents. In December 1942, *Fidelity* was involved in another operation off the Azores and was sunk by the German submarine *U-435* on 1 January 1943. None of her crew were ever seen again.

Amongst those lost were Costa, who had become Lieutenant Commander Langlais, and Madeleine Victorie Bayard who had adopted the English name of Madeleine Barclay WRNS and was the ship's First Officer. Lieutenant Commander Rene W. Doudet also died as did Lieutenant Jean Jacques Avencour and Paul R. Fontenay (true name Gauffriand). They are all commemorated on the Lee-on-Solent memorial.

* * *

Another unrecognised SOE agent was the Sudeten-German Richard Lehniger. He was born in 1900 and, as a member of the Social Democratic Party in Sudetenland, was opposed to Nazi policy and this led him to move to the UK when Hitler absorbed that area into his 'Greater' Germany. As a German speaker he was recruited by the SOE and began training in March 1941. At the end of the training course his assessor wrote: 'Pleasant, tough, a born revolutionary, quite without fear of any kind ... Not very intelligent, but he would be willing to do any dirty work, however dangerous ... In sum, he is the VC or the glass house type'.

Lehniger was seconded to the Small Scale Raiding Force (SSRF) and was involved in a raid upon the Normandy coast on the night of 12 September 1942, codenamed Operation *Aquatint*. The eleven-man-strong party landed on the wrong beach and was spotted by a German patrol. Most of the raiders were able to escape back to their little wood and canvas boat but it was sunk by gunfire as they rowed desperately back to the waiting Motor Torpedo Boat. All the raiders were either killed or captured. Lehniger drowned and was buried by the Germans in the cemetery in Saint-Laurent-sur-Mer with full military honours including a three-gun salute. This was filmed by the Germans for propaganda purposes. His personal SOE file can be found in TNA HS9/907/5.

Also killed in this operation were Captain March-Phillipps and Sergeant Allan Michael Williams, January Hellings and Abraham Opoczynki (see main entry) were captured.

Captain Graham Hayes escaped but was later captured in Spain and executed by the Germans in 1943.

The Small Scale Raiding Force was originally put together by the SOE in 1940 and though it later came under the operational command of Combined Operations, the men continued to be administered by SOE. Captain Geoffrey Appleyard who survived *Aquatint* died in an air crash, also in 1943, whilst working with the SAS.

* * *

The first SOE casualty of the war was the remarkable character Arnold Wienholt, a former member of the Australian Parliament and a big game hunter. He had operated with the South African Army as an Intelligence officer in the First World War and took a small party behind enemy lines in German East Africa (Tanzania). He was wounded and captured on 1 July 1916. He escaped six months later and spent fifteen days crossing enemy-occupied country to regain his own lines. For his gallantry he was awarded the Military Cross. Wienholt performed further successful reconnaissance missions for which he won the DSO and received a bar to his MC.

On the outbreak of the Second World War he sailed to Aden and offered his services to the British authorities. On 31 August 1940, he was sent overland from the Sudan to Ethiopia in charge of a small party of natives as part of SOE Mission 101 tasked with fostering rebellion against Italy. Ambushed and wounded, probably on the morning of 10 September 1940. It is variously stated that he was captured by the Italians and shot as a spy, despite being in uniform, or that he died from his wounds. He is remembered on the Khartoum Memorial.

* * *

Charles Gaskill was the Special Operations Executive Liaison Officer with the Soviet NKVD. He was killed in an aircraft crash on 5 November 1943.

* * *

Captain Howard Benjamin Burgess (born 15 April 1915) worked for the *Daily News* in London before being recruited into the Intelligence Corps and then the SOE. He became a member of the staff at the Beaulieu training school. On 9 April 1942, Burgess was sent to STS 103, the Canadian commando training installation on the shores of Lake Ontario. Also known as Camp-X, the facility was jointly operated by the SOE and the British Security Co-ordination to train SOE and OSS agents.

On 3 June 1942, when he was illustrating the techniques of avoiding gun-fire whilst crawling under barbed-wire, a live round hit Burgess in the head. He was twenty-six years old. He was buried at the Union Cemetery, Ontario.

* * *

Another SOE agent buried in North America is thirty-six-year-old Sergeant Henry William Clapinson – a New Zealander serving with the Royal Australian Air Force and seconded to the SOE Australian arm. He, along with six others, was engaged in Operation *Hawk* with Z Special Unit, which was a night assault upon the Japanese airbase of Babo in Indonesia. They took off for the mission from Fenton Airfield near Darwin at approximately 22.59 hours on 18 March 1944, on board a USAAF B-24. At 03.45 hours on 19 March the aircraft exploded in the air. The B-24 crashed to the ground at Fak Fak in the Philippines. All bar one of the bodies were recovered and later buried at St Louis (Jefferson Barracks) National Cemetery, Missouri, USA.

* * *

Hungarian-born Lieutenant Stephen Maitland (true name Steve Mate) from Ontario, Canada, was a member of the Canadian Armoured Corps who joined the SOE in October 1943. On 17 April 1944, he was en route from the UK to Hungary via Brindisi when the Warwick aircraft he was in (BV247 of 525 Squadron) exploded and crashed into the English Channel near Newquay, Cornwall. Maitland was killed as were SOE agents Lieutenant Colonel Ivan Watkins Birts (parent unit Royal Artillery) and the renowned archeologist Lieutenant Colonel Stanley Casson, who was acting as SOE Liason Officer, Greece. Also on board was Air Commodore George Lionel Dawson-Damer (Viscount Carlow) of 600 Squadron, who was attached to MI9. The three SOE men were buried at Newquay (Fairpark) Cemetery.

The details of all the individuals that died in the crash were not revealed to the public because of the secret nature of their employment and this led, remarkably, to the CWGC having *three* entries for Maitland. These are as follows:

Mate, Steve, Civilian War Dead
Mate, Stephen, Lieutenant, General List, Service No.8400
Maitland, Stephen, Lieutenant, Alias, Service No.8400

In some respects Maitland's story exemplifies the mystery surrounding many of the lost agents of the SOE – a mystery that continues to this day.

Source Information

Primary Sources

DOCUMENTS IN THE NATIONAL ARCHIVE, KEW

HS 9	Special Operations Executive: Personal Files (PF Series).
HS 4/129	Liquidation of Hungarian Collaborators and Contacts.
HS 7/121	Personnel Dropped by F Section.
HS7/244	France F Section Diary July–September 1942.
HS7/245	France F Section Diary October–December 1942.
HS8/811	Personnel: Casualties and Movements, Naval.
HS8/855	Casualties.
HS8/895 & 896	Casualties in the Field, January 1943 to December 1945.
HS8/1002	British Circuits in France, by Major Bourne-Patterson.
KV6/9-38	Security Service files, relating to individual cases referred to MI5 for investigation.

Secondary Sources

PUBLISHED BOOKS

Atkinson, Linda, *In Kindling Flame: The Story of Hannah Senesh* (Beech Tree Books, New York, 1992).

Auty, Phyllis and Clogg, Richard (Eds.), *British Policy Towards Wartime Resistance in Yugoslavia & Greece* (Macmillan, London, 1975).

Bailey, Roderick, *The Wildest Province: SOE in the Land of the Eagle* (Jonathan Cape, London, 2008).

Bailey, Roderick, *Forgotten Voices of the Secret War* (Ebury Press, London, 2008).

Ball, Simon, *The Bitter Sea: The Struggle for Mastery in the Mediterranean 1935 – 1949* (Harper Collins, London, 2009).

Beevor J.G., *SOE: Recollections and Reflections 1940-1945* (The Bodley Head, London, 1981).

Binney, Marcus, *The Women Who Lived for Danger: The Women Agents of SOE in the Second World War* (Hodder & Stoughton, London, 2002).

Blum, Howard, *The Brigade: An Epic Story of Vengeance, Salvation and World War II* (Simon & Schuster, London, 2001).

Boyce, Frederic and Everett, Douglas, *SOE: The Scientific Secrets* (The History Press, Stroud, 2009).

Buckmaster, Maurice, *They Fought Alone: The Story of British Agents in France* (The Popular Book Club, London, 1958).

Buckmaster, Maurice, *Specially Employed: The Story of British Aid to French Patriots of the Resistance* (Batchworth Press, London, 1952).

Burney, Christopher, *The Dungeon Democracy* (Heinemann, London, 1945).

Burney, Christopher, *Solitary Confinement* (Heinemann, London, 1951).

Butler, J.R.M., *History of the Second World War: Grand Strategy II* (HSMO, London, 1957).

Churchill, Peter, *Duel of Wits* (Hodder and Stoughton, London, 1953).

Churchill, Peter, *Of Their Own Choice* (Hodder and Stoughton, London, 1952).

Clarke, Freddie, *Agents by Moonlight: The Secret History of RAF Tempsford during World War II* (Tempus Publishing, Stroud, 1999).

Clutton-Brock, Oliver, *RAF Evaders*, (Grub Street, London, 2009).

Cook, Bernard (Ed.), *Women and War: A Historical Encyclopaedia from Antiquity to the Present* (Arc Clio, Oxford, 2006).

Cookridge, E.H., *They Came from the Sky* (Heinemann, London, 1965).

Cookridge, E.H., *Inside SOE: The Story of Special Operations in Western Europe, 1940-45* (Arthur Barker, London, 1966).

Cowburn, Benjamin, *No Cloak, No Dagger: Allied Spycraft in Occupied France* (Frontline Books, London, 2009).

Cunningham, Cyril, *Beaulieu: The Finishing School for Secret Agents* (Leo Cooper, London, 1998).

Dalton, Hugh, *The Fateful Years: Memoirs 1931-1945* (Frederick Muller, London, 1957).

Davidson, Basil, *Special Operations Europe: Scenes from the Anti-Nazi War* (Irwin, Toronto, 1980).

Dear, Ian, *Sabotage & Subversion: Stories from the Files of the SOE and OSS* (Arms and Armour, London, 1996).

Dear, Ian, *Escape and Evasion*, (Cassell, London, 2002).

Deroc, M., *British Special Operations Explored: Yugoslavia in Turmoil 1941-1943 and the British Response* (Columbia University Press, New York, 1988).

Dodds-Parker, Douglas, *Setting Europe Ablaze* (Springwood Books, Windlesham, 1983).

Dourlein, Peter (Trans. F.G. Renier and A. Cliff), *Inside North Pole* (Kimber, London, 1953).

Dufurnier, D., *Ravensbruck* (G. Allen & Unwin, 1948).

Elrlich, Blake, *The French Resistance 1940-1945* (Chapman and Hall, London, 1966).

Escott, Beryl, E., *Mission Improbable: A Salute to the RAF Women of SOE in Wartime France* (Patrick Stephens, Sparkford, 1991).

Escott, Beryl, E., *The Heroines of the SOE: Britain's Secret Women in France* (The History Press, Stroud, 2010).

Foot, M.R.D., *SOE in France: An Account of the Work of the Special Operations Executive in France, 1940-1944* (Frank Cass, London, 1966, reprinted 2004).

Foot, M.R.D., *SOE in the Low Countries* (St Ermin's Press, 2001).

Foot, M.R.D., *Resistance* (Eyre Methuen, London, 1976).

Foot, M.R.D., *SOE: An Outline History 1940-46* (Pimlico, London, 1999).

Ford, George H. (Ed.), *Frank Pickersgill: The Making of a Secret Agent* (Ryerson Press, Toronto, 1948).

Ford, Roger, *Steel from the Sky: Behind Enemy Lines in German-ccupied France* (Orion Books, London, 2004).

Fournier G. and Heintz, A., *'If I Must Die ...' From 'Postmaster' to 'Aquatint': The Audacious Raids of a British Commando 1941-1943* (Orep Editions, Cully, France, 2006).

Fuller, Jean Overton, *Madeleine: The Story of Noor Inayat Khan* (Victor Gollancz, London, 1952).

Fuller, Jean Overton, *The German Penetration of SOE* (William Kimber, London, 1975).

Giskes, Herman J., *London Calling North Pole* (William Kimber, London, 1953).

Grehan, John, *The Forgotten Invasion: The Untold Story of Britain's First Large Scale Combined Operations Offensive – the Capture of Madagascar 1942* (Historic Military Press, Storrington, 2007).

Hackett, David A. (Ed.), *The Buchenwald Report* (Westview Press, Boulder, Colorado, 1995).

Hamilton-Hill, Donald, *SOE Assignment* (William Kimber, London, 1973).

Helm, Sarah, *A Life in Secrets: The Story of Vera Atkins and the Lost Agents of SOE* (Abacus, London, 2007).

Howarth, Patrick, *Undercover: The Men and Women of the SOE* (Phoenix Press, London 2000).

Hue, André and Southby-Tailyour, Ewen, *The Next Moon* (Penguin, London, 2009).

Johnson, Stowers, *Agents Extraordinary* (Robert Hale, London, 1975).

Jones, Liane, *A Quiet Courage: Women Agents in the French Resistance* (Bantam Press. London, 1990).

Kramer, Rita, *Flames in the Field* (Michael Joseph, London, 1995).

Knight, Frida, *The French Resistance, 1940-1944* (Lawrence and Wishart, London, 1975).

Le Chêne, Evelyn, *Mauthausen: The History of a Death Camp* (Methuen & Co, London, 1971).

Lees, Michael, *Special Operations Executed, In Serbia and Italy* (William Kimber, London, 1986).

Mackenzie, William, *The Secret History of SOE: The Special Operations Executive 1940 – 1945* (St Ermin's Press, London, 2000).

Maclean, Roy, *Canadians Behind Enemy Lines 1939-1945* (UBC Press, Vancouver, 2004).

Marks, Leo, *Between Silk and Cyanide* (Harper Collins, London, 1998).

Marshall, Bruce, *The White Rabbit* (Pan Books, London, 1966).

Masters, Anthony, *The Summer That Bled: The Biography of Hannah Senesh* (Michael Joseph, London, 1972).

Mason, Wynne, *Prisoners of War* (Historical Publications Branch, Wellington, 1954).

Minney, R.J, *Carve Her Name with Pride* (Wyman, 1956).

Neave, Airey, *Saturday at M.I.9: The Inside Story of the Underground Escape Lines in Europe* (Pen & Sword, Barnsley, 2004).

Nicholas, Elizabeth, *Death be Not Proud* (White Lion Publishers, London, 1958).

Ottaway, Susan, *Violette Szabo, 'The Life That I Have ...'* (Leo Cooper, Barnsley, 2003).

Pawley, Margaret, *In Obedience to Instructions: FANY with the SOE in the Mediterranean* (Pen & Sword, Barnsley, 1999).

Perquin, Jean-Louis, *The Clandestine Radio Operators* (Histoire & Collections, Paris, 2011).

Perrin, Nigel, *Spirit of Resistance: The Life of SOE Agent Harry Peulvé DSO MC* (Pen & Sword, Barnsley, 2008).

Poller, Walter, *Buchenwald, Medical Block* (Souvenir Press, London, 1961).

Ransom, Candice F., *So Young to Die: The Story of Hannah Senesh* (Scholastic, London, 1993).

Saward, Joe, *The Grand Prix Saboteurs: The Extraordinary Untold Story of the Grand Prix Drivers who became British Secret Agents in World War II* (Morienval Press, London, 2006).

Seaman, Mark, *Bravest of the Brave* (Michael O'Mara Books, London, 1997).

Seaman, Mark (Ed.), *Special Operations Executive: A New Instrument of War* (Routlege, Abingdon, 2005).

Senesh, Hannah, and Marge Piercy (Foreword), *Hannah Senesh: Her Life and Diary* (Jewish Lights Publishing, Woodstock, 2004).

Smiley, David, *Albanian Assignment* (Sphere Books, London, 1984).

Stafford, David, *Britain and European Resistance: A Survey of the Special Operations Executive, with Documents* (Macmillan, London, 1980).

Stafford, David, *Secret Agent: The True Story of the Special Operations Executive* (BBC Books, London, 2000).

Stevenson, William A., *Man Called Intrepid: The Secret War* (Book Club Associates, London, 1976).

Sutherland, D. *He Who Dares: Recollections of Service in the SAS, SBS and MI5* (Leo Cooper, Barnsley, 1998).

Sweet-Escott, Bickham, *Baker Street Irregular* (Methuen, London, 1965).

Tickell, Jerrard, *Odette: The Story of a British Agent* (Pan Books, London, 1955).

Thompson, E. P., *Beyond the Frontier: The Politics of a Failed Mission; Bulgaria 1944* (Merlin Press, Suffolk, 1997).

Tomaselli, Phil, *Tracing your Secret Service Ancestors* (Pen & Sword, Barnsley, 2009).

Turner, John Frayn, *Awards of the George Cross 1940-2009* (Pen & Sword, Barnsley, 2010).

Webb, A.M. (Ed.), *The Natzweiler Trial* (War Crimes Trials series Volume V) (William Hodge & Co, London, 1949).

West, Nigel, *Secret War: The Story of SOE, Britain's Wartime Sabotage Organisation* (Hodder & Stoughton, London, 1992).

Wilkinson, Peter and Astley, Joan Bright, *Gubbins and SOE* (Leo Cooper, London, 1993).

Verity, Hugh, *We Landed by Moonlight* (Airdata Publications, Wilmslow, 1995).

Verlander, Harry, *My War in SOE: Behind Enemy Lines in France and Burma with the Special Operations Executive* (Independent Books, Bromley, 2010).

Vomécourt, Phillipe de, *Who Lived to See the Day* (Hutchinson, London, 1962).

Yarnold, Patrick, *Wanborough Manor: School for Secret Agents* (Hopfield Publications, Guildford, 2009).

INTERNET SOURCES

www.memorialgrove.org.uk
www.specialforcesroh.com
www.jewishvirtuallibrary.org
www.royalpioneercorps.co.uk
www.cwgc.org

Index